# FROM DAYTIME TO PRIMETIME

# FROM DAYTIME TO PRIMETIME

The History of American Television
Programs

JAMES ROMAN

GREENWOOD PRESS
Westport, Connecticut • London

**Library of Congress Cataloging-in-Publication Data**

Roman, James W.
    From daytime to primetime : the history of American television programs /
James Roman.
        p.   cm.
    Includes index.
    ISBN 0–313–31972–3 (alk. paper)
    1. Television programs—United States—History.   I. Title.
    PN1992.3.U5R64   2005
    791.45′75′0973—dc22          2004014142

British Library Cataloguing in Publication Data is available.

Library of Congress Catalog Card Number: 2004014142
ISBN: 0–313–31972–3

First published in 2005

Greenwood Press, 88 Post Road West, Westport, CT 06881
An imprint of Greenwood Publishing Group, Inc.
www.greenwood.com

Printed in the United States of America

The paper used in this book complies with the
Permanent Paper Standard issued by the National
Information Standards Organization (Z39.48–1984).

10   9   8   7   6   5   4   3   2   1

# CONTENTS

# ACKNOWLEDGMENTS

I'm grateful to the students of Hunter College for their spirit of inquiry and their pursuit of knowledge. I'd like to thank my wife, Mardee, my children and their wives, Matthew and Candi, Josh and Jenna, and my daughter Heather, who were always supportive and understanding during the time I spent researching and writing this book.

# INTRODUCTION: THE CULTURE OF TELEVISION'S CONTENT

Humankind has had a need to communicate to a wider audience since the dawn of time. Prehistoric man recorded his exploits in renderings drawn on the walls of caves. There was drama and pathos, all the elements of modern narrative, as exploits of the hunt appeared as images on stone. As civilization evolved, advances were made in mass communication. With the printing press, books and newspapers could produce text in volume, allowing the dissemination of material to a large audience. The advent of motion-picture photography, with the addition of sound, was one of the first means to communicate recorded moving images accompanied by audio to a significant audience. Point-to-point communication was made more spontaneous with the telegraph and telephone. However, radio was the first modern application of a mass-audience electronic medium.

The coming of radio captured the imagination of the American public. Before radio sets became mass-produced, the technology was available only to hobbyists who had the knowledge and aptitude to purchase the electronic components and build the first crystal sets. Eventually, companies like General Electric began building and selling affordable radio sets, and the public eagerly purchased them. Radio became a content provider and satisfied the needs of the ever-growing audience with serious drama; daytime serial drama (soap operas); news; sports; weather; presidential chats; election returns; and, of course, commercials. During World War II, radio kept the American public in touch with the war effort, bringing them news of Allied invasions, victories, and defeats.

As the audience grew, the magnitude of radio's influence on American culture became evident. It provided producers and advertisers with an object lesson in the power of an electronic mass medium and its ability to attract and persuade the public. For example, the entertainer Kate Smith, who introduced America to Irving Berlin's "God Bless America" theme song in 1938, used radio to sell $600 million in war bonds. Advertisers learned quickly that radio slogans and catchy tunes could move their products off the shelves.

Radio set the tone and influenced the content of television. As the technology of television became more sophisticated, it achieved both an immediacy and intimacy with the American public and the global community. And, like radio, it realized its potential as a merchandising tool in its ability to target the consumer and create the ultimate marketing tool, the home-shopping channels on cable television. Television learned quickly that advertisers were anxious to place their message on popular programs, so they developed a practice of alternating sponsorships. This allowed a particular advertiser to have exclusive announcements one week and switch with another advertiser the following week. As in radio, however, advertising agencies were very influential in producing programs and buying television time for their clients. And many of the programs had the client or sponsor's name in the title, such as *Philco Television Playhouse, Westinghouse Studio One, Goodyear Television Playhouse, Kraft Television Theatre*, and *The U.S. Steel Hour*. Many of the early television commercials that were broadcast in the 1950s used animation as a tool to sell their products. Like in radio, popular personalities were used to endorse products, such as Red Skelton demonstrating the virtues of Instant J-Wax, or Bing Crosby and his long affiliation with Minute Maid Orange Juice.

Celebrities like Bing Crosby and Red Skelton had a Hollywood presence moving to radio and then to television. The pioneering television producers, like the Internet providers of today, realized that content is king. In the late 1940s, the industry that had the most experience with providing filmed entertainment was Hollywood, although it was very suspicious of television and its competitive stature. Nevertheless, two men, Leonard Goldenson of ABC Paramount and Jack Warner of Warner Brothers, who were friends, forged a professional relationship that brought the Hollywood studios into producing films for television, forging an enduring bond that was both creative and profitable.

When Warner Brothers and other Hollywood studios entered the area of television production, they duplicated some of the success they had in theatrical films. One genre that was consistently popular was the Western. So eventually this became a popular programming format on television, with titles like *Cheyenne, Wagon Train, Sugarfoot, Maverick, Gunsmoke*, and *Bonanza*. The law-and-order theme also became a dramatic component of police, detective, and lawyer programming formats. Television was also ripe to explore the nuances of the medical profession, offering programs featuring doctors who dared to challenge traditional protocol for the welfare of their patients.

Soon it was apparent that television was a mass medium with enormous powers of persuasion. When Ozzie Nelson of *The Adventures of Ozzie and Harriet* show went searching in a television episode for tutti-frutti ice cream, the next day food stores reported a run on that flavor.

The study of television and its impact upon American culture has a number of themes associated with its influence. These include its impact upon children, issues of empowerment, portrayal of violence, dissemination of news, political manifestations, commercialization, and public access. In an effort to understand these issues, this book looks at television as the ultimate content provider. Examining various programming genres and how they evolved provides the reader with insight into television's ability to sustain its popularity and reinvent itself, conforming to the needs of an ever-changing audience.

As television grew and became a prominent form of entertainment on its electronic proscenium, it developed various genres of programming that not only reflected the cultural norms of American society but also addressed some of its ills. In addition, television became a mediator helping to determine behavior, and in some ways became a moderator of style and substance. In helping to define cultural determinism, the study of television's programming is an important variable, as it has become a force in advocating change in the dynamics of American society.

During a time when America's ideals are enduring the greatest test of the very fabric of their foundation, television provides a cohesive bond, acting as a healer while providing a window to the events impacting American society. Television cannot ignore this apocalyptic time, and indeed has woven these themes into the narrative of some programs.

This book attempts to analyze various television program genres as arbitrators of American values and their influence on behavior. There is little doubt about the influential role television has in setting an agenda and defining needs for its audience. It can range from the compelling to the sublime: the hottest Christmas toy, a challenging video game, branded sneakers, or a must-see concert or film. And with so many Americans relying upon television for news, it creates its own agenda, defining its importance within the context of national and international events.

News has become one of the most abundant of the content providers for television and the Internet. The compelling events of the geopolitical landscape have made the dissemination of news on television and the Internet a primary programming niche. More Americans get their news from television than any other source, and with CNN and other cable providers, news is a prominent commodity. And a lot of that news has to do with sports.

Indeed, television and sports have had a strong symbiotic relationship. Television created the highest-rated program in history, the Super Bowl. It also helped to popularize sports like tennis and golf, and gave the Olympics a cachet of compelling visibility. With the sale of television rights, baseball, basketball, football, and hockey have been able to afford the extravagant salaries paid to athletes. With long-running programs like *Monday Night Football* and *Wide World of Sports,* television has created a venue with a distinction for competition, achievement, tradition, and recognition.

Programming styles and genres have evolved as American mores have become more liberal. Situation comedies once reflected the innocence of a more rigid moral tone with the twin beds in the bedroom of a husband and wife (Lucy and Desi, Rob and Laura Petri). Of course, the entire landscape of sexuality on television has dramatically changed in language and the depiction of various situations. On both network and cable television there is more nudity and accommodation for sensuality than was ever perceived for the medium. And, of course, there's the tedium and pompousness of the reality shows with a new comedy twist. For example, NBC's *Average Joe* features overweight, balding nerds competing for the affection of a ravishing beauty, and *The Joe Schmo Show* on Spike TV uses a contrivance of actors and a real contestant who thinks he's competing against other contestants. And, in a reversal of roles and sexuality, there is the hit show on the Bravo cable network *Queer Eye for the Straight Guy,* where the fashion police consists of five gay guys who do a makeover on a style-impaired straight man.

Television is catering to the bread-and-circuses mentality and the huckster credo of selling the sizzle and earning the best bang for the buck. In some instances, it's catering to a universe of people who have the need to accommodate themselves to the basest type of programming within an atmosphere of abandon laced with a dereliction of morality. There is indeed a threshold of propriety that should be observed within the construct of disseminating images on broadcast television that may be perceived as inappropriate to certain audiences. Undeniably, those who wish to purchase programming to satisfy their prurient interest should be allowed to do so. However, in the realm of regularly scheduled broadcast and cable television programs at times when children are present in the audience, there should be boundaries of propriety that are respected and adhered to.

Issues of family values and what is perceived by some as inappropriate programming have precipitated advertising boycotts by various grassroots organizations concerned about the impact those programs have upon children. Clearly, parental advocacy groups have used the threat of boycotting products on questionable programs as a tool of empowerment to reach the hierarchy of decision-makers in the entertainment industry.

Today, the synergy created by television and the Internet has placed a great deal of emphasis upon content. Many television and cable channels have cross-platforms offering viewers an opportunity to access information. Local and network news programs have integrated the World Wide Web as an additional platform to disseminate information, urging their viewers to log on. Mergers and acquisitions in the entertainment and information industries have focused upon acquiring content and its need as a resource for success. Those involved in broadcasting from radio to television understand the need for developing content and its role as a tool for attracting audiences and advertisers.

Indeed, television's voracious appetite for programming has created a compelling need to create new genres or to recycle those programming concepts that were successful years ago. For example, when the Western television genre became dated and unpopular, the Western theme of law and order was updated by depicting the lives of modern-day police officers riding shotgun in their cruisers instead of on a stagecoach. Also, the situation comedy (sitcom), a stalwart of television's programming dynamic, was modernized to reflect the values of a sassy, younger, affluent, sexually enlightened audience.

The economics of television is also an important area of study. Production and talent costs have escalated while the television universe of providers has become extremely competitive. Licensing fees for programs acquired by television networks have become more expensive, reflecting the value of a successful product. Also, Hollywood, which churns out hundreds of theatrical feature-length films each year, has looked toward television as a profitable recyclable programming archive. Over the years, Hollywood producers have adapted many television concepts to theatrical release, creating profit centers for their studios. Some of these successful films based upon television programs are *Maverick, The Fugitive, Mission Impossible,* and *S.W.A.T.* Occasionally, producers attempt to resurrect a hit television series, as with the reincarnation of *The Fugitive* several seasons ago; however, the series failed to live up to the original (starring David Janssen) and the movie (featuring Harrison Ford).

The creative process involved in producing programs for television is also an interesting aspect of who sets the thematic and content agenda of programming. It's an interesting dynamic that involves a number of people contributing their efforts to the final product. Creating programming involves not only writers but also producers, directors, agents, and prominent corporate executives whose decisions give legitimacy to the creative talent and help to focus their input into various directions. The creative process and program development involve a complex of dynamics that are associated with personality, need, leadership, and tradition. Conceptualizing programming is an intimate process and one that is fraught with more failure than success.

There are, of course, many risks associated with prime-time programming development. Often the networks increase their chance of success by returning to successful producers who have validated their stature with hit shows. For example, Dick Wolf has taken the *Law and Order* (1990) concept and created a franchise of continuing series, including *Law and Order: Special Victims Unit* (1999), *Law and Order: Criminal Intent* (2001), and *Law and Order: Crime and Punishment* (2003). Other producers have also established a reputation with the networks for excellence, including Steven Bochco

(*NYPD Blue, Philly*), David E. Kelley (*L.A. Law, Picket Fences, The Brother-hood of Poland*), Chris Carter (*The X Files*), Joss Whedon (*Buffy the Vampire Slayer*), John Wells (*E.R., The West Wing*), Aaron Sorkin (*The West Wing*), and Kevin Williamson (*Dawson's Creek*).

Another tactic used to help quantify success is either spinning off a series from one that's a hit or offering a costar of a successful series a starring role in a new show. For example, *All in the Family* was spun off into three hit series: *The Jeffersons, Gloria,* and *Maude.* And Kelsey Grammer's character Dr. Frasier Crane became the hit sitcom series *Frasier.* However, being a costar on a megahit doesn't guarantee success for a stint at being a star. The three costars of *Seinfeld*—Julia Louis-Dreyfus, Michael Richards, and Jason Alexander—each dismally failed in their own attempts at playing a lead in a television series. However, the cocreator and writer of *Seinfeld,* Larry David, became an immediate television star with his quirky HBO show *Curb Your Enthusiasm.*

American television has also been a protagonist of change and an arbitrator of taste. It has progressed from the puritanical "gosh darn" separate marital beds of the 1950s to the in-your-face language and situations of MTV, *Big*

David Caruso and Dennis Franz star as New York City detectives in Steven Bochco's dramatic series *NYPD Blue.* (Photofest.)

*Brother, Survivor, Jerry Springer,* and *Sex and the City.* Indeed, television has become a showcase for tastelessness, perpetuating and defining a bread-and-circuses mentality into a feeding frenzy of garishness with a nod toward baseless voyeurism. Nudity, profanity, perversity, and a hint of pornography have become a part of the context of television, and yet audiences still worship television's golden age of virtue, now shown on Nickelodeon and TV Land. Is there a contradiction between the innocence of *The Andy Griffith Show*'s small-town family values and the sexual innuendo of *Dawson's Creek?*

Those same small-town values made an instant hit of *Peyton Place,* television's first prime-time soap opera. It was filled with sexual innuendo, provocative situations, and simmering libidos that made its audience sizzle with anticipation. But less was seen and more was imagined in those heady days of mining the audience's taste for passion. Today little is left to the imagination, and graphic depictions, along with highly stylized language, are a hallmark of television profanity. It's a measure of how our culture defines sexuality within the permissive context of heterosexual and homosexual relationships. Although these values are part of the dynamic of sexuality within the context of relationships, television had made it a reflection of the more tawdry aspects of gutter dynamics. It's a trend that reflects a culture of permissiveness, and boredom with the propriety that was defined by previous generations.

Any discussion of television programming cannot ignore the dilemma of balancing the elements of political determinism, religion, and morality. Indeed, these variables have caused a number of conflicts that have reverberated through the landscape of television, raising important issues associated with the First Amendment and ethics. There has always been concern about the content propriety of broadcast television and its degree of permissiveness. In addition to the representation of sexuality (heterosexual and homosexual), there are also concerns about violence, racism, and stereotyping. Although both cable and pay television are more permissive, broadcast television invokes more self-censorship because of its need to accommodate the concerns of advertisers and a mass audience. Indeed, in the 1950s, the industry trade organization, the National Association of Broadcasters (NAB), recommended a code of conduct for all members that included stringent guidelines pertaining to program content. If a station's programming complied with the guidelines, it could display the Seal of Good Practice at the end of the program and on the television screen at the end of the broadcast day. The code (not the NAB) was eliminated in the 1980s.

The issue of family values has become a recurring theme in the political construct of campaign rhetoric. Sexual explicitness, violence, abuse of women, and drugs have been prioritized in an agenda of debate and resolution. Religious groups and political parties are rallying around the call to purge television programming of these perceived illicit tendencies. Interestingly, there is a historical precedent to the reconciliation of moral values with

*Friends* cast (left to right): Matthew Perry (as Chandler), Jennifer Aniston (as Rachel), David Schwimmer (as Ross), Courteney Cox (as Monica), Matt LeBlanc (as Joey), and Lisa Kudrow (as Phoebe). (Photofest.)

the public taste. In the 1940s, the motion-picture industry, faced with scandal and rebuked by the Catholic Church's Legion of Decency, adopted a code for movies that became a tool for audiences to select appropriate films for their families. Over the years, the Motion Picture Association of America (MPAA) has adopted a rating code attempting to codify a rating system and provide guidance to parents and adult audiences about the explicit nature of motion-picture content. Although the process has been criticized, it nevertheless provides a sustained effort for oversight.

Looking toward Hollywood as a model for codifying a television content code, the industry turned to Jack Valenti, head of the MPAA, for guidance. In addition to creating an identifying process for determining the suitability of program content, the broadcasting industry adopted a technological tool called the V-chip, which was developed in Canada, to block programming deemed unfit for children. Legislation mandating that V-chip technology be integrated in every television set with a screen 13 inches or larger was passed as part of the 1996 Telecommunications Act. However, most parents are either confused by the ratings or simply ignore downloading the software to operate the system. Indeed, V-chip ratings labeled *The Oprah Winfrey*

*Show* and *Who Wants to Be a Millionaire* as educational, which is clearly stretching the validation of the rating system.

As television has moved into the realm of depicting more reality within the context of its programming, it has sustained a level of literal visual imagery and dialogue authenticity. For example, the HBO series *The Wire* uses the language of the street, with an abundance of expletives that are authentic to the drama. The concern for some critics is the provocative use of language and physical situations that are contrived for mere titillation. There should be a correlation between the use of adult situations and the structure of the story.

Another variable in the consideration of program content is advertisers. In the 1950s, television advertisers had a considerable amount of control over programming. At that time, the networks provided the time, and the advertisers and their agencies supplied the programming. That arrangement allowed the networks to plead innocent to any charges of complicity during the quiz scandals by claiming that they had no knowledge of the validity of the program content.

In today's television programming marketplace, advertisers, while not overtly prominent in program content, do exercise some control along with the network that licenses the program. Language, nudity, and references to religion, homosexuality, and abortion may raise a red flag and a cautionary warning to the program supplier. Producers may be encouraged to alter a reference or a scene that may be construed as offensive. Although the four broadcast networks have defined programming parameters in a more explicit way, they nevertheless must be sensitive to the concerns of their advertisers. Some advertisers are very concerned about associating the goodwill of their product with programming that may be construed as suggestive or provocative. Manufacturers who have spent years and a considerable amount of money on nurturing the image of their product are loath to risk any besmirching of how their merchandise is portrayed.

Television programming today is an amalgam of genres that meld into an aesthetic that is difficult to define. From the morning network television programs, with their gossipy celebrity interviews, to the afternoon syndicated talk shows, with their trash speech and confrontational nature, to the prime-time soap operas, quiz shows, dramas, sports, and leering reality programming, television is a hybrid of substance, innuendo, and Peeping Tom mentality. It paints with a broad palate of colors on a canvas that is celebrated for its diversity and style. Television is a showcase for both formulaic, episodic, routine programs offering little in substance to enriching dramas and documentaries that provide a measure of fulfillment that helps to enhance people's lives. It has many tentacles, embracing a myriad of enduring themes that are the subtext of American culture, providing a narrative of substantive ritual.

## ORGANIZATION OF THE BOOK

### Chapter 1, The Seeds of Television Programming: The Networks Steal from Radio

This chapter covers the origins of broadcast programming in radio, various genres that were developed, and radio's first stars. It also addresses industry leaders like William Paley, founder of CBS, and David Sarnoff, president of RCA (NBC). The chapter discusses the move from radio to television by various celebrities and how programming genres were transformed.

### Chapter 2, Tinseltown Comes to TV

This chapter reviews Hollywood's suspicion and resistance to television and its eventual embrace of it. Leonard Goldenson of ABC and Jack Warner of Warner Brothers are the prominent personalities that enabled a détente between the two industries. The chapter will review how ABC, as a struggling third network, was able to achieve competitive parity with CBS and NBC by working with Hollywood. It also discusses how the Hollywood studios, along with some independents, developed programming for television. Television changed America's consumer culture, closing movie theaters and restructuring magazine publishing. Popular magazines like *Life, Look,* and the *Saturday Evening Post* either went out of business or changed their publication schedule. As a mass medium, television had the ability to create a ringing endorsement of consumptive behavior by advertising consumer products and helping to build brand loyalty. These products were not only seen in commercials but were also prominently placed in programs.

### Chapter 3, From Prairie to Pavement: The Lawman's Lonely Ride

The American West has long been a staple for nurturing the romantic virtues of the frontier and its code of conduct. Writers like Zane Grey and directors like John Huston created a narrative that embraced the values of independence and a morality that reflected the ideals of strength and endurance. Early television incarnations included a fairly innocuous Roy Rogers and Hopalong Cassidy, whose singing cowboy characters were more consonant with the rhinestone glitter of Hollywood than the dry dust of the prairie.

Heroes came in many guises, and 1950s television allowed for the ethnic inculcation of stereotypes, albeit heroic ones, in the characters of Zorro and the Cisco Kid. Adventure and bravery were personified in the television programs of pioneers like Jim Bowie, Daniel Boone, and Davy Crockett. There was even the mystique of the superhero with the masked crusader the Lone Ranger.

Soon, Westerns became one of the most successful dramatic genres in television's early years. With the likes of *Wagon Train, Rawhide, Maverick, Have*

*Gun Will Travel, Gunsmoke, Bonanza, Bat Masterson, Cheyenne, Sugarfoot, Wanted Dead or Alive,* and many others, the portrayal of the American West became a revered television programming staple.

As American society evolved, the appeal of the Western changed. There was a momentous population move toward urbanization and the growth of cities. Lawmen traded their horses for cars and their six-shooter for semiautomatic weapons. Many of the themes were the same: good versus evil, corruption, jealousy, and greed. However, the crowded cities also brought new problems of drug abuse, homophobia, pedophilia, racism, and abuse of women, and television reflected these concerns.

They were expressed in a range of dramas that featured cops, crooks, and private eyes. These programs included *Dragnet, Highway Patrol, Peter Gunn, Hawaii Five-O, Streets of San Francisco, Chips, Adam-12, Starsky and Hutch, Mannix, The Untouchables, Baretta, Police Woman, Cagney and Lacey, Miami Vice, Nash Bridges, NYPD Blue,* and many more.

## Chapter 4, Medicinal Myopia: Television Makes House Calls

In the rhetoric of television, the roles of various professionals mediated by the narrative parameters of storytelling can create a heroic dimension to character portrayal. The medical and legal professions offered television producers an opportunity to present a romanticized version of doctors and lawyers as heroes expressing the virtues of healing and the heroics of courtroom drama. One of the first regularly scheduled medical-oriented programs was *Medic*, a reality-type program re-creating medical procedures.

Family medicine and its presentation of the doctor as teacher, social worker, healer, confessor, and saint were the themes of the immensely popular *Marcus Welby, M.D.*, starring Robert Young. Television medicine was institutionalized and moved into the complex dynamic of the hospital with programs such as *Dr. Kildare* (adapted from the movies), *Ben Casey, Medical Center, St. Elsewhere,* and *E.R.* Of course, daytime serial dramas have long been a repository for stories with a medical theme.

Courtroom drama and lawyers have also been a programming staple for television. A twist on the theme was *The Paper Chase*, an intelligent series about students at law school. The benchmark program that helped establish the genre was *Perry Mason*, starring Raymond Burr. Other programs include *The Defenders, L.A. Law, Law and Order,* and *The Practice.* Daytime television has also been a successful breeding ground for reality-oriented law programs. One of the first was *Divorce Court*. Contemporary incarnations include *Judge Judy, Joe Brown, People's Court, Greg Mathis,* and *Mills Lane.* The landscape for reality court-related shows has exploded with newer entries appealing to different audience demographics. These include *Arrest and Trial, Curtis Court, Judge Hatchett, Moral Court, Power of Attorney,* and *Singles Court.*

## Chapter 5, Mirroring the Melting Pot: Gender, Race, and Religion

Television was not always an inclusive medium. In its early days, when it attempted to be encompassing of minorities and women, it usually depicted their characters in stereotypical roles. With *Amos 'n' Andy, Beulah,* and *Molly Goldberg,* television featured the themes of black and Jewish culture, respectively. Unfortunately, the representations were more in step with the prejudices of the day. The presentation of these characters within the context of ethnic humor created an unsavory dynamic that was insulting and demeaning.

*The Jack Benny Show* featured the comedian along with other comic characters, including the role of his black houseman Eddie "Rochester" Anderson. Cast in the role as somewhat of a foil to Benny, Rochester could be snide and sarcastic. But Rochester was always on call, and although the humor was intended to be nonstereotypical, it managed at times to skirt the perimeter of racism.

There were programs that featured Latinos: *Popi; The Man and the City; Viva Valdez; A.K.A. Pablo;* and, of course, *Chico and the Man,* which starred Freddie Prinze and the veteran actor Jack Albertson. The civil rights movement provided the impetus to give a wider latitude to the portrayal of blacks on television. One of the first regularly scheduled prime-time television series to star a black actor in a recurring role was *I Spy,* with Robert Culp and Bill Cosby. Soon, color came out of the closet with the hit sitcoms *Sanford and Son, Diff'rent Strokes, The Jeffersons, What's Happening!!, The White Shadow, Julia,* and others.

Several programs that attempted to define socially responsible issue-oriented themes within the context of drama and comedy included *East Side, West Side; Maude;* and *All in the Family.*

## Chapter 6, The Sitcom: Innocence versus Urban Chic

The situation comedy on American television is a cultural icon with a global influence. Rightly or wrongly, it represents the values, morality, and aspirations that are indicative of the American psyche. In some ways it reflects an ideological mythology that depicts a highly stylized rendition of our society within the traditional roles of family and work.

The genre has evolved over the years to reflect the changing dynamic of American culture. It moved from the innocence of the 1960s, with the benign humor of *The Dick Van Dyke Show,* to the complex dynamic of twentysomethings and their relationships in *Friends,* and on to the sophistication, wit, and humor of *The Cosby Show* and *Seinfeld.* In the 1950s, television mirrored a perception of what the industry believed to be family values, as defined by programs like *The Adventures of Ozzie and Harriet.* This program was a carefully contrived portrait of a family with two teenage sons who pretended to be normal.

In opposition to the subtle humor of *Ozzie and Harriet, I Love Lucy* was a pantheon of slapstick comedy presented within the sitcom format. Lucy's physicality, along with Desi's malapropisms, presented itself as a vaudevillian exercise in borscht-belt humor.

Early television sitcoms also contrived to reinforce stereotypical gender roles in American society, with shows like *Father Knows Best, Make Room for Daddy,* and *My Three Sons.* Men were the breadwinners and women the housewives. In *The Honeymooners,* Jackie Gleason's Ralph Kramden was the self-defined man of the house who relied upon his wife Trixie to get him out of all the trouble he inevitably got himself into. Although Ralph was forever threatening Trixie to "send her to the moon" with his fist, by the end of the program they were expressing their mutual love for each other.

### Chapter 7, Television and the Comics

Comic-book characters in newspapers and magazines have been a part of American culture for years and have at times provided inspiration and sustenance to America's youth. Characters like Superman and Buck Rogers were immortalized on radio before they became prominent television stars in either live-action or animated programs. Cartoons and comics are well suited for the visual attributes of television, offering unlimited opportunities for expression. Indeed, many of television's situation comedies were inspired by the comics, adapting their style and form. And television has created its own genre of cartoon characters, challenging the traditions of program content with *The Simpsons* and *South Park.*

### Chapter 8, Television Drama: From the Golden Age to the Soap Factory

The 1950s are sometimes referred to as *the golden age of television* because of the substantive dramatic programming that was featured on a regular basis. There were many programs, such as *Playhouse 90* and *Armstrong Circle-Theatre,* that produced original programming or adaptations of classic American literature. And it was an exciting time for new writers like Rod Serling and Paddy Chayefsky, who wrote dramatic teleplays for television. That tradition, of course, lingers with prime-time drama, soap operas (prime-time and daytime) and miniseries. Network television provided an ambitious palate for expensive miniseries like *War and Remembrance* and *Lonesome Dove.* Cable television's HBO produced *Band of Brothers,* a tribute to the veterans of World War II's Charlie Company, at a cost of $120 million. And, of course, the regularly scheduled prime-time police, lawyer, and medical programs are still part of television's enduring programming mix.

### Chapter 9, Reality TV: Surviving the Trend

Although reality television is viewed as a new television genre, it has its roots in the 1950s with programs such as *Queen for a Day* and *Candid Camera*. It proves the adage that all programming is derivative, and nothing is truly original. Of course, the nuances of the reality genre have been massaged to suit the needs of producers who pander to the lowest common denominator. They've taken the innocence out of amateur-hour programs and reduced the format to debasing contestants with insulting commentary (*American Idol*). Audiences endured the frigid and harsh remarks of Anne Robinson of *The Weakest Link* and the banality of *Joe Millionaire, Are You Hot? The Search for America's Sexiest People, The Bachelor, Survivor, Big Brother,* and *Chains of Love.* It is a programming inventory that serves a voyeuristic agenda while rationalizing its sexuality within the context of entertainment. It has no greater substance than burlesque of the air waves, with no redeeming values except for titillation and temptation.

### Chapter 10, Talk TV: Running at the Mouth

Television talk shows owe their debt to radio and the intelligence and erudition of personalities like Barry Gray and Larry King. Radio provided an accommodating schedule for listeners and an opportunity for developing formats that could appeal to various niche audiences. It helped to influence talk trends on television with the evolution of Howard Stern and Don Imus, radio shock jocks who have sustained their popularity on radio while capturing an additional audience on television.

Conceptualizing the talk show as a programming staple and formatting it for national distribution on network television was the brainchild of NBC president Sylvester "Pat" Weaver, father of actress Sigourney Weaver, who served in that position from 1953 to 1955. Weaver helped to create *The Today Show* and *The Tonight Show,* successfully bookending the formats for morning and evening national distribution.

*The Tonight Show,* with successive hosts Steve Allen, Jack Paar, Johnny Carson, and more recently Jay Leno, has established a legacy for NBC that has endured as a programming and cultural phenomenon. The CBS television network, after trying for many years to duplicate the late-night talk format, has succeeded with David Letterman, who has managed to influence the American lexicon, replicating the famous "Here's Johnny" with his own identifying "Top Ten List."

Of course, the television landscape for talk has deteriorated into the daytime mayhem of bread and circuses, with leering audiences drooling over the lascivious and profane. Hosts and producers deliberately create inflammatory and potentially hostile confrontations to placate the more lecherous and demeaning members of the audience. But not all talk television is that debasing.

Programs coming out of the network news divisions, like NBC's *Meet the Press,* CBS's *Face the Nation,* and ABC's *This Week* and *Nightline* with Ted Koppel, offer intelligence, depth, and substance.

## Chapter 11, Kids, Cartoons, Puppets, and Muppets

While the debate over television's effect on children and its possible negative influence as yet remains unresolved, it has proven to be a fixture in their daily lives. Classic programs and cartoons have been recycled on dedicated cable networks like Nickelodeon, TV Land, and the Cartoon Network. Of course, the programming and its rationale have changed and become more sophisticated since the debut of Hopalong Cassidy, a 1948 series of recycled B movies that captured their imagination and spirit for adventure.

In the 1950s, puppets offered children a gentle blend of comedy and fantasy with popular programs like *The Howdy Doody Show; Kukla, Fran, and Ollie;* and, later, the endearing charm of Jim Henson's *The Muppet Show* and the pseudopuppetry of *Barney and Friends.* Ironically, the success of puppets or marionettes as a tool for entertainment on a mass medium was demonstrated on radio with the popular ventriloquist Edgar Bergen and his "sidekick," Charlie McCarthy. Even though the radio listeners couldn't see the dummy, they were nevertheless enraptured by his antics.

There was a tradition in newspaper publishing with the comics, or funny pages, and the first strip, *The Yellow Kid,* which was coveted by two major newspaper publishers. In the movies, cartoons became a popular form of entertainment, and Disney's characters, including Mickey Mouse, were audience favorites. Cartoons on television have endured as a popular form of children's entertainment and evolved to the domain of adult amusement. From *The Ren and Stimpy Show* and *The Simpsons* to *South Park* and *Beavis and Butthead,* cartoons have entered the realm of cutting-edge entertainment that is driven by attitude and chic.

At one time television was criticized for having too many animated children's programs and not enough live-action formats. Some animated shows, like *GI Joe,* were no more than program-length commercials for the licensed toy merchandise depicted in the program. There was a tradition for live hosts and their prosocial messages with shows like *Captain Kangaroo, Mister Rogers' Neighborhood,* and, of course, *Sesame Street,* which was an amalgam of live action, animation, and puppets.

## Chapter 12, Television's Telltale Tube: Fantasy, Science Fiction, and the Occult

Television has taken on many forms, and at times has lost its innocence to the midway antics of the snake-oil salesman with the carnival pitch boasting of elixirs that offer redemption and reconciliation. It has captured heroic ideals with the invincible crime-fighting antics of superheroes, explored the realm of darkness with *The Twilight Zone,* and taken its audience to far-off galaxies with *Star Trek.*

Like the movies, television is in the fantasy business, and its ability to stretch the canvas of reality and suspend the belief of the viewer provides it with a unique sense of the surreal. American television audiences have embraced these programs, and some, like *Star Trek,* have created a cult following, with their characters becoming cultural icons, spawning successful theatrical features and newly formatted television series.

Television's attraction to the occult and its lure of aliens predates *The X Files,* yet has an enduring programming presence. In its earliest incarnation, the amiable ghostly ghouls of the 1950s *Topper* series were role models for the modern rendition in *Touched by an Angel.* A humorous infatuation with aliens was the format for *My Favorite Martian* and *Mork and Mindy.* These programs were the progenitors of *3rd Rock from the Sun.*

With the superhero, television embraced the theme of good versus evil and the ethics of right versus wrong. Superman jumped from the comics to television, and the Man of Steel was joined by Captain Midnight, Batman, and later the Bionic Man and Woman. Their mission to rid the world of miscreants was embraced by television and applauded by a grateful audience.

## Chapter 13, Setting the Agenda: Television News Style and Substance

When news programming came to radio, newspaper publishers attempted to thwart it by eliminating radio listings from their newspapers. They also forbade the news wire services, which were dominated by the publishers, from distributing copy to the radio stations. However, after some bickering and negotiating, an agreement was reached between the parties that allowed radio to produce two 15-minute newscasts a day, one in the morning and another in the evening, after the requisite newspaper editions hit the newsstands. The agreement was short-lived, and radio became a mainstay for the dissemination of news.

Television's earliest attempt at news basically duplicated radio's technique, except with added pictures. Soon, however, television created its own unique news identity, with a style and substance that was developed by broadcast journalists like Edward R. Murrow.

Murrow, who started at CBS radio, defined the basic narrative components of broadcast news and helped to create a tradition of using television as a means not only for its dissemination but also as a tool for expressive editorializing. He helped to establish the format for documentary and newsmagazine programs and, in his pursuit of excellence, established an ethical and moral foundation for broadcast journalism. Eventually news became a staple of television, with local and national news becoming dominant forms of programming.

Television's appeal as a mass medium helped to create a culture of celebrity for national news anchors, who are viewed by their audience as stars. Indeed, one of the most trusted of these personalities was former CBS News anchor Walter Cronkite, who said that he didn't cover political candidates on the campaign trail because he was afraid of attracting more attention than they attract.

Televised news has become a dominant form of content and has evolved into a number of distinctive formats. Newsmagazines have replaced the long-form documentary, with *60 Minutes* and *20/20* setting the standard. There has also been a departure from legitimate journalism to tabloid, with an emphasis on "if it bleeds, it leads" stories.

Cable television and the Internet have provided new platforms for the dissemination of news. CNN has evolved from the "Chicken Noodle Network" to a mainstream 24-hour broadcast-news organization and a viable competitor to broadcast-network news. The NBC television network was one of the first to interface its three platforms of broadcast, cable (MSNBC), and Web into a cohesive information-provider unit.

## Chapter 14, Miniseries/Docudrama: A Delicate Balance

Creating a compelling long-form television narrative that attracts an audience weekly or nightly over weeks or even months can be a daunting task. The television miniseries, sometimes referred to in the trade as the *novel for television,* presented a unique opportunity for the networks to capitalize on the buzz of the series and build a loyal audience for its run. The miniseries concept was imported from England when *The Forsyte Saga,* a 26-part BBC series based upon the John Galsworthy novels of Victorian-Edwardian England, made its debut on public television in the 1969–70 season. That series helped to establish the miniseries as a viable genre of entertainment for American audiences. The most compelling example of the enduring legacy of the televised miniseries is the adaptation of Alex Haley's *Roots,* which appeared on the ABC television network during the last week of 1977.

After the success of *The Forsyte Saga,* public television licensed the miniseries *Upstairs Downstairs* from London Weekend Television. The Public Broadcasting Service created *Masterpiece Theatre* as a permanent niche for imported British programming, underwritten by the Mobil Corporation. The series proved to be a great success, and CBS attempted to duplicate the theme of class distinction in the American version, *Beacon Hill.* Although *Beacon Hill* did not fare well in the ratings, the miniseries format was recognized as a viable programming genre and became a staple of network programming.

Although once a popular programming format, docudramas have been one of the most controversial. Their blending of fact and fiction, along with the creation of composite characters and a manipulated chronology of events, has raised doubts about their reputed accuracy. Many of the subjects for these programs originate from screaming newspaper headlines with sexual themes and hostile confrontations. Perhaps the tawdriest examples were the three separate Amy Fisher movies produced by the television networks. The dynamics of the teenage mistress, assaulted wife, and philandering husband were too irresistible for television to neglect.

## Chapter 15, Sports and Television: The Tortoise Meets the Hare

There is a mystique associated with sports in this country that manifests itself at every juncture of American society. It defines various behavioral attitudes associated with work, family, leisure, economics, and politics. Perhaps more than any other activity, sports and their associated endeavors permeate our culture with an essence and texture that create an enduring presence. Professional athletes are nurtured and pampered within the context of their achievements with wealth and the lingering cheers of their fans. They are lionized for their achievements and cast in roles that define them as models for society.

Athletes have become symbols of merit, worth, discipline, morality, and commerce that make them icons of our culture. They wear signs of consumerism, branding themselves as tools of capitalism. As idols, they reflect the values that they embrace and are revered not only for their athletic prowess but also for business acumen and its associated success. As their likeness appears on billboards, television commercials, Web sites, and cereal boxes, there's a virtual presence permeating the boundaries of life while moving the psychology of the arena to every aspect of American culture.

Television has taken the excitement of sports into the intimacy of American homes and provided audiences with a unique view of the dynamics of competition. With its ability to selectively create the viewing experience, it has added a new dimension to how sports are appreciated. Television has created a sporting culture that projects an image of endurance and accomplishment within the context of consumerism.

Television has created a compelling broadcasting canvas, generating a drama and pathos associated with the thrill of competition and victory. It has taken what were once marginally popular sports, like golf and tennis, and built images and legends associated with those games. Television has created sports franchises such as *Monday Night Football*, World Series baseball games, Olympic coverage, Grand Slams, PGA tournaments, and the Super Bowl, providing a vernacular for narrative exposition and commentary.

The association of athletes with television as pitchmen and pitchwomen, commentators, and analysts is a long-standing one that presumes an identity of celebrity that is bought and paid for by television. It's a symbiotic relationship nurtured by greed, fame, and wealth for players, owners, and television networks. Television and sports are a volatile mix of business and competition that is finessed by the leagues, the team owners, television, and licensed product manufacturers to generate income that feeds a system of inflated egos and salaries.

## Chapter 16, Trends and Issues

There are a number of variables impacting the future of television programming. The first is the structure of television as it exists today. Several competitive technologies—like direct broadcast satellite (DBS), microwave (RCN), cable, TiVo/Replay (which allow for customized video recording), high-definition television (HDTV), and the Internet—threaten the dominance of broadcast-network television. The escalating cost of producing network television programs and the need to accommodate increasing demands from talent for equity, along with satisfying political priorities, will affect the programming environment and future trends.

# 1

# THE SEEDS OF TELEVISION PROGRAMMING: THE NETWORKS STEAL FROM RADIO

As radio grew and became a popular medium, it developed a number of programming genres that had antecedents in theater, music, and variety programs. The first radio stations, some of which were experimental and affiliated with universities, played records or had a live vocalist with a pianist accompaniment in the studio. The format was simple because of the limits of early radio technology.

Indeed, the economics of radio was envisioned by David Sarnoff, who, as a young man, worked for the American Marconi Company in New York City. He served as a telegraph operator and was on duty in 1912 when the ill-fated *Titanic* sank on her maiden voyage. Sarnoff was the critical link between the rescue ship *Carpathia* and the public as the names of survivors were being telegraphed to shore.[1]

The American Marconi Company was a foreign entity, and the United States Congress was sensitive to having it influence domestic telecommunications policy. Even when a branch of the military, under the auspices of Josephus Daniels, the Secretary of the Navy, lobbied for passage of a revision to the Radio Act of 1912 that would allow the government to control radio, it was rebuffed by Congress. To many, this was seen as a hostile move by a branch of the military to control the potential dominance of this mass medium.

## A CHOSEN INSTRUMENT

In 1919 the Radio Corporation of America (RCA) was created with the intention of becoming the American instrument for managing international communications policy. Edward J. Nally was installed as president, and David Sarnoff became the commercial manager. This allowed for the pooling or sharing of close to 2,000 valuable patents essential to the manufacture of radio sets. With the company's charter requirement that 80 percent of its stock be in American hands, RCA effectively removed the threat of the Marconi companies, which were foreign-owned, to manage ship-to-shore and other modes of international communication.

Under the terms of the agreement negotiated by Owen D. Young of General Electric, by 1921 the four partners in RCA (Westinghouse joined later) had equity under the following terms: General Electric, 30.1 percent; Westinghouse, 20.6 percent; AT&T, 10.3 percent; and United Fruit, 4.1 percent. Each of the prominent companies—G.E., Westinghouse, and AT&T—could build equipment for their own use; AT&T had the exclusive right to use radio telephony for hire (advertising), G.E. and Westinghouse could manufacture radios and supply them to RCA, and RCA would administer the patent pool (collecting royalties) and operate all maritime radio communication for hire.[2]

The first three of these companies dominated the American marketplace in electronics and telecommunications, while United Fruit found the wireless to be an invaluable tool in managing its far-flung plantations and bringing its products to market. All of these companies held patents in electronics that were needed for the manufacture of radio sets.

It was David Sarnoff who first perceived the potential of radio as a mass commercial medium. While employed by American Marconi as commercial manager, he wrote a memo to his boss, Edward Nally, in which he explained how "radio music boxes" could become a "household utility." In that same memo Sarnoff uncannily predicted yearly sales of radio sets over a three-year period.

There were a number of recommendations that were suggested in an effort to realize a feasible means to support radio and make it profitable, including voluntary audience contributions, purchasing seats for an invisible "theater of the air," annually taxing radio receivers, and direct advertising. The last of these approaches is what AT&T decided to pursue.

AT&T's attempt to create a commercial imperative for radio was called *toll broadcasting*. In its simplest form, AT&T would allow a person or entity to use the studio facilities at the radio station it owned, WEAF in New York, and for a per-minute fee broadcast a commercial message. The company, which was a part of the telephone group that consisted of AT&T and its subsidiary Western Electric, argued that under the patent agreements it had exclusive rights to manufacture and sell radio transmitters, sell time for advertising, and interconnect stations by wire for network or chain broadcasting. It was aggressively pursuing this posture, to the dismay of the radio group: RCA, General Electric, and Western Union. The first commercial message was broadcast on WEAF on August 28, 1922, for Hawthorne Estates, a cooperative housing community in Jackson Heights, New York City.

## NETWORK PIONEERS

A discussion of the historical roots of programming must include an understanding of the evolution of networking. As networking among radio stations prevailed, it created a need to provide programming to a growing audience. On September 9, 1926, RCA created a new network corporation, the National Broadcasting Company (NBC). It was owned by RCA (50%), General Electric (30%), and Westinghouse (20%), and Merlin H. Aylesworth, previously managing director of the National Electric Light Association, was named president. Several months later NBC purchased radio station WEAF from AT&T's Broadcasting Company of America for $1 million, removing AT&T from the broadcasting business.

Ushering in a new age of programming relevance within the context of networking, NBC had its premiere broadcast on November 15, 1926. It was a programming extravaganza, originating at WEAF from the Grand Ballroom of the Waldorf Astoria Hotel in New York, carried by 21 affiliates, linked by 3,600 miles of special telephone cable, and featuring the talent of humorist Will Rogers and numerous musicians and vocalists.

Shortly after the inauguration of the NBC network, RCA took control of WJZ in New York, which was the flagship station of the old Radio Group network. Using its facilities, RCA embarked on a second network. This network joined with WEAF in the January 1, 1927, broadcast of the Rose Bowl game between Stanford and Alabama. Soon, within the lexicon of the company hierarchy, the WEAF network was known as NBC Blue, while the WJZ network was known as NBC Red. Also, in 1927 NBC launched the Pacific Coast Network, which utilized as its foundation stations KGO and KPO in San Francisco. This network was short-lived because in 1928 NBC initiated full-time coast-to-coast programming on both the NBC Red and NBC Blue networks.

A complex web of maneuvering from 1926 to 1927 served as the pioneering efforts to create the Columbia Broadcasting System, the network that would compete with NBC. It started with Arthur Judson's Radio Program Corporation, a talent-booking firm that became United Independent Broadcasters and eventually merged with the Columbia Phonograph Corporation and was called Columbia Phonograph Broadcasting System. With the Judson Radio Corporation and United Independent Broadcasters on shaky financial ground, and a loss of $100,000 sustained by the Columbia Phonograph Broadcasting System during the first month, the record company opted out of the deal, and the name was changed to the Columbia Broadcasting System (CBS).

New investors were found to bail out the company; however, after continuing losses they grew disillusioned and offered to sell controlling interest in CBS-UIB. As is so often the case in business, a white knight was found, in the guise of a young vice president at a family-owned company. It was William Paley who convinced his family, which owned the Congress Cigar Company in Philadelphia, to advertise their La Palina Cigar on 26 programs over the CBS Network. That was in 1928, and soon after, Paley bought a controlling interest in CBS-UIB for $300,000, with subsequent family investments that brought the total up to $1.5 million. A shrewd negotiator and arbiter of talent, Paley was able to infuse his fledgling network with $5,000,000 in Paramount stock for 49 percent of his company.

An aggressive businessman, William Paley knew in the years 1948–49 that television was on the horizon and that much of the talent on radio would migrate to television. Faced with the prospect of fewer television station affiliates, Paley initiated what are known as *talent raids*. He and his accountants devised a clever plan that would allow radio stars to form their own corporations with themselves as the primary asset. Then CBS would buy the company at a considerable price, and instead of paying a tax on income or salary, the principal star would be taxed on the capital gain from the sale of the company. This tax would amount to less than a tax on income. In other words, they were taking their income in a capital gain.

The plan enticed some of the most prominent radio personalities to move from NBC and ABC to CBS. Perhaps the most notable were Freeman F. Gosden and Charles Correll, the voices of the wildly popular *Amos 'n' Andy*. They were lured from NBC to CBS by a $2 million payout. Other stars followed, including Jack Benny; Edgar Bergen and his dummy, Charlie McCarthy; Bing Crosby; and *The Adventures of Ozzie and Harriet*. Eventually, of course, NBC retaliated and recruited several CBS stars, including Groucho Marx, Bob Hope, Kate Smith, and Ed Wynn.

## HIS MASTER'S VOICE: TELEVISION'S PROGRAMMING ANTECEDENTS

By 1938 various radio programming genres had established themselves within the structure of network and local radio. More than half the programming on radio had some form of musical orientation. There was also talk, drama, news, religion, and special events. Network radio affiliates were receiving 70 percent of their programming from their network.

Musical programming proved to be a popular format in the early days of radio. It attracted sponsors that became so closely associated with the genre that often the sponsor's product name would appear in the title of the program. Programs like *Cliquot Club Eskimos* and *Michelin Tire Men* were indicative of this trend, which also occurred later in television.

For the sponsor, there was a cachet of distinction to be earned by being associated with a prestigious orchestra and the broadcasting of concert music. The NBC radio network attracted noted conductors like Arturo Toscanini and the New York Philharmonic. Toscanini later became the conductor of the NBC symphony orchestra. Several of these programs, like the Saturday afternoon broadcast of the Metropolitan Opera (a 72-year-old tradition) and the live broadcasts from Salt Lake City of the Mormon Tabernacle Choir, had such a loyal audience that they lasted for decades, and in some instances continue to be broadcast.

By the late 1940s the musical programming format had matured into a programming staple that included *Milkman's Matinee* and *Martin Block's Make-Believe Ballroom*. One of the most popular music-oriented formats was *Stop the Music,* which offered audience listeners substantial cash prizes if, when called, they could identify the music being played. This format is still being used as an audience-grabber, offering prizes to listeners on radio stations today.

While music was a popular format for radio programming, drama, in the guise of daytime serials, became an enduring genre. In 1935 the daytime serial radio drama, or *soap opera,* became a mainstay of network programming, with 75 hours a week and 9 out of 10 daytime sponsored hours. They were popular with women listeners, had permanent daytime scheduling berths, and had a running time of 15 minutes. Some of the most popular and enduring programs were *Back Stage Wife, Guiding Light, Our Gal Sunday, The Romance of Helen Trent, Ma Perkins,* and *Just Plain Bill.* These programs featured themes that had to do with frustrated love, balancing careers with marriage, and raising a family. The reason the genre became known as *soap opera* is because the programs had soap and food manufacturers as sponsors. A prominent force behind the production of these programs was the husband-and-wife writing team of Frank and Ann Hummert. Other contributors included Elaine Carrington and Irna Phillips.

## RADIO DRAMA: MARTIANS AND SUPERHEROES

Legitimate drama also evolved during the 1930s, with playwrights like Norman Corwin, Arch Oboler, and poet Archibald MacLeish writing provocative radio plays. Dramatic radio series included *Columbia Workshop, Lux Radio Theater,* and *The Mercury Theater on the Air.* In one of the most notable dramatic programs of the radio era, the obscure town of Grovers Mill, New Jersey, became a trial for the convergence of fiction and the power of the mass medium of radio.

When analyzing talent, there are few who measure up to the creative genius and innate grasp of drama of Orson Welles. When he was 23 years old, he became the creative force behind *The Mercury Theater on the Air.* In 1938, on October 30, the eve of Halloween, Welles broadcast a radio drama based on H. G. Wells's science fiction work *War of the Worlds.* In a clever narrative that took place entirely in a radio studio, Welles made it appear as if Martians invaded the earth and landed (where else?) in the "wilds" of Grovers Mill, New Jersey.

Although the program included three announcements indicating that it was a dramatization, some listeners either didn't hear it or tuned in late, as was the practice of some in the audience, who would listen to the first few minutes of Edgar Bergen and Charlie McCarthy on NBC.

The reaction by many listeners was unprecedented, as panic reigned with people fleeing their homes in an effort to avoid the gas attacks by the Martians. The next day the newspapers ran banner headlines about the broadcast. The *New York Daily News* on October 31 read, FAKE RADIO WAR STIRS TERROR THROUGH U.S., while the *New York Times* printed a story with the headline RADIO LISTENERS IN PANIC, TAKING WAR DRAMA AS FACT and the lead "Many Flee Homes to Escape 'Gas Raid From Mars'—Phone Calls Swamp Police at Broadcast of Wells Fantasy."

The program demonstrated the power of radio as a mass medium and the impact it would have on society. It also confirmed that radio was perceived by the audience as a corroboration of truth. Concerns about the merits of using radio in this manner prompted the Federal Communications Commission (FCC), which is responsible for determining policy and regulating radio and television, to issue a statement indicating it they did not consider such scare programs as broadcasting in the public interest.

Another popular genre of radio that also became prevalent on television was the thriller-adventure and situation-comedy formats. The evening crime-detective programs featured crime-fighting heroes with colorful names, tantalizing legends, and vivid costumes (albeit imaginary for radio). There was the Lone Ranger, the Green Hornet, and the Shadow (alias Lamont Cranston), whose hypnotic power would render him invisible. There were also programs based upon enduring literary characters, such as the famous detective Sherlock Holmes, whose exploits remained on radio for many years with different ensemble casts. Children had their own heroes, which included afternoon dramas featuring Captain Midnight and Hop Harriagan (both swashbuckling pilots), Jack Armstrong (the All-American Boy), Terry and the Pirates (based upon a popular comic strip), and the cowboy Tom Mix. Other children's radio heroes included Sky King, the singing cowboy Roy Rogers, and Space Patrol. Along with cowboys, Westerns proved to be popular with audiences, and *Death Valley Days,* an anthology series that made its debut in 1930, was one of the first to capture the myth for radio, along with the enduring presence of the adult Western *Gunsmoke,* which later became a hit program for CBS, running for over 20 years.

## SONG, DANCE, AND COMEDY

Variety programs were also popular on radio and usually featured a host along with guest artists. An audience favorite was the Fleischmann Yeast program featuring the popular crooner Rudy Vallee, which made its debut in 1929 and was sponsored by Fleischmann Yeast for 10 years. Radio nurtured one of the most popular variety-program hosts in the history of television, Ed Sullivan, who started on radio in 1931 and became a television cultural icon with his program *Toast of the Town*, which later became *The Ed Sullivan Show*. Other programs included *Dutch Masters Minstrels* and *National Barn Dance*.

The variety program concept also embraced comedy. Comedians like Eddie Cantor, whose show ran for 10 years; Al Jolson, who was featured in *The Jazz Singer*, the first talking picture; the husband-and-wife team of George Burns and Gracie Allen; Jack Benny; and Fred Allen were all stars of this genre. Indeed, Jack Benny, along with Burns and Allen, successfully made the transition from radio to television, enabling them to incorporate visual humor into their comedic routines within the context of situation comedy.

Situation comedy in radio had one of the most cherished programs to ever hit the airwaves, *Amos 'n' Andy*. The show featured two former vaudeville entertainers, Freeman F. Gosden and Charles J. Correll, who performed in blackface and used black dialogue. They brought their *Sam 'n' Henry* act to radio station WGN in Chicago and two years later, after unsuccessful salary arbitration with the station, changed the name to *Amos 'n' Andy* and moved it to station WMAQ. Shortly after, in 1929, the program moved to the NBC Blue network, which paid the team $100,000 a year. Gosden and Correll played all the characters associated with the Freshair Taxicab Company and the fraternal lodge Mystic Knights of the Sea.

Soon after the move to NBC, *Amos 'n' Andy* became a huge hit and a cultural phenomenon. Sponsored by Pepsodent toothpaste, the program was eagerly anticipated by a loyal audience who tuned in six times a week. As a testimony to the program's popularity, movie theaters would interrupt the evening's screening for 15 minutes so that the theatrical audience wouldn't miss the program.

Although by today's standards black audiences would find the exaggerated dialect, malapropisms, and mispronunciations offensive, especially as mimicked by two white actors, both blacks and whites were loyal listeners. With the coming of television, *Amos 'n' Andy* made the transition, albeit with an ensemble cast of black actors.

Ethnic humor, although stereotypical, was a popular format for radio in the 1920s and 1930s. *The Rise of the Goldbergs* (later shortened to *The Goldbergs*), written by and starring Gertrude Berg, was about an urban Jewish family facing different situations in each program. It helped to establish the role of an ensemble cast continuing from week to week in a series format. Other serial radio programs included the popular *One Man's Family*, which was the first program originating from the West Coast, and *Clara, Lu, and Em*.

Radio is an incubator for talk and commentary programs, and the genre is still popular today with shock jocks like Howard Stern. A humorist named Will Rogers, who was a successful performer, used radio to comment on the foibles of political leaders and the popular discontent with government. Will

Rogers was much more sophisticated and urbane than Stern is, and possessed a satirical and dry wit.

There were some popular hosts who were affiliated with various religious denominations and used radio as a pulpit to preach. In 1929 Harry Emerson Fosdick began the Protestant-oriented program *National Vespers* on the NBC Blue network, which was followed shortly after by the *Catholic Hour*.

## FIREBRANDS AND DEMAGOGUES

Just as today, these early radio talk programs could stir their share of controversy. One of the most notorious of these was the Catholic priest Father Charles E. Coughlin. He originated his broadcasts from his parish, the Shrine of the Little Flower, which was in Royal Oaks, near Detroit, Michigan. When he started his broadcasts over radio station WJR in 1926, his parish served only 28 families, but eventually Coughlin's audience grew larger and generated $500,000 a year in contributions. His bombastic attacks and anti-Semitic slurs caused CBS to cancel his program and end the policy of selling airtime for religious broadcasts. Instead, CBS created a multidenominational series entitled *Church of the Air,* which rotated clergy without charge for airtime.

Coughlin responded by organizing his own network of stations, bypassing CBS and NBC. In the mid-1930s his program had a loyal audience and could be heard throughout the country.

Another Catholic clergyman, who started in radio in 1928 with a regular program on the *Catholic Hour* but didn't attain a large following until his network television show *Life Is Worth Living* in 1952, was "Angel of the Airwaves" Bishop Fulton J. Sheen. He became an enormously popular television celebrity, at times threatening the ratings of his competition, "Mr. Television" Milton Berle, on an opposing network.

Just as the clergy recognized the power of radio, politicians also saw it as a tool to reach their constituents. *Share Our Wealth,* a program hosted by Senator Huey Long, the former governor of Louisiana, was a popular audience-pleaser. Long used radio to espouse his platform of providing every family with an income of $2,500 a year and a homestead worth $5,000. As radio had the ability to reach a mass audience, Long's Share-Our-Wealth clubs spread to thousands of cities and towns across the country. He criticized President Franklin Roosevelt and his initiatives in the New Deal administration, and in 1935 Long was assassinated.

In addition to demagogues, radio also became attractive to charlatans. Just as the patent medicine man of the Old West rambled into town in his rickety wagon hawking elixirs and snake-oil treatments, Dr. John Romulus Brinkley found a niche on radio to do the same. With questionable medical credentials, Brinkley freely dispensed advice and his own brand of numbered tonics to listeners of *Medical Question Box* writing in to station KFKB in Milford, Kansas, and describing their ailments. There is, of course, some similarity between

Brinkley's mode of treatment in absentia and using the Internet as a prescriptive tool.

With his lucrative pharmaceutical company and network of dispensing pharmacists, Brinkley had a thriving business duping his listeners. He also ventured into surgical transplants, using the gonads of goats to restore sexual rejuvenation, known as his notorious goat-gland operation. It became so popular that he needed a steady supply of goats! In 1930 the Federal Radio Commission (FRC) decided not to renew Brinkley's license because the Kansas State Medical Board revoked his medical credentials, which he received from a diploma mill. In defiance of the FRC's decision, Brinkley moved his broadcasting operation to the border town of Del Rio, Texas, and continued broadcasting from Mexico until 1940, when he was forced off the air.

## WITNESS TO HISTORY

Radio also served as a witness to history before television arrived, reporting newsworthy events. The first trial ever covered by the mass medium of radio is known as the "Monkey Trial." In 1925 John Scopes, a high-school teacher in Dayton, Tennessee, was charged with violating state law by teaching Charles Darwin's theory of evolution. It was a hot summer when battalions of journalists and photographers descended upon the small country mountain courthouse in Dayton, Tennessee, to witness two of the county's leading jurists, William Jennings Bryan (assisting the prosecution) and Clarence Darrow (aiding the defense).

In Chicago, where Darrow was from, there was a great deal of interest related to the trial. The *Chicago Tribune* station, WGN, brought in a telephone line at a cost of $1,000 a day for broadcast coverage of the trial. Its reporter, Quin Ryan, broadcast live from the stifling heat of the courtroom. Scopes was found guilty and fined $100 plus court costs, and several days later William Jennings Bryan collapsed and died.

Two years later, in 1927, radio covered the dramatic trans-Atlantic flight of Charles Lindbergh, the "Lone Eagle," in his single-engine plane, the *Spirit of St. Louis*. After 11 hours of tense waiting without a sighting, CHNS, a radio station in Halifax, reported that Lindbergh's plane had been sighted off Cape Race. Of course, the world celebrated when radio and the newspapers reported that he touched down in Paris at 5:21 P.M. and was hailed a world hero. Three weeks later, NBC radio covered Lindbergh's triumphant return and hero's welcome by President Coolidge at the Washington Monument, and the network provided live coverage reported by Graham McNamee of a ticker-tape parade in New York with Governor Al Smith and Mayor Jimmy Walker presiding.

As Lindbergh triumphed in the glory and celebration of his bold adventure, he would remain a hero and once again become the focal point of media attention five years later. In a tragic kidnapping involving his infant son,

Charles and Anne Morrow Lindbergh shared their anguish with the world. CBS and NBC sprang into action, with the first bulletin, received at 12:14 A.M., read by Harlow Wilcox from Chicago's WBBM. CBS ran a special line to Hopewell, New Jersey, location of the Lindbergh estate, and operated out of a vacant store, while NBC worked out of a local restaurant. Noted broadcast reporters of the day such as Lowell Thomas (NBC), Boake Carter (CBS), and Gabriel Heatter (WOR, Mutual) covered the search for the baby, the apprehension of the suspect Bruno Richard Hauptmann two and a half years later, the trial, and the execution.

Although microphones were not allowed in the courtroom, there were still- and motion-picture photographers. The decorum of the trial suffered as a result of the crowded courtroom and the celebrities involved. It was perhaps one of the most egregious violations of protocol within the annals of jurisprudence.

Decrying the carnival-like atmosphere, the American Bar Association adopted Canon 35, which closed courtrooms to photographers and was amended in 1963 to include radio and television.

Radio became a tool for instantaneous communication and distribution of news and events. On May 6, 1937, Herbert Morrison, a reporter from WLS Chicago, traveled to Lakehurst, New Jersey, to make an electrical transcription of an eyewitness account of the German dirigible *Hindenburg* on its 11th transatlantic crossing as it arrived for docking. Morrison and his engineer, Charles Nehlsen, witnessed the fire and explosion of 7 million cubic feet of flammable hydrogen. In one of the most dramatic and emotional descriptive narrative accounts in the history of radio, Morrison articulated what he saw and was overwhelmed by his emotion.

These radio programs, featuring news and entertainment, were role models for early television. They explored the limits of the medium, creating a language with a visual imperative that articulated the essence of the story to the radio audience. Using sound effects and descriptive narrative, these early radio programs were able to transport listeners to places they might never visit and introduce them to colorful, compelling characters. In many cases they served as the foundation for future television programming, creating enduring formats in a seamless arc of time.

## NOTES

1. Erik Barnouw, *Tube of Plenty: The Evolution of American Television,* rev. ed. (New York: Oxford University Press, 1982).

2. Christopher H. Sterling and John Michael Kittross, *Stay Tuned: A History of American Broadcasting,* 3rd ed. (Mahwah, N.J.: Lawrence Erlbaum, 2002).

# 2

## TINSELTOWN COMES TO TV

There were several variables that helped to shape and determine the direction of television programming in postwar America. They had to do with economics, technology, culture, networking, and Hollywood film studios. It was a harbinger of things to come when David Sarnoff, president of RCA, opened the television exhibit at the 1939 World's Fair. Visitors flocked there to see this new and wondrous form of entertainment. That same year, the first baseball game was televised, between Princeton and Columbia.

The radio networks—CBS, NBC, and later ABC (created from the NBC Blue Network in 1945)—were positioned to reap a bonanza of profits from television. However, the cost of building studios, equipping them, securing affiliated stations, and building or buying owned-and-operated stations was substantial.

An early means for the networks of providing television programming without ignoring their radio affiliates was to broadcast a live program over television while simulcasting the audio portion over radio. The first of the network television programs to successfully utilize simulcasting were *Arthur Godfrey's Talent Scouts,* which started its CBS simulcast on December 6, 1948, and NBC's *The Voice of Firestone,* September 1949.

Many successful network radio programs were moved to television, including *Ted Mack's Original Amateur Hour* on the Dumont Network (a continuation of the enduring *Major Bowes and His Original Amateur Hour*), and, on NBC, *Texaco Star Theater,* which became a vehicle for television's first big star, Milton Berle. The networks and advertisers made a conscious effort to sacrifice radio for television.

## THE NETWORKS MOVE TO TELEVISION

Most of early television programming was live and required expensive interconnection costs to reach affiliated stations. Some of the network stations were not interconnected, so kinescopes or tele-transcriptions, which were filmed recordings of the television program from the television monitor, were sent to those stations. This technique was a valuable tool prior to 1952, when coast-to-coast network lines were being constructed. Those stations that weren't interconnected needed programming, and advertisers needed additional markets for merchandising. In 1949 the networks distributed in excess of 2,000 hours of kinescoped programming to unconnected affiliated stations.

Not surprisingly, NBC, backed by the financial clout of RCA, was the first radio network to move toward television. With RCA's expertise in electronics and David Sarnoff's industry leadership, by 1946 it had four network stations, including its flagship station in New York, WNBT. By 1948 the network had grown to 25 affiliates in the Northeast and Midwest.

The CBS strategy was more deliberate. It moved into television by purchasing its flagship stations and devoting a great deal of effort and money to designing and implementing color television. Its rival, RCA (parent of NBC) was also racing to perfect a color television system.

In 1941 a new network was created, evolving from a divestiture order from the FCC that NBC sell one of its radio networks. After an attempt to block the order, it sold NBC Blue, the weaker of its networks, to Edward J. Noble, the inventor of Lifesaver candy, for $8 million, and he renamed it ABC (American Broadcasting Company).

Needing cash to finance its move into television, Noble was looking for prospective partners, and several suitors, including International Telephone and Telegraph and General Tire and Rubber, were interested. However, in a fortuitous move for ABC and the future of television, Noble aligned his company with United Paramount Theaters (the divested theater chain of Paramount) and its president, Leonard Goldenson.

United Paramount Theaters, an exhibition company, was spun off from Paramount by a court-ordered consent decree in 1949. Under the terms prescribed by the Justice Department, United Paramount Theaters, which was the former exhibition company for Paramount, had to reduce its ownership of theaters from 1,400 to 650 within five years. Most importantly, Paramount also promised $30 million for program development, and brought substantial experience in television management through its ownership of Chicago station WBKB, one of the earliest commercial television stations.

There were a number of critical economic issues that ABC had to circumvent before becoming competitive with NBC and CBS. In the early 1950s, ABC and Dumont were the weakest of the networks. Most significantly, ABC suffered from having fewer affiliated stations, some of which were in the hard-to-receive UHF band as opposed to the stronger VHF. In addition, their program clearance rate, which is the number of affiliated stations airing a live program, was only 34 percent in 1953, and increased to just 58 percent in 1955, with 84 affiliates. In comparison, CBS, with 121 stations, had a live clearance rate of 87 percent, while NBC, with 104 affiliates, managed a rate of 90 percent.

Therefore, ABC, under the guidance of Leonard Goldenson, proclaimed a five-year plan for building a prime-time schedule with a priority on developing new sources for programming and limiting the role of sponsors and advertising agencies. In the early 1950s, the television networks acted as repositories for programs developed by advertising agencies by merely selling them time with no creative or development control. Because ABC was the weakest of the major networks, the agencies would place programs with the least potential for success there, and if the program became popular, they would move it to either CBS or NBC. Indeed, the policy of having programs produced by advertising agencies was rationalized by the networks as their defense for the fraud perpetrated by the quiz shows.

Another concern for ABC was the expense of developing original programming and the reality that many of the stars were already under contract with one of its rival networks. Its new strategy was focused upon forging an alliance with Hollywood studios, licensing telefilms for exclusive distribution on ABC. The network's ace in the hole was, of course, Leonard Goldenson, whose reputation at Paramount and subsequently at United Paramount Theaters had earned him the respect of the Hollywood film community. However, Hollywood's disdain for television was so pervasive that Jack Warner, the head of Warner Brothers, forbade the presence of a television set in any at-home scenes of Warner features. But amid the undercurrent of hostility, Hollywood was staying close to developments in the television industry.

## HOLLYWOOD'S FIRST FLICKERS TOWARD TELEVISION

Indeed, Hollywood's investment acumen was especially perceptive when it came to the hardware and software of television. Viewing television as an alternate means for the exhibition of their feature-length films, studios like Paramount, Twentieth Century Fox, and Warner Brothers experimented with theater or pay television in the 1940s. Paramount was especially prescient in determining the potential value of television to the Hollywood studios. An executive of Paramount, Paul Raiborn, sat on the boards of two companies, American Scophony and the Dumont Television Network, each of which Paramount held significant equity as well as influence in. Indeed, in 1938, Allen B. Dumont, who developed the first practical television set, partnered with Paramount Pictures to build a network of broadcast television stations. However, Paramount embarked on its own ambitious plan to build television stations that did not distribute Dumont television network programs. The movie studio owned and operated television stations in Los Angeles and Chicago and held a number of patents on the television cathode-ray tube. Warner Brothers also had an interest in television, having purchased a majority position in Trans-American Television and Broadcasting Company.

With the movie studios being somewhat beguiled by the potential of theater or pay television as part of their strategy, they withheld talent and film product from broadcast television. In the interim, the FCC was less sanguine about the studios' pursuit of pay television and would not authorize any allocations or assignments to support the studios' endeavors throughout the 1950s. Indeed, the FCC in 1950 admonished the Hollywood studios for withholding film product and talent from television.[1]

Interestingly, the first experiment with pay television was in 1930 in Schenectady, New York. The following year, Zenith unveiled its Phonevision pay-television system; however, the FCC did not authorize a consumer demonstration until 1951. Implementing the test with 300 Chicago families, the system charged one dollar for each showing. After the three-month test period concluded, the Phonevision system lay dormant until 1962, when Zenith resurrected the system in Hartford, Connecticut. Repackaged as the Television Entertainment Company, the FCC sanctioned this experiment, which lasted until 1969 and was broadcast over RKO General UHF station WHCT-TV. Although this effort helped to lay a foundation for subscription television legislation, it failed to attract enough viewers to make the service profitable.

The FCC did authorize other companies to implement pay-television demonstrations, and, of course, Paramount was one of them. It created International Telemeter Corporation, which in 1953 initiated a five-month coin-box demonstration in Palm Springs, California. Predominantly owned by Paramount Pictures, the company from 1960 to 1965 operated a pay-television system in Etobicoke, Canada.

In the 1950s cable television was beginning to be utilized as a technology that could provide broadcast reception to communities located in valleys and other inhospitable television reception areas. Jerrold Electronics, a company headed by former Pennsylvania governor Milton Shapp, initiated the first pay cable experiment in 1958 by joining with Video Independent Theaters to serve the 30,000 people of Bartlesville, Oklahoma. The system premiered with the first-run feature *Pajama Game*.

Although the Hollywood studios were interested in pursuing the potential of television, they nevertheless had to be sensitive to the theater owners, who threatened to boycott their product if the studios became too intimate with television. Therefore, Columbia and Universal each used separate casts and crews, divorcing their telefilm from their theatrical production.

Hollywood was poised to supply product to television, and in 1948 Frederick W. Ziv, the largest packager and syndicator in the country, started telefilm production. Already accomplished in the radio transcription business, Ziv syndicated popular television programs like *The Man Called X, I Led Three Lives, The Cisco Kid, Boston Blackie,* and *The Falcon*. Another producer who switched from theatrical features to telefilms was Hal Roach Sr., who placed his son, Hal Roach Jr., in charge of the new company. Some of their programs included *Fireside Theatre, Public Defender, Duffy's Tavern, Code Three, Racket Squad, Passport to Danger, My Little Margie,* and a number of *Magnavox Theater* episodes. The first Hollywood producer to sell a series was Jerry Fairbanks Jr., who sold *The Public Prosecutor* to the NBC television network. He was an innovator who pioneered the multiple-camera technique of using several cameras at different angles shooting simultaneously. Other shows he produced included *Silver Theater, Bigelow Theatre* (also known as Bigelow-Sanford Theatre on Dumont, 1951), and *Front Page Detective*.

One movie studio that was active in the mid-1940s producing film for television was RKO. As a producer of commercials, RKO launched a series of filmed spots for the Bulova Watch Company. RKO-Pathe (merged in 1931) created two series for television in 1946: *Do You Know?* (a quiz show that utilized clips from the RKO film library) and *Ten Years Ago Today* (which cleverly used clips from old RKO-Pathe newsreels).

As early as 1950, Universal, which had purchased the Ziv Company, was using television to promote its films. Two programs, *Hollywood Flashes* and *Moviestar Album,* along with filmed commercials for products like Lux soap and Chevrolet, were produced by the studio for broadcast. By 1952 these deals left a chink in the armor of the Hollywood film community and its reluctance toward television. That year, Screen Gems, a wholly owned subsidiary of Columbia Pictures, entered into a $1 million deal with Ford Motor Company to produce 39 half-hour television films for *Ford Theatre*. In addition, they produced nine other television programs, including such enduring classics as *Father Knows Best* and *Rin Tin Tin*. Also, in 1952 Universal's United World Films and its Decca records distribution company, Republic's Hollywood Telefilms, and Monogram's Interstate Television all started producing telefilms. Independent producers like F. W. Ziv, Desilu, and Hal Roach Jr. aggressively entered television production by buying up studio lots.

Paramount utilized its wholly owned subsidiary television station KTLA for its filmed network, which distributed programs like *Time for Beany, Frosty Frolics,* and *Sandy Dreams* via Paramount Video Transcription. Later, Paramount became a major telefilm producer with *Lux Video Theatre* and utilized *The Colgate Comedy Hour,* with its stars Dean Martin and Jerry Lewis, as a showcase for its featured players, films, and musical scores.

Perhaps the most auspicious telefilm deal for ABC, and one that served as a model for the television industry, was its alliance with Walt Disney. After Disney's successful CBS Christmas special, the studio invited the networks to develop proposals for telefilm projects. The only hitch was that Walt Disney, who was building the Disneyland theme park in California, wanted a $500,000 contribution from the chosen network. Many in the television industry had little faith in Disney's "folly," but ABC was willing to spend the money and lose it just for the Disney franchise. However, that amount of money was just a drop in the bucket when it came to the $17 million investment to build Walt Disney's "Disneyland" in Anaheim, California. Both CBS and NBC had turned him down as potential investors, and the banks saw an amusement park as too risky for their support. However, with the influence that United Paramount Theater executives and Leonard Goldenson had with people in the motion-picture business, they were able to persuade Republic Pictures to put up $5 million toward the Disney theme park. After word of Republic's investment, the banks reconsidered, and Walt Disney was able to secure all of the financing to build Disneyland. However, unlike CBS and NBC, ABC's $500,000 had turned out to be a shrewd investment.

In exchange for its investment and ABC's position as guarantor for all the Disney loans, the television network owned 35 percent of Disneyland and took all the profits from the food concessions for 10 years. The jewel in the crown, however, was the Disneyland television show, which premiered in 1954 and tied into the different theme park venues, which included Frontier Land, Tomorrow Land, and Adventure Land. It was a seven-year deal with an option for an eighth, and at $5 million a year and a total of $40 million, it was the biggest programming package in television history, and the most expensive. Disney licensed the program to ABC for a fee of $2 million for 26 one-hour shows. Each *Disneyland* program cost $65,000 to produce, and there was an additional expense of $70,000 per broadcast for network line charges. The total cost, $135,000 per episode, had to be shared among several advertisers, which included American Motors, the American Dairy Association, and Derby Foods.

*Disneyland* soon became a tremendous hit for the ABC television network. The Disney studio shrewdly utilized the television program as a promotional tool for its upcoming feature films and for its amusement park. With only 20 original episodes per season, 20 reruns, and 12 repeated reruns, the series was extremely profitable. In 1955 ABC built on the successful Disney franchise with its first network afternoon show, *The Mickey Mouse Club*. It used the same ratio of original programs to reruns and was unabashedly flamboyant in its peddling of Disney's merchandise, films, and amusement park. It also raised the ire of some critics because of its 12 commercial minutes per hour and 22 advertisements per episode from four different sponsors. *The Mickey Mouse Club* was also an incubator for young talent like Annette Funicello and Frankie Avalon, who would also star in teen-oriented Disney features.

The numbers that Disney generated for ABC proved tantalizing for the rest of Hollywood. *Disneyland* was ABC's first show in the top 10, and *The Mickey Mouse Club* was responsible for half of the network's 1954 earnings and nearly a quarter of its earnings in 1955. The Disney programming was responsible for making 1955 ABC's first profitable year as a station owner and network.

Although MGM, a major Hollywood studio, was associated with CBS, in Ed Sullivan's 1952 tribute to the studio it was Warner Brothers that led the majors to television. Shortly after the merger between ABC and United Paramount Theaters, Goldenson made the Hollywood film studio rounds and was rebuffed by the fearful executives. After the Disney deal, Goldenson asked Jack Warner to lunch at the La Rue restaurant on Sunset Strip. They talked for four and a half hours and Warner expressed his reluctance to make "quickie" movies. Goldenson agreed and told Jack Warner that he wanted to use his film archives and put young management in charge. He also promised one minute in each program to promote Warner feature films.

For the 1955–56 season, Warner Brothers agreed to produce 40 one-hour programs at $75,000 per hour, with an additional $37,500 for 12 programs rerun during the summer. Concerned about hostility from his distributors and exhibitors over his move toward television, Jack Warner only agreed to the terms after a 10-minute segment titled *Behind the Cameras,* highlighting upcoming Warner films and stars, was to be included in the programs. Although the 10-minute segment assuaged Warner's guilt about submitting to television, it did not capture the interest of the television audience. Research showed that viewers turned away in wholesale fashion from these promotional segments, and after abbreviating their length they were finally dropped.

The ABC television series was called *Warner Brothers Presents,* like Disney providing the movie studio with a cachet of distinction. There were, however, three rotating programs within the series—*Casablanca, Kings Row,* and *Cheyenne*—all from Warner titles. *Cheyenne,* based upon an obscure Warner film, was wildly successful.

Clint Walker, who played Cheyenne Bodie, whose cool, unflappable indifference seemed to capture the audience perception of the American West, was a real audience-pleaser. After *Cheyenne* became a certified hit, the other two programs in the rotation were dropped. When agreeing to do television, Jack Warner complained that programs could not be made on such a tight budget; *Cheyenne,* however, proved him wrong. Most of these programs were produced in five days, and budgets were supplemented by using stock film footage. The venture was very profitable for Warner Brothers, as it earned residual payments that were not shared with the artists.

Warner's relationship with ABC provided the television network with a distinctive voice and created an intimacy between program supplier and exhibitor. The studio became a major force in defining the direction of ABC programming, and by 1959 was responsible for a third of ABC's prime-time network schedule. By the 1958–59 season, ABC reached a threshold of competitive parity with NBC and CBS in those markets where they enjoyed equal affiliation.

Of course, the other television networks took notice and moved to create programming relationships with Hollywood studios. At a program-scheduling meeting in early 1957 at NBC with David Sarnoff present, it was reported that an NBC executive turned to MCA vice president David A. "Sonny" Werblin and said, "Sonny . . . here are the empty spots, you fill them."[2] This was, in a sense, a capitulation to the strength of Hollywood's ability to sustain the volume of product necessary to fill the prime-time needs of network television. MCA, the powerful talent agency, which bought the Universal lot and eventually purchased the studio, obliged, producing the successful television programs *Tales of Wells Fargo, Wagon Train,* and *M Squad.*

CBS was also a part of the transition to Hollywood when it joined with the independent studio Desilu for the hit programs *I Love Lucy* and *December Bride,* along with *Schlitz Playhouse* from MCA and the classic *Perry Mason* from Twentieth Century Fox.

With the success of these programs, other Hollywood studios joined in the pursuit of television's pot of gold. Columbia Pictures, through its Screen Gems subsidiary, which was already affiliated with television through its *Ford Theatre* program, expanded its presence with *Rin Tin Tin, Captain Midnight,* and *Father Knows Best.* Robert Young, a veteran Hollywood film actor, played the lead in *Father Knows Best,* providing television with an air of legitimacy and distinction. The *Rin Tin Tin* series was based upon the successful feature films of the same name.

Other Hollywood studios followed in the dust of Warner Brothers. Taking their lead from *Warner Brothers Presents* yielded *MGM Parade* and *Twentieth Century Fox Hour.* The studios, albeit reluctantly, were embracing the potential wealth of television, but still relegating it to B-list stars and secondary sound stages. But the rush was on to supply product for the many hours television had to fill. One of the assets that Hollywood studios possessed was the vast film archive stored in their vaults. RKO was the first, in 1955, to sell its film library and studio for $25 million to General Teleradio, which was an offshoot of General Tire and Rubber Company. Soon, over 700 RKO feature films were being distributed to stations around the country, and the old RKO studio was acquired by Desilu, whose principals were the television stars Lucille Ball and Desi Arnaz. After the RKO deal, the floodgates opened, and in 1956 Warner Brothers struck a $21 million distribution deal, followed by a $30 million distribution arrangement with Twentieth Century Fox and a $50 million deal for Paramount features.

## THEATRICAL FEATURES AS TELEVISION PRODUCT

Perhaps the most valuable asset the Hollywood studios possessed in the 1950s was the treasure of theatrical features stored in their archives. Industry estimates in 1951 valued the over 4,000 features and 6,000 shorts and cartoons at close to $250 million. But prior to 1955 there appeared to be a reluctance by the studios to license these films to television. A number of factors influenced the studios' position, including greed and business priorities.

The studios had to consider the position of the movie exhibitors who owned the theaters that showed their films. They were concerned about television's competitive superiority and didn't want the studios to aid and abet them. The studios had their own agenda, which was driven by greed and power. Parlaying their position into one that was dependent upon the vagaries of government oversight pertaining to restraint of trade, they hoped to avoid an exhibitor boycott by having the Justice Department force them to release their 16 mm films to television. However, in 1955 the U.S. District Court rendered a decision protecting the motion-picture companies from intervention by the Justice Department.

British theatrical features found their way to television in 1948, while some from smaller American studios were licensed for broadcast in 1952. Some major studios, like Paramount, hoped to capitalize on subscription television and held their films from broadcast television in the hope of reaping huge profits.

In 1951 there was a breakthrough of A films to television when David O. Selznick released 12 of his films to syndication for a total of $2 million. He was the legendary producer of such critically acclaimed films as *Dinner at Eight* (1933); *A Star Is Born* (1937); *Rebecca* (1940); and, of course, *Gone with the Wind* (1939). That same year the Dumont television network purchased 26 high-end (although dated) films from the Quality Films distribution company for $1.8 million. By 1955 television had demonstrated its power as a mass entertainment medium, and the issue of withholding films became moot. By 1955 a turning point had been reached, and Paramount sold a package of 30 films produced by Pine-Thomas studios for $1.15 million. ABC created two programs, *Famous Film Festival* on Sunday evenings and *Afternoon Film Festival* on weekdays, that featured movies, some of which came from a package of 35 films bought from J. Arthur Rank for $45,700 each.

As the number of theatrical films sold to television increased, the hours that filled its airways rose from an initial trickle to a rush by major studios to cash in on their libraries. Television was now viewed as a cash cow with hours to fill and films to buy. RKO's vast library was sold by Howard Hughes to General Teleradio, a subsidiary of General Tire and Rubber company. There were 740 features and 1,100 shorts, and in 1955 General Teleradio sold the entire RKO library to C&C Television Corporation, keeping some product for its own exclusive use. Indeed, these vast film vaults were viewed as a kind of currency to be bartered and sold.

Columbia Pictures, through its Screen Gems subsidiary, realized a tidy sum of $9.7 million when it released 195 features in 1957. That same year Columbia's television subsidiary, Screen Gems, licensed the majority of Universal's film archive for seven years. The major Hollywood studios were starting to embrace television as a tool for the recycling of their films, allowing them to earn substantial residuals for product that was dusted off and resurrected for additional revenue enhancement. Indeed, Fox created a national advertising campaign around the theme of "See a movie tonight at home."

Some studios, in their haste to reap tidy sums from their archives, raced too quickly to the altar of avarice and sold off the rights to their product. Paramount deliberately delayed release of its film archives, waiting for the dust to settle. Eventually, in 1958, it sold off the rights to its library of 750 pre-1948 films to MCA for $50 million without retaining any equity in its product. By 1965 MCA had grossed $70 million on the Paramount films. It did this through a strategy of selling to local stations rather than networks and earning $70,000 per film. Being burned once, Paramount did not repeat the same mistake when negotiating the sale of rights to its post-1948 films.

A more sensible approach to the sale of film archives was pursued by Twentieth Century Fox. It sold exclusive rights to 52 films, and broadcast television rights to another 390, to National Telefilm Associates (NTA). In a shrewdly negotiated contract worth $32 million, Fox kept reversion rights after 7 to 10 years along with royalties above a fixed gross and a 50 percent interest in NTA's film network.

Most of the inventory of these films were pre-1948 and wholly owned by the studios, while the payments were in cash from distributors with certain guarantees. Television stations were quick to bid for the films and schedule them on their air, which allowed them to slash their operating budget by laying off staff, downsizing equipment, and showing films on a 24-hour clock. Programming schedules at local television stations reflected the new *rigueur* of the airwaves with stations like WOR-TV in New York City, which scheduled live drama every evening in 1954 and by 1956 had 88 percent of its schedule filled with mostly feature-length films. The film product was organized in a series format under titles like *Million Dollar Movie*. This format proved to be popular with viewers and successful with advertisers.

Hollywood had made its mark on television, providing much-needed product to fill hours and hours of programming. Indeed, by 1960, 40 percent of network programming was produced by the major studios. By the mid-1960s they received one-third of the networks' programming dollars. Recent theatrical feature films (two years old) came to network television in 1961 via NBC's *Saturday Night at the Movies*. These movies were being offered to the networks with ABC paying Twentieth Century Fox $20 million for 17 films and CBS paying MGM $52.8 million for 45 films. Two major theatrical events defined Hollywood's importance to television's success: the CBS showing of *The Music Man*, from MGM, for $1 million, and ABC's $2 million payment to Columbia for *The Bridge on the River Kwai*.

The dynamics of Hollywood's theatrical feature-film licensing provisions were drastically altered in 1972 when Home Box Office (HBO, then a subsidiary of Time Warner) distributed its first theatrical feature, *Sometimes a Great Notion,* via microwave to a cable system in Wilkes-Barre, Pennsylvania. Three years later, the pay-television service began satellite distribution. Soon, HBO was dictating film-licensing terms to the major Hollywood studios, and they were reluctant to comply, as hundreds of millions of dollars were at stake. In 1980 four movie studios—Columbia, MCA Universal, Paramount, and Twentieth Century Fox—along with Getty Oil created their own pay-television channel called Premiere. They hoped to bypass HBO and funnel the licensing fees directly back to the studios and withhold their films from distribution to other pay services for nine months. The Justice Department decided to investigate because of the studios' intention to withhold their product from the marketplace for nine months. Under that pressure, the studios decided to abandon the project.

Hollywood had made its mark on television, producing popular programs and supplying feature-length theatrical films and made-for-television movies to the networks. The studios diversified into television by dedicating facilities, talent, and divisions to the production and distribution of television programs. They hired distinguished producers and writers to lucrative development deals and created compelling dramas and sitcoms. Always the "dream factory," Hollywood had made television its stepchild, instilling it with the same virtues and values, creating an intimate proscenium of fantasy for the masses.[3]

## NOTES

1. William F. Boddy, *Fifties Television: The Industry and Its Critics* (Chicago and Urbana: University of Illinois Press, 1990), pp. 132–49.

2. Erik Barnouw, *Tube of Plenty: The Evolution of American Television,* rev. ed. (New York: Oxford University Press, 1982), p. 197.

3. Michele Hilmes, *Hollywood and Broadcasting: From Radio to Cable* (Chicago and Urbana: University of Illinois Press, 1990).

# 3

# FROM PRAIRIE TO PAVEMENT: THE LAWMAN'S LONELY RIDE

America has many cultural myths that are sustained by both legend and fact. The country's history is shaped by the deeds of heroic figures whose character is manifested in their exploits and adventures. The American West embodied many of these attributes and served as a rich canvas for the development of television programming in the 1950s. The character archetype was personified by the sheriff or marshal, a strong, silent type who upheld the law in the face of adversity. Other traits were also in evidence, and they included the tenacity and independence of the cowboy along with the endurance and fortitude of the gunslinger.

When Warner Brothers and the rest of Hollywood began producing telefilms for the networks, they intuitively used their experience in theatrical filmmaking to produce television programs. The studios had been successful with the Western genre, capitalizing on the rich themes of the Old West that directors like John Huston vividly captured in movies like *She Wore a Yellow Ribbon*. Actors like John Wayne portrayed these brave, gallant, and intrepid characters in Hollywood's vision of the Old West and its daunting development.

Initially, the first Westerns to reach television were repackaged from Hollywood's B-film archive. They included Hollywood's B-list of legendary cowboys, including Tom Mix, Hoot Gibson, Kermit Maynard, and Bob Steele. They appeared on local television whose target audience was children and were described in television logs with adjectives like *rootin', tootin', spine-tingling, hard-shootin',* and *hard-ridin'.* The popularity of these Western television programs in homes with children continued to increase, and by 1951 they were viewed at least once a week in 66.3 percent of those homes. Releasing these old films to television provided a profitable aftermarket for studios like Mascot, Monogram, Lone Star, Republic, and Columbia. The product was mostly from the 1930s and included titles such as *The Gay Buckaroo* (1932), starring Hoot Gibson; *Randy Rides Alone* (1934), starring John Wayne; and *Billy the Kid in Texas* (1940), starring Larry "Buster" Crabbe.

The television networks took an interest in the Western genre as programming targeted toward children. In 1950 *The Marshal of Gunsight Pass* premiered on the ABC television network. Produced out of a remodeled soundstage at the Vitagraph Studios in Los Angeles, it featured a weekly battle between the good guys and the bad guys. A serialized CBS drama, *Action in the Afternoon,* appeared from February 1953 to January 1954.

Early television also utilized the 15-minute programming format with some degree of success. One of these was *The Gabby Hayes Show,* which ran on NBC for three years in the 15-minute format and then on ABC in the summer of 1956 on a Saturday-morning half-hour show. Using old Western serials and B features edited for commercials and featuring the talents of Tex Ritter and Buster Crabbe, Gabby Hayes delighted his children audience with tall tales and legends.

In 1948 William Boyd began starring as Hopalong "Hoppie" Cassidy; Hoppie, striding his horse, Topper, became a phenomenal children's television hit. The Bar 20 Ranch was every child's fantasy of cowboy life. When he first started acting as a cowboy in 1935, Boyd couldn't ride a horse. However, by 1948, after 66 feature films, Boyd stopped making movies and turned to television. A shrewd businessman, he acquired the rights to his films for television and optioned exclusive rights to produce additional Hopalong Cassidy films for broadcast.

The program was first broadcast in New York and Los Angeles, and by 1949 it was being distributed nationally on NBC. It was a ratings success, beating out such competitive stalwarts as Ed Sullivan's *Toast of the Town* and *Stop the Music.* Boyd saw his career become reinvigorated by television, and, once again using his keen business acumen, he pioneered the sale of licensed product merchandise for television by celebrity endorsement, unleashing the first merchandising bonanza precipitated by the nascent medium. As testament to the popularity of the program, Boyd lent the Hopalong Cassidy imprimatur to products such as skates, soap, wristwatches, and wastebaskets. The Hopalong Cassidy juggernaut reached its height of frenzy when 1 million jackknives were sold in 10 days.

By 1950 Hopalong Cassidy films were on 57 television stations, and a half-hour radio program based upon the character was syndicated to 517 markets. A comic strip was created for the character and appeared in 72 daily and 40 Sunday newspapers. Always looking for an opportunity to ensure a consistent loyal following, Boyd created the Hopalong Cassidy Troopers Club. All the children members received a membership card, secret code, and the "Troopers News." In addition, the club espoused Boyd's code of morality, which was exemplified in his program by statements like "be kind to birds and animals" and "obey your parents."

For William Boyd and Hopalong Cassidy, ethics and morality were rather simply defined by the black-and-white world of good versus evil. Astride his fine white horse, Topper, Cassidy viewed the world from the knowing perspective of someone who can judge right from wrong and espouse positive values reflecting his perception of behavioral virtues. All that clean living paid off, as Boyd's net worth was conservatively estimated at $200 million.

A couple of other big-screen Western stars came to television. Both Roy Rogers and Gene Autry were under contract to Republic Pictures, a low-budget film studio. Seizing the opportunity to release their films to television, the studio created a subsidiary, Hollywood Television Service. The two Western stars sued in U.S. District Court in Los Angeles, attempting to block Republic from selling their films to Hollywood. The court upheld Rogers's request because his contract with the studio clearly prohibited the use of his name, voice, or likeness for advertising or promotion without his consent. The court, however, held that Gene Autry did not enjoy the same privilege, because the language of his contract was worded differently. Autry pursued the case but lost on appeal.

Autry's migration from the silver screen brought a lyrical sense of style to television. He helped usher in the era of the singing television cowboy. Sitting high on his horse, Champion, Autry in 1951 embodied the essence of the gentleman cowboy. The bad guys were respectful of his repertoire, never daring to step on one of his notes.

Autry was a good businessman, and he formed Flying "A" Productions to produce programs for television. In addition to producing his own television program, Autry's company made a number of other series, including *Annie Oakley, The Range Rider, Buffalo Bill Jr.*, and even a show featuring his horse, *The Adventures of Champion*. In explaining his rationale for deciding to turn to television, Autry spoke about the potential of television to reach a young audience. "Television had begun to seduce the whole country, and some of us saw it coming earlier than others. Around 1950, my company, Flying 'A' Productions, began developing ideas aimed at the kids market."[1]

In his approach to creating suitable programming for children, Autry developed his own code of cowboy conduct, which was a theme that was evident in all his programs. They included traditional adages, like

- A cowboy never takes unfair advantage, even of an enemy.
- A cowboy never betrays a trust.
- A cowboy always tells the truth.
- A cowboy is free from racial and religious prejudice.
- A cowboy is a patriot.

These, along with other tenets, made up Autry's creed, as he perceived his role as a model for youth and as a spokesperson for the new medium of television. He became very wealthy and invested in a number of radio and television properties in California.

Roy Rogers, the other cowboy crooner, moved into television with *The Roy Rogers Show*. He and his wife, Dale Evans, "Queen of the West," rode their horses, Trigger and Buttermilk, into the "Happy Trails" (the program's signature tune) of syndication heaven. Rogers, whose real name was Leonard Franklin Slye, lived with Dale at the Double R Bar Ranch near Mineral City.

Unlike some of the other heroes of television's Old West, Rogers had a more rough-and-tumble ideal associated with cowboys. His shows were filled with more violence, rationalized by Rogers's interpretation of the morality of the Old West. He viewed the cowboy as a six-gun savior who ploughed the land or road herd over the "doggies," always at the ready to defend his honor. Rogers explained his philosophy by his own interpretation of history and its manifestation as a morality play. "We only fire our guns when necessary. But, there's an evil force that always is challenging. And when that challenge comes you have to meet it with spirit and fire."[2]

He and Dale, an accomplished songwriter who composed their program's theme song, "Happy Trails to You," rode side by side, she on Buttermilk and he on his beloved Trigger. Indeed, both of these equines can be seen in all their splendor as products of the taxidermist at the Roy Rogers and Dale Evans museum in Victorville, California.

*The Roy Rogers Show* was, of course, targeted to children, so a number of liberties were taken with historical accuracy. Although the action took place in the traditional Western town of Mineral City, Roy's partner, Pat Brady, drove a post–World War II Jeep, and the town had telephones. Indeed, although the couple was married, their on-the-tube relationship was nurtured as a close friendship and nothing more. Some fans were outraged that Roy kissed his horse, Trigger, but never planted a kiss on the lovely Miss Evans. Indeed, in the 1946 newspaper the *World-Telegram*, an article reflected this frustration. "How that spurious cowhand can be content to kiss a horse when he has Miss Evans on the lot every day I cannot imagine. But the inflexible law of westerns is that the hero shall never smooch the heroine."[3]

At the height of their popularity in the 1950s they had over 2,000 fan clubs around the world and hundreds of licensed products, including lunch boxes and books that displayed their pictures or names. Indeed, the Roy Rogers name still had a presence in the 1970s and 1980s, with hundreds of fast-food restaurants bearing his name.[4]

One of the most enduring and beloved of the early television Westerns was *The Lone Ranger*. It started as a local radio show in 1933 and soon reached a national audience distributed by the Mutual Radio Network. It made its debut on ABC on September 15, 1949, and by 1950 it was the only ABC program in the top 15 A.C. Nielsen Company rankings.

Roy Rogers and his horse, Trigger. "Some fans were outraged that Roy kissed his horse, Trigger, but never planted
a kiss on the lovely Miss Evans." (Photofest.)

It was a classic tale of revenge and retribution, with John Reid, the only
surviving Texas Ranger, played by Clayton Moore, left for dead after an am-
bush by the notorious desperado Butch Cavendish that killed five others,
including his brother Dan. He was nursed back to health by Tonto, a friendly
Indian played by Jay Silverheels, a mixed-blood Mohawk born on the Six
Nations Reservation in Brantford, Canada. On the series, Tonto was portrayed as a Potawotamie Indian, and his signature phrase, *kemo sabe*, which
means "trusty scout," became a part of the pop-culture American lexicon.

The portrayal of Tonto as a Native American was sensitive to the history
of the American Indians as both warriors and as a subjugated people. Tonto
was seen as an assimilated Indian and one who was loyal to his friend and
demonstrated acts of bravery. The courageous aspect of his character was
profiled in an episode broadcast on January 17, 1957, entitled "The Courage
of Tonto." Indeed, as the story notes, it was Tonto who nursed the badly
wounded ranger from near death back to health.

The series aired from 1949 to 1957; however, because of a contractual
dispute, Moore was replaced by actor John Hart from 1952 to 1954. After

a public outcry, Moore returned, and also portrayed the Lone Ranger in two feature films after the television series ended. The show had all of the dramatic components for good television: the audience didn't see the face of the masked ranger; he used only silver bullets from his own mine; there wasn't a great deal of violence; the horses Silver and Scout were integral to the series; and, of course, the famous theme, the *William Tell* Overture by Rossini, accompanied the legendary opening narration:

> A fiery horse with the speed of light,
> a cloud of dust and a hearty "Hi-Yo Silver!"
> The Lone Ranger rides again!
> Return with us now to those
> thrilling days of yesteryear!

Interestingly, during the first year of *The Lone Ranger,* there was a significant amount of outdoor filming in Southern California. After the first year, various economies of scale were introduced using contrived indoor sets as a means to depict exterior scenes. These cramped studio sets were poor replacements for the great outdoors and gave the series a really cheap B look.

Although most of the early television Westerns featured men as leading characters, there was one that had a prominent female in the lead. In *Annie Oakley,* actress Gail Davis portrayed the hard-riding, sharpshooting Western heroine. With her pigtails and white-fringed Western outfit, she demonstrated that a woman can ride and shoot as good as or better than a man. "Bull's eye! Annie Oakley hits the entertainment bull's eye every week with her hard ridin', straight shootin', and suspense."[5]

Another Western series that attempted to portray women as strong Western figures was *Frontier,* which premiered in 1955. Conceived by the distinguished producer Worthington Miner, who had created shows like *The Goldbergs, Toast of the Town, Studio One,* and later *I Spy,* Miner said about *Frontier,* "Fifty percent of 'Frontier's' scripts are about women . . . 'Frontier' is about women with guts, not men with guns."[6] The show, however, failed to attract a significant audience.

A Western series that had an enduring presence on radio and television was *Death Valley Days.* Its development was intimately associated with the advertising industry and was created in 1930 by Ruth Woodman, a New York–based advertising scriptwriter, and controlled by the advertising agency McCann-Erikson. The program was created as a vehicle for its sponsor, 20 Mule Team Borax. For Woodman, the program became a career writing scripts for radio (1930–45) and television (1952–75). Although Woodman had never been to Death Valley, California, when she conceived the series, she subsequently made many trips to gather story material.

*Death Valley Days* was one of the first anthology series on television, with the Old Ranger, who introduced the program, as the only actor making a regular appearance. There were several actors throughout the 558 30-minute episodes who portrayed the ranger: Stanley Andrews (1952–65); Ronald Reagan (1965–66), who left after being elected governor of California; Robert Taylor (1966–68); Dale Robertson (1968–72); and Merle Haggard (1975).

The opening bugle call of the series provided a melodious counterpoint to the vivid scene of the 29-mule team pulling the Borax wagons out of the desert. Commercials, of course, featured Borax products and were pitched by Rosemary DeCamp. With such a large inventory of programming, the series has been syndicated under several titles with different hosts, including *Call of the West*, with John Payne; *Frontier Adventure*, with Dale Robertson; *The Pioneers*, with Will Rogers Jr.; *Trails West*, with Ray Milland; and *Western Star Theatre*, with Rory Calhoun. Several actors who later became movie stars appeared in episodes, including James Caan, in "Deadly Decision" (1963), and Clint Eastwood, in "The Last Letter" (1967).

In the landscape of Western drama, *The Cisco Kid* was a departure from tradition. It ran from 1950 to 1955 and starred Duncan Renaldo as the Kid and Leo Carrillo as his inveterate sidekick, Pancho. They were two benevolent bandits who aided the weak and poor. This television series was the first sold by Ziv, which had been the largest packager and syndicator of radio programs. Frederick W. Ziv explained his rationale for creating the series and why it was successful.

It was obvious to all of us who had our fingers on the pulse of the American public that they wanted escapist entertainment. . . . We did not do high brow material. We did material that would appeal to the broadcast segment of the public. And they became the big purchasers of television sets. And as they bought television sets, the beer sponsors began to go on television. And the beer sponsors, for the most part, wanted to reach the truck and taxi driver, the average man and woman. They were not interested in that small segment that wanted opera, ballet or symphony.[7]

Although it was the first television series featuring Latino characters, it didn't pay homage to their culture. At times it presented a view of Latinos as heroic, villainous, and foolish. Part of the enduring quality of *The Cisco Kid* was the fortuitous decision to film in color, which added to its value in syndication.

Another program featuring a Latino hero was *Zorro*. It was produced by Walt Disney and ran from 1957 to 1959. Zorro was played by actor Guy Williams, whose real name was Armando Catalando. The program today is criticized for its negative portrayal of Hispanics, although Zorro, of course, was a heroic figure whose deeds were measured by courage and benevolence.

## ADULT WESTERNS

Adult Westerns addressed themes and had more complex characterizations than children's Westerns featuring stars like Gene Autry and Roy Rogers. The genre appeared first on radio with programs like *Gunsmoke* (CBS radio, 1952–61) and *The Six Shooter,* featuring James Stewart (NBC radio, 1953–54). The first adult Western on television was the off-network *Stories of the Century,* syndicated in 1954. It featured the actors Jim Davis and Mary Castle, who portrayed two investigators for the Southwestern Railroad.

As they featured themes that appealed to mature audiences, adult Westerns nevertheless maintained their propriety. Instead of cereal companies, these programs had sponsors that included Greyhound, Kaiser, Buick, Ford, Procter and Gamble, and various tobacco companies that advertised cigarettes (L&M, Chesterfield).

One network that appeared to embrace the genre was CBS. In the early 1950s, the network experimented with television programs like *Fort Laramie* (1956), starring Raymond Burr; *Luke Slaughter of Tombstone* (1958); *Frontier Gentleman* (1958); and a radio adaptation of *Have Gun Will Travel* (1958–60).

The defining moment for the adult Western was the entrance of the Hollywood studios and their production of telefilms. That effort was pioneered by Jack Warner of Warner Brothers, with a gentle prodding from Leonard Goldenson of ABC.

When Jack Warner, the head of Warner Brothers, agreed to produce telefilms for the ABC Television Network to air in the 1955–56 season, the original terms called for three rotating series, *Kings Row, Casablanca,* and *Cheyenne. Cheyenne* rotated with *Conflict* in the second season and in the third with another Western, *Sugarfoot. Sugarfoot,* also known as *Tenderfoot,* ran from 1957 to 1960 and starred Will Hutchins. The first two were based upon successful Warner properties, while *Cheyenne*'s theatrical success was more obscure.

Bill Orr, Jack Warner's son-in-law, was put in charge of television at the Warner studio. ABC wanted Warner's George Montgomery to play Cheyenne in the television series, but Orr was reluctant to cast a noted Hollywood film actor for the part. An agent referred a little-known actor, Norman Walker, to be tested for the lead role of Cheyenne. Walker was a spear-carrier at Paramount and had been under contract to DeMille for a short time. The producer of *Cheyenne* thought little of Walker's acting ability, calling him a "rank amateur." Nevertheless, Jack Warner liked him, and Norman Walker got the part.

Name changes are always a part of Hollywood legend, and Walker was no different. The producers felt that Norman was not the right name for a Western star. Remembering Gary Cooper's portrayal of Clint Maroon in the film *Saratoga Trunk,* the producers came up with the name Clint Walker.

Creating a one-hour dramatic telefilm was basically uncharted territory, and there were some difficulties associated with the development of *Cheyenne.* The producers had to invent a new form, because doing radio with pictures would not work on television. After a few of the hour-long *Cheyenne* episodes were produced but not yet aired, Monsanto Chemical, the program's sponsor, wrote a lengthy telegram, the size of a small telephone book, criticizing the program and saying that it was not going to pay for it. Another writer-producer, Roy Huggins, who would become a major influence in television programming, was brought in, and he immediately changed the format, which was aimed at children. He got rid of Cheyenne's sidekick, changed his occupation from mapmaker to drifter, and created adult themes. *Cheyenne* was the first Western series made for television.

Surprising everyone, *Cheyenne* was a hit, and *Kings Row* and *Casablanca* were eventually dropped from the rotation. Warner Brothers received $75,000 for each episode of *Cheyenne,* which was usually shot in five days. In an effort to economize and expedite production, stock film footage of cattle drives, Indian fights, and barroom brawls was incorporated into the original telefilm. In addition, Warner Brothers received $37,500 for each of 12 summer reruns. By 1956 *Cheyenne* was one of the most popular shows on television, and advertisers were knocking on Clint Walker's door to pitch their products. When an advertising agency approached Warner Brothers to have Walker advertise cigarettes, it was told that Cheyenne doesn't smoke. Indeed, Warner Brothers would not allow the actor to appear in any commercials. Of course, this policy did not last very long. In 1958 Walker left the show, but by mid-1959 he had returned.

Other Westerns followed in the trail blazed by *Cheyenne,* which lasted for seven years. By 1959 there were 28 prime-time Westerns on the three television networks. The popularity of *Cheyenne* and its contribution to the programming schedule of ABC made Roy Huggins think about developing the genre while departing from the traditional format. He was working on a show called *Conflict,* where a minor character was a worthless con man with an ironic attitude toward himself and life. Bill Orr urged him to use actor James Garner for the minor role. Having used Garner for a bit part in *Cheyenne,* Huggins thought that he was a terrible actor. Orr persisted and Huggins agreed, and it turned out that Garner was perfect for the part. Huggins was so smitten with Garner's portrayal that he wanted to conceptualize his character into a lead for a Western. It would be about a "gentle grifter" whose values would be the direct opposite of the traditional Western hero. Huggins wrote a script and, noting the character's divergent traits, he called him and the show *Maverick.*

*Maverick* broke all the rules that had been inspired by the literature and films of the West. When faced with a hostile threat, the Maverick brothers would rather surrender their winnings than face the dire consequences of a fight or a bullet. Huggins was very certain of his character's foibles and vulnerabilities: "he's a little bit of a coward, he's not solemn, he's greedy and not above cheating a little, he's indifferent to the problems of others. He's something of a 'gentle grifter,' but we couldn't use that title because O. Henry used it first."[8]

In the interesting dynamics of television, *Maverick,* one of the most successful programs in television history, almost never made it to the air. ABC had to find a sponsor for the show, and as a struggling third in the network-television hierarchy, it was no small task. The network called upon its brilliant 38-year-old president, Ollie Treyz. He zeroed in on Henry Kaiser, a crusty old man and the millionaire head of Kaiser Aluminum. Kaiser loved the pilot, envisioning himself as a "maverick," and when Treyz suggested that the title was a working one and would be changed, Kaiser indicated that he loved the title. Kaiser was almost hooked, but his son Edgar was less confident. And executives from the Young and Rubicam advertising agency were about to make Kaiser the offer of a lifetime. They came with a proposal offering Kaiser half of *The Ed Sullivan Show* on CBS, the number-one network at the time. However, like the plot in so many Westerns, there was a deadline of noon the next day for him to accept. Treyz had to make the ultimate pitch to sell an untested program in place of a show that consistently earned a 35 rating. The Y&R people were pushing hard, and Treyz got Jack Warner on the speakerphone and asked him to tell Kaiser whether or not he could produce a hit program. Jack Warner, never one to mince words, said, "My show isn't out yet. You give me the stage, and I'll be the fucking winner."[9]

*Maverick* was a smash hit, beating out the competition, both *Ed Sullivan* and *Steve Allen.* However, there were some production issues that threatened the stability of the show. Each hour of *Maverick* took seven days to produce, but Warner Brothers couldn't afford to pay crews overtime on weekends. So two days from the following week had to be used to complete each *Maverick* episode. Huggins quickly calculated that in order for ABC to receive all of the 26 contracted episodes, there would have to be simultaneous productions of *Maverick,* and since James Garner could not appear in both, Huggins hired actor Jack Kelly to appear as Bart Maverick, brother of Bret. It too turned out to be a brilliant but costly move. Henry Kaiser, who owned a third of the series, asserted that he had never been informed about the change, and in the end ABC had to pay him $600,000 to placate his ego.

*Maverick* ran for seven years, and the brothers, with their mischievous smiles and rakish good looks, were perfect foils when they appeared in the same episodes together. Indeed, the concept was so enduring that it became a feature film in 1994, starring Mel Gibson and James Garner.

Another Western that was a departure from the traditions of the genre was *Gunsmoke.* It had been a successful CBS radio program (1952–61) starring William Conrad (a heavyweight in more ways than one); however, the actor, although a talented radio artist, was not deemed right for the part. Eventually, Conrad would become a television star with his own series. The network would have been delighted if John Wayne accepted the lead of Matt Dillon, U.S. Marshal, but it was 1955 and he wasn't interested in leaving the silver screen. But he did recommend another actor named James Arness, who was under contract to Wayne's production company. Arness didn't have too many film credits, having a small part with Wayne in an anticommunist propaganda film and his singular achievement as a giant, growling, alien vegetable in *The Thing.*

Tall and handsome, Arness excited CBS executives after testing for the part. He and his agent, who knew little about television, were, however, reluctant to commit to the series. With no other prospects looming, Arness eventually said yes. Then, after sets were ordered and a cast was hired, just before shooting was about to begin, Arness called and said he was no longer interested. Indeed, he had already started in a Western for Republic Pictures.

The recalcitrant actor was then contacted by William Dozier, CBS West Coast director of programming. He expressed his displeasure with Arness and warned that his behavior was unprofessional. After a visit to Dozier's resplendent Beverly Hills estate, Arness reconsidered. As Dozier later recollected, he had to "pump some sunshine up his ass."

Labeled an "adult Western," *Gunsmoke* dominated the 10 P.M. Saturday-night time period for 12 years and made James Arness a multimillionaire. Its original ensemble cast included Amanda Blake as the good-hearted saloon keeper and love interest Kitty; Millburn Stone as the wise Doc; and Dennis Weaver as the limping, loyal Chester. Later in the show's iteration, Ken Curtis replaced Dennis Weaver as Festus Haggen, and Burt Reynolds appeared as Quint Asper, a blacksmith. (Reynolds went on to star in *Riverboat,* another television series, which ran from 1959 to 1961, and appeared in movies.)

In *Gunsmoke,* the audience was drawn into a weekly morality tale based upon the virtues and foibles of its characters. But these characters were portrayed as humanistic figures who had a clear sense of right and wrong. None of the principal characters had a family, so their reliance on each other became a compelling feature of the program. Matt Dillon personified the stolid, stoic hero who sometimes would question the need for action but always performed his duty. His relationship with Kitty was measured by only the most noble of intentions. Doc was the judicious and prudent adviser whose judgment was trusted. Chester and his limp served as a perfect foil to the strength and fortitude of Marshal Dillon. Where Dillon was strong, Chester was weak and vulnerable. As Dillon reeked of stoicism, Chester's emotions became a palette for Dillon to experience and react. These integrated qualities, along with superb writing, made *Gunsmoke* a unique Western drama and one of the longest-running programs in television history.

The character of Matt Dillon was carefully molded to make him susceptible and vulnerable to error and poor judgment. At CBS, vice president Hubbell Robinson articulated the nurturing of the character and the need to make him "human." "We worked on the character of Matt Dillon. We made him a man with doubts, confused about the job he had to do. He wondered whether he really had to do that job. We did the same for Chester and Doc. They're not just stooges for Matt."[10]

According to producer-director Norman MacDonnell, Dillon's character was contrived to have shortcomings, including anger and errors in judgment. They did not want to make their lawman a heroic invincible figure. If that started to happen, then it was time to write a script that would reveal his idiosyncrasies. "Poor old Matt gets outdrawn and outgunned and pulls every dumb trick in the book. It makes him, and us, human."[11]

Expressing his views on the success of *Gunsmoke* and how the television audience embraced the Western genre, its star, James Arness, talked about some of its unique aspects. "People like Westerns because they represent a time of freedom. A cowboy wasn't tied down to one place or one woman. . . . they tune into western shows to escape conformity. They don't want to see a U.S. marshal come home and help his wife wash the dishes."[12]

Indeed, the series was almost canceled. In the 1957–58 season, *Gunsmoke* was the highest-rated show on television, continuing that dominance until the 1961–62 season. That year new programs were seen on Saturday nights and reruns aired on Tuesday evenings. As time passed, *Gunsmoke* slipped more and more in the ratings, and in the 1966–67 season was ranked 34th. Another problem that the series faced was the loss of the valuable 18–49-year-old audience demographic. The longer a program stays on the air, the older its audience gets. And so the program was canceled.

However, as any television viewer knows, there is often a heroic white knight waiting in the wings, poised for the rescue. In this case it was William Paley, the CEO of CBS. He loved *Gunsmoke* and was at his Bahamian estate when he was notified of the cancellation. Paley's instinct for talent and programming was legendary, and on his recommendation *Gunsmoke* was moved to Monday evening. There had already been the requisite final cast party and the principals in the series, who were all wealthy, had to be re-signed to new contracts. Of course, their negotiating latitude benefited from Paley's interest in seeing the show back on the CBS prime-time schedule.

The move worked, and *Gunsmoke* jumped from 34th to 4th place the following season and managed to stay in the top 10 for the next five years. The final season for the series was 1974–75. According to Mike Dann, who for years was the CBS senior vice president for programming, *Gunsmoke* had the worst demographics pertaining to a young audience for any show on television. However, with such a large audience, Dann rationalized, "Who cared whether they all wore dentures?"

Another early Western series that was considered adult, *The Life and Legend of Wyatt Earp* (1955–61) made its debut on September 6, 1955, on the ABC television network, just a few days before *Gunsmoke*. It was on Tuesday evenings from 8:30 to 9:00. The first episode, "Mr. Earp Becomes a Marshal," introduced his trademark Buntline Special pistols, the marshal's weapon du jour. Actor Hugh O'Brien portrayed the legendary lawman for the length of the series. Although O'Brien was the only actor to stay the course for all six seasons, writer Frederick Hazlitt wrote scripts for the show during its entire run.

Although John Wayne wasn't interested in moving to television, another Hollywood legend did make the transition: Henry Fonda, who played Marshal Simon Fry in *The Deputy* (1959–61). Actor Robert Redford made his first television appearance in this series, on an episode entitled "The Last Gunfight," which was broadcast on April 30, 1960. Fonda waited a decade before he again ventured into series television with *The Smith Family* in 1971.

One of John Wayne's closest friends, actor Ward Bond starred in the successful series *Wagon Train* (1957–65) as Major Seth Adams. It was so popular that it challenged *Gunsmoke* as the leading Western series from that era. It ran for eight years and was number two in the ratings until the 1961–62 season, when it became the top-rated program on television.

There was one Western television series that personified the independent iconoclastic nature that was associated with the myth of the Western hero, and it was *Wanted Dead or Alive* (1958–61). As a bounty hunter named Josh Randall, actor Steve McQueen embodied the essence of the solitary, self-reliant figure confronting evil. McQueen played Randall with a defiant swagger but with an amiable touch. He wanted us to know that he was different, and to that end, rather than toting a six-shooter, Randall carried an 1892 44/40 center-fire Winchester carbine on his right hip. Commenting on his role as the bounty hunter Josh Randall, McQueen discussed the essence of the hero. "There's a certain honesty and realism in this series. The hero isn't always a nice guy—you didn't stay alive in the Old West being nice."[13] McQueen went on to Hollywood and starred in his first feature, *The Magnificent Seven* (1960), a Western.

The television Western featured many stereotypes that were established in both literature and in the movies. The good guys wore white, and the bad guys wore black. Gunslingers were sometimes sinister villains or heroic figures, like Alan Ladd's portrayal of the benevolent professional gunman in the movie *Shane*. A Western that captured the essence of the enlightened gunfighter was *Have Gun Will Travel* (1957–63), starring Richard Boone. It premiered on September 14, 1957, on CBS, and was scheduled just before *Gunsmoke*.

As the gunslinger Paladin, Richard Boone played a character that was a departure from the tradition. He was a connoisseur of fine wine and women as well as a devotee of literature who would quote Shakespeare and Socrates. Paladin was somewhat narcissistic and surrounded himself with luxury living in a suite at the Hotel Carlton in San Francisco, dressing in the finest clothing, drinking only premium brandy, and smoking the best cigars.

He defied the symbolism of good and evil, dressing entirely in black when he worked. His calling card featured the emblem of a chess piece, which also appeared as a silver ornament on his holster. It was the knight, the most versatile piece on the board, as it moves in eight different directions and over other pieces. The name he chose, Paladin, means a knightly supporter and medieval prince.

At the hotel, Paladin read the newspapers, and when he saw a story that revealed a potential client, he'd clip the article and enclose his business card. Hey Boy, who usually brought Paladin news of a client's response, was played by Kam Tong. Noting no gender bias, he was replaced for a season (1960–61) by Hey Girl, played by Lisa Lu.

Richard Boone was a versatile actor appearing in feature films and early television dramas. His first starring television role was on *Medic* (1954–56), where he played Dr. Konrad Styner. After *Have Gun Will Travel* ended its run, he hosted the short-lived *Richard Boone Show,* which featured the same ensemble of actors in a different play every week. In the early 1970s, he returned to television and starred in the Western *Hec Ramsey.*

The program *Have Gun Will Travel* was conceived by two Hollywood feature-film writers, who brought their idea to James Aubrey, who was manager of CBS programs in Hollywood. Aubrey and Hunt Stromberg Jr. (son of the movie director) took the idea to Hubbell Robinson, CBS network vice president for programming in New York. The idea of a benevolent gunman who believed in justice intrigued him, and the show was put into production and became a hit for CBS. It ranked in the top-rated four programs four years running, and for three of those years it was third most popular, behind *Wagon Train* and *Gunsmoke.*

Western characters like Paladin were offbeat and original, which added to their attraction. Another Western series that featured inspired characterization was *The Wild Wild West* (1965–69), and Hunt Stromberg Jr. was also involved in bringing it to television. The development of the concept can be credited to two writer-producers, Michael Garrison and Gregory Ratoff. In 1956 they sensed that the novels of Ian Fleming's 007 agent James Bond could be developed into high-concept commercial films. They purchased the rights to one of Fleming's earliest Bond novels, *Casino Royale.*

In somewhat of an ironic twist, network television had already managed to produce a live drama of *Casino Royale* in 1954 as part of *Climax Mystery Theater* on CBS. However, that version featured Barry Nelson as an American secret agent and was clearly a departure from Fleming's original work. After the unexpected death of Gregory Ratoff, the rights to *Casino Royale* were eventually acquired by the team of Broccoli and Saltzman, who popularized the Bond character and made him into a cultural icon. The Bond films were a commercial juggernaut, with *Goldfinger* (1964) becoming the third-largest-grossing film of the 1960s. The rerelease of *Dr. No* (1962) and *From Russia with Love* (1963) as a double feature became the most successful double bill in movie history.

Although Garrison was no longer developing the Fleming novels, he conceived of the idea of secret-agent cowboys that was later pitched as "James Bond in the West." The two agents, James T. West (Robert Conrad) and

Artemus Gordon (Ross Martin), worked exclusively for President Ulysses S. Grant. In many ways, the villains were parodies of those that appeared in the 007 films, and featured some of the best character actors, including Victor Buono, Jonathan Winters, and Avery Schreiber.

As America tuned to the cold war, the television screen was consumed with a variety of spy programs, including *The Man from U.N.C.L.E., I Spy, Secret Agent, Get Smart, The Prisoner, Mission Impossible,* and *The Avengers.* However, *The Wild Wild West* was a delightful variation of the genre, combining the fantasy of science fiction with the rough-and-tumble of the Old West. The executives at CBS, including Hunt Stromberg Jr., the head of programming, and Ethel Winant, associate director of program development, loved the concept, and CBS president James Aubrey gave it the nod with Michael Garrison producing.

The producers were considering actor Rory Calhoun, a tall, handsome leading man, for the lead character of James T. West. However, his screen test didn't go well, and Conrad got the part. Although they didn't know each other prior to the show, the chemistry between Conrad and Martin was especially good. One issue that disturbed some of the executives at CBS was the level of violence. The show had some terrific stunts, many performed by the two leads, Conrad and Martin. They were integral to the narrative of the program and in some cases dangerous. Although *The Wild Wild West* was successful, it was canceled because of the network's sensitivity to congressional concern about the level of violence on television. In 1999 a feature film based upon the television show was released, starring Will Smith, Kevin Kline, Kenneth Branagh, and Salma Hayek. The movie's total domestic box office gross was $111 million, once again demonstrating that popular television shows have an enduring shelf life.

As the Western genre began to mature, it attracted young, talented writers, one of which was David Dortort. Starting out as a novelist living in New York City, Dortort began contributing scripts to *Suspense, Public Defender, Racket Squad,* and other early television series. After relocating to Hollywood, he combined his writing talents with producing and created his first television Western, *The Restless* (1957–59), on NBC. That network was looking for a program to compete with the crushing success of *Perry Mason* and *Gunsmoke* on Saturday night. That effort was to be *Bonanza,* with the pilot program written and produced by Dortort and premiering on NBC September 12, 1959.

Envisioned as a family drama enriched with the moral leadership of the patriarch Ben Cartwright, the series would sometimes address such serious themes as racial prejudice, mercy killing, and various psychological problems. In creating the character of Ben Cartwright, David Dortort eschewed the influence of women and the presence of a female influence. He explained his intent as a means to strengthen the resolve of all the male characters. "He is not led around by the nose by anybody. We do not have any Moms built into our show—or for that matter, any women. We are, as it were, anti-Momism."[14] Each of the sons—Adam, Hoss, and Little Joe—had starkly different personalities and were devoted to their father and the Ponderosa, their ranch.

Since there was a great deal at stake in trying to outmaneuver the competition on CBS, NBC executives wanted to have established actors in the lead roles. Dortort, however, felt differently, arguing that unknown actors would establish themselves in the starring roles: Lorne Green, a Canadian radio actor, as father Ben; Pernell Roberts as Adam; Dan Blocker as Hoss; and Michael Landon as Little Joe. Dortort's instinct was prescient, as the characters and program became enormously popular after being moved to Sunday night after its second year.

Another of Dortort's hunches paid off when he insisted that the show be filmed in color. He felt that capturing the beautiful dramatic vistas of Lake Tahoe, where the exteriors were filmed, would add an exciting dimension to the series. Color television was just starting to be available, and the patent owned by RCA, which also owned NBC, made the rationale for the decision both corporate and artistic. *Bonanza* became the first network prime-time series to be filmed in color and was the benchmark for series that served as the catalyst for the move to all-color on NBC and the other networks.

*Bonanza* ran for 14 years and successfully continued after the departure of Pernell Roberts at the conclusion of the sixth season. The series, however, was dealt a mortal blow with the death of Dan Blocker in 1972. The program hobbled along for another season on Tuesday nights and broadcast its last episode on January 16, 1973. However, its popularity and color cinematography have made it a worldwide syndication favorite.

Dortort distinguished his career with another television Western, *The High Chaparral* (1967–72), on NBC, which featured Latino leads in starring roles, and in 1979 was co-executive-producer of *The Chisholms,* a 12-hour CBS miniseries.

A part of the Western's mystique was the way it personified the value of the open range and the freedom it manifested. In *Bonanza,* the ranch known as the Ponderosa was more than a piece of land, but assumed a character of its own, one that was nurtured and cherished by the Cartwright family from any threat or harm. American audiences were enamored with the concept of the ranch owner and his commitment to family, the land, and his cattle.

The popularity of *Bonanza* and its paternalistic family values became a model for other land-based Westerns. *The Virginian* (1962–70) was the first 90-minute Western and featured the sprawling Shiloh ranch in Medicine Bow, Wyoming. Based upon Owen Wister's 1902 novel, the series starred James Drury as the Virginian, the chief ranch hand, and Doug McClure as Trampas, his sidekick. The program featured such veteran actors as Lee J. Cobb as Judge Henry Garth, who, with his family, was the first resident of Shiloh.

Other well-known Hollywood actors included Charles Bickford, Jeanette Nolan, and Stewart Granger.

One of the most distinguished Hollywood actresses to star in a television Western series was Barbara Stanwyck, who played matriarch Victoria Barkley in *The Big Valley* (1965–69). Stanwyck's career accounted for almost 90 feature films and included the classics *Double Indemnity* (1944) and *Sorry, Wrong Number* (1948). It was a reversal of the *Bonanza* theme, as Stanwyck played the widowed mother to four sons. Barbara Stanwyck's Western persona was honed on the silver screen with starring roles in *Annie Oakley* (1935), directed by George Stevens; *Union Pacific* (1939), directed by Cecil B. DeMille; *Cattle Queen of Montana* (1954), directed by Allan Dwan; and *Forty Guns* (1957), directed by Samuel Fuller. In *Cattle Queen of Montana,* one of her costars was Gene Barry, who later starred as the legendary lawman Bat Masterson (1958–61) on television.

*The High Chaparral* (1967–72) was created and produced by David Dortort, who was the inspiration behind *Bonanza*. High Chaparral was a large ranch in the Arizona territory of the 1870s that was overseen by Big John Cannon, played by Leif Erickson. After his first wife is killed by an Indian arrow, he marries a Latina, Linda Cristal, who played Victoria Cannon. Big John's two sons, Buck and Billy Blue, were played respectively by Cameron Mitchell and Mark Slade. Victoria's brother, Manolito Montoya, was played by actor Henry Darrow.

Two Westerns, *Wagon Train* (1957–65) and *Rawhide* (1959–66), epitomized the harshness of the West and the ruggedness of the men and women who tried to tame it. They each featured actors who were making a transition—Ward Bond to television, and Clint Eastwood to the movies. Ward Bond, the star of *Wagon Train,* came from Hollywood after acting in over 200 films, including distinguished Westerns like *The Searchers* (1956), with his buddy John Wayne, directed by another close friend, John Ford. The show appeared on NBC and was an audience favorite and the number-two program, after *Gunsmoke,* for three years running. During the 1961–62 season, it became the highest-rated show on television. While acting on the series, Bond made his final Western film, *Rio Bravo* (1959). He died in 1960 at the age of 57 and was replaced on the show by John McIntire.

*Rawhide* featured Clint Eastwood on television's perpetual cattle drive. The television series may have been inspired by the classic Howard Hawks film *Red River* (1948), which was about a turbulent cattle drive and the opening of the old Chisholm Trail. Eric Fleming played Gil Favor, the trail boss, and Eastwood was Rowdy Yates, his "ramrod." The cast also included Raymond St. Jacques, who became a featured regular in 1965 and the first black actor to have a recurring role in a television Western. Although Eastwood had appeared in many B movies before *Rawhide,* it was his work in the Sergio Leone spaghetti Western *A Fistful of Dollars* (1964) that made him a movie star. He also became a respected director and repeatedly returned to his Western roots with films like *High Plains Drifter* (1973), *Pale Rider* (1985), and his Academy Award–winning film for best picture and director, *Unforgiven* (1992).

The Western as a popular television genre reached its peak in the 1950s and 1960s. However, at the end of the 1980s and beginning of the 1990s, television revisited this genre with a major miniseries event and a popular television series with a woman in the starring role.

Although network television had become disillusioned with the miniseries format because of its high cost and weak ratings, in 1988 the CBS television network committed itself to a $20 million, eight-hour Western miniseries. It was based upon Larry McMurtry's Pulitzer Prize–winning 843-page trail-drive novel, *Lonesome Dove*.

The project was a monumental epic based upon a 373-page teleplay. It had a 16-week shooting schedule involving about 1,400 head of cattle and 89 speaking parts, with massive location shifts. The eight-hour miniseries was originally broadcast over four nights during a sweeps month, starting on February 5, 1989. It featured famous screen actors in leading roles, including Tommy Lee Jones, Robert Duvall, and Danny Glover.

*Lonesome Dove* was a smash hit for CBS, far exceeding the rating and share estimates projected by the network, and spawned a number of sequels, including *The Return of Lonesome Dove* (CBS, November 14, 1993), *The Streets of Laredo* (CBS, November 12, 1995), *Dead Man's Walk* (CBS, 1996), *Lonesome Dove: The Series*, and the series' second season, *Lonesome Dove: The Outlaw Years*.

Although the success of the *Lonesome Dove* franchise did not act as a catalyst for the wholesale return to the Western genre on television, it did help in the nurturing of one of the most successful Western-themed series programs of the 1990s, *Dr. Quinn, Medicine Woman*. It ran for six seasons from 1993 to 1998 on CBS, and its creator and producer was Beth Sullivan. The story was about Dr. Michaela Quinn, who, with her father, practiced medicine in Boston circa the 1860s. After her father's death, she answers an ad for a town doctor in Colorado Springs. Once there, she must overcome the town's resentment toward a woman doctor.

With the female lead played by Jane Seymour, the television series addressed issues of gender associated with women in professional roles. It also touched upon alternative medicine (Cheyenne herbs) and Native American issues. Although its ratings were not consistently high, it remains as one of the most enduring Westerns of the 1990s.

There's a vast body of literature about the Old West that became part of American culture in novels, film adaptations, and on television. These books proved to be a rich resource for narrative development, and the stories they told were popularized for mass consumption. Authors like Jack Schaefer (*Shane*), Owen Wister (*The Virginian*), and Zane Grey had their work adapted for film with remarkable success. *Shane* is considered one of the greatest Western films of all time, earning six Academy Award nominations in 1953 and starring Alan Ladd as the quiet gunfighter along with Jean Arthur, Van Heflin, Brandon De Wilde as the child Joey, and Jack Palance.

The success of Western theatrical films provided an incentive for television to pursue that genre. The American television Western personified a landscape of values associated with the ruggedness of the Old West and its dogged pursuit of independence and virtue. Many of the stories evolved around didactic lessons of morality, integrity, and justice that were an inherent part of the behavior on the prairie. Of course, television romanticized these events and portrayed the characters in a heroic posture based upon a loose interpretation of history (just as the movies had). Nevertheless, this genre helped to define television as a prominent tool for dramatic storytelling and assisted in its evolution as a mass medium.

## MERCHANDISING THE WESTERN

Television's ability as a tool to merchandise products themed to a particular program was realized by *Davy Crockett* (1954–55). It was presented in three separate hour-long segments of the *Disneyland* program, so it was not a typical television series. The show, starring Fess Parker as Davy, was a phenomenal hit and pioneered the technique of selling tie-ins, with the coonskin cap becoming a national craze. The first program, "Davy Crockett Indian Fighter," was broadcast on December 15, 1954, followed by "Davy Crockett Goes to Congress" on January 26, 1955, and ending on February 23 with "Davy Crockett at the Alamo."

In that short time, Davy Crockett merchandise became the rage. Over $100 million of Davy Crockett merchandise was sold, including 4 million copies of the record "The Ballad of Davy Crockett," 14 million books, and millions of coonskin hats. There was an inventory of about 3,000 different Davy Crockett products, because Disney did not have exclusive rights over his name and likeness. Parker kept his costume in mothballs and returned to television in 1964 to star as Daniel Boone, another legendary American hero. That show ran until 1970.

Interestingly, television was a quick learner when it came to generating revenue from television tie-ins and advertiser promotions. For example, General Mills offered an "atomic bomb ring" to any viewer who sent in 15 cents and a Kix cereal box top to *The Lone Ranger.*

## COPS AND ROBBERS AND GUMSHOES

At the same time that television glorified the dusty prairie and its frontier code of justice, it also dramatized the virtues of modern-day crime-fighters and the romantic notion of the private eye. Indeed, there are many similarities between Westerns and cop shows. Each features nonconformist characters who act as arbitrators of justice, interpreting the law and applying its code. The lawman, high on his mounted steed, patrols a vast territory, searching for evil while sustaining the virtues of morality. He plays many roles, mediating disputes, facing off with malcontents, and maintaining a level of civility within the context of daily living.

The themes of law and order and frontier justice were updated for television audiences in the portrayal of police officers on patrol in their cars, serving the public and fighting crime. Although they weren't mounted on horses and didn't carry six-shooters, their mission was to patrol the urban prairie. The characteristics of these modern-day crime-fighters were similar to their Western counterparts, as they displayed the same rugged individualism.

There is a romantic sensibility associated with the fiction of the Western that lends itself to various interpretations within the context of the crime-fighting drama. It is imbued within the structure of the narrative, integrating the heroic virtues of bravery, strength, and resourcefulness. These attributes are universal constructs that are part of the mystique of the law enforcement genre and are what make these programs so attractive to television audiences.

Television heroes are created within a realm of fiction that articulates their personality as a virtuous characteristic of the traditions associated with law enforcement. Whether riding a horse or driving a patrol car, the dynamics of the genre provide a compelling story that touches upon many nuances of drama. Just as Westerns once dominated the television airwaves, police and detective programs have also been a prominent part of television's programming landscape. From *Dragnet* to *Police Woman* to the gritty realism and physical intimacy of *NYPD Blue* and the measured restraint of *Law and Order*, the lawman is an icon of television and its perception of justice.

Early programs featuring the exploits of the police were created with a keen eye toward reality. One of the most successful serial programs was *Dragnet*. Based upon actual case files of the Los Angeles police department, *Dragnet* avoided the depiction of violence while concentrating on the pursuit of the perpetrator.

As its star, along with being the show's producer and director, Jack Webb personified the no-nonsense but compassionate law-enforcement officer: "Just the facts, ma'am." Many of the stories still have relevance today, including the pursuit of a child beater, stolen white rats injected with a plague germ, the threatened bombing of police headquarters, and a high-school pornographic-picture ring. (Indeed, in the post-9/11 quest for "comfort programming," a remake of *Dragnet* appeared in the fall 2002–2003 television season.) Characterized by his staccato, flat delivery, Webb's Sergeant Joe Friday was a strictly business type of guy who was always on the job with only an occasional dalliance with a woman. He and his partner, Ben Alexander, never abused their power (pre-Miranda) and were always sensitive toward the needs of their victims.

Harry Morgan as officer Bill Gannon and Jack Webb as Sergeant Joe Friday in Universal Television's *Dragnet*. (Photofest.)

Produced for Liggett and Myers and sponsored by their Chesterfield brand of cigarettes, *Dragnet* was a phenomenal hit for NBC. The opening theme music, "dum da dum dum," composed by Walter Schumann, became a musical icon of the 1950s, offering a signature melody associated with the program.

From its pilot episode in 1951, the critics raved about the solid writing, acting, and production values of *Dragnet*. It leaped from radio to television with a compelling narrative structure and gripping drama. "Returning for the fall season with a new series, Jack Webb's 'Dragnet' remains one of the smoothest, classiest telepix packages on the air, due chiefly to star director Webb's penchant for realism and restraint."[15]

In 1953, a reviewer for *Variety* called *Dragnet* one of the best-produced series on the channels.[16] Another *Variety* reviewer mentioned that it was "solid and earthy without being crime ridden."[17] Its television success was the impetus for a feature-length film produced by Warner Brothers. Because of Webb's attention to detail, *Dragnet* had the best production values of any show on television during the 1950s. Webb was unrelenting in his pursuit of excellence, and his professionalism and attentiveness left an enduring television legacy.

The first police drama to be shot on location on the streets of New York City was *The Naked City*. Filmed on the streets of Manhattan, this program was one of the first to break the boundary of the Hollywood studio. It had a strong cast, led by veteran actor John McIntire, and solid writing by Stirling Silliphant. Each program ended with a voice-over intoning, "There are eight million stories in the Naked City. This has been one of them." That tagline made the program recognizable and provided it with an imprimatur. In 1960 the show moved from a half hour to an hour on ABC.

Detective programs became a feature of television in the late 1950s and 1960s. The ABC television network helped to pioneer these trendy, hip shows. On ABC it was known as the *caper trend,* starting with *77 Sunset Strip, Bourbon Street Beat, Adventures in Paradise,* and *Hawaiian Eye.* Writer-producer Roy Huggins, who had worked on *Cheyenne,* had written a novel after World War II called *77 Sunset Strip.* He decided that he would write the series' lead character, a detective, against type. Instead of a hard-boiled tough guy, he chose a sophisticated, bright personality played with charm and elegance by the actor Efrem Zimbalist Jr.

In the 90-minute pilot for the program, originally broadcast in October 1958, entitled "Girl On the Run," a 19-year-old sociopath who combed his hair before he murdered his victims became a subsequent principal of the series. During the film editing of the sequence, each time the sartorial murderer entered the frame, he was referred to as the "kook" by Huggins and producer Bill Orr. The actor portraying him was Edward Byrnes, and during a theatrical test of the film he was surrounded by young admirers. The feature pilot was successful, and ABC bought the series from Warner Brothers. In October 1958 a review that appeared in the entertainment newspaper *Variety* praised the program.

Warner Bros. put its best foot forward with a splashy, impressive 90-minute preem for its new hour long series "77 Sunset Strip." "Girl On the Run," originally made for theatrical release and as a pilot, is an excellent, well-conceived show, and the series should be a real winner for the Burbank lot if subsequent episodes even approach the standard of the initial one.[18]

The two other ABC programs in the network's spin cycle of breezy detective yarns were *Hawaiian Eye* and *Surfside Six.* These were referred to by reviewers as "comic strip adventure" and "formulaic," the basic formula being three male private eyes, a pretty girl, edgy dialogue, and a villain. In the Hawaiian version, Robert Conrad played the sexy male lead, and the Miami version served as a star vehicle for adolescent heartthrob Troy Donahue.

In the realm of creativity and originality, the most urbane detective drama of the late 1950s and early 1960s was *Peter Gunn,* starring Craig Stevens. It was a moody amalgam of a suave gumshoe and a city filled with creatures of the night crawling on the perpetually wet and shiny asphalt. The characters were a reflection of this inner sanctum, mirthlessly reveling in the nausea of their self-indulgent lives as addicts, prostitutes, swindlers, and murderers.

The series was a tribute to Raymond Chandler's detective hero Phillip Marlowe, and creator-producer Blake Edwards embodied Gunn with many of Marlowe's character traits. The show was instilled with a textured resonance that gave it a unique presence in the detective genre. In its murkiness it created a synergy between the narrative, the environment, and the sound track that provided a seamless entrée into Gunn's world of controlled mayhem. The composer Henry Mancini created a punctuated jazz theme for the show that embodied the stylized components of the series, making it a model for what is known today as the music video. From its cutting-edge opening credits to the slick editing and edgy dialogue, *Peter Gunn* was a fascinating mix of cool and hip.

The writing is classic for the genre, weaving a poetic cadence that matches the mood of the series. A client complains to Gunn after being presented with a thousand-dollar invoice for one night's work. "A thousand dollars! For a night's work? I didn't think the job was that hard." Gunn's response: "Not hard. Dirty."

In the underworld of Gunn's idiosyncratic informants, which include a pool shark midget, an avant-garde composer, and an artist whose body of work is uniquely devoted to self-portraits, the language is especially colorful and expectant. Gunn asks the artist about his quirky body of work.

You ever paint anything but yourself?
Why should I? I'm so infinitely complex.

The ensemble cast also includes Herschel Bernardi as Lieutenant Jacoby, whose timing seems perpetually off as he arrives at the crime scene after Gunn has usually resolved the problem with his snub-nosed .38. And, of course, there's the requisite girlfriend, Edie, played by Lola Albright, who provides the sexy interludes.

In all there were 114 30-minute episodes of *Peter Gunn,* which premiered on NBC on September 22, 1958, and ran on that network until 1960. For its last season, 1960–61, the series moved to ABC.[19]

The detective genre continued its aggressive pace on network television with *Staccato,* on NBC, starring veteran actor John Cassavetes as an ex–jazz musician turned gumshoe in New York's Greenwich Village. On CBS, the Four Star Film Company, with principal owner film star Dick Powell, supplied *Richard Diamond, Private Detective,* starring David Janssen. Interestingly, Powell played the role on radio early in his career. Sponsored by Maxwell House Coffee and P. Lorillard, Janssen played a smooth, suave, urbane private dick. A sexy twist to the series was the role of Sam the telephone girl, whose only identifying characteristic was her voice and her shapely legs, played by actress Mary Tyler Moore.

Of course, David Janssen went on to star in *The Fugitive,* one of television's most popular programs. It wasn't a traditional cops-and-robbers yarn, as it was about a physician wrongfully accused of murdering his wife. The series' creator, Roy Huggins, who had been writing for Westerns like *Cheyenne* and created the concept for *Maverick* and other series, wanted to do a more contemporary program. His intention was to integrate the independence and free spirit of the Western hero into the character of Dr. Richard Kimble. Most of the reaction to his idea for *The Fugitive* was negative. As a result, Huggins had decided to return to school and pursue graduate studies when a former associate called him, saying that Leonard Goldenson, the CEO of ABC television, wanted to talk to him. Huggins reluctantly agreed to take the meeting. Once there, feeling he had nothing to lose, he pitched his idea for *The Fugitive,* and once again was met with negative resistance. One ABC executive called the idea un-American. As the room fell silent for several seconds, one man spoke up, and all eyes were on Leonard Goldenson. He said, "Roy I think it's the best television concept I have ever heard in my life."

In the fall 2000 television season, CBS hoped to capitalize on the former success of *The Fugitive* franchise and the hugely successful theatrical film starring Harrison Ford. In a review of the recycled series that appeared in the *New York Times,* Stanley Fish was less than sanguine about its prospects. The original ran on ABC from 1963 to 1967 and, as Fish noted, it was about the formation of character in situations of intense and private moral choice. In David Janssen's portrayal of Dr. Richard Kimble, all the people he touched were somewhat changed by the experience. The new series had shallow character studies and focused more on action sequences designed to increase tension through articulated stunts rather than substantive narrative plotting. Apparently the television audience was equally unimpressed, as the new version was surely not improved, and the show was canceled.[20]

The iconoclastic characteristics of police detectives and their provocative stylistic behavior were clearly defined in the successful CBS drama *Kojak,* starring Telly Savalas. His portrayal of Lieutenant Theo Kojak of the Manhattan South 13th precinct was defined by the swagger and arrogance that television audiences found endearing. The series was produced by MCA Universal television and ran on CBS from 1973 to 1978. It started with a three-hour pilot, "The Marcus Nelson Murders," which was based upon the brutal 1963 "Career Girl Murders" of Janice Wylie and Emily Hoffert on Manhattan's East Side. From 1985 to 1989, seven two-hour movies were produced with Telly Savalas reprising his role as Inspector Theo Kojak.

Equally imbued with streetwise allure and self-assurance, Robert Blake's portrayal of undercover Manhattan cop and master of disguise Tony Baretta in ABC's *Baretta* ran on the network from 1975 to 1978. Featuring his pet cockatoo Fred and his street stoolie Rooster, the program struck a resonant chord with viewers.

Veteran screen actor Karl Malden was lured to the rigors of television-series work with the ABC police-detective series *Streets of San Francisco.* He co-starred as Lieutenant Detective Mike Sloane, with Michael Douglas playing his college-educated rookie partner, Steve Keller. The series, which was a Quinn Martin production, was filmed entirely in San Francisco and was broadcast for four seasons from 1972 to 1976. Actor Michael Douglas left the series after the third season and became a successful producer and movie star.

Other variations on the crime programming genre included lawyers who not only advanced their arguments within the halls of justice but also utilized their skills as sleuths to help solve crimes. One of the most notable and enduring of these was *Perry Mason,* based upon the stories of Erle Stanley Gardner. The series made its debut in September 1957 on CBS and faced some very stiff competition from Perry Como on Saturday nights. In a review of the first program in the series, Raymond Burr's portrayal of the legendary detective-lawyer was praised. "This is the first time that the Gardner-created unorthodox attorney has hit the video screens and, in the portrayal by Raymond Burr in 'The Case of the Restless Red Head' he comes off as an appropriate reincarnation."[21]

Shortly after the final gavel fell on *Perry Mason,* Raymond Burr moved on to *Ironside,* another successful series, this time on NBC. Burr's character, Chief of San Francisco Detectives Ironside, was confined to a wheelchair, providing an added sense of tension and drama to the program. It started its run on September 20, 1967, on Thursday evenings at 8:30, and was hailed by critics as a fresh and innovative police drama.

One of the most literate and realistic dramas profiling lawyers was Reginald Rose's *The Defenders,* starring E. G. Marshall and Robert Reed as father-and-son attorneys. The series dealt with issues of substance concerning the law and delved into the lives of the people touched by it. The intellectual nature of the program was heralded by critics, who praised it as innovative and challenging.

Testing the mettle of the producers and the CBS television network was a 1962 *Defenders* program entitled "The Benefactor," a pro-abortion program. It was about a doctor championing abortion rights at a time when it was illegal in the United States. Refusing to respond to public and advertiser pressure, the network ran the program as scheduled, with 12 of its affiliated stations declining to air the episode. It was this kind of courage that made *The Defenders* so compelling.

"The Defenders" is one of the best series on telefilm. The greatest surprise is that this intellectual, sometimes fragilely executed program continues to maintain such a high share of audience.[22]

"The Defenders," entering its third season, still shapes up as the most thoughtful dramatic show on network television. Week after week, the series maintains an unusually high standard for scripting literacy and production values. Even more importantly, the series has demonstrated that a TV show can be loyal to its subject matter, in this case the law, and still be dramatically cogent.[23]

Another CBS series that pushed the envelope in addressing issues of substance was *East Side, West Side*. The executive producer was David Susskind, and the lead and part-owner of the program was noted stage and screen actor George C. Scott. He played a crusading social worker, along with his costar, noted black actress Cicely Tyson, attempting to help those lost to the safety net of society. It was a gritty program and was green-lighted by the chairman of CBS, William Paley, over the objections of his programming head, James Aubrey, also known as "the smiling cobra." Aubrey's candor about the program was revealed in a meeting with Susskind when he berated the concept of *East Side, West Side*. "Get that fucking show out of the ghetto. I'm sick of it, the public's sick of it and it doesn't work. They've got just as big social problems on Park Avenue and that's where I want the goddamn show to be."[24]

When Susskind indicated that Scott would not be receptive to the change, Aubrey told him to have the actor meet with him and that he would straighten him out. The meeting took place at CBS headquarters in New York. As Aubrey went through his litany of rationales for changing the program, Scott listened quietly, poised to eat an apple. (He had once again given up smoking and usually munched on an apple to calm his nerves.) When Aubrey confirmed that he had finished his presentation, Scott removed a knife from his pocket, pressed a button and, after the glistening blade popped up, he speared a piece of apple. Holding the blade precariously close to Mr. Aubrey's nose, he said, "The show is staying right where it is. Good-bye, Mr. Aubrey, we are not meeting again."[25]

Actors and producers do not have the ultimate power in television, and shortly after their meeting, Aubrey canceled the show at the height of its popularity.[26]

As frequently happens in television, two networks, CBS and ABC, vied for the same audience when, in 1970, they debuted two very similar lawyer programs: *The Young Lawyers* (ABC) and *Storefront Lawyers* (CBS). Each program featured idealistic young attorneys helping the poor and indigent resolve their personal and professional dilemmas.

Television's fascination with the legal genre continued into the 1980s with *L.A. Law*, which was created by Steven Bochco, who was also responsible for the successful gritty police series *Hill Street Blues*. This drama focused on the lives and cases of a spirited cadre of attorneys at the high-powered L.A. law firm of Mackenzie, Brackman, Chaney, and Kuzak. Its characters provided a mix of men and women whose emotions sometimes betrayed their professional ethics.

One of the most endearing television series about students of the law was *The Paper Chase*, which was based on the movie and starred veteran actor John Houseman as the feared and revered Professor Charles W. Kingsfield. It was broadcast on CBS from 1978 to 1979 and rerun on PBS. The series was resurrected on Showtime in 1983 as *The Paper Chase: The Second Year* and in 1985 as *The Paper Chase: The Third Year.*

Programs featuring lawyers are a foundation of network television's programming mix. David E. Kelley's *The Practice* is about defense attorneys at the law firm of Donnell, Young, Dole, and Frutt; another of Kelley's law-themed programs, *Girls Club,* on Fox, about a trio of twentysomething women who were best friends in law school and work and live together, was canceled early in the 2002–2003 season. Apparently the allure of these sexy young lawyers was not enough to sustain audience interest in the program.

One of the biggest television hits in the cops-and-robbers genre was a program called *The Untouchables.* It first appeared on the CBS television network as a two-part special on *The Desilu Westinghouse Playhouse* in 1959. Two ABC executives, Dan Melnick and Tom Moore, saw the segment and agreed that it would be a great acquisition for ABC. Noted producer Quinn Martin (*The Fugitive*) produced the series, and it became a huge success for ABC. Starring Robert Stack as federal agent Elliot Ness, the series used a documentary-style narrative approach to its storytelling technique. Syndicated columnist Walter Winchell, a noted voice in radio, was effective as the voice-over narrator.

There was some concern that *The Untouchables'* use of violence and sex was too realistic for family audiences. A reviewer in *Variety* put the issue in perspective. "Violence and sex become legitimate qualities of adult fare when the story is realistic and believable, and that's the charm of the quasi documentary technique with a series that bases more or less on fact."[27] There was also concern expressed by some in the Italian American community about the portrayal of Italians as gangsters and members of the Mafia. This was illustrated when 30 distinguished Italian Americans visited the office of Leonard Goldenson, the CEO of ABC, and protested the characterization that all Italians were gangsters. Goldenson assured them that he would look into the matter. Shortly after, Terry Klein, a representative for the advertising agency McCann-Erickson, called to cancel its two minutes of commercial time on the program. The audience, however, had expressed its opinion by watching *The Untouchables,* and its numbers helped to ensure the success of the series.[28]

The dramatic context and narrative structure of the television Western and police drama are similar in design and function. Heroes are portrayed as courageous individualists, sacrificing personal gain for the glory of public service. They are a unique breed, invested in their duties and service to their community. These ideals continue to flourish on television, albeit with a more current cultural perspective. For example, the *Law and Order* series, with its dedicated franchises, uses newspaper headlines as a foundation for many of its episodes. In addition, the situations and language of police dramas in both broadcast and cable are more realistic and vivid. Programs on cable like *The Wire,* about a West Baltimore homicide and narcotics department, are graphic in their representations associated with issues of crime.

Audiences respect the rugged determinism of these individuals, and whether the character is portrayed as a lawyer, detective, or cowboy, the actions they take are measured by a precedent of self-reliance as defined by television.

## NOTES

1. A. C. Nielsen, Jr. Online Research Center, The Museum of Broadcast Communications, www.museum.tv/archives.

2. A. C. Nielsen, Jr. Online Research Center, The Museum of Broadcast Communications, www.museum.tv/archives.

3. The Library of Congress, New York World Telegram & Sun Newspaper Photograph Collection, www.loc.gov/rr/print/coll/130_nyw.html.

4. James Barron, "Dale Evans, No-Nonsense Queen of the West, Dies at 88," *New York Times,* 8 February 2001, p. A28.

5. Fifties Web, Candace Rich, www.fiftiesweb.com.

6. *Worthington Miner—Interviewed by Franklin J. Schaffner* (Metuchen, N.J.: Scarecrow Press, 1985).

7. William Boddy, *Fifties Television: The Industry and Its Critics* (Chicago and Urbana: University of Illinois Press, 1990), p. 72.

8. J. Fred MacDonald, *Who Shot the Sheriff?: The Rise and Fall of the Television Western* (New York: Praeger, 1987), p. 63.

9. Leonard H. Goldenson and Marvin J. Wolf, *Beating the Odds* (New York: Charles Scribner's Sons, 1991), p. 160.

10. MacDonald, *Who Shot the Sheriff?,* p. 62.

11. Ibid., p. 65.

12. Ibid., p. 75.

13. Ibid., p. 52.

14. Ibid., p. 73.

15. *Variety,* 15 September 1962.

16. *Variety,* 8 September 1953.

17. *Variety,* 12 February 1954.

18. *Variety,* 13 October 1958.

19. Frank Lidz, "The Private Eye by Twilight," *New York Times,* 7 April 2002, p. AR26.

20. Stanley Fish, "Running Away from a Daunting Television Legacy," *New York Times,* 22 October 2000, p. 27.

21. *Variety,* 25 September 1957.

22. *Variety,* 19 September 1962.

23. *Variety,* 2 October 1963.

24. Robert Metz, *CBS: Reflections in a Bloodshot Eye* (Chicago: Playboy Press, 1975), p. 228.

25. Ibid.

26. Ibid.

27. *Variety,* 19 October 1959.

28. Goldenson and Wolf, *Beating the Odds,* p. 173.

# 4

## MEDICINAL MYOPIA: TELEVISION MAKES HOUSE CALLS

The dynamic of the television hero is made up of distinct characteristics that have various similarities associated with different roles. Their heroism is based upon their deeds and the goodwill that they extend to others. Even if they are fugitives like Dr. Richard Kimble (David Janssen in ABC's *The Fugitive*), they can have a profound impact upon other people's lives.

American society has always viewed the role of the physician as somewhat reverential. Their ability to heal the sick and provide emotional comfort to the ailing provides a rich source of dramatic material for television. As such, in both prime-time and daytime television, portrayal of doctors has been a consistent part of the programming mix.

The first series to capture the idealism of the medical profession and build on the mythology of the genre was *Medic*, a 30-minute program on NBC starring Richard Boone, which made its premiere in September 1954. Using a dramatic documentary style similar to *Dragnet*, it was described as being factual and educational in content with a dramatic kick. Sponsored by Dow Chemical, with Worthington Miner as the executive producer, the premiere episode, "White Is the Color," was controversial because it was about a pregnant woman diagnosed with a deadly case of leukemia and the effort made to save her baby.

Utilizing authentic medical case histories, *Medic* wove an intricate, compelling narrative of people facing severe trauma with doctors and staff providing support and aid. It helped set a standard for dramatic television within this genre while addressing realistic themes and situations faced by medical professionals every day.

Although a stylistic departure from *Medic*, *Dr. Kildare*, starring Richard Chamberlain as an idealistic intern, became a hit program for NBC television. Based upon the popular theatrical features of the same name starring actor Lew Ayres in the title role, the television version, produced by the same studio, MGM, was true to form. While some critics dismissed the program as saccharin-coated soap opera, others were more generous, calling it interesting and wholesome. The show made its debut in 1961, following on the heels of its competitor, *Ben Casey*, on the ABC television network. In the late 1960s, a syndicated half-hour *Young Dr. Kildare* program made its debut, featuring a different cast, which included Mark Jenkins, Gary Merrill, and Andrew Duggan.

With *Ben Casey*, ABC and the program's producers, Jim Mosher and Meta Rosenberg, came up with a gritty, realistic program about a young, passionate resident neurosurgeon. Not surprisingly, Mosher had been a writer on *Medic* and was now poised to integrate some of that program's character into his new medical drama. There were similarities to *Dr. Kildare*, with Casey also having an older doctor as a mentor, Dr. Zorba, played by actor Sam Jaffe.

At ABC television, Dan Melnick was supervising the production of the *Ben Casey* pilot and had cast all of the roles except for the lead. When he mentioned it to his wife, she reminded him of a B movie they had seen several weeks before featuring a criminal played by Vince Edwards. They arranged a screen test, and Edwards landed the part that made his career.[1]

For some actors who were matinee idols on the silver screen, moving to leading roles in television was viewed as a professional step down in their careers. However, television was responsible for resurrecting and rejuvenating the careers of many of Hollywood's film stars. One of them was actor Robert Young. He appeared as a leading man in many Hollywood films and moved to television with a starring role in *Father Knows Best*.

When another network declined the script for *Marcus Welby, M.D.*, it was submitted to ABC by Universal Television. At the network, Len Goldberg liked the script and envisioned actor Lee J. Cobb in the leading role. As is so often the case in television, one's initial perception of a character doesn't always accord with the actor chosen to play him. After reading the script, Robert Young became very interested in the role of Marcus Welby. However, Goldberg felt that Young's charming, sophisticated manner would not suit the character of the older, struggling general practitioner. Persistent, Young called Goldberg several times and finally asked if he could test for the part. An actor of Robert Young's stature testing for a television role was unprecedented, so Goldberg conceded. His portrayal of Marcus Welby was right on target, and that role became one of Young's signature characters.

*Marcus Welby, M.D.* made its premiere on ABC in the fall of 1969. Its first appearance, however was as a two-hour program on ABC-TV. In one of those rarely noticed ironies of television, actor Lew Ayres, who played young Dr. Kildare in the movies, was cast as a hospital director for the two-hour feature.

The program was a hit and was a formidable contender for ABC's prime-time Tuesday-night schedule.

A popular medical program that became a hit for CBS television in 1970 was *Medical Center*. It started as a two-hour feature entitled *University Medical Center* in 1969 and starred Richard Bradford as the dedicated, attractive bachelor Dr. Gannon. Its premiere in 1970, as often happens, had Chad Everett in the lead as the handsome Dr. Gannon, with a spanking new title, *Medical Center*. The guest star on the first episode was O. J. Simpson (then a college player and recent acquisition of the Buffalo Bills), who received highly favorable reviews in his first acting role.

The doctors at St. Eligius Hospital on the NBC series *St. Elsewhere* were accustomed to handling chaos as a routine. Led by actor Denzel Washington, who played Dr. Chandler, the series premiered on NBC in October 1982 and ran for six seasons. Of course, Denzel Washington launched a successful movie career after the demise of the series.

The medical theme on television was nuanced by different programming orientations, including the Korean War and the Vietnam era, as portrayed by *M*A*S*H* and *China Beach*. In many ways, *M*A*S*H*, which ran for 11 seasons, satirized the purpose of war and its futility for a generation of television viewers. The lead character, Dr. Benjamin Franklin "Hawkeye" Pierce, portrayed by Alan Alda, was a spokesperson for a disaffected generation. On *China Beach,* Dana Delany played army nurse Colleen McMurphy, who was trying to survive the daily grind of her tour of duty in Vietnam.

In yet another iteration—but a more frivolous one—associated with medicine, Neil Patrick Harris portrayed the title character of *Doogie Howser, M.D.,* a boy genius who graduated from Princeton at the age of 10 and became a licensed physician at the ripe old age of 16. Television managed to treat almost every discipline in medicine, including that of the forensic medical examiner played by actor Jack Klugman, who gave viewers a weekly anatomy lesson for seven seasons, starting in 1976, on *Quincy, M.E.* Not unlike *Quincy, M.E.,* CBS's *Diagnosis Murder,* which ran for eight seasons (1992–2001), featured seasoned television veteran Dick Van Dyke as Dr. Mark Sloan, a physician who moonlighted as a forensic medical specialist and helped his son, Detective Steve Sloan, solve various crimes. The series served as a proscenium for displaying the talent of the Van Dyke family, with Dick's son Barry portraying Steve Sloan and nephew Shane Van Dyke as a medical student.

The hospital-medical drama continued as a life force for television into the new millennium with the series *E.R.,* helping to resuscitate the genre's image. The show, which was a star vehicle for actor George Clooney (who has since left the series), was a consistent ratings winner for the NBC television network. Its lengthy television run of more than twelve seasons includes a George Foster Peabody Award and more than 17 Emmys. Featuring an ensemble cast, the program focuses on young interns at the fictional County

Hospital in Chicago. Stories follow traditional soap-opera themes, highlighting the romantic, professional, and personal nature of their lives.

To heighten the drama of a season premiere in 1998, *E.R.* debuted with a live broadcast that was presented twice, for the East Coast and West Coast time zones. The series also made news when the cast demanded higher salaries and the production company Constant c Productions, whose principal is Michael Crichton, author of *Jurassic Park* (and creator of *E.R.*), significantly increased the show's license fee paid by NBC to more than $10 million per episode. Coproducers of the program are Amblin Television and Warner Brothers Television.

Building on the success of *E.R.*, John Wells, an executive producer of the series, created *Third Watch*, which premiered on the NBC television network in 1999. This popular series focused on the police officers, firefighters, and paramedics of New York City's fictional 55th precinct. It is also syndicated on the A&E network.

A similar hospital series, CBS's *Chicago Hope*, starring Adam Arkin, was a competitor to *E.R.* It also featured a cast of young actors who played doctors at a large urban hospital in Chicago. Attempting to thwart the ratings juggernaut of *E.R.*, CBS tried to compete with *L.A. Doctors* (1998–99), about four young, idealistic doctors who take on the system in their practice, bending the rules to accommodate their patients' needs. The series ran for only one season. The network, however, had more success with Jane Seymour's portrayal of the title character in *Dr. Quinn, Medicine Woman* (1993–98) as a woman doctor in the rough-and-tumble frontier town of Colorado Springs. For the 2002 season, CBS premiered the series *Presidio Medical*, produced by John Wells, Lydia Woodward, and Chris Chulack, the team responsible for *E.R.* The series was a departure from tradition in that most of the prominent characters are women, including Blythe Danner, playing Dr. Harriet Lanning, an ob-gyn specialist who also provides a sympathetic ear to the women on her staff in this private practice. Other notable actresses portraying doctors in the series include Dana Delany (*China Beach*), Anna Deavere Smith (*The West Wing*), Sasha Alexander (*Dawson's Creek*), and Julieanne Nicholson (*Ally McBeal*).

An ambitious hospital drama series that premiered in the 2000 season, *Gideon's Crossing* featured the talented actor Andre Braugher, who had been on *Homicide: Life on the Street*. The action for this drama was not in Chicago but at a fictional New England teaching hospital. Facing difficult competition during its time period, the series was canceled in April 2001.

In an effort to stay competitive within the rigors of cable, broadcast, and satellite television programming schedules, while assuming that the audience taste for medical drama hadn't waned for more of the same, several new programs made their debut beginning with the 2000 television season. One of the first, *Strong Medicine*, premiered on the Lifetime television network on July 23, 2000, and featured the rivalry between two woman doctors working at a women's clinic in south Philadelphia. In *Doc,* which debuted on the PAX cable network on March 11, 2001, country crooner Billy Ray Cyrus ("Achy Breaky Heart") portrayed Dr. Clint Cassidy, who is transplanted from a rural practice in Montana to a bustling New York City HMO.

For the 2001 season, NBC premiered *Scrubs,* a series about ambitious medical interns moving toward their residencies, and in 2002 on ABC, *MDs* made its debut, portraying a group of antiestablishment doctors at the fictional Mission General Hospital who are determined to practice medicine according to their own agenda. The latter series proved to provide viewers with more base titillation when in one episode a pager was used as a sex toy.

## REAL MEDICINE

As reality programming became a trendsetting television phenomenon, broadcast and cable networks moved toward initiating programming that would accommodate the audience appetite for this fare. The Lifetime cable network distributed the documentary *Women Docs,* about 12 University of Washington female physicians with different specialties. Other reality series about medical professionals on The Learning Channel include *Trauma: Life in the E.R., Code Blue,* and *Maternity Ward.* At the ABC television network, summer programming during the 2000 and 2002 seasons included two compelling nonfiction medical programs revolving around doctors and their patients at two prestigious hospitals, Johns Hopkins (*Hopkins 24/7*) and Memorial Hermann Hospital at the University of Texas Medical School (*Houston Medical*). Both of these narrative nonfiction series offered producers unprecedented access to the medical staff and their patients. Both were six parts, with producers at Hopkins having access during three months of filming; at Memorial Hermann Hospital, the access was for one year in the critical care unit and level-one trauma centers. These programs provided a realistic portrait of the stress physicians and other medical professionals face in balancing their professional, personal, and family lives.

## DAYTIME SOAP DOCS

Daytime serial television (soap operas) have been a fertile programming landscape for the distribution of long-running medically oriented programs. The longest running of these serial dramas is *General Hospital,* which premiered on the ABC television network on April 1, 1963. The setting for the drama is the fictional upstate New York seaside town of Port Charles, where the wealthy and influential Quatermaines family presides over the town's business and affairs of the heart. Over the years, *General Hospital* has won numerous awards for its story lines, which feature prominent health issues associated with breast cancer, HIV/AIDS, and sexual responsibility.

Another vintage medically oriented soap opera that ran on the NBC television network was *The Doctors* (1963–82). It started as an anthology series, and by 1964 became a regularly scheduled daytime serial drama. The series featured soon-to-be movie stars Alec Baldwin (1980–82) and Kathleen Turner (1978–79).

Perhaps the finest of television's medically themed dramas was the 10-part 1983 PBS *Masterpiece Theatre* adaptation of A. J. Cronin's biographical novel *The Citadel,* starring British actor Ben Cross as Dr. Andrew Manson, who begins his medical career in the squalid conditions of a Welsh mining town and then internalizes the guilt of his success with a fashionable medical practice in London's West End. It offered the television viewer an outstanding portrayal of early medicine and the conflict between idealism and reality.

## TALK DOCS

For some time, radio and television have provided a forum for doctors to offer advice and counsel. However, there were also instances when the airwaves were used by charlatans masquerading as medical professionals and using broadcasting technology to nurture their own greed. When radio was a fledgling mass medium in the 1930s, an enterprising swindler named John R. Brinkley, a self-anointed doctor, used radio as a platform to cheat listeners. Although he never received a diploma from the one-room school he attended in Tuckasiegee, North Carolina, Brinkley pursued medical studies at two dubious medical "colleges," Bennett Medical College of Chicago and Eclectic Medical University of Kansas City, both known as diploma mills. Although his credentials were suspect, he was licensed by Arkansas and went on to practice in Milford, Kansas. In 1918 he began performing his goat-gland operation, a controversial procedure to rejuvenate male sexual potency and virility via the implantation of goat glands into male gonads. A talented promoter, Brinkley soon was performing 100 of these procedures a week at a cost of $750 for each patient.

His wealth increased as a result of the goat-gland operation and the patent medicines he dispensed through his pharmaceutical business. In 1923 he built KFKB, the radio station in Kansas that he used to broadcast his popular program *Medical Question Box,* where he presumed to diagnose the ailments of listeners who wrote in describing their medical problems. He had an array of patent medicines identified by number that he readily prescribed over the radio. Listeners could purchase these elixirs at one of the Brinkley pharmacies or at a participating location. In addition to his program, the station also carried fundamentalist preaching and country music.

Outraged by "Dr." Brinkley's presumptuous use of the radio for making diagnoses and prescribing patent medicines, Dr. Morris Fishbein of the American Medical Association attacked Brinkley's credibility, and as a result, in

1930 the Kansas State Medical Board revoked his license and the Federal Radio Commission refused to renew his broadcasting license.

Not easily daunted by authority, Brinkley ran for governor as an independent and lost in a close election. His gubernatorial attempts in 1932 and 1934 also failed. An enterprising businessman, Brinkley received permission from Mexico to build a powerful transmitter with the call letters XER at Villa Acuna, Mexico, across the river from Del Rio, Texas. Then, in a bold move, he relocated his staff and facilities to the Roswell Hotel in Del Rio. Using his new station as an aggressive marketing tool, Brinkley successfully convinced his listeners to visit his clinic and purchase worthless ampoules of high-priced colored water. He also performed numerous prostate operations and, instead of the goat-gland operation, devised a new protocol of Mercurochrome shots and pills as a restorative of youth. He became even wealthier and pursued a lifestyle of the rich and famous, but was plagued by malpractice suits and by the pursuit of the Internal Revenue Service for back taxes. He declared bankruptcy in 1941 and died of heart failure in 1942.

## NEW AGE PRACTITIONERS

### Dr. Ruth

Although the Internet may be the new platform of choice for dispensing rejuvenating drugs like Viagra, radio and television offer a provocative proscenium for individual medical practitioners to pursue their discipline. One of the modern-day pioneers, first on radio and later on television and the Internet, was Dr. Ruth Westheimer, known affectionately as Dr. Ruth. She received her master's degree in sociology in 1959 and in the 1960s worked at Planned Parenthood, earning a doctorate in education at Columbia Teachers College in New York City.

Her interest was in psychosexual therapy, and she trained with noted sex therapist Dr. Helen Singer Kaplan and opened her own practice in 1980. She made radio history in September 1980 when her 15-minute midnight program *Sexually Speaking* premiered on New York's WYNY. The program became a phenomenon and soon was carried by 78 stations. Fan mail increased in volume, and Dr. Ruth started answering questions over the air. By the end of the first year she was taking telephone calls from listeners on an expanded hour-long radio broadcast. Her cable television programs include *The All-New Dr. Ruth Show* and *What's Up, Dr. Ruth,* and she's the author of 15 books.

### Dr. Laura

In the realm of media pop-culture psychology, one of the most popular practitioners is Dr. Laura Schlesinger. Her syndicated radio program reaches

20 million listeners daily and is distributed over 450 radio stations. She's also created a cottage merchandising industry that includes books (such as *Ten Stupid Things Men Do to Mess up Their Lives*) and a line of jewelry. Although her doctoral degree is in physiology and not psychology, she readily dispenses advice on a wide range of personal issues and family dynamics. Also, estimates place the number of male listeners in her radio audience at between 53 and 57 percent. One of her favorite phrases is "Tell me what you think, not what you feel."

On September 11, 2000, *Dr. Laura* moved to television and was syndicated by Paramount Domestic Television. Prior to her television debut she had referred to homosexuality and lesbianism as "deviant" and a "biological error" on her radio show. This brought about sharp, vocally pointed rebukes from the gay and lesbian community and others who found her comments to be reprehensible. Indeed, the Gay and Lesbian Alliance against Defamation boycotted her program and those who advertised on it. This led many television stations to move the program from daytime to the middle-of-the-night graveyard schedule. Not surprisingly, while her radio ratings remain strong, her television program was canceled in April 2001.

## Dr. Phil

One does have to speculate about the value of advice dispensed en masse by pop icons of media mediation. Of course, there's a legacy associated with offering guidance to millions of people. The syndicated newspaper columnist Esther Pauline Lederer, writing under the name Ann Landers, reached 90 million readers daily in 1,200 newspapers. And her twin sister, Pauline Esther Phillips, was also a popular syndicated advice columnist with *Dear Abby*.

Defining an image on the crowded television spectrum can be a daunting task. It always helps to have a celebrity endorsement validate your image. That's exactly what happened to Dr. Phillip C. McGraw, better known as Dr. Phil. A psychologist who grew tired of practicing traditional therapy, he founded a company called Courtroom Sciences, consulting on the dynamics of winning in court. One of his clients was Oprah Winfrey, who was battling the beef industry in 1998 after swearing off hamburgers. She was victorious both in the legal courtroom and in the court of public opinion, and the good doctor became a regular guest on her show. He became a television celebrity in September 2002 with his own program, *Dr. Phil,* which was launched with a 97 percent television station clearance rate, making it the second-most-popular syndicated program, after *The Oprah Winfrey Show.* It's produced by Harpo Productions, Oprah's production company, and either precedes or follows her program in most markets, but never competes.

## Dead Doctors Don't Lie

Radio provides a rich resource for the pursuit of merchandising related to the alleged medicinal value of alternative medical products. For Dr. Joel D. Wallach, a veterinarian and naturopathic physician, the syndicated radio program *Dead Doctors Don't Lie* provides a means to promote his American Longevity Colloidal Mineral Products Line. In addition to a daily live radio program, Dr. Wallach also promotes his self-help audio tapes during the live broadcast.

## INFOMERCIALS

There are many infomercials on television, some of which make dubious claims. An infomercial is a program-length commercial for a product or service. It features a spokesperson, sometimes a fading celebrity, who endorses the product or service and explains its merits. Viewers of infomercials must be alert to the claims they make and the terms of payment that they arrange. It's a classic case of "Let the buyer beware." This is especially true for any form of medical treatment, vitamins, herbs, or apparatuses that are featured in the infomercial. For example, the Federal Trade Commission invoked a $3 million fine on Blue Stuff Inc. for making unsubstantiated claims that their products Blue Stuff and Super Blue Stuff, which each sold for $59.95 for an 8-ounce jar, relieved pain. There are, however, legitimate doctors, products, and services, like Dr. Lee Bosley of Bosley Medical, who specializes in hair transplants and is featured on television in an infomercial.

The medical profession has provided many opportunities for television to nurture its fictionalized canvas of heroes and champions. Doctors are heralded for their status as healers and saviors who sometimes practice in a hostile environment. They are challenged by their commitment to save life and their dedication to treat it with dignity, respecting the realities of death. Their quest to define the limits of their ability and challenge the traditions of accepted practice is what makes for the tension and conflict in medical television drama.

The medical show, whether it features crusading doctors with individual practices or physicians in a hospital setting, is a staple of television programming. The world of medicine has always had a fascinating allure for viewers, and its plots and themes remain a tantalizing reservoir for compelling story ideas. As viewers, we look into the doctors' world as people who can identify with the patients and illnesses they treat. We are part of the larger dynamic of medicine, and through television are attempting to understand its virtues and deficiencies. The television audience is a consumer of programming content that is at times entertaining and instructive. Medical programs, once jokingly referred to as "disease of the week," sometimes provide viewers with an understanding of medical protocol and procedures. As entertainment, these programs have interesting characters in compelling dramatic situations that are nuanced by fiction and fact.

## NOTE

1. Leonard H. Goldenson and Marvin J. Wolf, *Beating the Odds* (New York: Charles Scribner's Sons, 1991), pp. 151–52.

# 5

## MIRRORING THE MELTING POT: GENDER, RACE, AND RELIGION

Like the movies, television has not always been sensitive to issues of gender, race, and religion. Stereotypes prevailed not only in their assumption of roles but also in the context of behavior. Hollywood established boundaries that were predicated upon values and mores popularized by tradition and bias. Indeed, *Birth of a Nation,* Hollywood's first great film epic, embodied the tenets of racism as perceived by southern whites. Adapted from Thomas W. Dixon's novel *The Clansman,* D. W. Griffith, a Kentuckian whose father was a Confederate officer, parlayed his contempt for black Reconstruction and the Negro's pursuit of voting rights, along with the fear of miscegenation, into a 12-reel, two-and-a-half-hour film in which the Klan was portrayed as the heroic knights preserving the heritage of white America. For the Camerons, the South Carolina family featured in the film, the blacks are the essence of evil, raping white women, executing Confederate officers, and looting white southern homes.

Although the film was well received and most audiences cheered the efforts of the Klan, there were some who mounted conspicuous objections. Ohio banned the exhibition of the film. The National Association for the Advancement of Colored People (NAACP) objected to its pronounced racism in Boston and elsewhere. Their action in many ways was a precursor to future confrontations with Hollywood and the television industry over the portrayal of African Americans in the media.

Another film epic based upon the Civil War, *Gone with the Wind,* captured the imagination of America and presented blacks in a more sympathetic role, albeit one that was based upon historical stereotypes. Produced by David O. Selznick, it won the Academy Award for best picture in 1939. In an auspicious recognition of talent, Hattie McDaniel, the black actress who played Mammy, won an Oscar for best supporting actress.

In television, there was a need to create relevant and entertaining programming for a mass audience. Unlike the movies, television was perceived by its audience as free entertainment that could be accessed in their home on demand. In most cases, television producers decided to play it safe and pursue the same ideology toward race and gender that Hollywood had sustained over the years.

During the 1950s television predominantly featured white talent and focused upon the myth of racial tolerance through a process of exclusion. It created its own behavioral mythology of American society based upon the fiction of Hollywood and its perception of American values.

The television families of the 1950s—the Nelsons of *The Adventures of Ozzie and Harriet* (1952), the Andersons of *Father Knows Best* (1954), the Cleavers of *Leave It to Beaver* (1957), and the Stones of *The Donna Reed Show* (1958)—were an idyllic representation of an institutionalized bias. It was a personification not only of race but of gender, as women dutifully tended to their roles as homemakers and yielded to their husbands' needs. Indeed, in some instances women were marginalized as scatterbrains and unsuited for anything more than household chores, as in the case of Gale Storm's role in *My Little Margie*.

When black actors were featured in television programs, their roles were stereotyped as domestics or buffoons. For black women actresses, portraying an affable maid to a white household became de rigueur in the television landscape of the 1950s and 1960s. In *Beulah* (1950–53), black actresses like Ethel Waters, Hattie McDaniel, and later Louise Beavers played the role of loyal domestics, smiling and humming as they happily attended to the drudgery of their chores. Ever loyal to the white Henderson household, Beulah was respectful to "Mr. Harry" and "Miss Alice" but was less tolerant of the friends in her black universe. Indeed, those characters—like the dull, empty-headed Oriole, the maid next door, and the cloddish boyfriend, Bill—appeared as severe racially denigrating stereotypes.

There were other television families that featured black maids as foils for white talent. One black actress sustained quite a career playing a domestic on radio and television. As the maid on the radio version of *The Great Gildersleeve*, Lillian Randolph spent a decade with the show and then played the same character when it became a syndicated television program. She also played the maid Louise in the hit television series *Make Room for Daddy*, which later was renamed *The Danny Thomas Show*.

One television series that demonstrated the offensiveness of racial stereotyping, *Amos 'n' Andy* (1951–53), evolved as a vehicle for white actors portraying blacks in radio and then became the first sitcom television series with an all-black cast. It established some of the basic ingredients of the situation comedy, but its pursuit of humor at the expense of denigrating race caused a great deal of controversy.

The male characters in *Amos 'n' Andy* were portrayed as either scheming or dull, while professionals were inept and unscrupulous. Women were shrewish, somewhat vulgar, and domineering. Even as the series first went on the air, in June 1951 on CBS, the NAACP attempted an injunction in federal court to prohibit the network from distributing the program. There were protests from unions and other professional organizations. The criticism of *Amos 'n' Andy* included the inferior treatment of Negroes; their portrayal as lazy, clownish, and criminal; the portrayal of women as screaming shrews; and the acceptance of these traits by white America.

Among all the protest against *Amos 'n' Andy,* there were some who viewed it as bound by the classic traditions of American humor. One black scholar described it as "race-consciousness" but not racism. Interestingly, an informal telephone poll in 1987 on the Black Entertainment Television channel found that when asked if they'd like to see the series back on television, 80 percent of respondents voted affirmatively. The program was taken off the air in 1953 and by 1966 was removed from television syndication.

Perhaps one of the most telling statements of the need for television to sustain the racial status quo of the era was *The Nat King Cole Show* (NBC, 1956–57). Cole was the consummate entertainer and had captured the hearts of America with his romantic ballads "Mona Lisa" and "Unforgettable." Unfortunately, as a black entertainer who originated from the South—and one of its most bigoted and racially defiant states, Alabama—he led a life that was anything but unforgettable.

Soon after the success of his hit "Nature Boy" in 1948, Cole purchased a home for himself and his family in the white suburb of Hancock Park in Los Angeles. In an effort to keep him out, the homeowners formed the Hancock Park Property Owners Association. Although Cole eventually prevailed and moved into the English Tudor-style house, he had to endure the racial hostility of a community intent on discriminating against him. "How would you like it if you had to come out of your home and see a Negro walking down the street wearing a big wide hat, a zoot suit, long chain, and yellow shoes?"[1]

In 1956, the same year Cole was to become the first black to host a variety program on national television, he was attacked by a group of white men while performing before a segregated audience in Birmingham, Alabama. The emerging civil rights movement made television advertisers acutely sensitive to sponsoring programs featuring Negro performers. Although Cole's television program was popular, even in the South, its inability to attract a national sponsor sounded its death knell. Another obstacle impeding the program's success was that it was aired opposite *Robin Hood,* a hit series on the CBS television network.

The intrinsic dilemma for *The Nat King Cole Show* was securing consistent advertising. It started on NBC as a 15-minute program with sporadic sponsorship by Arrid deodorant and Rise shaving cream. In an effort to make the show more competitive, NBC reconfigured it into a half-hour format and introduced it during the summer of 1957. Unfortunately, it was once again placed opposite a powerful competitor on CBS, *The $64,000 Question.*

In an effort to build the show's audience, famous entertainers from that era like Pearl Bailey, Mel Torme, Peggy Lee, Sammy Davis Jr., and Harry Belafonte offered their talents for the minimum union wage allowed. The camaraderie among performers making an effort to help struggling African American talent succeed on television was not unique to the Cole show. Some of the most popular television stars of the late 1940s and early 1950s, including Ed Sullivan, Steve Allen, and Eddie Cantor, were outspoken and demonstrated their support by showcasing black talent on their programs. Indeed, when Eddie Cantor invited the Will Mastin Trio, featuring 24-year-old Sammy Davis Jr., to his *Colgate Comedy Hour* on February 17, 1952, he said of Sammy Davis in his introduction that he was "one of the greatest hunks of talent I've ever seen in my life." With the start of the fall season, *The Nat King Cole Show* was moved to Tuesday evenings at 7:30.

In addition, network executives, attempting to assuage the sensibilities of their southern constituency, made insulting demands of Cole, including eliminating his black backup singers and maintaining a "respectful" relationship with white female guests. Nat King Cole could not acquiesce to such demands, and the program was canceled after one season. Reflecting on these circumstances, Cole was somewhat rueful and sarcastic when he said publicly that "racial prejudice is more finance than romance."[2]

## PHANTOM BLACKS AND ISSUES OF EMPOWERMENT

In the 1960s there were some black artists that passed through the cultural threshold of television, but they did not have a defining influence on the medium. Indeed, the noted black author John Oliver Killens was highly critical of the monochrome landscape of television in the 1960s. Referring to this deficiency, Killens reflected that a black person could

stare at television and go to an occasional movie and go through the routine from day to day, month to month, and year to year and hardly (if ever) see himself reflected in the cultural media. It was as if he had no real existence, as if he were a fragment of his own imagination, or, at best, if he had an existence it wasn't worth reflecting or reflection.[3]

A televisual existence for blacks was viewed by some as a cultural means for greater assimilation and acceptance by white society. Writing about television's ability to communicate with an indulgent audience and embrace blacks into the mainstream of American culture, Robert Lewis Shayon, a columnist for the *Saturday Review,* saw television as a virtue toward greater acculturation.

If Negroes were seen more frequently on television—and in featured roles comparable to those played by white actors—their real-life employment picture might be favorably affected. Television's power to change mass habits and attitudes appears to be significant. An improvement in the Negro image on television might be a very important step toward real integration.[4]

Although Killens acknowledged that some progress had been made, he rejected the notion of Shayon's quantification of black images on television and spoke to the need for providing an authentic reflection of the African American social experience and the quality of the imagery; not the quantity.

In assessing the virtues of a realistic depiction of the African American social experience, it is interesting to look at some of the pioneering programs and series featuring the first black television stars. The Dumont television network, which was a struggling competitor to the other networks because of its deficient number of station affiliates, in the summer of 1950 featured jazz pianist Hazel Scott, who hosted a 15-minute show.

Many black artists, like Lena Horne, Ella Fitzgerald, and Harry Belafonte, performed on variety programs like Ed Sullivan's *Toast of the Town*. One of the first network series featuring black talent was an hour-long variety program on CBS, *Sugar Hill Times*. Unfortunately, the show, hosted by New York radio personality and noted bandleader Willie Bryant, suffered from the reality of competition. His career included some of the most distinguished jazz musicians and performers of the era, including Bessie Smith, Eddie Durham, David "Panama" Francis, and Teddy Wilson. Several years later, another program committed to the black television presence was *The Billy Daniels Show* on ABC. Appearing in the fall of 1952 as a musical variety program, it was distributed in some of the major television markets in the nation, including New York, Boston, Chicago, Philadelphia, Los Angeles, and San Francisco. The national broadcast was sponsored by a single advertiser, the Vitamin Corporation of America. It was a 15-minute program on Sunday nights and ran for only half a season, or 13 weeks.

As television became a means for black artists to reach the American public, it was also a tool to perpetuate the stereotypical myths of "coon" mentality. This was manifested in behavioral acting techniques, including rolling the eyes, shuffling the feet, and making high-pitched utterances in pidgin English. The perception of blacks as shiftless, happy-go-lucky, and dull was providing rewarding employment for actors like Willie Best. Although Best was a multitalented performer, his roles in the television series *Trouble with Father, My Little Margie,* and *Waterfront* were a personification of the racist vision of blacks confirmed by the mass medium of television. He was known as the younger embodiment of Stepin Fetchit, nicknamed "Sleep 'n' Eat."

Somewhat of a renaissance for black television talent began in the 1960s. It started with the program *I Spy* (1965–68), the first prime-time network dramatic series to star a black actor, Bill Cosby, on NBC. As a tennis coach and globe-trotting secret agent, Cosby broke the traditions of black stereo-types, portraying a smart, suave, sophisticated character. The producer of the series, Sheldon Leonard, had played a hunch using the relatively unknown comedian.

Interestingly, *I Spy* was not the first detective series to feature a black actor. In 1954 *Harlem Detective,* based upon the mystery novels of Chester Himes (*If He Hollers Let Him Go*), was a local program series in New York that featured black talent; however, it was not distributed on network television. It was also the first dramatic television series with an integrated cast. Being on a network provided Cosby with national exposure and gave him an op-portunity to build a loyal following. He won three Emmys and was recog-nized as one of the most popular stars on television.

The program also provided Cosby with a platform to present a positive role model of blacks to white audiences. While giving credit to individuals and groups who were campaigning for civil rights, Cosby praised them for their dedication and accomplishment articulating his position. "My way is to show white people that Negroes are human beings with the same aspirations and abilities that whites have."[5]

Indeed, the program portrayed Cosby's character, Alexander Scott, as bright and energetic. It also made a statement about the interracial friendship between Cosby and actor Robert Culp, making a profound statement about the limitless boundaries of respect beyond the threshold of color.

The series also created scripts that featured other black talent and attracted actors like Eartha Kitt, Barbara McNair, Ivan Dixon, Cicely Tyson (who ap-peared in the acclaimed series *East Side, West Side* with George C. Scott), and Leslie Uggams. These actors often appeared in nontraditional roles.

Although there were a number of programs in the 1960s featuring black talent, some took issue with the way blacks were portrayed as assimilated characters. Some blacks were highly critical of these characterizations, saying that "they're just shows with black people acting white" or "they're just white folks masquerading in black skin." One program that seemed to personify these concerns was *Julia,* starring Dihann Carroll. When the series first ap-peared, in 1968, it coincided with a tumultuous time in American culture. There were civil rights demonstrations and hostile police facing off with ad-amant demonstrators. In her world as a professional nurse, war widow, and single mother, Julia was educated, articulate, and almost devoid of any "black" qualities: a "white Negro." Indeed, Carroll articulated these feelings in 1968: "At the moment we're presenting the white Negro. And he had very little Negro-ness."[6] Nor did the context of the program address any of the civil rights issues of the day. While defending the series as a means of reaching a mass audience with a positive image of a professional black woman, Carroll also spoke of its personal benefits, including the money. "Money is power in this country, and power means freedom . . . to do what I want to do."[7]

While the program had many critics, Hal Kanter, its creator-producer, defended the series. He argued that it was an entertainment show that did not advocate a point of view. "This is not a civil rights show. What we're driving at is escapist entertainment, not a sociological document."[8] *Julia* was canceled in 1971, but in its first season it was the seventh-highest-rated program on prime-time network television. At its peak, the program reached an average weekly audience of 14 million households. By the end of the 1960s, *Julia, The Bill Cosby Show,* and *The Flip Wilson Show* simultaneously became the most popular shows in television's history to feature black talent.

In the 1970s there were a number of very successful television shows with leading black characters created by Norman Lear and Bud Yorkin (working as a team and individually). They included *Sanford and Son, Good Times, The Jeffersons, What's Happening!!, Carter Country,* and *Diff'rent Strokes.* Perhaps the most controversial of these programs was *Good Times.*

It generated critical debate because of the nature of the portrayal of a central character known as J. J., played by comic Jimmy Walker. His buffoonery, along with behavioral antics that were perceived by some critics as

Desmond Wilson (left) and Redd Foxx star as Lamont and Fred Sanford in NBC's *Sanford and Son.* (Photofest.)

reminiscent of racial stereotyping, created some tension among the costars, which included veteran actors John Amos and Esther Rolle. Some suggested that there was an association between J. J. and Kingfish from *Amos 'n' Andy*. The facial mannerisms and the use of the oaths *holy mac'l* by Kingfish and *dy-no-mite* by J. J. resonated in the syncopated harmony of another time. Walker's face was described as silly putty, "with a set of buck teeth that could have come from a joke store," and having "the bulb-eyed glare of an aggravated emu."

Although Walker's character helped make the show a hit, the values associated with him, including his laziness (he was unemployed) and ignorance, were sore points among cast members. Costars Esther Rolle and John Amos found the humor offensive and were upset by the negative stereotypes. Rolle, in an interview with *Ebony Magazine*, spoke about her concerns. "He's eighteen and he doesn't work. He can't read or write. He doesn't think."[9] John Amos, who was eventually fired from the series for being a disruptive influence, was also harsh in his criticism. "Little by little—with the help of the artist, I suppose, because they couldn't do that to me—they have made J. J. more stupid and enlarged the role. Negative images have been slipped in on us through the character of the oldest child."[10]

An attempt to reconcile the motives and objectives of black programs speaks to many issues, including those of artistic control. One of the most successful in portraying the subtle nuances of black culture has been Bill Cosby. On *The Bill Cosby Show* (1969–71), he played teacher Chet Kincaid, who embodied this essence by identifying himself with blacks artistically and professionally. Throughout his career, Bill Cosby has demonstrated a commitment to the values of the black community.

As executive producer, Cosby brought blacks into the technical and craft unions that worked on the show. He attempted to use black writers, but only one episode was written by a black. According to Cosby, his show—with an integrated cast that included blacks, whites, Asians, and Latinos—was trying to tell an American story.

I'm aware that the show will have a negative meaning for people who are really militant about any story with a black person in it—black viewers included. But you can still pick a guy's pocket while he's laughing, and that's what I hope to do.[11]

Later, Bill Cosby's television career led to a defining moment for the sitcom and its relevance toward the black community. *The Cosby Show* (1984–92) spent eight seasons demonstrating the positive virtues of the Huxtables, an upper-middle-class black family. The parents were professionals—Cliff a doctor and Claire a lawyer—with five children. In addition to the portrayal of a close-knit black family, the series also dealt with issues of respect, prejudice, drugs, sibling rivalry, teenage lifestyles, and parental authority.

As a producer of the show, Bill Cosby made an extraordinary effort to screen out stereotypical humor. To that end, he hired Alvin Poussaint to review scripts that made demeaning references or perpetuated racial prejudices.

Interestingly, when the show was being shopped to the networks, ABC rejected it on the grounds that American audiences were not ready for an upwardly mobile professional black family. Although NBC bought the series, it was cautiously optimistic and initially ordered only six episodes. The program became a phenomenal hit and a ratings blockbuster for NBC. Although the show was criticized by some for its middle-class orientation, noted black scholar Donald Bogle praised Cosby, because he "had a perspective and stood by it."[12]

## ROOTS

It was a television phenomenon based upon a bestselling novel by author Alex Haley. When it premiered on ABC (January 23–30, 1977), *Roots* averaged a 44.9 rating and a 66 percent share of audience. Most revealing was the fact that of the 130 million Americans that watched the series for 12 hours over eight nights, 120 million of them were white. The program, with its story about slavery through the generations of a single family, captured the pathos of the American television audience. It bore witness to the experience of African Americans and their abiding attempt to maintain their dignity while struggling to stay alive.

Although the network was enthusiastic about the series and extended it from 8 to 12 hours, executives were concerned about its impact upon black and white audiences. Unsure of the reaction, they scheduled the series at the end of the prime-time segment so as not to impact negatively on the earlier part of the schedule. Because of the uncertainty, advertisers on *Roots* received a discounted rate, which was one of the biggest advertising bargains in television history.

No one could predict the overwhelming response. Viewers altered their routines so that they could be in front of a television set at the appointed hour. Movie theaters, bars, and restaurants suffered a decline in business during the eight consecutive nights of broadcast. In addition, for the northern part of the country it was the coldest week of the year.

For blacks, it was truly a showcase of achievement as their talent, not only as singers and dancers but as actors, was seen on a worldwide stage. There was also some criticism about blacks not having more of a creative role (other than that of on-screen talent) in the writing and producing of the series. *Roots* was seen by some as a validation of the need to provide more opportunity for blacks to assume a greater role in television both behind and in front of the camera. However, even with the production of a sequel, *Roots: The Next Generations* (February 18–23 and 25, 1979), the sentiment among the black community was that it was back to business as usual, with blacks taking on their ordained roles with little change associated with issues of empowerment.

One of the issues permeating the ways blacks are portrayed on television is the establishment of a middle-class facade that is a construct for their assimilation, and the need to show them within the dynamics of their own culture, including the blemishes and strengths. Several shows in the 1990s helped to establish blacks as intelligent television personalities, while some brought harsh criticism from the black community.

Both as a celebrity and a producer, Oprah Winfrey represents the kind of positive force that can create provocative, intelligent programming addressing themes and issues that are pertinent to the African American experience. Taking her local Chicago talk show into national syndication in 1986, Winfrey formed Harpo, her own production and distribution company. She produced *The Women of Brewster Place* for ABC in 1990, which delved into the professional and domestic challenges of inner-city women. Her short-lived series *Brewster Place* was a sobering look at the lives of African Americans in a poor Chicago neighborhood.

While Oprah Winfrey established herself as the premier daytime talk-show host, Arsenio Hall became a respected host of a late-night talk show. As a comedian, Hall had the presence and wit to banter with guests and integrate humor into the dialogue. He also had an air of confidence and intelligence that was equal to other hosts like Jay Leno and David Letterman.

One of the most controversial programs of the 1990s was *In Living Color,* produced, written, and directed by Keenen Ivory Wayans. The humor was satirical, irreverent, sharp, and sometimes offensive, and was a departure from traditional skit comedy. There were some blacks, however, that were critical of the program and its attempt to perpetuate bigoted assumptions based upon behavior and language. A black comedian and writer for the program, Franklyn Ajaye, left at the end of 1990 because of what he saw as "glorification of the ghetto." "This whole street, urban rap thing needs to be pulled back some. The ghetto is being glorified, and there's nothing good about a ghetto except getting out of one."[13]

Taking someone out of the ghetto and moving him in with wealthy relatives was the premise of *The Fresh Prince of Bel Air,* which premiered in the fall of 1990. The wisecracking rapper Fresh Prince, played by Will Smith, was a reminder to his bourgeois uncle of where he had come from. Defending the series from criticism that it was a poor reflection of black sensibilities and values, Smith remarked that the show would enlighten white viewers holding the perceived bias that "what black means is chicken, watermelon and a big radio." Executive producer Quincy Jones commented about the power of comedy and the clashes of cultures. "It's a very powerful dramatic vehicle for comedy to have this type of clashes of cultures—from a ghetto kid in a very affluent black family—inside the same family."[14]

But Don Bogle saw in its irreverence the same biases and racial stereotyping that were intrinsic in earlier television programs that were demeaning to blacks. He spoke of "Negro street niggs" and minstrel-show elements. "He bodaciously enters the room outlandishly dressed in old style coon fashion. Throughout, the hip hop clothes, language and culture—which could be a real fashion/cultural statement—are mainly used to make him look silly and cartoonish."[15]

In his criticism of the program, Bogle also speaks of the lack of respect for the black family that was manifested by the Fresh Prince character. According to Bogle, Hollywood has misunderstood blacks and their cultural behavior: that they don't always use slang, and that they do have manners.[16]

Interestingly, even amid the criticism that *The Cosby Show* endured because of its upper-middle-class portrayal of the black family, that same theme was revisited midseason in 2001 with a sitcom entitled *My Wife and Kids*. Starring Damon Wayans of *In Living Color*, the program is a testament to Cosby and the tradition of family humor and African American values that it depicted.

Playing an upper-middle-class businessman married to a stockbroker with three children and a Hispanic nanny, he, like Cosby, at times feels unappreciated. Just like *The Cosby Show*, there are universal themes in this sitcom that go beyond racial boundaries and are applicable to many families.[17]

Perhaps the biggest concern for black sitcoms is their inability to cross over to a white audience. This has diminished their presence on network television and made the television networks somewhat wary of scheduling them. The decline has been dramatic since 1997, when the number of prime-time black comedy series numbered 15. As this book goes to press, several prominent black-themed sitcoms have been canceled, including *Moesha* (1996–2001, UPN), *The Parkers* (1999–2004, UPN), *The Hughleys* (1998–2002, UPN), and *The Steve Harvey Show* (1996–2002, the WB). Those known to be returning for the 2004–2005 season include *The Bernie Mac Show* (Fox), *My Wife and Kids* (ABC), and *Girlfriends* (UPN).

Like *My Wife and Kids*, these canceled shows had a distinctive middle-class orientation. *Moesha* typified the wholesome family values of a middle-class family. *The Parkers* was a spin-off from *Moesha* and is more gritty in its humor. In this show, a mother and daughter wound up attending the same junior college and becoming roommates, with the humor ensuing from the rivalry that prevails between the two. In a hearkening back to Sherman Hemsley of *The Jeffersons* and Archie Bunker of *All in the Family*, Mr. Hughley of *The Hughleys*, an unrepentant bigot, moved his family to a white neighborhood.[18]

For blacks, there is still a great deal that eludes them, as measured by their success as actors, writers, directors, and producers. As television has evolved, it has demonstrated a willingness to integrate black talent into its milieu, but only to a certain extent. African Americans have struggled with issues of empowerment related to their ability to create, manage, and produce television programs. Those that have the latitude to be involved in the decision-making process, like Bill Cosby and Damon Wayans, are the exception and not the rule. While the color line has been broken on the proscenium of television's stage, it still asserts an influence behind the scenes.

Every creative field has an enduring hierarchy that sustains a level of mythology associated with its entry. There are issues of boundaries established as creative signposts that all are expected to obey. Sometimes even those with the best talent and creative energy are denied access. Fortunately, African Americans have been recognized for their talent and achievement; however, there has been a rather sluggish embrace to empower them within the structure of the television industry.

These issues have been addressed by the government, the Federal Communications Commission, and by various guilds and unions that have created programs to provide more access. The television networks have also indicated a desire to provide more opportunities for minorities to become writers, producers, and part of management. These efforts are laudatory; however, as of the present, they have not made a significant difference in the empowerment of African Americans, women, and other minorities.

## LATINOS AND CROSSOVER PROGRAMMING

Although historically the presence of Latinos on American prime-time broadcast television has been defined by neglect and bias, the process of exclusion has not always been deliberately sustained. Indeed, two of television's earliest successful series featured either Latinos in prominent roles or Anglos acting as Latinos. Desi Arnaz, a Cuban, costar and creator of *I Love Lucy,* was a sustaining presence on network television for six seasons from 1951 to 1957. While his character, Ricky Ricardo, may be viewed as an assimilated stereotypical personification of Latino culture, his portrayal was the closest most of the white television audience of the 1950s would come to identifying with Hispanic culture. Indeed, Desi's role as the bandleader at the Tropicana was featured prominently in many episodes, with a musical arpeggio that clearly had a Latin beat. In addition, there were several shows in the series that were themed to Latin influences, including a 1952 episode, "Cuban Pals," featuring a hot-blooded Renita, Ricky's former Cuban dance partner; a 1955 program known as "Bullfight Dance"; a 1956 segment, "The Ricardos Visit Cuba"; and "Lucy Does the Tango" in 1957. Although *I Love Lucy* cannot be viewed as a tribute to Latino culture, it did help to establish Desi Arnaz as the first Hispanic television star. Within the context of a white Anglo audience, *I Love Lucy* at the very least helped to define a Latino character as upwardly mobile and successful.

*I Love Lucy* was a hit for CBS, and when the series ended in 1957, NBC attempted to capitalize on the popularity of Latin bandleader Ricky Ricardo by creating a variety show for Xavier Cugat. Although Cugat was a real-life personification of Ricky Ricardo, NBC allocated only 15 minutes to this musical variety program to fill in the balance of its half-hour nightly news program. Cugat was a colorful character, and his wife, dancer Abbe Lane, had a consummate amount of verve and panache. The show ran only from February to May 1957 but was significant because it starred a Latin entertainer.

Network television's inability to create successful crossover prime-time programming featuring Hispanic themes and characters may be rooted in the conceptualization of earlier programs. At that time, producers were most interested in filling vacant airtime and not particularly sensitive to the needs of any minority. Indeed, as one views the decade of the 1950s, it yields a number of Hispanic-themed television series that were successful with Anglo audiences and thus perhaps could be defined as crossover television programming.

*The Cisco Kid*, which aired in syndication from 1950 to 1956, presented a view of Latinos as heroic, villainous, and at times foolish. However, the series was popular with a wide audience demographic, and although it did little to enhance a modern cultural image of Latinos, it nevertheless provided a proscenium for an adventure program that had a popular entertaining appeal.

Another Hispanic-themed television program from the 1950s was *Zorro*. Although the program today is disdained for its negative portrayal of Hispanics and the casting of Anglo actors in the leads (Guy Williams played Don Diego), it too provided a manifestation for the popularization of Latinos or Latino characters on television of the 1950s, which was targeted to the white majority viewing audience. *Zorro* was produced by Walt Disney and appeared on the ABC television network from October 1957 to September 1959.

The Disney studio also produced *Nine Lives of Elfego Baca*, featuring actor Robert Loggia as a New Mexico peace officer. It was a part of the Walt Disney limited-run series, with six episodes premiering in October 1958 and additional programs the following season.

Although there's no data on the number of Latinos present in the television audience of these programs, one can assume that it was minimal based upon the Latino population in the United States at that time. Therefore, one may not necessarily view these programs as crossover, although they were influential in helping to shape the programming canvas of early television.

Almost five decades later, there have been a number of significant changes in the landscape of broadcast television that have inexorably altered its product, distribution, and organization. Competitive media such as cable television and the creation of additional broadcast networks have drastically impacted network television's audience share, decreasing its universe and redefining its positioning. No other time in broadcast television's history has witnessed such a dramatic shift in viewing audience and the aggressive pursuit of viewers.

Placed within this context of competition is the Hispanic television audience. There are many facets to the character of Hispanic viewers that make them an attractive asset to traditional broadcast networks. Most notably, as a group, Hispanics average greater overall television entertainment viewing than Anglos, and number 9 million American television households. In addition, they look toward television as a primary tool for keeping informed. More importantly, the Hispanic audience appears to be more satisfied than Anglos that the broadcast media are fulfilling their functions. Why, then, have the broadcast networks failed to address the needs of this audience?

Like African Americans before them, Latinos were viewed as an invisible part of the television audience. Indeed, from 1955 to 1986, as blacks increased their television presence—nearly tripling it, from 6 percent to 17 percent by 1992–93—Hispanic portrayals dropped from 2 percent to 1 percent. A content-analysis study examining character portrayals in 1992 found that Hispanics on television, when compared to African Americans and Anglos, were low in number and social status. In the 1994–95 season the visibility of Hispanics in prime-time television increased from 1 to 2 percent of all characters, still underrepresenting the 10 percent of Americans with Hispanic ancestry. The most recent census indicates that Hispanics are nearly 12.5 percent of the American population, yet according to a study by Children Now, the number of Hispanic characters represented on prime-time television decreased from 3 percent to 2 percent between 1999 and 2000.

Today, however, the Hispanic television audience is perceived as a valuable asset. Indeed, the recent purchase of the Hispanic network Telemundo for $1.98 billion by General Electric, parent of NBC, is a clarion call to the industry, which for years ignored the Hispanic television market. Also, the growth of the Hispanic daytime television audience was recognized when CBS was the first to simulcast a daytime serial drama, *The Bold and the Beautiful,* in Spanish and English. Indeed, a recent ratings sweeps period in the Miami market demonstrated the strength of the Hispanic audience. Univision-affiliated station WLTV was the number-one station from sign-on to sign-off in Miami, which is 35 percent Hispanic. In other markets— including Los Angeles; Dallas; Fresno, California; Houston; San Francisco; and Phoenix—Univision affiliates routinely surpass the broadcast networks. Univision is the network of choice for Hispanic audiences over broadcast, cable, and any other English or Spanish network in any day part. It reaches 92 percent of Hispanic television households. Launched in 1961, it uses a programming foundation of steamy *telenovelas* (soap operas) produced in Mexico and Venezuela.

An important trend in language identified with the Hispanic community is a move toward bilingualism. With the Hispanic population in the United States growing by 60 percent in the last decade, the significance of its influence upon the media marketplace is profound. While the broadcast television networks have largely ignored these trends, Hispanic television has not. Indeed, *Hispanic Business Magazine* reported that in 1997 advertisers spent $1.4 billion trying to reach Spanish-speaking and bilingual consumers, and Univision accounts for over $800 million in advertising sales.

Spanish television is addressing this trend by creating some programs that simultaneously use Spanish and English. In addition to television, magazine publishing, radio, and the music industry are creating crossover content that embraces the Latin bilingual experience. A talk program distributed by Telemundo and hosted by the Cuban-born actress Maria Conchita Alonso often mixes both Spanish and English. Galavision, Univision's premium pay cable network, broadcasts a bilingual two-hour lineup of Sunday-night programs that are nearly all in English with some Spanish phrases. They include *Funny Is Funny,* a half-hour stand-up comedy show; *Café Ole,* a half-hour talk program featuring *Access Hollywood* cohost Giselle Fernandez; and reruns of a 20-year-old PBS bilingual generational sitcom, *Que Pasa USA?* The programs, except for *Que Pasa,* are produced by Si TV, a production company specializing in producing bilingual programming for Hispanic television. Galavision has reported that the response to the programming has been overwhelming. The premium cable network, which is available to 1.7 million Hispanic households, found that the English-oriented programming attracted an additional 55,000 viewers in its first six weeks of broadcast. These figures are impressive, especially when factoring in the popularity of the 20-year-old *Que Pasa.* They are also indicative of the value that this programming genre can have for the mainstream traditional broadcast networks. Barry Diller, one of the foremost media barons in the United States, made another successful attempt at bilingual programming. His cable network, USA Networks Inc., began Citi Vision at local Miami station WAMI. It's a local programming effort reaching a bilingual audience and features *Generation ñ,* a bilingual magazine program based upon a popular bilingual magazine.

The reality of marketplace forces has contributed to a move toward more English-language-oriented programming. According to Alex Nogales, chairman of the National Hispanic Media Coalition, economics and politics are conspiring to make Hispanics embrace English more readily. He cites the recent move of voters in California to exclude bilingual education in schools. In addition, the objective of these programs is to reach the youth market because of their rapid assimilation into American culture and a slowdown in immigration.

Apparently, the Hispanic television audience wants more quality and educational content associated with the programming they watch on Spanish television. This finding was compiled in a survey of 1,000 Hispanics in five major U.S. markets conducted by *American Demographics* magazine. In addition, the survey revealed that while Spanish-language soap operas persist in popularity, 97 percent of respondents said that there is either the right amount or too much of this programming on Hispanic television. More than 8 in 10 of those participating in the study said that there are not sufficient cultural programs, and 64 percent wanted more family shows. These findings are pertinent to the broadcast networks because of their relevance toward creating niche programming appealing to a wider, more diverse multicultural audience.

## PAST IMPERFECT

American network television has somewhat of a tainted legacy associated with the development and production of Latino-oriented programming. Indeed, when compared to black-oriented network television programming, there is a significant difference in the gap of representation. While black representation on television nearly tripled from 1955 to 1993 (from 6 percent to 17 percent), Hispanic portrayals dropped from 2 percent to 1 percent. From the 1970s to the 1980s, the black-to-Hispanic ratio of television characters grew to more than three to one. The difference in black and Hispanic character portrayals became even more pronounced in the 1992–93 season, when the cultural imbalance reached a profoundly prominent gap of 17 black characters for every Hispanic character on television. Although there are issues associated with how Hispanics are portrayed on television, that is an area that goes beyond the scope of this section.

The landscape of American network prime-time television programming is littered with failures in crossover Hispanic-oriented programming. However, there were also some successes that demonstrate the viability of the genre along with the potential substance of the programming. One variable that is evident from a historical review of Hispanic programming genres from the 1970s to the 1990s is that, unlike black programs, television shows featuring mostly Latino characters fare less well than those with a racially mixed cast.

Programs like *Popi* (CBS), *The Man and the City* (ABC), *Viva Valdez* (ABC), *Condo, A.K.A. Pablo, I Married Dora,* and *Trial and Error* had prominent talent associated with the projects but barely lasted more than a season. These programs either featured a strong Latino character or an ensemble cast of Latino characters and actors. However, there were some programs featuring Latinos in a racially mixed format that proved popular with audiences.

*Chico and the Man* was broadcast on NBC from September 1974 to July 1978. The concept and talent behind the program appealed to a crossover audience. Jack Albertson and Freddie Prinze were perfect foils, parrying wisecracks and delighting audiences with their wit and charm. Other programs that were successful in presenting Hispanics in featured roles or as positive role models included *The High Chaparral, Miami Vice* (which balanced portrayals with law enforcement characters and drug lords), *L.A. Law, Law and Order, The Hat Squad, NYPD Blue,* and *Nash Bridges.* While these programs don't reflect the rich diversity of Latino culture, they do offer Latino actors and characters some presence on the proscenium of entertainment.

A recent example of an attempt to create a Latino sitcom on Fox and its failure provides a look at the politics, economics, and culture of programming

Detectives Tubbs (Philip Michael Thomas, left) and
Crockett (Don Johnson) from NBC's police drama
*Miami Vice*. (Photofest.)

on network television today. A Hispanic stand-up comedy group known as
Culture Clash was brought to the attention of Latino comic Cheech Marin
(formerly half of Cheech and Chong). Fox expressed an interest in developing
the project, and veteran writers were brought in to develop the concept. The
featured comics, all Latinos, weren't given the opportunity to write for the
program, although the characters they portrayed were based on their original
idea. The first program had several T and A ("tits and ass") jokes and made
demeaning references to lettuce picking and rampant barrio crime. That was
enough for Fox, and the show never made it to the fall schedule. The three
principals of the program agree that *Culture Clash* was a bad show and that
Fox was right to pull the plug. However, they maintain that because they
were closed out of the creative process and had no input (because of their
inexperience as television writers), the stereotypical humor was a product of
"experienced" Anglo writers. As an added rebuke to their heritage and creative sensibilities, one of the writers brought her Salvadoran maid to one of
the writing sessions.

Issues of empowerment define the entertainment industry, both television
and film. There are instances when celebrities like Cheech Marin and Paul

Rodriguez can initiate a project and interest a studio or network in its development. However, in an industry that has an aversion to risk, there must be compelling factors for a network to take a chance with novice talent and Latino-themed programming. The competition facing the traditional broadcast networks today, and their need to attract viewers, provides a challenging opportunity for risk and the development of crossover programming that can appeal to Latinos and the general television audience.

The broadcast networks are determined to avoid any projects that they perceive as risky, and so it shocked no one when CBS decided not to develop a series about a Mexican American family entitled *American Family* (2002–2004). After investing a million dollars in the pilot, CBS withdrew from the project, but indicated that it would donate the pilot program to PBS (Public Broadcasting Service) if it could raise the money to finance the series. At PBS, Pat Mitchell, its president and chief executive, raised the $13 million needed for the 13 programs of the first season by tapping into the PBS discretionary program fund and enlisting the sole sponsorship of Johnson and Johnson as the corporate underwriter. In an effort to reduce production costs, the creator of the series, filmmaker Gregory Nava, cut salaries, limited locations, and moved from 35 mm to high-definition digital video to record the program.

As a filmmaker, Nava produced notable features such as *El Norte* (1984), *My Family* (1995), and *Selena* (1997). The series premiered on January 23, 2002, on most PBS-affiliated stations and became the first Hispanic-oriented weekly drama on broadcast television. It evolves around the Gonzalez family: Jess (Edward James Olmos); his soon-to-be-deceased wife, Berta (Sonia Braga); and their five children—Nina (Constance Marie), a lawyer and advocate for people from the barrio; Estaban (Esai Morales), a former gang member on parole and a single dad; Vangie (Rachel Ticotin), a successful fashion designer; Conrado (Kurt Caceres), a doctor; and Cisco (A. J. Lamas), an aspiring filmmaker. Also featured in the cast is Raquel Welch as Aunt Dora, who is portrayed as an almost Hollywood star.

Although the series at times exhibits the same manipulative dramatic techniques as daytime serial dramas, it addresses values and themes that go beyond cultural barriers. While the Gonzalez family is Hispanic, the struggle they face has a universal dimension that relates to matters that are germane to all minority groups and include assimilation, education, family dynamics, and upward mobility. Placing these themes within the context of the Latino American experience provides an indelible portrait of a family that experiences the same pangs of cultural dissonance as other ethnic groups attempting to partake of the American Dream while rationalizing it with the traditional values of their culture.[19]

On Showtime, the pay cable network, *Resurrection Blvd.* (2000–2003) made its debut in June 2000. It features a number of notable Latino actors who portray characters that face both physical and emotional challenges. The Santiago family, led by patriarch Roberto (Tony Plana), has a rich tradition in the boxing ring. While some of the narrative structure is familiar, such as the shooting of son Carlos (Michael DeLorenzo), who is about to get a title bout, other elements are touching and provocative. As Bibi, Roberto's sister-in-law, Elizabeth Pena has her usual flair of rough-hewn drama and bristly humor. After she's forced to close her beauty salon and cut hair from her home, Bibi tells one of her clients that she's going to squeeze the landlord's cojones until his eyes bulge out if she doesn't get her security back.

The series demonstrates the need for a programming vehicle that expresses the Latino voice as part of the dynamic of American culture. As the fastest-growing minority in the United States, Latinos are woefully underrepresented on television, experiencing a withering ignorance of their culture. The actor Edward James Olmos expressed his frustration over the profound limitations frustrating the Latino creative community.

We've gone backward. We were 3 percent of the images that were performing last year; this year, we're less than 2 percent. It's a disaster that's going to have an impact on every single one of our lives because there are so many more of us here and there are so many more of us coming and there's so much fear because there's no knowledge of us.[20]

"Fall Colors 2001–2002," a report addressing diversity in prime-time programming released by Children Now, a child research and action organization, found that service worker, unskilled laborer, and criminal made the top-five-occupation lists for Latino and African American primary recurring characters. As a Latina actress, Lupe Ontiveros, who has portrayed a maid in several movies and sitcoms, is a vivid example of this trend. By her estimation, she has played a maid in at least 150 films and television shows, including *As Good as It Gets, Veronica's Closet,* and *Leap of Faith.* She disdains the short-sighted view toward Latino characters and makes it abundantly clear that they are "very much a part of this country and [they] make up every part of this country."

Maids, of course, are not her only role, as Ms. Ontiveros has been a featured actress in *Real Women Have Curves,* earning a jury prize for acting at the Sundance Film Festival; has been awarded the National Board of Review Award for best supporting actress in the film *Chuck and Buck;* and has received excellent reviews for her portrayal of the maid Consuelo in Todd Solondz's *Storytelling.*

Although the "Fall Colors" study found that Latinos in the 2001–2002 season increased to 4 percent of the entire prime-time population, they represented only 2 percent of the opening-credits casts, no increase over the previous year. In announcing the fall 2002–2003 television season, the network programs featuring Latino characters included NBC's *Good Morning Miami,* with Tessie Santiago and Lucia Rojas Miller; the WB's *Greetings from Tucson,* about a Mexican Irish family; and CBS's *C.S.I.: Miami,* featuring Hispanics in the ensemble cast.[21] For the fall 2004–2005 season, the only sitcom on the broadcast networks featuring a Latino cast is *The George Lopez Show* on ABC.

## ASIAN AMERICANS FROM HOP SING TO LIN WOO

The visibility of Asian Americans in American film and television has been influenced by a myriad of cultural, political, and ethnic factors. Feature films of the Old West and the rise of railroads depicted Chinese laborers as nothing more than human chattel whose lives had little value. For Americans, Asian culture has been defined by geopolitical constructs that have been shaped by American policy and propaganda. The relationship between the United States and China has evolved from a total absence to one of cautious rapprochement.

The movies have often portrayed Chinese as enigmatic characters spouting proverbs and speaking in riddles. Hollywood's embodiment of the Asian hero in the 1930s was Charlie Chan. Portrayed by a series of Caucasian actors (Warner Oland, Sidney Toler, Roland Winters), Chan was an Oriental Sherlock Holmes in pursuit of justice with a nod to civility and grace. There were also television incarnations that included *The Amazing Chan and the Chan Clan* (1972–74), a cartoon series produced by Hanna-Barbera that appeared on television with one of the voices supplied by actress Jodie Foster, portraying Anne Chan. Also, in 1979 *The Return of Charlie Chan*, a television feature, was produced.

On early television programs, Asians, if they were seen, were usually relegated to domestics like Hop Sing (Victor Sen Young), on *Bonanza;* Hey Boy (Kam Tong), who served one of the most eclectic gunfighters on television, Paladin, on *Have Gun Will Travel;* Kato (Bruce Lee), the Japanese houseboy on *The Green Hornet;* and Mrs. Livingston (Miyoshi Umeki), the Japanese housekeeper on *The Courtship of Eddie's Father.*

As the civil rights movement empowered African Americans, it had an impact on other minorities as well. During the 1960s and 1970s, Asians took on more prominent television roles, such as George Takei's Mr. Sulu on *Star Trek* and Jack Soo's Sgt. Nick Yemana on *Barney Miller.* A prime-time dramatic police show that starred Pat Morita, a Japanese American, was *Ohara* (1987–88). He was not new to television, having had a featured role playing Arnold on *Happy Days* (1975–76, 1982–83), and Morita was nominated for an Academy Award for the feature film *The Karate Kid.*

Recently, Asian Americans have had a greater presence on network television, and their characters have been more demonstrative of America's cultural milieu. They are no longer bound by the traditions of their culture and have been integrated into the televisual representations that had been relegated to Caucasians. The first prime-time network series about an Asian American family was *American Girl* on ABC (1994–95), starring Margaret Cho. The program's theme evolved around the issue of assimilation and the clash between the values of a teenage girl growing up in a traditional Korean family.

A compelling change in the number of Asians appearing on prime-time network television occurred during the 2000–2001 season. There were 11 network prime-time series featuring Asian American talent, including Lucy Liu of *Ally McBeal*, Ming Na of *E.R.*, and Garrett Wang of *Star Trek Voyager*. There was also the syndicated program *Relic Hunter* (1999–2002), starring Tia Carrere as globe-trotting college professor Sydney Fox, a female counterpart of Indiana Jones hunting down lost or stolen artifacts. Other programs with Asians in featured roles included *DAG, Gideon's Crossing, Gilmore Girls, Level 9, Deadline,* and *Daddio.* (As of this writing, some of these programs have been canceled.) In broadcast journalism, Connie Chung has been the most visible female Asian, and Ann Curry has established herself as a news anchor on *The Today Show* and *Dateline NBC.*

Asian American men, who in the past have been typecast in martial-arts films, have fared less well and are featured in only a few prime-time network television programs. One canceled CBS series, *Martial Law,* featuring Sammo Hung as a Chinese martial-arts star, was praised for its depiction of Asians in more mainstream roles. However, the show's creator, Carlton Cuse, expressed his concern about the ability to cast an Asian American actor as a lead in a television series that is not about martial arts. In the 1972 hit series *Kung Fu,* David Carradine portrayed the half-Chinese lead character.

Asian Americans have increased their visibility, appearing in television commercials and making guest appearances on prime-time programs. The Internet has also spawned a popular animated site at Icebox.com called "Mr. Wong," about the antics of an 85-year-old Chinese houseboy.[22]

## LADIES-IN-WAITING/SITCOMS

Like other disenfranchised groups, women have had to struggle for a sense of empowerment as talent, writers, and producers on television. During the 1950s their television personae included roles as housewives, weather girls, and pitch ladies. In most sitcoms they were devoted housewives who dutifully administered to their husbands' needs. If they were included in a professional environment, they appeared unprepared and ill at ease. However, women on early television sitcoms (pre-*Roseanne*) were the embodiment of family values and stalwarts of tradition. Quite often they were also the foils of their husbands or significant others who in the end upstaged their male counterparts with their intellect, poise, and bravado.

Interestingly, as television programming matured, the role of women changed, and the perception of the single independent woman evolved. One of the first programs featuring a young single woman was *My Little Margie,* starring Gale Storm. The character was somewhat mischievous and scatterbrained as she tried to fix up her widowed father with potential dates. The program ran from 1952 to 1955 on CBS and NBC.

Women were also featured as objects of desire, and actor Robert Cummings personified this trait in several early sitcoms: *My Hero* (NBC, 1952–53), *Love That Bob* (NBC, 1955; CBS, 1955–57; NBC, 1957–59), *The Bob Cummings Show* (CBS, 1961–62), and *My Living Doll* (CBS, 1964–65). In *Love That Bob,* Cummings played a lecherous photographer surrounded by beautiful models who had amorous intentions toward him. His costars were veterans of the small screen and included Rosemary DeCamp, who played his widowed sister, Margaret, whom he lived with, and Dwayne Hickman (*The Many Loves of Dobie Gillis*) as her son, Chuck. In his final television incarnation, *My Living Doll,* Cummings played a psychiatrist who has a live-in female government-issued robot in the guise of sexy Julie Newmar. It was the 1960s, an era that embraced free love and promiscuity, so the premise of a single man living with an exquisite woman, albeit a robot, was acceptable.

Teenage angst and the active male libido were the themes for *The Many Loves of Dobie Gillis* (CBS, 1959–63). The series starred Dwayne Hickman as the lovesick Dobie in hot pursuit of self-centered, egotistical Thalia, played by a youthfully seductive Tuesday Weld. For a short time Warren Beatty was in the show, portraying the self-indulgent playboy Milton Armitage. Dobie's best friend was beatnik Maynard G. Krebs, his imperfect foil, played by actor Bob Denver, who later gained fame in *Gilligan's Island*. Women were a plot device, and their sexuality was articulated in an amorous dynamic of unfulfilled desire.

One program that served as a cultural icon for the perfect American family was *The Adventures of Ozzie and Harriet*. It was the longest running sitcom in television history, first starting on radio from 1944 to 1949 and then appearing on ABC television from 1952 to 1966. Ironically, Harriet Nelson, the real-life mom on and off television who appeared as the ideal homemaker, always wearing an apron and blissfully making sandwiches in the kitchen, had been a sultry blond bombshell nightclub performer. Appearing in vaudeville when she was three and on Broadway as a teen, Harriet Hilliard Nelson was a free-spirited, independent woman. She hung around New York's Cotton Club, started smoking at 13, and briefly married an abusive comedian. On television she became the embodiment of the perfect wife and mother, tending to her family and genuflecting to her husband's authority.

What was so intriguing about *Ozzie and Harriet* was that they were a real family whose dynamics unfolded on television. The series was the first taste of reality television, with every nuance of behavior recorded for an audience. Although the plots were contrived, the actors were indeed part of the same family. This created tension on and off the set. Ozzie Nelson was an authoritarian figure whose work ethic often clashed with the needs of his two sons, Rick and David Nelson. More than anything, the Nelson television family was perfect for sustaining the idealistic moralistic values envisioned by their patriarch, Ozzie Nelson. Indeed, always the consummate businessman, Ozzie, realizing his son Ricky's fledgling musical talent, had him perform on the program. Using television as a merchandising tool for Ricky Nelson's band was a stroke of genius and catapulted Ricky into musical stardom, at times surpassing Elvis in record sales and popularity. Although it appeared as if the Nelsons were an idyllic family, their television personae were not part of their off-screen relationships, which was a dysfunctional manifestation of their celebrity.

There were, however, some women in early television who sustained themselves with strong characterizations and leadership. In *The Rise of the Goldbergs,* which started on radio in 1929 and moved to television (CBS, NBC, Dumont, 1949–53), Gertrude Berg played the indefatigable Molly, never at a loss for words. She was the foundation of the family and was a stalwart whose resolve never waned in the face of adversity.

Indeed, Berg's determination as the fictional Molly was a realistic portrayal of her own personality. She was the creator, lead writer, and producer of the NBC radio series *The Rise of Goldbergs* (later shortened to *The Goldbergs*). It was a 15-minute nightly program that ran Monday through Friday for 20 years, compiling an archive of over 5,000 scripts, most of which Berg wrote. When the program moved to television, she continued as its creative force. As a star of radio and later television, Berg was unique in that she was one of the first women to be empowered with unfettered control over her program. Indeed, when her costar Phillip Loeb was a victim of the McCarthy-era blacklisting crusade, she refused to fire him. He resigned to avoid the program's cancellation and eventually committed suicide. After the network run ended, Berg attempted several short-lived revivals, including *Molly* (1954–55) and *The Gertrude Berg Show* (1961–62).

With *The Honeymooners,* bus driver Ralph Kramden (played by comedian Jackie Gleason) and his wife, Alice (portrayed by Audrey Meadows; Pert Kelton, Sue Ane Langdon, and Shelia MacRae also had short stints playing Alice), were, to say the least, a feisty couple. The show began as part of *Cavalcade of Stars,* a low-budget live variety show broadcast on the Dumont Television Network. It began as a six-minute sketch and eventually became a featured segment. In 1952 Gleason left the Dumont Television Network and signed with CBS, where *The Honeymooners* became a segment on the new *Jackie Gleason Show.* During the next two years, *The Honeymooners* sketches gradually increased in length, with some equaling 30 minutes. In 1955 CBS offered Gleason one of the most generous contracts in show-business history to produce *The Honeymooners* as a half-hour program. He filmed two live shows a week using multiple cameras at the Adelphi Theatre in New York City. Gleason, who had total control, ended the show after 39 episodes and sold the library to CBS for $1.5 million. These 39 programs became one of the most lucrative syndication packages in television history.

There were a number of resurrections, and Gleason returned to the variety format in 1962 and moved production permanently to Miami Beach in 1964. A television special and a remake of *The Trip to Europe* were broadcast during the 1966–67 season, and in the 1970s four one-hour *Honeymooners* specials reuniting most of the original cast were broadcast on ABC, including a Christmas show in 1977 and one for Valentine's Day in 1978. In 1985 Gleason and Audrey Meadows taped a special for NBC featuring clips from 67 "lost" episodes that Jackie Gleason had in a basement air-conditioned storage vault and later sold to Viacom.

Although in *The Honeymooners* Alice was a dutiful wife who made sure that dinner was waiting for her husband when he returned from work, she nevertheless asserted herself when she had to. With all his scheming and threats, Ralph couldn't fool Alice, and she refused to be manipulated by him. She was relegated to the role of a housewife, which was a cultural expression of the 1950s. However, while she subordinated herself to her husband's needs, Alice was not threatened by Ralph's bluster. She validated herself as a woman and could equal his wisecracks, measure for measure.

There was unique comedic resonance in the original cast of *The Honeymooners*. For example, Art Carney's portrayal of dull sewer worker Ed Norton proved to be a perfect foil for Ralph's failed get-rich-quick schemes. As their wives and best friends, Alice and Trixie were a blend of patronizing respect and cutting sarcasm. They loved their husbands but understood their limitations. Other than the living room of Archie Bunker's home in *All in the Family*, the spartan Kramden kitchen is probably the most remembered television set in sitcom history.

One of the most popular and enduring situation comedies of the 1950s was *Father Knows Best* (CBS, 1954–55; NBC, 1955–58; CBS, 1958–60). It was originally created for radio by producer Eugene Rodney and Robert Young and was a staple for five years before moving to television. The two men supposedly based the premise for the series on their experiences as husbands and fathers. Actor Robert Young, who was respected for his roles in feature films, was the only original cast member from the radio program to follow the series to television. He played Jim Anderson, an insurance salesman, and his wife, Margaret Anderson, was played by Jane Wyatt. She was a professional housewife who took care of her family and was always there for them. Rarely did she venture from her domestic chores, and when she did, it was associated with the needs of her family. However, the sense of the series and how it approached the patriarch of the family were articulated in the punctuation of the original title of the radio program: *Father Knows Best?* Quite often, Father was not the touchstone of knowledge, and the women of the family, wife Margaret (Jane Wyatt) and daughters Betty (Elinor Donahue) and Kathy (Lauren Chapin), demonstrated their character as formidable foes in the ubiquitous landscape of the Anderson family.

Another program that featured a dominant leading male figure was *Make Room for Daddy* (1953–64), starring Danny Thomas as Danny Williams and Jean Hagen as Margaret Williams. Almost all of the family-oriented sitcoms, including *The Donna Reed Show,* were of the same cookie-cutter variety. The plots were redundantly simple and revolved around the rather tame dynamics of 1950s family life. Indeed, in an *Ozzie and Harriet* episode, a central theme was Ozzie's nighttime search for some tutti-frutti ice cream. The program was so popular that the next day ice-cream stores all over the country experienced a rush for the flavor.

There were, of course, departures from the family sitcom mold, and they did prove to be refreshing. For example, *The Real McCoys* (1957) was about plain country folk from West Virginia relocating to California. The series featured veteran movie actor Walter Brennan and noted television actor Richard Crenna, who had appeared in *Our Miss Brooks* (1952) with Eve Arden, which in many ways was a tribute to schoolteachers. The concept of *The Real McCoys* was revisited in the 1970s with the hit program *The Beverly Hillbillies.*

Perhaps one of the most original comedy programs of the 1950s was *Topper* (1950), starring Leo G. Carroll as Cosmo Topper and Robert Sterling and Anne Jeffreys as the resident ghosts, the Kirbys. The cast also included Neil, the martini-drinking ghost dog. While *Topper* was unique as a situation comedy featuring lead characters as spirits (ahead of its time), the most popular show on television during that era was *I Love Lucy* (1951–57), which was the number-one-rated show during four of its six seasons.

Although some may view the character of Lucy Ricardo as a frustrated housewife who must succumb to the wishes of her husband, she also demonstrates a drive to be somewhat liberated. Integrating her unique talent for comedy, Lucy embarks on plan after plan to become more self-sufficient and break into Hollywood. Though all of her attempts fail in some manner of hilarious circumstance, she nevertheless provides a foundation for a married woman to be more than just a hausfrau.

The show also explored universal themes of loyalty, friendship, marital tension, and the balance of career and family. The Ricardos and the Mertzes, Fred and Ethel, forge a close friendship that at times is tested by their shortcomings and foibles. Lucy's closest friend, Ethel Mertz, is her unwitting ally in her brazen schemes. In her own life, Lucille Ball was a shrewd businesswoman. In return for shooting the series with three cameras on film in Hollywood, Ball and her husband, Desi Arnaz, took a cut in pay from CBS and became the owners of their television show. *I Love Lucy* was the basis for the creation of their production company, Desilu, which became a television programming powerhouse in the 1950s and 1960s. Indeed, after their divorce, Ball bought Desi Arnaz's share of Desilu Productions and became the first woman to head a major studio. In her private life, Lucille Ball personified the independent woman, and some of those qualities were reflected in her character. She was not a pushover, a pansy, or an ingenue. Her strength was her comedy, which she pursued with a classic style and verve.

As the roles of women changed in American society, television, always a mirrored reflection of our culture, also changed. The 1960s was the Age of Aquarius, which helped to define it as an era of dissent. Women took their place marching in civil rights rallies, burning their bras, and rallying to Gloria Steinem's call for independence. Not wanting to be defined as *Miss* or *Mrs.,* they established a new salutation, *Ms.,* which created a different dynamic for the way that they interacted with men.

Perhaps one of the most idiosyncratic television programs that helped to set a foundation for the "new woman" was *Mary Hartman, Mary Hartman.* Created by Norman Lear (*All in the Family*) as a parody of the soap opera and eventually of contemporary life, the program, starring Louise Lasser, became a cult favorite. Mary broke from the conventional persona of the sitcom housewife to become her own person, with a willingness to satisfy her own needs and sexual desires. When her husband rejected her romantic overtures because he was turned off by her rights of initiation, Mary, having resisted the allure of potential suitor policeman Tom Hartman, succumbs to her desire.[23]

Another Mary, Mary Tyler Moore, in *The Mary Tyler Moore Show* (1970–77) became the embodiment of the independent woman with newly defined limits and an exuberant sense of optimism. Her character achieves a rapport with men within a dynamic of respect and professionalism. Ms. Moore was also a principal, like Lucille Ball before her, with her then husband, Grant Tinker, in MTM Enterprises, which was responsible for producing compelling dramas and situation comedies, including *The Mary Tyler Moore Show, Rhoda, The Bob Newhart Show, Lou Grant, Hill Street Blues, St. Elsewhere,* and *WKRP in Cincinnati.* These programs helped to define a new rhetoric in television by reflecting cultural values that were more in concert with the times.

However, not every 1960s sitcom featuring a female lead was as expressive promoting an agenda of liberation. In the ABC series *That Girl* (1966–71), starring Marlo Thomas as Ann Marie, a single woman living in the city, the focus was on a glamorized, chaste portrayal of the main character. Struggling to be an actress, her independence was reliant upon a precarious employment ritual. The network was also concerned about her sexuality as a function of her lifestyle. Therefore, they pressed Marlo Thomas to marry her television boyfriend, Don Hollinger, played by Ted Bessell. To her credit, Thomas resisted the move, but eventually conceded to a 1970 broadcast engagement. Although tame by today's standards, *That Girl* created a precedent for validating the ability of a woman to survive an agenda of independence in the big city and was a precursor to the more explicit HBO series *Sex and the City.*

One of the most prolific and respected producers in television, Norman Lear, created *All in the Family* and its spin-off *Maude* (1972–78). The lead characters in each of the series, Archie Bunker and Maude Findlay, were a unique departure from the sitcom norm. Bunker was a bigot, and Maude a sometimes meddling liberal. As Maude, Beatrice Arthur was a feminist with a verve for the pleasures of life. She was the guiding force of her family, which included her husband, Walter; divorced daughter, Carol; grandson, Phillip; and her maid. Maude could be crusty and had an in-your-face unassuming demeanor. She personified an inner strength, fortitude, and stability while dealing with having an abortion, going through menopause, struggling with her husband's alcoholism, and bankruptcy. After several major cast changes and declining ratings, in 1978 Beatrice Arthur decided to leave the show.

In *All in the Family,* Edith (Jean Stapleton) was no slouch when it came to understanding her husband Archie's faults and nurturing his needs. He may have called her a dingbat, but Edith had shrewd survival instincts that were sustained by her ability to adapt to her changing environment. And his daughter, Gloria (Sally Struthers), was a woman with a liberal bent not above criticizing her father for his bigoted ways.

Although sitcoms helped to define the status of women and the changed perception of them in American society, other programming genres also contributed to this effort. While some may view the show *Charlie's Angels* (1976–81) as a step backward for women and as the reconstitution of their stereotypical roles as sex objects, it nevertheless presented these women as a force to contend with. Of course Kate Jackson, Farrah Fawcett-Majors, and Jaclyn Smith were attractive and sexy, but they were also articulate, smart, and athletic. Stuck in dead-end jobs after graduating from the police academy, the three lead characters, Sabrina, Kelly, and Jill, are recruited by the never-seen Charlie Townsend to use their guile, wit, and charm to apprehend criminals. In November 2000, a feature film based upon television's *Charlie's Angels* was produced starring Cameron Diaz, Lucy Liu, and Drew Barrymore.

Crime-fighting was usually the purview of male dominance in film and television. However, the 1970s produced two shows with a nod to women's equality, *Police Woman* (NBC, 1974–78) and *Get Christie Love* (ABC, 1974–75). Portraying Sgt. Suzanne "Pepper" Anderson in *Police Woman,* actress Angie Dickinson brought a sexy, stylistic, edgy tone to the role. She had been a featured character in an episode of *Police Story* that was successfully transformed into a starring vehicle for her. The premise for *Get Christie Love* was a feature film with the same title. In this iteration, Teresa Graves played the no-nonsense, sassy black detective Christie Love.

A more serious attempt to show women in law enforcement, *Cagney and Lacey* (1982–88; in 1981 six episodes were produced with Meg Foster playing Cagney), was created by Barney Rosenzweig (a producer of *Charlie's Angels*). It was one of television's first attempts to create a dramatic professional situation between two women who interact as friends and colleagues. In a departure from male-dominated police formats, the characters are strong women with a commitment to their careers (Cagney) and family (Lacey). Both Sharon Gless (Cagney) and Tyne Daly (Lacey) are women in law enforcement who demonstrate that they can be more than prostitute decoys and serve as detectives on major cases.

The show addressed detective Lacey's family life and her marriage to Harvey, a frequently unemployed construction worker. As the dominant force in her family, Lacey's character is expressive of the changing dynamic of working women in our culture. In opposition, but clearly not adversarial, is Cagney, who is a single woman in her late 30s, somewhat insecure about being unmarried and childless, but wedded to her career and expressive of her sexuality.

In its attempt to address important issues faced by women, *Cagney and Lacey* dealt with themes such as date rape, abortion, birth control, guarding a celebrity feminist, sexual harassment, terrorism at an abortion clinic, alcoholism, spousal abuse, and breast cancer.

Another police series that featured strong women characters was *Hill Street Blues* (1981–87). In addition to creating a stunningly new visual dynamic, this program provided an opportunity for women to demonstrate their ability to cope within a male-dominated environment. These women—including the sexy, feisty public defender (Veronica Hamel); the tough uniformed police officer (Betty Thomas, now a noted film director); and the captain's ex-wife (Barbara Bosson)—recognized the bias in the system and strove to succeed within those limitations.

Perhaps one of the most larger-than-life fictional characters in television history was Murphy Brown (1988–98). Like Mary in the *Mary Tyler Moore Show,* Murphy, played by Candice Bergen, worked in television on the show *FYI* and became a symbol for women's liberation. In one of the most bizarre fictional narrative incantations to transcend reality, Murphy's pregnancy as a single woman became an issue for both national debate and Washington politics. In 1992 *Murphy Brown* was criticized by then vice president Dan Quayle for having a baby out of wedlock. The vice president was especially demonstrative about his position when he said, "It doesn't help matters when prime time TV has Murphy Brown . . . mocking the importance of fathers by bearing a child alone and calling it 'just another lifestyle choice.' "[24] Murphy's single-mother status was also the subject of a White House press conference.

While the country debated the morality of Murphy's decision to be an unwed mother, the producers cleverly created an episode dealing with the controversy, and CBS quickly raised the advertising rates to $330,000 for a 30-second commercial, the highest during the 1992–93 season. Murphy had her baby and went on to recover from substance abuse (alcoholism) and survive breast cancer. As the old Virginia Slims cigarette commercial stated, "You've come a long way, baby."

One series that may have influenced the Murphy Brown character was *The Days and Nights of Molly Dodd,* starring Blair Brown. Created and produced by Jay Tarses, who was also responsible for the irreverent *Buffalo Bill* and *The Slap Maxwell Story,* Molly Dodd was a recently divorced single woman living on Manhattan's Upper West Side. As the program title implies, the story line followed her at work and leisure. Unlike Murphy Brown, Molly wasn't as self-assured about her life or career, held a number of jobs, was unemployed for a time, and had some romantic involvement—one an interracial affair resulting in a pregnancy.

The characters that influenced Molly's life included Davey, the elevator operator in her building; Molly's mother, Florence; her ex-husband, Fred; her best friend, Nina; her boss, Moss; and an African American police detective, Nate. The distinctive quality of *Molly Dodd* is its realistic portrayal of the urban lifestyle of a single woman.

The insecurities of Molly Dodd became even more pronounced in the character of Ally McBeal. This popular Fox series on the WB network, created by award-winning producer-writer David E. Kelley, revolves around Ally, a single attorney who works in a practice with two ex-boyfriends. Like so many other sitcoms that predated this one (*Rhoda*), Ally is a thirtyish neurotic on a constant prowl for Mr. Right. As a liberated woman, Ally has many romantic interludes, some made in haste rather than with thoughtful deliberation.

This series has an edge and deals with issues of work, family, and sexuality within the context of modern society. Issues involving infidelity, relationships, and workplace ethics are themes for various episodes. As a means to express Ally's insecurity and self-doubts, the show uses fantasy sequences with flashbacks and voice-overs.

A radical change in the empowerment of women television writers and executives has resulted in a redefined sense of postfeminist sitcoms. These women are a hybrid of career professional and wife and mother, embracing neither of these roles with any sense of vigor. Their characters are more complex, reflecting a greater sense of realism within the daily construct of their lives.

These changes were slow in being realized, as women writers and producers fought against an industry with a pronounced male bias. Caryn Mandabach, president of Carsey-Werner, which produced *3rd Rock from the Sun, The Cosby Show,* and *Men Behaving Badly,* noted that television networks want male comedies because they earn more money.

As an executive producer of *3rd Rock from the Sun,* Bonnie Turner was pleased to create Sally, a television character who was neither a victim nor especially cute. Instead she is a complete woman, with a balanced combination of strengths, foibles, and vulnerabilities. Of course, Sally is also an alien who is a man on her home planet.

In *Dharma and Greg,* series creators Chuck Lorre and Dottie Dartland wanted Dharma to be less neurotic and cynical and not as overwhelmed by life as so many female lead characters before her. As Lorre acknowledged, there's a lot of humor that emanates from the stereotypical portrayal of women on sitcoms. The struggle, according to them, was not to dumb down Dharma and to fight to keep her bright and aware. This issue is one that Sharon Lawrence had to face in the sitcom *Fired Up* on NBC. She felt her character had been dumbed down to suit a male audience. Indeed, for many involved in network television, the perception is that women will watch a man's show but that men will not watch a woman's program.

Interestingly, *Ally McBeal* and *Dharma and Greg* are both very popular with men. In addition to the sexy portrayals by Calista Flockhart and Jenna Elfman in their respective roles, the writers have given these characters a sophisticated edge. Ally, the Harvard-educated lawyer, is admonished by a judge for wearing short skirts to court and calls him a pig, while Dharma lovingly sees to Greg's needs. For many women, these shows illustrate that a woman doesn't have to be ugly to be funny on television.

Ally, however, does have her critics. Some women feel that the program is antifeminist. While acknowledging that Ally and Veronica of *Veronica's Closet* are strong, intelligent women in the workplace, their behavior in relationships and with body language are considered stereotypical and somewhat insulting. In addition, some critics feel that a woman constantly on the prowl for men (and in some cases harassing them) is demeaning.

Most women writers agree that the bias against them is more subtle than overt. When Yvette Lee Bowser, producer and creator of *Living Single,* a show with an ensemble cast that appeared on Fox, pitched it to the network, she was told that it wouldn't get to air unless it had a strong male presence. When it finally made it to the network, there was an attempt to focus on the dating aspect of the women's lives. While Bowser felt that dating was important, she also felt that issues like careers also had a place in their lives.

According to producer Caryn Mandabach, each decade presents a new presumption of what makes a woman strong. She says that too often women are victims and that there is a misunderstanding that strength is power and being right all of the time. More than ever before, women writers and producers are creating television programs with women characters that reflect their values and judgments.

More women in commanding network positions, and their increased visibility in development deals, has made them prominent leaders in programming. In 2001 three women held the top programming jobs at the WB, Fox, and CBS: Suzanne Daniels, Gail Berman, and Nancy Tellem, respectively. Women also held leadership roles in network programming, including comedy development, at ABC; prime-time series development at NBC; and comedy development at Fox. Most women writers and producers agree that women write women differently than men do.

In the past, some women observed that women were hired for story and character while men were hired for jokes. That has changed, especially for the 2000–2001 season, which saw the most significant rise in women-developed sitcoms. In the 1980s women were the driving force in creating successful television sitcoms, including Susan Harris (*The Golden Girls*), Diane English (*Murphy Brown*), and Linda Bloodworth-Thomason (*Designing Women*). But the latest sitcoms featuring women reflect values of a postfeminist generation. Although some of the programs didn't survive, they were nevertheless the inspiration of women who were integral to their development.

On *The Geena Davis Show*, Ms. Davis played a single career woman thrust into the role of motherhood after becoming engaged to a widower with two children. On *Three Sisters*, the siblings represented an array of behavioral patterns expressed by the modern woman. One sister was married and a new mother, another a single career woman, and the last a free twentysomething.

The success of the HBO ensemble female series *Sex and the City* had a dramatic impact on how the television networks perceived a program featuring women without a strong male lead. Created by Darren Star and based on the writings of Candace Bushnell, its frankness about women and their attitudes toward sex created a buzz and became a popular show with men and women. They took notice by offering two of the series' executive producers, Cindy Chupack and Jenny Bicks, lucrative exclusive development deals.

As network competition has heated up, and audience erosion by cable, Internet, and satellite distribution has changed the complexion of the audience, the networks have had to reconceptualize their attitudes about how they define their viewers. Instead of broad-based comedies with a mass audience appeal, they have become interested in niche programming for targeted groups of viewers.

Taking a lesson from cable television and its success with programs like *The Sopranos, Sex and the City*, and earlier hits like *Dream On, The Larry Sanders Show*, and *Tales from the Crypt*, the networks are attempting to develop programs that have a more defined target audience. For the fall 2001 season there were several new series with female leads that were well positioned in the network schedules. They included *Emma Brody* on Fox, starring Arija Bareikis as a young Ohioan involved in international intrigue; *Crossing Jordan* on NBC, starring Jill Hennessy as a crime-solving woman coroner set in the mold of the 1970s series *Quincy*, starring Jack Klugman; and *Philly*, a Steven Bochco creation on ABC starring Kim Delaney (formerly of *NYPD Blue*). Women have become empowered with a sense of professionalism and the respect that it generates. With that comes entitlement as equals in the television landscape that defines the dynamics between men and women as characters in a dramatic context.

Creating a sense of programming symmetry within the context of feminist values is an important priority in the evolving matrix of the perception of women in our society. Recent data has articulated a significant change in America's family structure, with households headed by women outpacing the growth of traditional families. Television has a responsibility to be sensitive to these changes and reflect those values in programming.

## NOTES

1. Suzanne E. Smith, *Dancing in the Street: Motown and the Cultural Politics of Detroit* (Cambridge, Mass.: Harvard University Press, 1999), p. 134.

2. Ibid.

3. Phillip Brian Harper, "Extra Special Effects, Televisual Representation and the Claims of the Black Experience," in *Living Color: Race and Television in the United States,* ed. Sasha Torres (Durham: Duke University Press, 1998), p. 70.

4. Ibid.

5. Ibid., p. 67.

6. J. Fred MacDonald, *Who Shot the Sheriff?: The Rise and Fall of the Television Western* (New York: Praeger, 1987), p. 125.

7. Harper, "Extra Special Effects," p. 69.

8. MacDonald, *Who Shot the Sheriff?*, p. 126.

9. Billy Ingram, http://www.tvparty.com.

10. Ibid.

11. MacDonald, *Who Shot the Sheriff?*, p. 127.

12. Donald Bogle, *Primetime Blues: African-Americans on Network Television* (New York: Farrar, Straus and Giroux, 2001).

13. MacDonald, *Who Shot the Sheriff?*, p. 290.

14. Ibid., p. 292.

15. Bogle, *Primetime Blues,* p. 387.

16. Ibid.

17. Julie Salamon, "A Wayans as a Father, Not a Brother," *New York Times,* 28 March 2001, p. E5.

18. Robert F. Moss, "The Shrinking Life Span of the Black Sitcom," *New York Times,* 25 February 2001, p. AR19.

19. Andy Meisler, "A Hispanic Drama, Rejected Once, Finds a Home," *New York Times,* 16 December 2001, p. AR33; Julie Salamon, "Latino Family Values, Beyond the Tortillas," *New York Times,* 23 January 2002, p. E1.

20. Tim Goodman, "Big Networks, Cable Ignore Latinos; Showtime's Drama 'Resurrection Blvd.' Stands Out as an Exception," *San Francisco Chronicle,* 16 September 2001.

21. Meisler, "Hispanic Drama," p. AR33; Salamon, "Latino Family Values," p. E1; Mireya Navarro, "Trying to Get Beyond the Role of the Maid," *New York Times,* 16 May 2002, p. E1; Children Now, "Networks Lose Ground on Diversifying Prime Time Picture, Study Shows," press release, 15 May 2002.

22. Alan James Frutkin, "The Faces in the Glass Are Rarely Theirs," *New York Times,* 24 December 2000, p. AE31.

23. Anita Gates, "When TV Began to Be about TV," *New York Times,* 28 May 2000, p. 33.

24. Dan Quayle, speech given to the Commonwealth Club of California, San Francisco, May 1992.

# 6

## THE SITCOM: INNOCENCE VERSUS URBAN CHIC

One of the manifestations of American culture is the experiences that it exports via its theatrical films and television programs. The situation comedy, or *sitcom,* is an enduring television programming genre that weaves a narrative of humor within the context of a perception of domestic routine. In some cases the humor is associated with the dynamics of a relationship between a husband and wife, the siblings, or extended family and friends.

The sitcom first appeared on radio and was embraced by audiences for its wit, charm, humor, and appeal. In 1939 *Li'l Abner,* based upon the Al Capp comic strip featuring the loveable characters from Dogpatch, debuted on NBC. Comic strips, by their nature, were good sources for comedy, drama, and superhero radio programs. Along with *Li'l Abner* in 1939, CBS placed *Blondie* on its network radio schedule. Also based upon a popular comic strip, this one by Chic Young, *Blondie* dramatized the exploits of a bumbling Dagwood Bumstead and his wife, Blondie. The legendary actress-comedian Fanny Brice was the star of the radio sitcom *Baby Snooks,* whose title character was a terror of a child, causing countless episodes of trouble for her father and her baby brother, Robespierre. Adolescents also had their moments in radio with the misfortunes of *Henry Aldrich,* whose title character was characterized by his cracking, high-pitched voice.

As the 1940s approached, radio sitcoms endured with new characters and situations. The idea of spinning off a character from a popular sitcom was an idea from radio. For example, *The Great Gildersleeve* was a spin-off from the popular *Fibber McGee and Molly* radio series. Two radio programs featuring sitcom characters that made the transition from radio to television were *The Adventures of Ozzie and Harriet* and *The Life of Riley.*

The Nelson family (left to right): Ricky, Ozzie, Harriet, and David, of *The Adventures of Ozzie and Harriet,* the longest-running situation comedy in television history. (Photofest.)

The first television sitcoms had themes that incorporated some religious, ethnic, and status stereotypes. In *The Life of Riley,* William Bendix played one of the first blue-collar workers to appear on television. Many of these characters were portrayed as good-hearted schnooks who sought more legitimacy in their lives. Another sitcom that featured a working-class character was *The Honeymooners,* starring Jackie Gleason, Art Carney, and Jane Meadows. The setting was a New York City tenement building where Ralph and his wife, Alice, had a modest apartment. Bus driver Ralph Kramden, played by Gleason, was always conspiring with his bumbling pal Norton, a sewer worker played by Art Carney, in schemes that would backfire. Each effort to hide the truth from their respective wives, Alice and Trixie, would result in disaster, and the two men would always be admonished for not telling the truth. In this conceptualization of middle-class life, the working man was relegated to a subservient position dependent upon the goodwill and kindness of the smarter woman.

*The Honeymooners,* which started as a part of the variety program *Cavalcade of Stars,* became a half-hour show in 1955. It succeeded because of a fine ensemble cast, with actors who had great timing and writers that were sharp and witty. It was a great success on CBS and made Jackie Gleason a television star.

Ethnic humor was also a part of the sitcom landscape. Two radio programs that became popular because of their characters' association with religion or race were *The Rise of the Goldbergs* and *Amos 'n' Andy*. As the star and writer of *The Rise of the Goldbergs*, Gertrude Berg created an immensely popular radio sitcom that began in 1929, moved to CBS in 1949, and ran until 1953. The Goldbergs were a poor Jewish family living in the Bronx, and Molly was at its foundation. She managed to persevere and rise above the most difficult circumstances.

That resiliency was a part of Gertrude Berg's personality, which was evident in her real life. At a time, in the 1950s, communism was feared, and accusations made Berg come to the defense of her costar Phillip Loeb, who played

Jackie Gleason (right) and Art Carney, as bus driver Ralph Kramden and sewer worker Ed Norton, in the situation comedy *The Honeymooners*, which first began as a part of the *Cavalcade of Stars* variety show. Audrey Meadows, who played Ralph's wife, is also pictured here. (Photofest.)

Jake. He was labeled as a communist, and she defended his innocence. As the creator and owner of the series, Berg was able to delay Loeb's firing, but the sponsor, Sanka coffee, ended its support, and the program was dropped. The show eventually moved to NBC without Loeb but with another sponsor. Tragically, unable to get radio, television, or theatrical work, Loeb committed suicide by taking an overdose of sleeping pills. Real life and its true dilemmas had intruded into the fiction of television.

One of the most successful and beloved radio sitcoms was *Amos 'n' Andy*. It was created by two Caucasian vaudeville performers, Freeman Fisher Gosden (Amos) and Charles J. Correll (Andy). They started on radio at a small station in a Chicago hotel, using a blackface routine in exchange for free meals. Their act was called *Sam 'n' Henry*, and it was picked up by the *Chicago Tribune* station, WGN, for 600 episodes over two years. Wanting more money and being denied their request, they took their program to radio station WMAQ, but WGN, while releasing them from their personal contract, wouldn't allow Gosden and Correll to use the *Sam 'n' Henry* title. So Gosden and Correll changed the name of their program to *Amos 'n' Andy*.

Both Gosden and Correll had a unique talent for mimicking voices and played the roles of all of the characters associated with the community of the Freshair Taxicab Company and the fraternal lodge Mystic Knights of the Sea. Five-minute segments were syndicated on 78 rpm records to smaller stations, giving the program broader coverage. In 1929 *Amos 'n' Andy* was acquired by the NBC Blue radio network, with the team of Gosden and Correll receiving $100,000 annually, and quickly became one of the most popular programs on radio.

By today's standards the working-class dialect adopted by the two white actors portraying different black characters would seem offensive. However, black and white audiences were avid listeners and became devoted fans of the program. Indeed, the program was so popular that it went from five to six nights a week, and movie theaters would suspend their operations for 15 minutes and play the show over their loudspeakers so that the audience would not miss the radio broadcast.

In a move precipitated by CBS chairman William Paley to bolster the talent pool of his network at the expense of NBC, he raided NBC's stable of performers, and the first to defect were Gosden and Correll, in 1948, for $2 million. A shrewd businessman, Paley was also looking toward the future and the content needs of television. To that end, *Amos 'n' Andy*, with an all-black cast, made its debut on CBS in June of 1951. The program's depiction of blacks proved very controversial, and it ceased its network run in 1953 and was removed from syndication in 1966.

Ethnic and religious sitcoms have at times created controversy. One program, *Chicken Soup*, starring comedian Jackie Mason and actress Lynn Redgrave, stirred the cauldron of religious tolerance. The program, about a Jewish bachelor who falls in love with an Irish Catholic widow with three children living in the apartment next door, barely lasted the 1989 season on ABC. Another program that suffered a similar fate, also concerning an interfaith marriage, was *Bridgette Loves Bernie,* which was an update of *Abie's Irish Rose.* It was about a poor Jewish boy who marries an Irish girl from a wealthy family and his struggle to be a successful writer while driving a taxi in New York City. Although it was riddled with clichés, the audience liked the program, but CBS removed it from the schedule after a number of Jewish groups protested the theme of intermarriage. Ethnic humor has also had its successes with programs like *Seinfeld; Fresh Prince of Bel Air; The Jeffersons;* and, of course, *All in the Family.*

## I LOVE LUCY

There are moments in television that reverberate through time and space, providing treasured memories of fun, warmth, and laughter. Looking through the *I Love Lucy* cookbook and seeing recipes for Vitameatavegamin and Babalu Black Bean dip provides a link to the past and a situation comedy whose humor remains timeless.

The concept for *I Love Lucy* evolved from the radio program *My Favorite Husband,* starring Lucille Ball, on CBS radio. In 1948 a writer named Jess Oppenheimer, who had been writing for the legendary comedienne Fanny Brice, the star of *Baby Snooks,* was asked by an executive from CBS if he would join the *My Favorite Husband* team. At the time he was approached, the *Snooks* program was off the air because of a salary dispute involving Brice. *My Favorite Husband* had only been on the radio for a few weeks, and Oppenheimer was unfamiliar with it. He listened to the program, read several scripts, and wrote his own. In his script, however, Oppenheimer made the lead character, Liz Cugat, played by Ball, a little more childish, like the Snooks character, and more scheming. That approach was successful and broadened the appeal of the program.

Other changes made by Oppenheimer brought the concept of *My Favorite Husband* even closer to *I Love Lucy.* He brought less sophistication to the lead characters and introduced another couple, Rudolph and Iris Atterbury (George's boss at the bank), to act as foils to Liz and her husband, George, played by Dick Denning. The couple was played by the versatile actors Gale Gordon and Bea Benaderet. In a move to make the Cugats more of a plain, everyman couple, Oppenheimer changed the last name to Cooper and made sure that the audience knew that George didn't earn a lot of money at the bank.

In his direction of Ball, Oppenheimer, who was disappointed in the way she was reading her lines with little physical movement before the live radio studio audience, gave her a ticket to *The Jack Benny Show* and told her to go to school. When she returned, her performance style changed, and she became the physical comedienne that made her famous—so much so that the

The cast of *I Love Lucy* (left to right): Vivian Vance (as Ethel Mertz), William Frawley (as Fred Mertz), Desi Arnaz (as Ricky Ricardo), and Lucille Ball (as Lucy Ricardo). "What made *I Love Lucy* so endearing was a unique blend of talent, writing, and production values that provided a lighthearted view of domestic life." (Photofest.)

critics took note and wrote how the new medium of television would be perfect for her talent.

CBS made a pitch for her to transfer her radio program to television, but Ball would only agree if her husband, Desi Arnaz, was made her costar. The network didn't think much of the Cuban bandleader and turned down the proposal. To prove them wrong, she and Desi created Desilu Productions and formed a vaudeville act with summer bookings while she was off from her radio series. The act was called "Desi Arnaz with Band and Lucille Ball." It was a resounding success, and the advertising agency of Young and Rubicam, which represented General Foods, sponsor of *My Favorite Husband,* became interested and advised Lucy and Desi to produce the television program themselves and sell it to the highest television-network bidder. They had difficulty conceptualizing the format and finding the right script. After NBC expressed an interest in the television show, CBS capitulated and placed

Desi under contract. Also, Ball insisted that Jess Oppenheimer be her producer and head writer.

The network wanted a pilot television program as soon as possible, but there was no concept, no title, and only tentative names for the characters, Lucy and Larry Lopez. Of course, they knew that they couldn't use the format of *My Favorite Husband* for the new, as yet untitled television show because no one would believe Desi in the role of a banker. After a lot of brainstorming, Oppenheimer came up with the idea of a working-class bandleader who, after a day at the club, likes nothing better than to come home to his wife. The conflict, of course, was that Lucy was not a stay-at-home wife and had an unrequited desire to be in show business, and schemed her way with hilarious results.

As for the title, after an arduous dialogue about billing credits with Desi Arnaz, Oppenheimer decided upon *I Love Lucy;* Eliot Daniel, Rudy Vallee's pianist, wrote the signature tune, and the characters' names were changed to Lucy and Ricky Ricardo. At the time the pilot was shot, no contract had been signed with CBS. After completion of the pilot episode, the kinescope (a low-quality 16 mm film version of the live show) was sent to CBS in New York, and Oppenheimer, Lucy, Desi, and the crew all eagerly awaited the network's reaction.

*I Love Lucy* became a seminal program and the foundation for television situation comedy not only because of creative genius but also because of business necessity. The initial CBS reaction to the *I Love Lucy* pilot was disappointing; however, it was sold to Milton Biow, advertising agency for the Philip Morris Company. The plan was to broadcast the program live from the West Coast and transmit the filmed 16 mm kinescope via cable to the East Coast. This was a time before the invention of videotape, and the *kine,* as it was called, had poor resolution quality because it was recorded on film off of a television picture tube.

In the 1950s most of the live television programs were produced in New York, reflecting the majority of television homes on the East Coast. Both Phillip Morris and the Biow ad agency were insistent that the production be moved to New York because they feared that the low-quality kinescopes would alienate the majority of the audience. Although they were insistent, Oppenheimer prevailed by promising a high-quality filmed program, as was being done for *Amos 'n' Andy.*

The broadcasting business, like any other, is cost-conscious, and in turn the network insisted that Lucy and Desi cut their joint salary from $5,000 to $2,000 per program in order to compensate for the increased production costs that the use of film would incur. In a shrewd business decision, Desi agreed to the terms but stipulated that Desilu Productions must own 100 percent of all the film negatives. He was looking toward the sale of the program overseas to make up the difference in their salary. CBS agreed, and, of course, ownership of the programs, which are still being seen on television today, proved to be a financial bonanza for Desilu.

Shortly after the pilot program was sold, Oppenheimer realized that Lucy and Desi had to have dramatic foils, another couple that they could relate with on the program. This concept worked well on the radio program *My Favorite Husband,* and Oppenheimer approached costars Gale Gordon and Bea Benaderet to play the Mertzes, an older couple that would be the Ricardos' best friends. The two actors had other commitments by the time *I Love Lucy* was sold, and so Oppenheimer had to search for another couple. He settled on the perfect match, William Frawley and Vivian Vance. Although a veteran actor having appeared on Broadway and in 103 films, Frawley hadn't been working much. He called Lucille Ball and made a pitch for the role of Fred Mertz. Everyone thought he was perfect, but when Phillip Morris and CBS found out, they objected because of his alleged drinking problem. He did get the part and promised Desi Arnaz that he would be a reliable, professional part of the team and would never miss a call. An avid baseball fan, Frawley had a unique clause in his contract allowing him leave to attend the World Series if the New York Yankees were playing. This happened for seven out of nine seasons in his role as Fred Mertz.

In another serendipitous happening, Marc Daniels, the director of the show, suggested Vivian Vance, an actress he had worked with in movies, for the part of Ethel Mertz. She was appearing in a revival of *The Voice of the Turtle,* and after seeing her on stage, Daniels, Oppenheimer, and Desi Arnaz agreed that they had found Ethel Mertz.

The technical components for shooting *I Love Lucy* were challenging and at times daunting. Indeed, in the early years of television one had to have a sense of bravado and a pioneering spirit along with being an entrepreneur and innovator. These were qualities that were needed to adapt the principles of theatrical motion-picture production to television.

Although the filmed version of *Amos 'n' Andy* produced a high-quality print, the single-camera cinematic style was not suitable for *I Love Lucy.* For the *Lucy* show, a live audience was an essential ingredient to the production. On *Amos 'n' Andy* there could be no live audience because scenes were shot out of chronological order, then edited and shown before a live audience, after which the laugh track was inserted. As a result, the actors had to anticipate and time their pauses to where they expected the audience to laugh. Often those moments were ill timed, and the final results were awkward and out of sync.

Resolving the problem for *I Love Lucy* meant thinking out of the box, which is how Oppenheimer et al. solved the problem. In these nascent days of television, few programs were being filmed before a live audience, but there was one, Ralph Edwards's *Truth or Consequences,* a game show that used three motion-picture cameras. Following that lead, Oppenheimer adapted the same technique. On a recommendation from Lucille Ball and a whim, he contacted Karl Freund, an Oscar-winning cinematographer.

As a cinematographer, Freund's work in film was legendary. He won an Oscar for *The Good Earth* and was director of photography on the film classics *Metropolis, All Quiet on the Western Front, Camille,* and *Dracula*. As a director, Freund directed eight feature films, including *The Mummy* (1932). He was also an innovator and was the first to place a camera on a dolly and move it while filming a scene.

A brilliant innovator and inventor, Freund developed the Norwich light meter and the process shot. His work had made him quite wealthy and head of his own company, Photo Research Corporation of Burbank, California. He had worked with Lucy on the MGM feature *DuBarry Was a Lady,* helping to make her look spectacular.

Freund was a respected and demanding craftsman, devoted to the art of film and somewhat suspicious of television. Loving a challenge, the 61-year-old came out of semiretirement and created the shooting technique that is still used in television today. As director of photography, Freund's ability to light the set from overhead (unlike a film set, which has floor lamps) and coordinate the simultaneous filming of three film cameras mounted on dollies made it technically feasible to shoot before a live studio audience.

Another challenge was the search for a space that would be suitable for accommodating the production and the live audience. At first a traditional theater was considered, but when none could be found, once again thinking out of the box, a film soundstage was considered. A bankrupt company, General Service Studio, was looking for a tenant, and the space was perfect for the *I Love Lucy* set and its audience.

Television history was made on October 15, 1951, with the CBS television network premiere of *I Love Lucy*. From the moment of the rarely seen opening animation segment to the appearance of Lucille Ball, Desi Arnaz, William Frawley, and Vivian Vance, television took on a new form, creating a foundation for years of situation comedy programming.

What made *I Love Lucy* so endearing was a unique combination of talent, writing, and production values that provided a lighthearted view of domestic life. The many nuances of Lucy's character as a schemer who shuns the typical role of an obedient wife by defying her husband's caution about staying out of show business set the tone for the series and its comedic direction. As her foil, Desi Arnaz proved to be no less of a talent and exhibited a sense of great timing and physical dexterity. As a coconspirator, Vivian Vance as Ethel Mertz could be a stabilizing force at times, but most often became an active protagonist in her many plots. Making the Mertzes, Ethel and Fred, an older couple was another stroke of genius. As the landlord of the apartment building, Fred was a curmudgeon who viewed life and marriage through a somewhat jaded lens. A die-hard vaudevillian, he shared a sense of excitement with Lucy toward show business.

The characters, plots, and celebrities created a compelling dynamic for endless humor and physical comedy. There weren't any subtle messages in the humor of *I Love Lucy*. In her defiance, she got into all kinds of trouble punctuated by hilarious consequences. As a comedienne, Lucy had a singular talent to make people laugh. Even today her humor is a timeless manifestation undated by any topicality but sheer frivolity and delight. The endless reruns of *I Love Lucy* are a joy for each new generation and a tribute to the creativity and resilience of the programming.[1]

## FATHER KNOWS BEST AND ALL IN THE FAMILY

Although Lucille Ball was the biggest television star in the 1950s, close behind her was Robert Young. While they were very different in character, both had a charisma that made them popular with the American television audience, and both came from the world of Hollywood. In the show *Father Knows Best,* Young played the role of Jim Anderson, a manager at the General Insurance Company and the consummate father. In that role he exuded a warmth and confidence that endeared him to the fans of the program. The show was a testimony to the intimacy of the American family and its cherished traditions. There was no doubt that Jim was a faithful husband to his wife, played by Jane Wyatt; a good provider; and an understanding father to his three children, Betty (Princess), James Jr. (Bud), and Kathy (Kitten).

The concept for the series was created by Ed James in 1949 for radio. It moved to the CBS television network in 1954, and after performing poorly in the Sunday 10 P.M. time slot, it was canceled by the network. Viewers protested the cancellation, and NBC picked up the program, placed it in an earlier time slot, and had a certifiable television hit (NBC, 1955–58; ABC, 1962–63). The production techniques for *Father Knows Best* differed greatly from *I Love Lucy*. The show, a Screen Gems (subsidiary of Columbia Pictures) production, was shot on a closed set (not before a live audience) using one 35 mm camera. This enabled the construction of sets with four walls (instead of the usual three), which added a sense of reality and intimacy to the Anderson household scenes.

A great deal of attention was paid to detail, and every effort was made to provide the audience with a familiarity and intimacy with the characters and their sense of family. The executive producer of the series, Eugene Rodney, had high standards of excellence, and along with head writers Roswell Rogers and Paul West and directors Peter Tewksbury and William D. Russell, he strove to create the consummate family program. This dedication was also inherent in the casting of talent that was not recurring. If Rodney felt that a particular New York actor was well suited for a part, he would fly him to Hollywood for the one-time effort. The series ran from October 1954 to April 1963, with a total of 203 episodes that were originally broadcast. There are presently about 190 episodes in syndication; the others were lost or recut into other segments.

*Father Knows Best* became a fixture of American pop culture, touching the fabric of our institutions. Its ability to clearly enunciate family values and promote civic responsibility was viewed as a valuable asset on the part of the government. This was clearly articulated in 1959 when the United States Treasury Department commissioned an episode to be produced promoting the purchase of savings bonds. Although never broadcast, this program, "24 Hours in Tyrantland," was distributed to civic institutions, schools, and church groups. In it Young's character, Jim Anderson, is chosen to head Springfield's savings-bond drive and is greeted with less than an enthusiastic response from his children. To teach them a lesson in civics, he declares their home a communist state for 24 hours and offers them each the cost of a savings bond to spend as they please if they don't change their mind. As a result of their harsh treatment under "communist" rule, the children are made aware of their civic deficiency and taught a didactic lesson on the need to support democratic principles. The strong family fabric and traditional parental roles in *Father Knows Best* made it a perfect vehicle for the dissemination of propaganda.

In the multicultural society of today, there is a vast gulf that exists between the modern world and the lives of the Anderson family. Their universe rarely included people of color and revolved around issues that were mundane and inconsequential. But this was a time when situation comedies had no subtext or message other than to make people feel good or make them laugh.

With the advent of the civil rights movement, the Kennedy assassination, and the Vietnam War, America lost its innocence. Humor became more topical and irreverent, and a television program about a bigot was a huge hit. As is so often the case, timing and serendipity all played a part in the development and success of Norman Lear's *All in the Family*. In the late 1960s, CBS had lost its luster and lead in the three-network race. It was no longer the prime-time network of choice, and its audience demographics skewed toward the 50-and-over population with programs like *The Red Skelton Show, The Jackie Gleason Show, Petticoat Junction,* and *Hee Haw.*

With Bob Wood assuming the reigns as the new network president, he canceled those programs and was looking for material with greater relevance for a more urbane audience in the 18–34 demographic. He found it, of course, with *All in the Family*. But the program's road to network television was riddled with potholes.

Writer-producer Norman Lear had seen a BBC program in London called *Till Death Us Do Part*. It featured Alf and Elsie Garnett, two loveable racists from London's East End. Enamored with the concept, Lear bought the rights for the United States and created a program that he entitled *Those Were the Days*. Two pilots were filmed, the first one taped in New York City in January 1969 and the second in March of the same year, with the roles of Mike and

Gloria recast, with Sally Struthers and Rob Reiner joining Carroll O'Connor's portrayal of Archie Bunker and Jean Stapleton as his "dingbat" wife, Edith, both brilliant adaptations of their characters. Even with the cast changes, ABC declined to pick up the series. Lear approached Wood at CBS and received an enthusiastic reaction, albeit one that was somewhat guarded because of the explicit language and stereotypical references.

The pilot program, shot in Hollywood, set the tone for the series, and its frank portrayal of sex and the use of racial epithets shocked some veteran CBS executives. As the executive producer and writer, Norman Lear was committed to a full disclosure of all of Archie's foibles in the first broadcast episode along with a vivid introduction of the other members of the family. The network wanted the first episode to be less controversial, but Lear refused. CBS demurred but came back with a request to cut 80 seconds from the pilot. Again Lear refused, explaining that there was a need for CBS to experience the entire force of the program.

I felt we had to get the network wet completely. Once you're completely wet you can't get wetter. I wanted the audience to hear all of Archie's epithets, to see his sexual hang-ups, to meet the whole family.[2]

In the pilot program, while Edith and Archie Bunker are at church, Mike attempts to convince his wife, Gloria, to have sexual intercourse in the middle of the day. The couple returns home early and Archie, annoyed with the sermon, begins a diatribe against student subversives, welfare cheats, Jews, blacks, and atheists. Then he moves on to praise the virtues of premarital celibacy.

When your mother-in-law and me was goin' around together—it was two years—we never—I never—I mean absolutely nothin'—not till the wedding night.

Edith, with her deadpan looks, answers:

Yeah, and even then . . .

At the CBS office of Standards and Practices, a euphemism for the network's censors, the mood was solemn and concerned. The head of the department was William Tankersley, a no-nonsense veteran of CBS programming oversight whose sobering personality earned him the nickname "Mr. Prohibition" at the network. Even though Bob Wood had committed to the program after seeing the pilot, Tankersley articulated his concern about Bible-Belt network affiliates and the use of words like *Yid*, which he believed could never be used on network television.

The concern over scheduling *All in the Family* reached up the corporate hierarchy to William Paley, the chairman of CBS. Initially it was thought that he was opposed to it. He agreed, however, to provide a commitment of 13 weeks even though the program did not fare well during preview testing. Although he personally loved the show, Bob Wood had some lingering

Jean Stapleton (as Edith), Carroll O'Connor (as Archie), Rob Reiner (as Mike), and Sally Struthers (as Gloria) compose the cast of CBS's groundbreaking situation comedy *All in the Family*. (Photofest.)

doubts, so he scheduled *All in the Family* as a February replacement show during the 1970–71 season on Tuesday nights at 9:30. Its competition was NBC's *Tuesday Night at the Movies* and ABC's *Movie of the Week*. Initially, most reviews were positive, but ratings were low and there was some viewer protest. One of the most vivid was a note scrawled by a viewer on an empty Kotex box after the broadcast of an episode about Gloria's menstruation. The next season, CBS scheduled the program on Saturday night at 8:00 P.M., and on that day in that time slot, *All in the Family* became one of the greatest television hits of all time.

With the success of *All in the Family*, Norman Lear established a reputation as a producer-writer of television sitcoms that had a distinctive tone and cutting-edge humor. He used the success of his signature sitcom to launch other series based upon characters developed for *All in the Family*. Two successful spin-offs were *The Jeffersons* and *Maude*. George Jefferson, the head of the black family that moved next door to the Bunkers, and Archie couldn't stand each other. Although the two men hated each other, their wives became good friends. The Jefferson characters were a natural for their own series, which Lear developed for CBS.

In *The Jeffersons,* George becomes a successful businessman and owner of a dry-cleaning business, moving his family into a luxury apartment building in an all-white neighborhood. Having an affluent black man in a prosperous white neighborhood flaunting his wealth and his anger toward white people provided a catalyst for conflict and humor.

Another character that had the breadth and depth for a spin-off series of her own was Archie's oft-married cousin, Maude, played by Bea Arthur. She was an outspoken women's libber who was on the opposite pole of the political spectrum from her conservative, bigoted cousin, Archie Bunker. *Maude* addressed issues that were at one time considered off-limits on television. In a famous two-part episode, Maude, who considered herself past childbearing age, learns that she's pregnant. After struggling with the decision, she decides to have an abortion. This, of course, was a hot-button issue for 1970s television to address, and CBS stood by the broadcast and reran it at a later date.

The stable of Lear-produced successful sitcoms also included *Sanford and Son,* which NBC quickly bought. The show featured black comedian Redd Foxx, a nightclub performer known for his off-color humor. He played a loveable curmudgeon junk dealer that was given to musings like "Just because he's white doesn't mean he's stupid." This series was not a spin-off and was a successful component of NBC's comedy schedule.

## COUNTRY MOUSE MEETS CITY MOUSE

Many of the sitcoms on television today have defined an urban sensibility glamorizing city life, its challenges, and its rewards. While American cities are indeed vast population centers, there is also an expansive rural community integrated into the power structure of the culture. At times there appear to be considerable differences in how urban and rural populations view politics and religion. These are concerns that are sometimes reflected in programming decisions made by national television networks. Programs reflecting rural themes have been successful on radio and television. For some, these programs express homespun family values that are not always reflected in the slick tradition of urban comedy.

As political tensions increased in the 1960s and civil unrest rocked the nation, television programming moved to address more comfortable, nostalgic themes. This is not a surprising accommodation to the needs of a nervous public and was demonstrated again after the tragic events of September 11, 2001. On November 26, barely two months after the attacks on the World Trade Center and the Pentagon, CBS aired a special entitled *The Carol Burnett Show: Show Stoppers,* reuniting the original cast of *The Carol Burnett Show,* which concluded its CBS run in 1978. The special attracted almost 30 million viewers, stunning industry executives already reeling from dealing with the trauma of terrorism. It was the fourth-most-watched prime-time broadcast-network television show of the season, bettered only by the final game of the World Series and two episodes of the sitcom *Friends*. The clips and outtakes surpassed the ratings of *E.R.*, the remaining games of the World Series, and all of *Monday Night Football*, making it one of the highest-rated programs of the season to date.

The program featured *bloopers*, or unscripted outtakes by the cast, a concept not entirely new to television. The idea of using these unrehearsed moments hearkens back to the days of radio and *The Jack Benny Show*, when George Burns would start laughing when Jack Benny stared at him. In 1981 NBC produced a special called *TV's Censored Bloopers*, and with its success created a series, *TV's Bloopers and Practical Jokes*, with hosts Dick Clark and Ed McMahon. The blooper format also appeared on ABC as *Foul-Ups, Bleeps, and Blunders*.

Another unexpected result of the program was its popularity among younger audiences in the 18–49 age group. CBS executives had expected the special to reach the over-50 viewers, but the 13 million viewers in the younger age group were a surprise. Those associated with the program speculated about its popularity. Indeed, Ms. Burnett had approached CBS with the idea in the summer of 2001. The network liked the concept and made it a part of a highly promoted event called *Laugh Your Head Off Monday*.

Ms. Burnett offered her thoughts on the show's success, describing it as "perfect, just mindless silliness." She also added, "I think with everything that has happened, a lot of people just want to go back to a time when maybe life was a little more innocent."[3] Judging from the success of other CBS retrospective specials, including a November 11 look back at *I Love Lucy*, a November 13 special featuring Michael Jackson, and another Carol Burnett special, "Let's Bump Up the Lights," in May 2004, Burnett's observations are probably correct.

At CBS, David F. Poltrack, executive vice president for research, noted that audiences appeared to savor entertainment that they had enjoyed in the past and that with more people staying home, more families are watching television together. At CBS, other executives offered similar points of view, pointing out that during uncertain and frightening times, audiences seek out the comfort of familiar things, including television programming.

The return to the more mundane sensibilities of comedy unencumbered with the angst of messages also seemed to satisfy the needs of television audiences in the 1960s and 1970s. During this time CBS developed the theme of rural (or "hick") sitcoms, which seemed to hit a responsive chord with audiences. The idea wasn't new. Indeed, *Ma Perkins*, a radio soap opera with a homespun countrified theme, ran for 7,065 episodes, realizing its final broadcast on November 25, 1960, with Ma telling her loyal listeners, "Goodbye, and may God bless you."

In the early years of television, the ABC network helped to define the status of rural comedy with the 1957 sitcom *The Real McCoys*. It was a portrayal of a self-reliant rural clan with strong values and quaint customs. Well suited for his role as grandpappy Amos, Walter Brennan, a veteran film actor, was the wizened leader of the family. Actor Richard Crenna, who was a cast member of an earlier sitcom, *Our Miss Brooks*, and was a young veteran of television, played Luke, and actress Kathleen Nolan was also a featured player.

In 1959, under the leadership of newly appointed network president James Aubrey, the tone and substance of CBS programming changed. Under his guidance, CBS acquired one of television's greatest hits and longest-running sitcoms. Combining the themes of rural humor and urban chic, *The Beverly Hillbillies*, which began its network run in 1962 and lasted for nine seasons, was the highest-rated television program for the first two seasons it was broadcast.

The program's concept had some similarities to *The Real McCoys*, but this time the Clampett family, led by widower Jed (played by veteran actor Buddy

The cast of *The Beverly Hillbillies* (left to right): Donna Douglas (as Elly May Clampett), Irene Ryan (as Daisy Moses), Buddy Ebsen (as Jed Clampett), and Max Baer Jr. (as Jethro Bodine). (Photofest.)

Ebsen), became rich from oil found on their land and moved to Beverly Hills. As in *The Real McCoys,* there had to be a senior character, in this case Irene Ryan as Granny. The younger members of the clan were played by Max Baer and Donna Douglas. The program struck a comic chord with audiences, who reveled in the down-home behavior of the Clampetts and their ability to best the conniving city slickers who tried to take advantage of them.

The chairman and founder of CBS, William S. Paley, who was a patron of the arts and often espoused the need for literacy on television, defended the program to his friends and the critics. He spoke about *The Beverly Hillbillies'* mass audience appeal and the nature of its humor. "I like it because it is very funny. It's a slapstick comedy—a form of entertainment that amuses me and many other people of low and high taste in other matters."[4] The program was a huge success for Filmways, the studio that brought it to CBS.

One notable sitcom that predated *The Beverly Hillbillies* and helped perpetuate the success of rural comedy was *The Andy Griffith Show,* which premiered on CBS in 1960. It was about an easygoing sheriff, a widower with a young son and a doting aunt, in the small town of Mayberry, which was populated by some very unique and distinctive characters. His deputy, Barney Fife, portrayed with comic genius by comedian Don Knotts, had great aspirations, only to be daunted by his own ineptness. Realizing this, Sheriff Andy, who doesn't carry a weapon, allows Barney to carry an unloaded gun while keeping a single bullet for him locked up. Another denizen of Mayberry and friend to Andy and Barney was the somewhat dimwitted Gomer Pyle.

*The Andy Griffith Show* was one of the first to create spin-off programs based upon the concept or its characters. After Griffith left the show in 1968, it continued without him as *Mayberry R.F.D.* (1968–71). For this series incarnation, Ken Berry played Sam Jones, George Lindsey was Goober Pyle, and Frances Bavier reprised her role as Aunt Bee (1968–70). In addition, Jim Nabors (Gomer Pyle) became the star of his own sitcom, *Gomer Pyle–USMC.* Although not a spin-off character, Ron Howard, who played Andy's young son in the original *Andy Griffith Show,* later starred in the successful *Happy Days* series and today is an accomplished film director.

The bucolic theme of CBS sitcoms endured with the series *Petticoat Junction.* It started on CBS in 1963 and featured Bea Benaderet, who played cousin Pearl on *The Beverly Hillbillies.* She played a widow with three pretty, available daughters, Bobbie Jo, Billie Jo, and Betty Jo Bradley, who ran the Shady Rest, a small down-and-out family hotel situated near a long railroad spur unused except for the antique train the Cannonball. In some ways this series gave credence to the old joke of the traveling salesman coming upon a widow with three sexy daughters and spending the night.

A tribute to the country genre of sitcom programming was *Green Acres* (CBS, 1965–71) and its cult of mindless bumpkin humor. In this CBS incarnation (produced by Filmways), stressed-out Manhattan lawyer Oliver Wendell Douglas, played by Eddie Albert, moves his upwardly mobile trophy

The cast of *The Andy Griffith Show* (left to right): Don Knotts (as Deputy Barney Fife), Andy Griffith (as Sheriff Andy Taylor), and Jim Nabors (as Gomer Pyle). "The show was one of the first to create spin-off programs based upon the concept or its characters." (Photofest.)

wife to a ramshackle farm in the backwater hamlet of Hooterville. These characters, played by the same actors, were also featured in *Petticoat Junction*. Actress Eva Gabor (Zsa Zsa's sister) is perfectly cast as the fish out of water who must adapt to the local denizens, including her neighbor's television-watching pig, Arnold. Also in the cast were famous character actors known for their rustic portrayals: Edgar Buchanan, Pat Buttram, and Bea Benaderet (who starred in *Petticoat Junction*).

There were other programs that attempted to capitalize on this theme with less success. In a reconceptualization of the *Green Acres* theme, *Apple's Way* (1974–75) starred Ronny Cox as George Apple, who moves his wife and family from the big city to Appleton, Iowa, his hometown. Everyone must adjust to the new realities of small-town life. *Cade's County* (1971–72) starred film actor Glenn Ford as the sheriff of Madrid County, who was tough yet compassionate and exemplified the virtues of small-town life. The series also featured actor Edgar Buchanan. By the mid-1970s the American television audience had grown somewhat weary of television's depiction of small-town life. However, once over, a winning television format can reinvent itself and become successful using the building blocks of the past.

This was the case for David E. Kelley's *Picket Fences* (1992–96). The setting was the small town of Rome, Wisconsin. Although it was a drama and not a sitcom, the characters and narrative structure had similarities to successful rural programs like *Green Acres* and *The Andy Griffith Show*. The series centered around the Brock family, with Tom Skerritt as sheriff Jimmy Brock and Kathy Baker as his wife, town doctor Jill Brock. Rome was peopled with characters that had idiosyncrasies and traits that helped to fuel the success of the series, and they were portrayed by notable character actors like Fyvush Finkel as Douglas Wambaugh and Ray Walston (the Martian in *My Favorite Martian*) as Judge Henry Bone.

On the WB network, *Gilmore Girls*, which premiered in 2000, has a new take on small-town life. In this series Lauren Graham plays 32-year-old Lorelai Gilmore, a single mother raising her 16-year-old daughter, portrayed by Alexis Bledel. The twist is that the mother and daughter are often mistaken for sisters. Actress Sally Struthers, who played Archie's daughter in *All in the Family*, is featured as Babette Dell.

## FLIGHTS OF FANCY

They flew and disappeared, were benevolent monsters and friendly aliens, and cast harmless spells. They were objects of fantasy and frivolity, capturing the lighthearted spirit of the American television audience. It was sheer escapism from a world that was at times harsh and unforgiving. But these programs provided respite from the drab routines of life and supported the notion that audiences, adults and young adults, were enamored with the fiction of fairy tales.

One of the first to successfully combine these elements beyond the characters of comic-book heroes (*Superman*) was *The Flying Nun*. Based upon the novel *The Fifteenth Pelican* by Tere Rios, the series starred actress Sally Field as Sister Bertrille, a nun at the convent San Tanco in Puerto Rico. She discovers that her light weight combined with the wind gusts and her ornate headdress and habit allow her to "fly." As Sister Bertrille notes, "when lift plus thrust is greater than load plus drag, any object can fly."

Of course, there were also the supporting characters, which were somewhat stereotypical yet good-natured, including the stern mother superior; Gaspar Formento, the police captain; and even a local playboy, Carlos (Alejandro Rey), who was smitten by the pretty flying nun. This series was also successful in creating merchandising tie-ins to the program, which included flying-nun dolls and paper-doll sets. In addition, the Catholic Church recommended the series to its members, endorsing the program's moral virtues and serving in an advisory capacity to the program.

*The Flying Nun* was not Sally Field's first starring television role. She made her television debut in the short-lived ABC series *Gidget* (1965–66), based upon the successful Sandra Dee movies of the same name about a fun-loving, boy-crazed teenager. Of course, her career took a turn from television into movies, where she matured as a leading lady and became an Academy Award– winning actress.

Perhaps the earliest example of a fantasy-oriented television sitcom was *Topper,* starring Leo G. Carroll as Cosmo Topper, the stern banker who has three fun-loving ghosts just a step behind. The television series was based upon the 1937 movie starring Constance Bennett as Marion Kerby and Cary Grant as her husband, George. The playful television poltergeists include the drunk St. Bernard, Neil, equipped with a keg of spirits, and George and Marion Kerby, portrayed by Anne Jeffreys and Robert Sterling, who playfully tried to make Cosmo's life a bit more fun and carefree. His wife, Henrietta, wonders about Cosmo's strange behavior while the ghosts of George and Marion, who can only be seen by Cosmo, relish every moment of their pranks. Even with the rudimentary visual attempts at special effects, *Topper* was a leading example of the fantasy sitcom.

The ghost theme was revisited in the 1968–69 television season with *The Ghost and Mrs. Muir* on the NBC television network. It was based upon the 1945 novel of the same name and a 1947 feature film starring Gene Tierney and Rex Harrison. After a single season NBC canceled the series, and it was picked up by ABC, where it ran for the 1969–70 season and then was canceled.

In their pursuit of fantasy sitcoms, the television networks explored an array of themes that included a Peter Pan orientation, which embodied the humanization of cartoonlike characters. One of these was aptly rendered by the 1960s sitcom *I Dream of Jeannie* (NBC, 1965–70). In many ways the program fulfilled the fantasies of young adult and mature men longing for the beautiful woman who is a slave, catering to their whims. It brought reality to all of the "Jeannie in a bottle" jokes that had been and are so popular. In this iteration, it is astronaut Major Anthony Nelson, played by Larry Hagman, who, while stranded on a desert island because of a spacecraft malfunction, finds an odd bottle and releases the gorgeous 2,000-year-old Jeannie from ancient Babylon.

Played by Barbara Eden, this Jeannie is a sexy lady wearing a revealing costume, showing off her assets while revealing a bare midriff. It was a daring undertaking for 1960s television, not only because of Eden's physicality but also because of the concept of a single man cohabiting with a woman, even though she lived in a bottle. In addition, there were the special effects that were needed to make Jeannie appear and disappear, which added an additional $6,000 to the cost of each episode.

Another attractive actress, Elizabeth Montgomery, played a benevolent witch, Samantha Stephens, in *Bewitched* (1964–71), married to advertising executive Darrin Stephens, played first by Dick York (1964–69) and then by Dick Sargent (1969–72). With the wrinkle of her cute nose, Samantha can perform feats beyond the ability of mere mortals. Ignoring the objections of her mother, Endora (actress Agnes Moorehead), she marries mortal Darrin Stephens, and he learns of her identity on their honeymoon. She promises not to use her supernatural powers while they're married, but circumstances and plot needs prevail, making for some funny situations.

Adding to the comedy and drama of the series was the eventual birth of a daughter, Tabitha, who was half witch and half mortal, and a son, Adam, who was a human without any powers. Samantha's vain sister, Serena, was also played by Elizabeth Montgomery. During its run the series built an inventory of 256 episodes.

In 1982, 10 years after *Bewitched, Tucker's Witch* (CBS) made an attempt to combine the somewhat ethereal powers of a sorcerer with a cops-and-robbers theme. The Tuckers ran a private-detective agency, and Amanda's (Catherine Hicks) supernatural powers came in quite handy helping to solve crimes. The success of *Bewitched* and the television audience's attraction to the occult made this concept one that could be retuned for a younger, hip audience. In 1996 *Sabrina the Teenage Witch,* starring Melissa Joan Hart, premiered on the WB network. The character was created for the *Archie* comic books and was featured in a 1971 cartoon series. In the live-action series, Sabrina matured into an attractive young woman, and her latest challenge, besides curbing her benevolent witchy powers, was living on her own while pursuing a career in journalism.

Challenging evil and overcoming its wrath is the domain of the crusading witches in *Charmed* (WB, TNT, 1998). The three crusading young witches—Phoebe, Piper, Prue (deceased), and Paige—abide by the motto "The power of three will set you free." Quite a mission for three young women who must save the world!

While witches and genies romped through the sitcoms of television land, empowered to create their own world driven by flights of fancy, writers and producers looked toward the heavens for other characters who could conjure up an equal amount of chuckles from the audience. They literally found a vehicle for such comedy in a show called *My Favorite Martian* (CBS, 1963–66). Of course, Hollywood had a fascination with aliens and Martians, making movies about their visits to earth. In some instances their interpretation was hostile, with the aliens taking on grotesque shapes. However, Ray Walston, who played Exodus in *My Favorite Martian,* had a human appearance; spoke English; was telepathic; had kinesthetic abilities; and, of course, could become invisible. His one-man space capsule had crash-landed, and newspaper reporter Timothy O'Hara, played by Bill Bixby, befriended him and had him move into his apartment in Mrs. Brown's rooming house under the guise of his Uncle Martin. Of course, Tim thought he had the story of a lifetime, but "Uncle Martin" would not admit to being an alien to anyone but Tim. In its three years the series produced 107 episodes, and in 1999 it became a theatrical feature film.

Fairy tales are a part of classical literature, and from them children delight in the human qualities that animals assume. They talk and have families, behaving like people that children and adults can identify with. Although television cartoons, theatrical features, and some movies made for television have included fantasy characters and themes, there was one live television series, *Mister Ed,* that featured a talking horse.

The pilot program for the series was entitled "The Wonderful World of Wilbur Pope" and was produced by veteran comedian George Burns. It was never broadcast, and in 1961 *Mister Ed* became a syndicated television series. Produced by Filmways Pictures, it was picked up by CBS, making its debut on October 1, 1961, and ending its run on September 4, 1966.

After moving to a farm, architect Wilbur Post, played by Alan Young, finds a chatty palomino in his barn who will talk only to him. Soon, to the surprise of his wife, Carol, played by Connie Hines, he moves his architect table into the barn to carry on regular conversations with Ed. In addition to talking, Mister Ed has an adventurous side, aspiring to human activities like driving and surfing.

Of course, one could analyze this kind of relationship as being dysfunctional and deranged; however, at the time of *Mister Ed,* America was a nation facing civil unrest, assassinations, and the quagmire of Vietnam. Talking to an animal who had good "horse sense" could be far more rewarding than communicating with people. The audience seemed to agree, and the show won a Golden Globe award in 1963. The familiar voice of Mister Ed was provided by actor Allan "Rocky" Lane. Prior to *Mister Ed,* adults on live-action programs frequently talked to animal puppets, like on the programs *Andy's Gang; Kukla, Fran, and Ollie;* and later on *The Muppet Show.* Also, live-action talking animals have been prominent in television commercials and featured in movies like *Babe.*

Monsters of all shapes, sizes, and personalities have inhabited literature and the screens of American film. Such classic performances as Boris Karloff as Frankenstein and Bella Lugosi as Dracula are coveted as the personification of how horror can fascinate audiences. But television's sitcom monsters had a different agenda. They wanted to pursue their ghoulish ways while attempting to be part of mainstream society.

One of the most successful of these television adaptations was inspired by a series of cartoons by Charles Addams that ran in the *New Yorker.* It featured a family of ghouls who were a loveable lot that became television's first regularly scheduled monsters of mayhem. *The Addams Family* ran on NBC from 1964 to 1966, featuring some very unique characters, including Morticia (Carolyn Jones); Gomez (John Astin); Uncle Fester (Jackie Coogan); the children, Pugsley and Wednesday; Lurch, the seven-foot butler; and Thing, a disembodied hand that lived in a black box.

The concept eventually led to the development of five television shows, three live-action and two animated, and two feature-length theatrical films, *The Addams Family* (1991) and *Addams Family Values* (1993). The films starred Anjelica Huston as Morticia and Raul Julia as Gomez. The first animated series appeared on NBC from 1973 to 1975 (64 episodes, plus one special in 1977) while the second cartoon featuring Addams characters was broadcast on ABC from 1992 to 1995.

Television audiences enjoyed the quirky nature of these fiendish, good-natured demons, and *The Munsters* (1964–66) made its debut almost simultaneously with *The Addams Family*. It was developed and produced by Joe Connelly and Bob Mosher, veteran television producer-writers of *Amos 'n' Andy* and *Leave It to Beaver*. The writing was sharp, and the programs had lots of funny sight gags. The head of the family, Herman Munster, was portrayed by Fred Gwynne, who starred in a successful earlier series, *Car 54, Where Are You?* Veteran screen actress Yvonne DeCarlo played Herman's wife, Lily, and Al Lewis played Grandpa. In addition to the television series, there was a theatrical feature film, *Munster Go Home,* and two television movies, *The Munsters' Revenge* and *The New Munsters.*

Some of the fanciful situation comedies were silly and devoid of any substance, yet they became very popular with television audiences. An example from the school of the absurd is the sitcom *Gilligan's Island* (CBS, 1964–67). When it premiered, the critics scathingly condemned it. The *San Francisco Chronicle* echoed what many other newspapers wrote: "It marks a new low in the networks' estimate of public intelligence."

The series was created by Sherwood and Elroy Schwartz and had the well-worn premise of seven people getting stranded on an uncharted island. The twist was that the individuals marooned on *Gilligan's Island* were distinctly different from each other, with some being so vacuous as to have few redeeming qualities. Also, they were off on a three-hour pleasure cruise when their small craft was hit by a hurricane. There was the billionaire couple, Thurston Howell III and his upwardly mobile, socially prominent wife, Lovey (Jim Backus, the voice of cartoon character Mister Magoo, and Natalie Schafer); the sexy movie star, Ginger Grant (Tina Louise); the Professor, Dr. Roy Hinkley (Russell Johnson); the innocent girl from Kansas, Mary Ann Summers (Dawn Wells); the skipper of the SS *Minnow,* Jonas Grumby (Alan Hale Jr.); and, of course, his "little buddy" and first mate, the hapless Gilligan (Bob Denver, who was also in *The Many Loves of Dobie Gillis*).

Although it was successful as a first-run series, *Gilligan's Island* became one of the most profitable syndicated television programs. There were 98 episodes, 36 black and white and 62 color. There were also three television movies, *Rescue from Gilligan's Island* (1978), *The Castaways on Gilligan's Island* (1979), and *The Harlem Globetrotters on Gilligan's Island* (1981). In addition to the live-action features, there were also two animated films, *The New Adventures of Gilligan's Island* (ABC, 1974) and *Gilligan's Planet*

(CBS, 1982). In hindsight it's interesting to note that *Survivor*, the hit reality program on CBS, used the same concept as *Gilligan's Island*, isolating a group of disparate individuals on an island or another remote area while testing their survival instincts, ingenuity, and camaraderie. Maybe the concept wasn't so silly after all.

What with ingratiating ghouls, bickering castaways, and talking horses, it didn't take long to come up with *My Mother the Car*. This time it was Jerry Van Dyke as Dave Crabtree, who is the lucky soul and the only person who is able to hear the voice of his reincarnated mother (voice of Ann Sothern, from *Private Secretary*) through the car radio of a 1928 Porter convertible. While car shopping with his family for a station wagon, Dave spots the old Porter and buys it. Although the show was ridiculed for its banality, it had the cachet of two Emmy Award–winning writers, Allan Burns and Chris Heyward of *He and She* and *The Mary Tyler Moore Show*.

The critics were unforgiving in their condemnation of the show and its attempt to combine the "U.S. fascination with cars, sex and Mom," labeling it as one of the worst television series of all time. For Jerry Van Dyke, Dick's brother, it was another disappointment in his career.

The success of *Mister Ed* brought about the creation of *Me and the Chimp* (CBS, 1972), which competed with *My Mother the Car* for worst-program status. As star of the show, Ted Bessell was well known to television audiences through his five years in the role of Donald Hollinger, Marlo Thomas's boyfriend in *That Girl*. That series had a successful five-year run, which was ended by Ms. Thomas's decision not to continue in the series. CBS offered Bessell a lucrative contract to star in *Me and the Chimp* six months after *That Girl* left the network schedule.

The premise was simple. Suburban dentist Mike Reynolds's (Bessell) two children find a "stray" chimpanzee, and he and his wife, Liz (Anita Gillette), allow the children to keep it as a pet. Hiding it from the neighbors, he's perpetually engaged in trying to keep the animal secret while tending to the mishaps it causes. The original title of the program was *The Chimp and I*, but Bessell wouldn't take second billing to a toddling primate, and so the title was changed.

Like *My Mother the Car*, this series also had good "bones," having been created by Garry Marshall and Tom Miller, who were responsible for the hits *Happy Days* and *Laverne and Shirley*. For Bessell, *Me and the Chimp* sank his career, and he eventually became a television director on programs like *The Tracey Ullman Show*.

One of the more quirky and successful sitcoms of the 1990s that owed an allegiance to those of the 1960s was *3rd Rock from the Sun*. The concept had been done before: aliens trying to behave like humans but not with such verve and style. It also owed a debt of gratitude to *The Beverly Hillbillies*, which had aliens of a sort in the affluent and conceited world of Beverly Hills.

When *3rd Rock* premiered in the winter of 1996, NBC had achieved considerable success with cutting-edge, youthful sitcoms showcasing the humor and acerbic wit of Manhattan singles, which included *Seinfeld, Mad about You,* and *Friends.* Although it was out of place, in context the writing was sharp and the humor, without much subtext, was downright funny. The casting was an inspiration, with John Lithgow as Dick Solomon, the leader and college-professor poseur; Kristen Johnston as Sally, the sexy, beautiful female alien; William Shatner as the lecherous, drunken boss alien; French Stewart as the dull Harry; and Joseph Gordon-Levitt as Tommy, the boy. The featured humans were played by Jane Curtin (as Dr. Albright) and Wayne Knight (as Don Leslie Orville, the overweight cop). Interestingly, Jane Curtin had been a regular on *Saturday Night Live* when the concept of "The Cone Heads" was born. They also were aliens hoping to take over Earth when they crash-land and must adapt to their new environment as pseudohumans in suburban New Jersey. It was released as a feature film in 1993.

The series had originally been developed at ABC with the husband-and-wife creative team of Terry and Bonnie Turner. However, NBC felt so

"In the 1970s the traditional standup comedy of Bob Hope and Jack Benny led to the more irreverent style of *Saturday Night Live.*" (Photofest.)

strongly about *3rd Rock* that they managed to squire it away. The series ran for six years and was canceled in May 2001 after occupying 13 different time slots. Perhaps Jeff Zucker, the president of NBC entertainment, aptly described the show when he announced its cancellation.

We're grateful to "Third Rock's" producers and the out-of-this-world cast, who provided NBC with so many seasons of sheer lunacy. Their loopy and creative humor will make this one of the classic series of the 1990's.[5]

## SITCOMS AND THE NUCLEAR FAMILY

As the sitcom evolved as a popular television genre, it created its own mythology about family life. Shows like *Father Knows Best, The Donna Reed Show,* and *The Adventures of Ozzie and Harriet* reflected the values of traditional families, albeit in a highly stylized way. Family values became a resounding theme of the 1970s and 1980s with programs like *The Waltons* and *The Cosby Show* celebrating family tradition and the bonds they forge. In time, however, television producers also found value in pursuing what they considered then as nontraditional families led by single men or women, on programs like *My Three Sons* and *Julia.* And so, over time, television has explored the configuration of the American family, attempting to imbue it with the sensibilities of a culture that evokes less cohesive stability in family life. Indeed, according to the 2001 U.S. census, traditional families with married couples and children are no longer the predominant family structure, whereas single-parent households are.

In the fall season of 2001, Children Now, an advocacy group that measures and analyzes media content targeted at children, found that only 11 percent of recurring television characters on the six networks are parents. Indeed, the trend of urban, hip shows like *Seinfeld* and *Friends* are clearly an indication supporting the data compiled by Children Now.

Network television has long portrayed the dysfunctional nature of families in its daytime serial dramas, but it also has integrated those themes and others into prime-time situation comedies. Of course, the pioneering television program in departing from the traditions of family was *All in the Family.*

The 2001–2002 television season was indicative in demonstrating these trends. On *The Bernie Mac Show,* a Fox sitcom featuring the comedian of the same name, a childless couple (by choice) becomes the instant parents of three children, nieces and nephews, after the children's mother enters rehab. At the WB network, a surprise hit of the season was the show *Reba,* starring country-music singer Reba McEntire. She plays a suburban Texas soccer mom who is facing the disintegration of a 20-year marriage to her dentist husband, who has impregnated his young dental hygienist. As she struggles to hold her family together, she must deal with her 17-year-old daughter's pregnancy, have her future dimwitted high-school jock son-in-law move in, and endure the abuse of her 12-year-old daughter, who is having a difficult time facing puberty. This sounds, of course, like the well-explored landscape of soap opera, but the writing is sharp with veteran producer Allison M. Gibson (*Home Improvement* and *Boy Meets World*) at the helm.

The concept of family is one that takes on different dimensions within the orientation of character and structure. This is the case of *Malcolm in the Middle,* about a neurotic family with a chaotic lifestyle. Malcolm, portrayed by Frankie Muniz, is a gifted child in a dysfunctional family. His older and favorite brother Francis is boarded at a military school to keep him out of trouble but is always getting into difficult situations. Malcolm's take on being assigned to the gifted Krelboyne class after he is tested with an IQ of 165 is "Around here being intelligent is exactly the same as being radioactive." His parents, Hal (Bryan Cranston) and Lois (Jane Kaczmarek), exhibit somewhat bizarre behavior, like when Lois thinks Monday is Sunday and keeps Malcolm, his older brother Reese (Justin Berfield), and younger brother, Dewey (Erik Per Sullivan), home from school.

In *Everybody Loves Raymond,* creator Philip Rosenthal came up with a smart, quirky sitcom starring comedian Ray Romano and Patricia Heaton as middle-class suburban Long Island couple Ray and Debra Barone. They have twin toddler sons and a daughter. He's a sportswriter and she's a full-time mother. The series presents the subtext of marriage and the tensions that prevail. Of course, there are the meddlesome and bickering in-laws, Marie and Frank Barone, Ray's parents, played with a sparring allure by Doris Roberts and Peter Boyle. The writing is harsh yet funny. In one scene Marie is in Debra's kitchen washing dishes as Debra and Ray are getting ready to leave. Debra tells Marie not to bother with the dishes, and Marie responds with a terse, "Even the ants are laughing." Ray's parents live across the street with Ray's unmarried brother, a little too close for comfort for Debra. Ray's older brother, Robert (Brad Garrett), is a New York City cop. It's a marriage under siege, which creator Phillip Rosenthal has conceived as an adult sitcom with discussions about sex (she's "too tired") and domestic responsibility (he's "too busy").

There have been other adult sitcoms that evolved around the lives of a young professional married couple. One of the most notable of these was *The Dick Van Dyke Show,* starring the actor of the same name and Mary Tyler Moore. At times this show was zany, poignant, and physically funny. Its supporting cast included television pioneers Mory Amsterdam, Carl Reiner, and Rose Marie. The show was created by Carl Reiner and based upon his life as a comedy writer and comedian and was produced by veteran actor-producer Sheldon Leonard.

As Rob Petrie, Dick Van Dyke portrayed a comedy writer for *The Alan Brady Show,* with Carl Reiner playing Brady. Rob's wife, Mary Tyler Moore, was one of the last of 60 actresses to be considered for the part. Indeed, at one time the producers considered Johnny Carson for the role of Rob Petrie.

The show premiered on October 3, 1961, and ran for three months from 8:00 to 8:30 on Tuesday nights. That time period was considered too early in the evening for an adult sitcom, and the show followed a rerun of *Gunsmoke* and didn't even place in the top-70 program list. After three months of dismal ratings, *The Dick Van Dyke Show* was moved to Wednesdays from 9:30 to 10:00, following *Checkmate*, and then followed *The Beverly Hillbillies* after *Checkmate* was canceled.

It wasn't until the new season that *The Dick Van Dyke Show* would follow *The Beverly Hillbillies.* Prior to that CBS considered canceling the show. Its producer, Sheldon Leonard, convinced the network to allow the show to run another season. He was assisted by the advertiser Procter and Gamble, which threatened to withdraw its advertising from the CBS schedule of daytime soap operas if a place for *The Dick Van Dyke Show* was not found on the fall schedule.

In a tribute to the style and humor of *The Dick Van Dyke Show,* comedian Paul Reiser modeled his adult sitcom *Mad about You* (1992–99) after its predecessor. In one segment the reference is clearly visible, when Reiser's character, Paul Buchman, who is a documentary-film producer, interviews "celebrity" Alan Brady, the Carl Reiner character from the original *Dick Van Dyke Show.*

Another sitcom with a *Dick Van Dyke* twist, *Imagine That* (originally *The Hank Azaria Show*), with Hank Azaria playing Josh, a comedy writer, premiered on NBC in January 2002. Dealing with a somewhat unstable marriage, Josh creates fantasy characters similar to those on *Ally McBeal* to relieve the stress at home and at work. These sketch characters include a caricature of a marriage counselor, whom he imagines as a macho, smart-ass, gold-chained therapist as the couple awaits their turn. The show attempts to combine sketch comedy with the dynamics of a fantasy environment, with characters that may be more suitable for a cartoon than a live sitcom.

## TRIED AND NOT SO TRUE

Television-sitcom-land has its own set of values that at times measures its creativity by its association with the past. This attitude is embodied in the perception of talent and the programming vehicles that are created for them. In typical fashion, there is a bias toward established actors from movies or television who have successfully navigated the orbit of stardom. However, the attempt to nurture success based upon past performance has repeatedly failed to attract an audience.

Establishing a starring role for a costar of a successful television sitcom series has been a popular technique in television for decades. Actors have been successfully cloned into roles that their characters have popularized in the original series. Those efforts have been less successful when costars are taken out of character and moved to a new environment embedded in an unfamiliar dynamic. That's what happened to John Goodman, who played Dan Conner on *Roseanne,* and Michael Richards, who played Kramer on *Seinfeld*. Both actors created memorable, enormously popular characters, but their attempt to redefine themselves as distinctly different individuals met with utter failure.

In the 2000 sitcom *Normal, Ohio,* John Goodman portrayed Butch, an openly gay man who returned to his hometown to live and interact with his ex-wife, son, parents, and friends. Although the setting is different, Butch still had the blue-collar values and even a wardrobe similar to Dan's. Beside the strained gay jokes and the choppy writing, the audience wouldn't separate Goodman's Butch from Dan, the character they had a relationship with.

That same year, *The Michael Richards Show* premiered and was also short-lived. Although Richards played the hapless private eye Vic Nardozza, the seeds of *Seinfeld*'s Kramer were prominently portrayed. In an attempt to limit their risk, the producers and writers failed to create a clear delineation between Vic and Kramer, sharing the nuances for both characters. Morphing Kramer's character into a private detective was a stretch for the viewer's imagination, and the show was eventually canceled after nine episodes.

With the Boot Hill of sitcoms littered with monuments to the fallen heroes of television, the quest to create derivative television programming vehicles for movie stars is equally challenging. Making the transition from the larger-than-life theatrical movie screen to the smaller, more intimate television tube can be a sobering experience for a celebrity. Classic film stars like James Stewart, Loretta Young, and Dorothy Malone had difficulty transferring their large-screen personas to television. However, Robert Young was a television sensation with *Father Knows Best* and *Marcus Welby, M.D.,* two long-running television series. Conversely, television actors have also found it difficult to move to theatrical features. Some have had it easier than others, like James Garner and Steve McQueen.

For Bette Midler, Geena Davis, and Gabriel Byrne, the move to television was surely a sobering one. In the fall of 2000 each of them starred in their own sitcom: *Bette, The Geena Davis Show,* and *Madigan Men,* respectively. With the first two titles defining the personality of the headliner, the audience expectation was predetermined.

In *The Geena Davis Show,* Ms. Davis played Teddie Cochran, owner of a public-relations firm, who is living with her widowed boyfriend (soon to be her husband) and two of his children: Eliza, a cute 6-year-old girl, and Carter, a precocious 13-year-old boy. She's a miniskirted, well-coiffed woman with an eye trained on her lover and career. The concept was a simple one: take a sophisticated New York single woman and have her meet an attractive widower and become an instant mom. But it was old hat, formulaic and all too familiar. The writing, according to critic John Carman, "is only a click above dreadful." Davis played a harried, somewhat frenzied professional, the type who leaves for breakfast half-dressed in a cheeky nightshirt. She's also the one who, while on a family sing-along in their van, doesn't know the words to the songs. The critics panned the show: "By dint of her dimples, Geena Davis keeps her new ABC comedy from being the unqualified disaster it otherwise is. 'The Geena Davis Show' is the most insulting and condescending of the season's new series."[6]

One of the most anticipated new sitcom series of the 2000 television season was *Bette,* starring the actress and comedienne Bette Midler. Both CBS and Columbia Tri-Star had huge hopes for the failed show. In this iteration Midler played herself, a star balancing work and family. A documentary about the actress would probably have been more funny than the sitcom. The writers and producers tried to take a page from reality and create a fiction from the character of a popular living celebrity.

Early in the season there were problems with the show. The daughter Rose, originally played by Lindsay Lohan, was replaced by Marina Malota. Then, after 10 episodes, Robert Dunn, who played Bette's husband, Oscar, left after a disagreement about the direction his character was taking. The actor Robert Hays, who replaced Dunn, may go down in the *Guinness Book of World Records* as the shortest-lived costar in a prime-time network sitcom, as he made his debut in March on the same day the show was canceled. Although the series had a 22-episode commitment, it was canceled after 18 shows.

The writing showed a lack of imagination and used tedious, hackneyed allusions to a scatterbrained female character who hammered and stomped on frozen waffles and was obsessed and self-absorbed. Although the characterization of women as scatterbrained and domestically challenged was popularized successfully on television by Lucille Ball, that era ended long ago, and women are now portrayed as savvy and career-oriented. Perhaps Midler said it best during a November 2000 appearance on *The David Letterman Show,* when she dissed her starring vehicle as "the lowest thing that ever happened to me in my life . . . I'm like a dung beetle pushing this ball of dung up a mountain."[7] One could not be more explicit than that.

Another sitcom, *Madigan Men,* starred film actor Gabriel Byrne as Ben Madigan, a divorced architect living with his dad and teenage son. Although it tried to touch upon contemporary themes, *Madigan Men* appeared to be a throwback to male-lead sitcoms of yesteryear like Danny Thomas's *Make Room for Daddy.* In a scene where Ben talks to his son about his relationship with his ex-wife's boyfriend, he nervously adds too much sugar to his coffee. An audience raised on sitcom humor can anticipate what may happen next. It's an old routine, dating back to the Three Stooges and the Marx Brothers.

Of course, the program also had the office-pal loser who tells Ben how to get dates. As the father, Roy Dotrice mimics every clichéd reference to an Irish dad perpetuated by the myths of the movies. The series didn't last long and was an early casualty of the 2000 television season.

When the 2001 television season approached, the broadcast networks were once again saluting established celebrities and hoping for shooting stars. They were looking toward Jason Alexander, who played George Costanza on *Seinfeld;* Emeril Lagasse, the noted television chef; Ellen DeGeneres; and Academy Award–winning actor Richard Dreyfus.

On the ABC sitcom *Bob Patterson,* Alexander played a successful dysfunctional motivational guru whose personal life is a mess. He's ranked the third best in the country, and his manager, Landau, played by actor Robert Klein, wants him to try harder and become number two. Added to his troubles is that his beautiful ex-wife (Jennifer Aspen) wants to move back with him and practice celibacy. And the writers, in an attempt to accommodate the physically challenged, race, and gender, created Claudia, Bob's newly hired black wheelchair-bound secretary, played with a tough edge by Chandra Wilson. The concept was a stretch, and although Bob displayed some of the same neuroses as George Costanza, the routine writing and stale humor were enough to keep audiences away. The average audience for the show on ABC was near 7 million, barely a blip on the ratings radar screen. It was canceled after five episodes.

For Julia Louis-Dreyfus, another *Seinfeld* alumnus, the rigors of re-creating herself as Ellie for her sitcom *Watching Ellie* was a challenging effort. Undaunted by the failure and wreck of her former *Seinfeld* costars, the show made its debut in February 2002 to good reviews. Her husband, Brad Hall, who created the short-lived *Single Guy,* is the creative force behind *Watching Ellie.* Its premise was a narrative depiction of real-time events in Ellie's life as a clock in the corner of the screen counted down the 22 minutes in each episode.

Ratings for the program were impressive: 17 million viewers its first week and a 7.1 rating among adults 18–49. However, afterward there was a precipitous drop, and by March 2002 there was a decline to 9.5 million viewers with a rating of 3.6 among the 18–49 group, a drop of 50 percent from the opening week. Once again the aura of *Seinfeld* was being tested, and after a hiatus the series returned in spring 2003.[8]

What happens when you take an experienced chef with no acting credits and poor comic timing and make him a star of a prime-time network sitcom? You have a recipe for disaster. That was what was served up on NBC's *Emeril,* starring television chef Emeril Lagasse. With just a million more viewers than *Bob Patterson, Emeril* was sinking faster than a falling soufflé.

The popular New Orleans chef, who has created an industry of books, videos, and restaurants, could not conjure up the right ingredients for the show even with the help of master producer-writers Harry and Linda Bloodworth-Thomason. The concept for *Emeril* evolved around his cooking show and was about as exciting as a wilted string bean. One episode dealt with the cast being stranded on the set overnight during a snowstorm. Unfortunately, talented actor Robert Urich, cast as Jerry McKenney, was wasted on this show. In *Emeril,* Mr. Lagasse clearly demonstrated the "fish out of water" adage, and should have never left his studio kitchen.

During the 2001 television season, CBS was the only broadcast television network to have some sitcom success with established stars. One of these was *The Ellen Show,* starring Ellen DeGeneres as Ellen Richmond, a gay former dot-com executive who returns to her small hometown of Clark after her company goes bust. The theme sounds curiously similar to the previous season's gay-themed failure, *Normal, Ohio.* In this reincarnation, noted actress Cloris Leachman portrays Ellen's eccentric mom. Once home, she lives with her mom and unlucky-in-love sister, Catherine, played by Emily Rutherford. Needing to find meaningful employment, she returns to her old high school, where Mr. Munn, played by Martin Mull, is still the principal, and she is hired as a guidance counselor. Of course, there's a former beau, Rusty, portrayed by Jim Gaffigan, who was Ellen's prom date and is in denial about Ellen's sexual inclinations. He just doesn't seem to get it! And Ellen has come out for faculty, family, and friends.

According to the producers, the emphasis on Ellen's being gay was played down for the show—probably because the original *Ellen* experienced a precipitous decline in ratings during its final 1997 season, when Ellen emerged from the closet—but in an early episode of the new show, Ellen does have a "close encounter" with a lesbian gym teacher. According to Ms. DeGeneres, she wanted her show to be more wholesome and traditional. "The shows I loved growing up and want to emulate are things like 'The Mary Tyler Moore Show' and 'Carol Burnett,' good old-fashioned shows where you're not doing something that's mean-spirited."[9] In January 2002 the show was placed on hiatus after production of 18 of the 22 scheduled episodes.

As *The Ellen Show* demonstrated, even a former sitcom television star with a proven track record is vulnerable to failure. For actor Ted Danson, the sitcom rewards were sweet. As the star of *Cheers,* portraying former baseball player Sam "Mayday" Malone, Danson logged more than 10 years (1982–93) as a sitcom star. His return to sitcom television as Mike Logan in the ill-fated *Ink* (1996–97) once again demonstrated the risks of television and changing audience tastes. The show was about a newly divorced couple (Danson and Mary Steenburgen, who played Danson's wife), both journalists working at the same newspaper; through a series of coincidences, she winds up being his boss. But Danson was determined to return to the small screen (he had a part in the blockbuster *Saving Private Ryan*).

In 1998 Ted Danson returned in *Becker,* a CBS sitcom about a cantankerous, dedicated doctor, John Becker, who runs a practice in the Bronx and readily speaks his mind. Although he has a gruff exterior, Dr. Becker has an endearing manner toward his patients and friends. Although somewhat conventional, with a cast of predictable characters like Jake (Alex Desert), the blind local newsstand proprietor, the show was a successful vehicle for Danson's return to prime-time network sitcoms.

Creating a new television sitcom is associated with all kinds of risk. Scheduling and competition can kill even the best concept with the biggest star.

So when CBS decided on *The Education of Max Bickford,* starring Academy Award winner Richard Dreyfus, they had a celebrity, a good time period on Sunday nights after *60 Minutes* (formerly occupied by *Touched by an Angel*), and a good concept.

As an aging widowed college professor at an all-girls school, Dreyfus, who has been passed up for promotion, is facing a midlife crises. Talent, of course, also helps, and he is surrounded by an excellent cast, including Eric Ian Goldberg as his wiseass son, Lester, and Katie Sackhoff as his rebellious daughter, Nell. Added to the dynamics of the show is Helen Shaver, who plays Max's best friend, who returns from a sabbatical as the transgender Erica. As they say in show business, the show had good "bones," and was created by Dawn Prestwich and Nicole Yorkin, whose credits included *Touched by an Angel, Judging Amy, Ally McBeal,* and *Chicago Hope.* During most of the 2001 season, the series had a very respectable audience of 14.6 million viewers. It also provided an alluring sense of compelling humor and drama to a television sitcom landscape predicated on sexual misanthropes guided by an innuendo of mediocrity. Unfortunately, intelligence and sophistication are not hallmarks of American sitcoms, and the series was canceled after one season.

One of the standout successes of the 2000–2002 television season was Larry David's HBO series *Curb Your Enthusiasm.* As a creator and writer for *Seinfeld,* Larry David showed a keen sense for wry humor, inventive comedy, and sarcasm. These qualities became a touchstone for his new series as creator, writer, and star. In it, David plays himself as a misanthrope who defies normal social conventions while pursuing a dynamic of confrontational misjudgment. On the golf course he won't retrieve a wayward golf ball because he doesn't care for the golfer's hat. He's hostile to a hostess at a dinner party, calling it "the dinner party from hell," and argues over the seating arrangement in a movie theater. All of these antics provide for an entertaining mix of witty comedy, funny situations, and sharp writing.

There's a great deal of cross-pollination between television and film, with television serving as a foundation for successful feature films (*The Fugitive, Mission Impossible, Maverick*) and vice versa (*M\*A\*S\*H, Ferris Bueller, Casablanca*—although the last two were not successful). The most recent example is *My Big Fat Greek Life* (CBS), which is based on the movie and features most of the actors from the film who portrayed the Portokalos family, including creator and star Nia Vardalos, Lainie Kazan, and Michael Constantine. A hit film doesn't necessarily guarantee that the television adaptation will be successful, because of the limitations that the small screen offers in time and space. However, the concept of the film owes a debt to the formulaic style of American sitcoms with its stereotypical humor and thin plot. Therefore, continuing the exploits of the family is more suitable for television than making a sequel to the film.

Another theatrical feature film, *Back to the Future,* influenced the development of two sitcoms, *Do Over* on the WB network and *That Was Then* on

The last episode of *M\*A\*S\*H*, "Goodbye, Farewell, and
Amen," was feature-movie-length. (Photofest.)

ABC, each making its debut in September 2002. In each case the main character is a disaffected thirtyish man who attempts to alter the present by changing the past. In *Do Over*, Joel Larson (Penn Badgley) is returned to the year
1981 and his status as a high-school student and attempts to change the
events that shaped his life. In another twist, he's a 34-year-old man trapped
in a 14-year-old body, hinting at the movie *Big*, where Tom Hanks portrayed
Josh Baskin, a child in a man's body. The premise for *That Was Then* had
Travis (James Bulliard) as a 30-year-old loser living with his mother and still
dreaming of his high-school sweetheart, who married his brother. In this
rendition of the *Back to the Future* theme, Travis moves back and forth in
time and sees how what he altered in the past doesn't really help in the
present.

Blue-collar comedy was created by Jackie Gleason's *Honeymooners* and had
a more modern iteration with *Roseanne*. The trend continued with *The King
of Queens* (CBS, 1998) starring stand-up comic and *Everybody Loves Raymond*
alumnus Kevin James as a parcel-delivery man living in the borough of
Queens, New York, who must endure living with his zany father-in-law (Jerry
Stiller).

Moving the blue-collar ethic to Chicago with a family called the Millers is the CBS comedy *Still Standing*. Of course, Bill Miller (Mark Addy) is laid back, and his wife, Judy, is the one with the firm hand. The "crises" the family faces include their teenage daughter wanting a belly-button ring and Judy's concern that her husband will intrude on her private sanctuary at the hair salon and violate the trusting bond that she shares with her hairdresser, Gary. What compelling narratives!

Lily tries to get her driver's license, Claudia plays a super-violent video game, and Sean worries about the beer distributor: these are some of the compelling narratives in the WB's *Grounded for Life,* another attempt at postulating the struggle of blue-collar life. In this version, Donald Logue plays Sean Finnerty, married at 18 with three children and a beautiful wife. And just like so many other family sitcoms, he has a misdirected brother, a meddling father, and three children who behave as if they're doing the parenting.

Upward mobility and dual ethnicity are the themes of the WB's *Greetings from Tucson,* about an ethnically mixed marriage—he's Mexican American and she's Irish Catholic, and dad just got a big promotion at the copper mine. Their 15-year-old son, David (Pablo Santos), tries to understand the nature of his combined heritage while his sister Maria denies her Mexican roots and tells everyone she's Spanish. There's also the matriarchal grandma, Magdalena, played by Lupe Ontiveros, who's aching to get out of the nursing home and move in with the family.

Ethnic mismatches are not new to sitcom-land, and one of the most glaring examples of disastrous failure is *Chicken Soup* (ABC, September–November 1989), starring comedian Jackie Mason and Lynn Redgrave. She played the Irish widow with three children, and he was the short Jewish bachelor next-door neighbor. Of course, he had a meddling Jewish mom and she was saddled with a bigoted brother. What else is new? Nothing in sitcom-land; it's all derivative.

Bringing back successful sitcoms with more current cultural themes is the métier of *Family Affair.* The original series, starring Brian Keith as uncle Bill Davis and Sebastian Cabot as his English butler, Mr. Giles French, ran from 1966 to 1971. On the WB network, actor Gary Cole portrays the single, affluent uncle Bill, who must care for his twin nieces, and Tim Curry plays his erstwhile butler.

## RESURRECTING A WINNER

Although many sitcoms are celebrity-driven and suffer the fate of cancellation after the star exits, there have been instances when a program manages to continue with a replacement in the lead. Such was the case with *Spin City,* which was created for Michael J. Fox and premiered on the CBS network in 1996. It became a hit for the network and a moneymaking asset for the production company, DreamWorks SKG.

When Fox left the series to battle Parkinson's disease, the studio was faced with the prospect of losing its only series on network television along with the loss of a syndication revenue stream. Fortunately, through a set of serendipitous circumstances, the actor Charlie Sheen was chosen to replace him. Although their style and technique are different and distinctive and Sheen was recovering from alcohol and drug abuse, his new character, Deputy Mayor Charlie Crawford, clicked with audiences and earned him a Golden Globe Award in 2002.[10]

## LIVING COLOR

As sitcoms evolved, they were defined by various cultural parameters that addressed business, personal, and professional lives. These constructs changed as American society moved into a dynamic of changing cultural mores, and minority groups, including blacks, became newly enfranchised. The television sitcom began to reflect the values and attitudes of young upwardly mobile blacks who were engaged in the struggle to succeed in white society.

The move of blacks into starring sitcom roles proceeded at a measured pace but was clearly articulated by creating leading roles for black comedians. This trend started in 1972 with the sitcom *Sanford and Son,* starring black comedian Redd Foxx (née John Elroy Sanford). After Foxx earned success as a nightclub performer with a lewd, vulgar, but funny act, producers Norman Lear and Bud Yorkin noted his portrayal of the elderly junk dealer in the movie *Cotton Comes to Harlem* and cast him as Fred Sanford. The producers had already parlayed talented black comedians into successful sitcoms, which included *The Jeffersons* and *Good Times,* and had licensed the successful format from the British producers of *Steptoe and Son,* which featured a cockney junk dealer. The program ran on NBC from 1972 to 1977 and became one of the most successful sitcoms on television. It also set a benchmark for being the first hit sitcom featuring a mostly black cast since the cancellation of *Amos 'n' Andy* nearly 20 years earlier.

The next ripple of change in black-oriented sitcoms came with the enormously popular *Cosby Show.* Although Bill Cosby had an excellent rapport with the American television audience, both black and white, his success as a leading character on television was less spectacular. His first starring vehicle, *I Spy* (1965–68), costarring with Robert Culp, was an audience-pleaser, but his later attempts, *The Bill Cosby Show* (1969), *The New Bill Cosby Show* (1972), and *Cos* (1976) were disappointing failures. When Marcy Carsey and Tom Werner, former programming executives at ABC, shopped the concept to the networks, only NBC was willing to commit. The rest, of course, is television history: broadcast from September 1984 to June 1992, a total of 200 episodes realized some of the highest sitcom ratings in television history.

It was a departure from other black-oriented sitcoms in that it stressed family values and challenged the stereotype of the dysfunctional black family, featuring a professional couple: Bill Cosby as a successful gynecologist and Phylicia Rashad as Clair, his wife, who was a practicing attorney. Although criticized for being just as homogenized as *Father Knows Best* and selling out to white sensibilities, the show nevertheless provided a benchmark of sophisticated humor nuanced by depth and character.

A sassy, more irreverent style associated with black sitcoms evolved in the 1990s. These shows featured successful black stand-up comics who integrated their cultural humor and body language into a genre of wisecracking, edgy comedy. One of the first was Martin Lawrence in *Martin* (1992–97), who portrayed Martin Payne, a clever Detroit talk-show host. His interaction with his buddies and girlfriend, Tisha (Gina Waters), provided for the funny dynamic among the characters.

In order to accommodate the needs of the talent, some of the program formats appeared familiar and contrived. In *The Hughleys* (1998–2002), starring D. L. Hughley, the character mix includes an amalgam of Archie Bunker and George Jefferson. Here, D. L. Hughley plays Darryl, a self-made, affluent businessman (vending machines) who moves his family to an upscale white neighborhood. There's a white couple, the Rogerses, who are neighbors that they befriend, and the requisite jokes associated with race and culture.

On the United Paramount Network (UPN) the Monday-night prime-time schedule is blocked with African American sitcoms, including *The Parkers, One on One,* and *Girlfriends,* each depicting a nuance of family life that challenges traditional norms. A spin-off of *Moesha, The Parkers* features Countess Vaughn as Kim Parker and Mo'Nique as Nikki Parker, a mother and daughter who compete for attention and classes at Santa Monica Junior College.

The premise of single parenthood is the theme for *One on One,* featuring Flex Alexander. He's a single dad who's a sportscaster active in the dating scene and raising a teen daughter, Breanna (Kyla Pratt). The two have a strong bond, and Dad is willing to give his daughter the freedom she expects providing she recognizes the consequences.

In *Girlfriends,* there's a sense of the daytime serial drama (soap opera) with its alluring women who struggle with the challenge of dating, drugs, marriage, and business. The series features Tracee Ellis Ross, Golden Brooks, Jill Marie Jones, and Persia White as friends who deal with the day-to-day dynamics of dealing with men, family, and their professional lives.

One of the most successful programs featuring a stand-up black comedian is *The Bernie Mac Show,* featuring comic Bernie Mac. When he and his sitcom wife (Kellita Smith) must raise his sister's three children, the dynamics challenge his traditional parenting views. It also crimps their style of living, as he is a successful stand-up comic and she's a busy corporate executive. There's a zany mood to the show, with the child actors very adept at stealing scenes.

Interestingly, *The Bernie Mac Show* has many similarities to *My Wife and Kids* (ABC), featuring comedian Damon Wayans as a successful owner of a delivery-truck company; his wife, Janet Marie (Tisha Campbell-Martin), a former homemaker who is transformed into a successful stockbroker; and three sassy children with more than enough attitude to go around. Once again it clearly articulates the premise that television sitcoms are derivative, with only a rare instance of originality.

In *Abby,* actress Sydney Poitier plays Abby Walker, a young, hip West Coast sports reporter who is living with her ex-boyfriend while pursuing other relationships. The story line has the weary familiarity of sitcom purgatory with her coanchor and best friend, Max Ellis (Randy J. Goodwin), who harbors a secret crush on her, and Abby's dealing with an overbearing boss, portrayed by Sean O'Bryan.

## FINAL EXIT

Television programs and characters have a unique ability to become an intimate part of a household and family. Today, the rituals of popular television programs include a farewell episode that provides closure for the audience. Popular sitcoms have earned blockbuster ratings in their final outings. These numbers are a testament to the close association that the audience has developed with the program and its stars.

In the early days of network television, when popular sitcoms ended, if there was any indication of their finality, it was a retrospective episode of scenes from the run of the series. It wasn't until 1967 that the television industry realized the psychological attachment that viewers cultivated with what they saw on television.

After a spectacular five-year run, *The Fugitive,* on ABC, was ending because David Janssen, portraying Dr. Richard Kimble, was leaving the series. No one at the network except Leonard Goldberg, president of programming at ABC, wanted to mark the occasion as a special event. At the time it was a novel idea to write and produce a program that would wrap up the thematic components of the series. The show had been so popular that viewers were at the edge of their seats to learn the truth about the one-armed man.

Since such an event had never been created for a series ending, Goldberg confronted a lot of resistance from ABC. He was determined to bring *The Fugitive* to resolution and closure. "I said we owe it to the people who have been watching for four years to complete the circle for them. I was kind of a lone voice. People at the network said, 'They don't care, they just watch it.' "[11]

Executives at the network also expressed concerns about what they perceived to be the diminished value of the series if the suspense was removed because of the resolution of the conflict. The network felt that if the audience knew what happened at the end of the series, viewers would not tune into prime-time summer reruns or daytime broadcasts.

ABC finally acquiesced to Goldberg's request but scheduled the two-part series finale in the summer "ghetto" of television, late August, after summer reruns had been completed. When the ratings came in for the final episode, Goldberg's prescience proved to be right on target. It was broadcast on August 29, 1967, and was watched by 45.9 percent of homes with television. It held the audience record for 13 years until the final episode of *Dallas,* "Who Shot J. R.?," was broadcast in 1980.

While it was dramatic television that created the concept of resolving program issues to a conclusion, sitcoms have adapted this programming technique with great success. Final sitcom episodes have attempted to place characters and themes into a denouement of resolution, like the firing of the newsroom staff of WJM on *The Mary Tyler Moore Show.* For *The Odd Couple,* Felix Unger moved out of Oscar Madison's apartment and remarried his ex-wife. In the sitcom *M\*A\*S\*H,* the final episode was feature-movie length and entitled, "Goodbye, Farewell, and Amen." Following the series for 10 years, viewers were anxious to see the end, and CBS anticipated its popularity by charging advertisers $450,000 for a 30-second spot. There was also a lot of audience interest in the final episode of *Seinfeld,* which was the number-one-rated program when it ended its run in 1998. In *Seinfeld*'s case, viewers and critics were disappointed with the episode, indicating how anticipation can result in frustration.[12]

## COMFORT TV

Television has often been referred to as the *electronic hearth.* This description became even more relevant after the events of September 11. The sitcoms of television's past offered audiences a return to a time of idyllic innocence and mirth. Returning to the adventures of the Ricardos and the Mertzes, the sheer buffoonery of the Clampetts, the nebbishness of Barney Fife, and the charm of Mary Richards provided a safety net from fear and apprehension.

While some may mock that time of virtue as being an unrealistic portrayal of American culture, the programs and characters demonstrated a singular commitment to American values. As the character of television programming has evolved into a more issue-oriented, thematic, journalistic style taken from screaming headlines, some of its content has become more confrontational and hostile.

The tragedy of September 11 unfolded on television screens across America, and the world's eyes were glued to the TV in disbelief, fear, and anger. After such an event, critics wondered if America would laugh again. Of course, Americans are resilient and become strong in the face of adversity. But there was also a television programming archive of humor and fun that could inspire and comfort.

Nostalgia has become a programming niche on television. There is American Movie Classics (AMC) on cable, along with Turner Classic Movies. Vintage television programming is represented by TV Land (owned by Viacom's MTV Networks), the Cartoon Network, and the Sci Fi Channel. On the

The cast of *Seinfeld* (left to right): Julia Louis-Dreyfus (as Elaine), Jerry Seinfeld (as Jerry), Michael Richards (as Kramer), and Jason Alexander (as George). (Photofest.)

Cartoon Network one can follow the antics of Barney in *The Flintstones,* and on the Sci Fi Channel audiences can return to Rod Serling's chilling tales from *The Twilight Zone.* Of these networks, TV Land is solely dedicated to distributing classic television programs. And their popularity has grown over the years and become more accelerated after September 11.

Even for generations of viewers who weren't born at the time of *I Love Lucy, The Andy Griffith Show,* or *The Beverly Hillbillies,* there is an association based upon generational influence. The stylistic humor is a lingua franca of comedy that viewers young and old can enjoy. Often they had no agenda nor did they attempt any substantive commentary about life and family. Yes, they were wholesome and sometimes unforgivably silly and bland. However, their redemption was a simplicity that left viewers with a beguiling sense of security. Those early sitcoms indulged our sense of fantasy with a narrative tradition that provided an essence of whimsy that explored the limits of humor. Whether it was folksy or physical pie-in-your-face sketch comedy, it provided viewers with distraction and fun.

In times of crisis, people retreat into the familiarity of routines that provide comfort and security. They want to feel safe within the boundaries of their environment and interact with those things that have virtue and that they trust. Television is, of course, a window on the world, but it is also an archive resonating with sounds and visions from another time. One day what we see today will be a part of the visions of tomorrow and provide others with a sense of calm, trust, and faith.

## LANGUAGE, SEX, AND VIOLENCE

Advertisers are concerned about gratuitous sex and violence on television, and although defining *family* is difficult, they nevertheless became advocates for family programming by creating the Family Friendly Programming Forum, an endowment for script development and scholarships. Sponsored by the Association of National Advertisers (ANA), the Forum seeks the development of programs that deal with issues in a family-friendly way and cites role models such as *The Cosby Show* and *Seventh Heaven*.

Indeed, the ANA initiative was greeted by both houses of Congress with a joint resolution commending the group of 33 advertisers for undertaking an active role in the development of more family-friendly programming. The text for the congressional joint resolution was sponsored by Senators George Voinovich (R-OH) and Joe Lieberman (D-CT) along with Representatives Rob Portman (R-OH) and Ed Markey (D-MA). Senator Voinovich placed the mission of the Forum within the context of America's children.

Since the future of our country depends upon our children, we must do all that we can to limit their exposure to negative influences and provide them with as safe and nurturing an environment as possible. Therefore I encourage efforts that will expand the number of quality family programs that are shown on television, and I congratulate The Forum for Family Friendly Programming on their leadership towards that goal.[13]

Some of the corporate sponsors of the Family Friendly Programming Forum include the largest multinational corporations in the world: the Procter and Gamble Company, Ford Motor Company, General Motors Corporation, Hershey Foods Corporation, Johnson and Johnson, IBM, Kellogg Company, and the Coca-Cola Company.

With its endorsement of the script-development fund, the Forum provides seed money for the creation of family-friendly scripts. The money is given to networks and production companies for writing scripts and for the production of a pilot program. If the pilot is picked up by the network, the money is reimbursed to the fund for the funding of other projects. The first sitcom produced from the fund was *Gilmore Girls* on the WB, which was a charter member, along with ABC, CBS, and NBC.

American radio and television have a rich tradition of humor associated with situation comedies. They can be a reflection of cultural mores that imbue their audience with irreverence about traditions and values. As society evolved into a more permissive environment, sitcoms mirrored those changes. We moved from the innocence of *Leave It to Beaver* to the adult-oriented themes and promiscuity of *Coupling*. Yet each generation defines its own sensibilities and virtues in the sitcoms that they want to see. Roles for men and women are viewed in different ways, with gender and sexuality being articulated within the context of a new dynamic. As a genre, the sitcom is an enduring part of American culture and plays into the dynamics of the moment. Its situations, characters, and plots may be ritualistic, but are nevertheless a signpost for change.

## NOTES

1. Jess Oppenheimer, *Laughs, Luck . . . and Lucy*, with Gregg Oppenheimer (New York: Syracuse University Press, 1996); Bart Andrews, *The I Love Lucy Book* (New York: Doubleday, 1985); Joyce Millman, "The Good, the Bad, the Lucy: A Legacy of Laughs," *New York Times*, 14 October 2001, p. 30.

2. "The Classic Sitcoms Guide to . . . All in the Family, The Pilot Episodes—1968–69, Season One: 1970–71," http://www.classicsitcoms.com/shows/family1.html.

3. Bernard Weinraub, "Turning Bloopers into Comedies of Errors," *New York Times*, 30 November 2001, sec. E, p. 3.

4. William S. Paley, *As It Happened: A Memoir* (Garden City, N.Y.: Doubleday, 1979), p. 256.

5. Craig Tomashoff, "Farewell to 'Third Rock,' Truly Out of This World," *New York Times*, 13 May 2001, p. AR21.

6. Bernard Weinraub, "Low Ratings Haunt Sitcoms with High-Profile Stars," *New York Times*, 15 October 2001, p. E1.

7. Lynn Hirschberg, "Meta-Midler," *New York Times*, 8 October 2000, sec. 6, p. 78.

8. Caryn James, "There's a Lot of Elaine in This Star's New Sitcom," *New York Times*, 26 February 2002, p. E1; Bill Carter, "Another Short Second Act for a 'Seinfeld' Alum?" *New York Times*, 25 March 2002, p. C1.

9. http://www.ellen-m-site.com.

10. Jim Rutenberg, "Charlie Sheen's Redemption Helps a Studio in Its Struggle," *New York Times*, 4 February 2002, p. C1.

11. Leonard H. Goldenson and Marvin J. Wolf, *Beating the Odds* (New York: Charles Scribner's Sons, 1991), pp. 238–42.

12. Stephen Battaglio, "The Big Business of Fond Farewells," *New York Times*, 29 July 2001, p. AR23.

13. George V. Voinovich, http://voinovich.senate.gov.

# 7

## TELEVISION AND THE COMICS

### SUPERHEROES

#### The Man of Steel

Newspaper comics and comic books have provided a rich resource for live-action and animated television programs. Of course, some comic-book heroes had already been immortalized on radio when they made the transition to television. One of the first to move to the cathode-ray tube was Superman, in *The Adventures of Superman* (1952–57), which became one of the most valuable character franchises in entertainment history. In its television incarnation, George Reeves played the Man of Steel, Phyllis Coates (1952–53) and later Noel Neill (1953–57) played Lois Lane, and Jack Larson portrayed Jimmy Olsen. After *The Adventures of Superman* went off the air, producer Whitney Elsworth created *The Adventures of Superboy* to continue the narrative of the superhero. In this version, Clark Kent/Superboy, played by John Rockwell, is a high-school student in Smallville, and the show ran for 13 episodes. In 2001 the WB network premiered *Smallville,* a successful adaptation of the superhero theme, once again portraying a young Clark Kent, played by Tom Welling, as a high-school student. Familiar characters in youthful apparitions populate the series, including a young Luthor (Michael Rosenbaum) and Lana Lang (Kristin Kreuk).

#### Jungle Fever

"Jungle fever" became a popular theme on television in 1955 with the arrival of the syndicated series *Jungle Jim* and *Sheena, Queen of the Jungle.*

After completing his final *Tarzan* film, *Tarzan and the Mermaids* (1948), Johnny Weissmuller returned to the tropics as Jungle Jim in 16 low-budget adventure films produced by Sam Katzman. The character was based upon the comic version created in 1934 by Alex Raymond. In 1955 *Jungle Jim,* produced by Screen Gems, moved to television, where Weissmuller was joined by Norman Fredric as Jim's able and loyal friend, Kaseem, and Martin Huston as his son, Skipper. There were 26 television episodes of the series. That same year there was a gender-inspired adaptation of another superhero, the female counterpart to Tarzan, *Sheena, Queen of the Jungle*. She was portrayed by the sexy Olympian Irish McCalla in 26 episodes. Her costars were Christian Drake (as the trader Bob) and Chim (her friendly chimpanzee). In Great Britain *Sheena* (2000–2002) was resurrected as a live-action television series starring *Baywatch* babe Gena Lee Nolin.

Her jungle counterpart Tarzan didn't arrive as a regularly scheduled television series until Ron Ely's portrayal in NBC's *Tarzan* (1966–68). In addition to the animated versions—*Tarzan, Lord of the Jungle* (1976–80), *Batman/Tarzan Adventure Hour, Tarzan and the Super Seven,* and *Disney's The Legend of Tarzan*—live-action stories returned to the small screen with *Tarzan,* starring Wolf Larson, and *The Epic Adventures of Tarzan,* featuring actor Joe Lara.

### The Dynamic Duo

One of the most enduring comic-book heroes is Batman, created by Bob Kane for DC Comics in 1939. A huge success in print, *Batman* was also a hit when it came to television on the ABC network in 1966. Its campy, stylized rendition, with animated titles like *bang, pow,* and *bop* appearing in comic-style balloons, was a drawing card for adults and children. And in the first season, the producers manufactured a cliffhanger effect like the old theatrical movie serials, with two broadcasts a week (Wednesday and Thursday) with a resolution by the Thursday broadcast. It also featured a number of notable character actors, including Frank Gorshin and John Astin as the Riddler, Burgess Meredith as Penguin, Cesar Romero as Joker, Victor Buono as King Tut, and Vincent Price as Egghead. A sexy Catwoman was alternatively played by Julie Newmar, Lee Ann Merriweather, and Eartha Kitt. The leads were Adam West as Bruce Wayne, alias Batman, and Burt Ward as the Boy Wonder, Robin. In an effort to boost ratings, the character of Batgirl (Yvonne Craig) was introduced in the 1967–68 season. The series ran for three seasons (120 episodes) and was canceled in 1969. For more than 30 years the original series has been running in syndication. There were also animated television programs featuring Batman (CBS, 1968), and another in 1977 with the voices of Adam West and Burt Ward.

The *Batman* franchise also created five theatrical features, starting in 1966 with Adam West and Burt Ward starring in a television pilot, followed by

Tim Burton's *Batman* (1989), *Batman Returns* (1992), *Batman Forever* (1995), and *Batman and Robin* (1997).

## Through a Web, Darkly

Of course, Spider-Man is another superhero cult favorite who transcends the printed page and made a successful transition to television, mostly via animation. There have been several televised animated series featuring the webbed creature, including *Spider-Man* (1967–69), *The Amazing Spider-Man* (1977–79), *Spider-Man and His Amazing Friends* (1981), and *Spider-Man the Series* on MTV prime time. There was, however, an attempt at a live-action *Spider-Man* series on the CBS television network from 1977 to 1979. Thirteen episodes were produced, which were broadcast on an irregular basis, starring Nicholas Hammond as Peter Parker (alias Spider-Man) and Ted Danson as Major Collins.

## The First Techno Cop

Perhaps Chester Gould, who originated the comic-book character Dick Tracy, was a visionary when he equipped his hero cop with a two-way wrist radio. And his hero became a pop-cultural idol when the character was introduced in 1931. From its introduction as a comic book to 1934, when it moved to radio, the Dick Tracy character was an engaging addition to the landscape of heroes. His adversaries were a compendium of evildoers with colorful names like Pruneface, Mumbles, and Flattop. The radio program circulated among the networks (NBC, CBS, ABC, and Mutual) and ran from 1934 to 1948. It was also a feature-length film and ran as a movie serial starring Ralph Byrd. In 1950 a low-budget live-television-studio version was broadcast on the ABC television network. Later, 39 television episodes were syndicated by United Television Productions. In 1967 there was a made-for-television movie featuring the square-jawed detective and, of course, the feature film *Dick Tracy* in 1990, directed by and starring Warren Beatty.

## Hunting the Hulk

In the annals of comic-book history, the beginning of *The Incredible Hulk* in 1962 by its creators Stan Lee and Jack Kirby is a rather recent arrival. Nevertheless, the character has been popular in comic books, television, and in the movies. The Hulk character first appeared on television in the 1960s under the umbrella title of the animated series *Marvel Super Heroes*. A live-action adaptation of the comic character approved by creator Stan Lee premiered on CBS (1978–82, 85 episodes) starring Bill Bixby as Dr. David Banner and Lou Ferrigno as the Incredible Hulk. The evolution of the Hulk character has contextual similarities in literature to Robert Louis Stevenson's

Dr. Jekyll and Mr. Hyde. Indeed, the unfortunate Dr. Jekyll has similar fits of violence, like the Hulk, after a laboratory experiment goes awry and the doctor has difficulty reversing its tragic consequences. In the updated *Hulk* scenario, Dr. Banner, through a similar lab mishap, is overexposed to gamma radiation and when angered transforms into the Hulk. Also, borrowing from the successful thematic style of *The Fugitive,* Banner travels around the country seeking a cure and is pursued by Jack McGee, a seedy investigative reporter. Reruns of the series have appeared on the Sci Fi cable network, and three made-for-television *Hulk* movies have been produced and seen on NBC (*The Incredible Hulk Returns, The Death of the Incredible Hulk, The Trial of the Incredible Hulk*). From 1996 to 1997 an animated Hulk appeared on the UPN cable network, featuring the voice of Lou Ferrigno. The first feature-length film of the Incredible Hulk, starring Eric Bana and directed by Ang Lee, was released in the summer of 2003.

## SEXY ADVENTURERS

The first comic strip to offer sensuality, suspense, and realism was *Terry and the Pirates,* created by Milton Caniff in 1934. He went on to create another adventure strip entitled *Steve Canyon* in 1947. Both of his concepts were eventually adapted for television but were short-lived. From June to November 1953, *Terry and the Pirates* ran on the Dumont television network, starring John Baer as Terry Lee, William Tracy as Hotshot Charlie, and Gloria Saunders as the sensual Dragon Lady. There were 18 episodes and the sponsor was Canada Dry Ginger Ale. On NBC, *Steve Canyon* ran from September 1958 to June 1959 for 34 episodes, starring Dean Frederiks in the lead role and Jerry Paris as Major Williston. Interestingly, Mary Tyler Moore, who later became a legendary television personality, was featured in the first episode as Mary Moore.

## SPACE CADETS

### Buck Rogers

Both film and television have been enamored with the subject of science fiction and the fantasies associated with that genre. Indeed, the success of films like *Star Wars* and *Close Encounters of the Third Kind* are indicative of the influence that earlier incarnations in the comics, radio, and later television have had. Two of the earliest space adventurers were Buck Rogers and Flash Gordon. The first appearance of Buck was in a novelette entitled *Armageddon—2419* A.D. by Philip Francis Nowlan, which was published in August 1928 as part of the *Amazing Stories* series. A year later Buck became a popular comic-book character, and Nowlan was joined by cartoonist Dick Calkins. The theme of the comic book centered around Buck, the former air-force officer, and his five-century-long sleep. When he awakes he learns that the United States has been invaded by Mongols. Buck's adventures came to radio on November 7, 1932, when *Buck Rogers in the Twenty-Fifth Century*, a 15-minute early-evening program, was broadcast Monday through Thursday on CBS. The radio program was an immediate hit with children because of the popularity of the comic strip syndicated in newspapers around the country. Children were fascinated by the adventures of Buck and his copilot, Lieutenant Wilma Deering, along with hearing the fascinating sounds of Buck's sophisticated space weapons, which included death rays, incendiary missiles, space guns, gamma bombs, psychic destruction rays, and a mechanical mole. The nature of radio afforded a greater ease of creating an illusion of these weapons—for example, the sound of the psychic destruction ray was created by a Schick electric razor. The cast included John Larkin as Buck and Adele Ronson as Wilma.

Although audience research wasn't too sophisticated in the early 1930s, a means of determining the popularity of a radio program was by offering listeners a mail-order premium. When the program offered a map of the planets, the station received 125,000 requests. Another offer for a cardboard space helmet required more due diligence by depression-era children. To receive it they had to purchase a can of Cocomalt, the show's sponsor, and send in a metal seal from the can. Undeterred, Buck's loyal audience sent in 140,000 strips of tin. The radio program concluded its run in 1939. Buck's popularity became a featured exhibit at Chicago's 1935 World's Fair, where a short 10-minute film was shown to large audiences. Cereal companies like Kellogg's and Cream of Wheat, especially interested in promotional opportunities, were eager to license the Buck Rogers name and accompanying assets. Some of the valuable collectibles include a Buck Rogers pocket watch and a Solar Scouts Badge.

In 1939 Buck's exploits were released in a 12-part movie serial starring Buster Crabbe, which proved to have an enduring distribution presence and was reedited and rereleased several times as *Planet Outlaws* (1953), *Destination Saturn* (TV movie, 1965), and most recently on video and DVD. Buck's first television exploits were featured on the ABC television network broadcast on Saturday evenings from 6:00 to 6:30 and ran from April 15, 1950, to January 30, 1951. The cast included Kem Dibbs, who was later replaced by Robert Pastene, as Buck, and Lou Prentis as Wilma.

In 1979, following on the popularity of space-genre films like *Star Wars*, Universal Studios released the motion picture *Buck Rogers in the Twenty-Fifth Century*, starring Gil Gerard as Buck and Erin Gray as Colonel Wilma Deering. Shortly after, an NBC television series featuring the two leads from the movies ran on the network from September 1979 to August 1981. Some of the guest stars on the series included Buster Crabbe (*Tarzan, Flash Gordon*), Jamie Lee Curtis, Julie Newmar, and Jack Palance.

## Flash Gordon

Flash Gordon, who saved the world when he fired a rocket at the planet Mongo when it was on a collision course with Earth, had been a popular character in comics before he transitioned to other media. He was created in 1934 by Alex Raymond, who also originated *Jungle Jim* and *Rip Kirby*. The comic strip was distributed in Hearst newspapers and today is drawn by Jim Keefe. On radio, in a 1935 broadcast on the Mutual Network, the Hearst organization produced 26 episodes of *The Amazing Interplanetary Adventures of Flash Gordon* from 1935 to 1936.

Shortly after the debut of the comic strip, Universal purchased the rights to the Flash Gordon character and produced 13 serials (a total of 245 minutes) starring Buster Crabbe as Flash and actresses Carol Hughes and Jean Rogers as Dale Arden, produced from 1936 to 1940. In 1951 the serials were syndicated to television and broadcast on the Dumont television network on its *Serial Theater* series. Critics and parents were appalled at the level of violence portrayed in the serial, and as a result the program was pulled from the network. This was the first instance of a television program ceasing broadcast because of parental and critical pressure. However, the serial returned a few months later without any protest on another New York television station.

In 1954 a joint production venture representing three countries, the United States, Germany, and France, created a Flash Gordon syndicated television series distributed by a company called Motion Pictures for Television (MPTV), which broadcast 39 30-minute episodes from October 1954 to May 1955. The stars of this series were Steve Holland as Flash and Irene Champlin as Dale. One of the writers for this series was Bruce Geller, who later went on to create two highly successful television series, *Mannix* and *Mission Impossible*. An animated television program, *The New Animated Adventures of Flash Gordon,* produced by Filmation Associates, appeared on the NBC television network from 1979 to 1980 and again in reruns from 1982 to 1983. A feature-length film, *Flash Gordon,* was produced in 1980 by Dino De Laurentis and starred Sam J. Jones as Flash and Melody Anderson as Dale and also featured Timothy Dalton and Max Von Sydow. Interestingly, Flash Gordon was one of the first comic strip characters to have been immortalized by the U.S. Post Office on a postage stamp!

## Captain Midnight

Although this captain was not a space explorer, he was nevertheless a champion crime-buster to children. The character was created for radio and did not emanate from a comic book; however, his heroic crime-fighting efforts nevertheless made him a popular media figure. The Captain Midnight character evolved from a 1939 radio show on the West Coast entitled *The Air Adventures of Jimmy Allen,* which was sponsored by Skelly Oil. Out west,

Captain Midnight was portrayed by Bill Bouchey, while Ed Prentiss was the voice of the captain on Mutual radio. In 1940 the radio program was nationally distributed and sponsored by Ovaltine. The moniker Captain Midnight was for undercover agent Jim "Red" Albright, who piloted a cargo-passenger plane and was gathering information on a gang of criminals, including his nemesis, Ivan Shark. When the captain moved to network radio, there were wholesale cast changes and the title was changed. The program moved to the CBS television network (1954–56) and starred Richard Webb as Jim Albright/Captain Midnight.

The televised version of *Captain Midnight* was one of the first to offer premiums to the children who signed up as members of the Secret Squadron, and were featured in the program. These included decoder badges and code-a-graphs, which were offered on the Ovaltine jars' foil tops and labels. The series was popular with children who enjoyed the participatory nature of using the "tools" of the captain while watching the show.

Interestingly, the Screen Gems studio produced the program, while Ovaltine owned the title, *Captain Midnight*. In syndication this proved to be somewhat of an inconsistency, with Screen Gems selling the program under a different title—*Jet Jackson, Flying Commando*—roughly eliminating any audio reference to *Captain Midnight*.

### Captain Video

The irony behind the development of *Captain Video and His Video Rangers* is that it evolved out of the necessity of using 12-minute segments of old 60-minute B Westerns on the Dumont television network. The challenge was that children in the audience weren't familiar with these Western relics, and so the 12-minute segments had to be integrated into a child-friendly format. It was James Caddigan, Dumont's program director, who approached producer, director, and writer Larry Menkin to conceptualize a programming vehicle that would accommodate the vintage Westerns along with an entertaining story concept for children. As a result, Menkin's genius and creativity created one of the first and most enduring of all children's science-fiction programming.

As the show was distributed live from a studio, there was limited time and space for ambitious action sequences. So when the program started to drag, Richard Coogan (who was succeeded by Al Hodge in 1951), the first Captain Video, would switch to Ranger Headquarters, where cowboys like Sunset Carson and Bob Steele would appear as Rangers in their B-film exploits. This was also one of the first children's programs to articulate pro-social Ranger messages dealing with the Golden Rule, freedom, and nondiscrimination.

The program was conceptualized as a daily evening television serial broadcast from 7:00 to 7:30 P.M. By 1951 it was distributed on 24 stations to 3.5 million viewers. With the growing popularity of *Captain Video*, the producers created *The Secret Files of Captain Video,* a 20-episode prequel and separate series written by some of the best and youngest science-fiction writers of that era.

In many ways, *Captain Video* foreshadowed the themes and culture of modern science-fiction movies and television. He patrolled the universe in *Galaxy,* his space vehicle, representing the Solar Council of the Interplanetary Alliance. Blending scientific fact with fiction, *Captain Video* was the first intergalactic television explorer to enter a black hole, discover a planet ruled by a supercomputer, and encounter an enormous space ark traveling in space for generations. These plots should sound very familiar to science-fiction fans. The program was sponsored by Powerhouse Candy, Skippy Peanut Butter, and Post Cereals, and it ran from 1949 to 1955 on the Dumont television network.

### Tom Corbett, Space Cadet

Set in the year 2350, *Tom Corbett, Space Cadet* featured teenagers at an all-male high school who were training as cadets to enter the Solar Guard as officers. The radio and television series were inspired by two writers: Robert Heinlein, author of *Space Cadet,* and Joseph Greene, who wrote *Dig Allen, Space Explorer.* Guest appearances featured a who's who of aspiring young actors, some of whom later became television stars, including Tom Poston, William Windom, Jack Lord, and Jack Klugman. Both the radio and television show were very successful. The 52-episode radio series was distributed on ABC in 1952 and was sponsored by Kellogg's. On television, the series first appeared on CBS (October 2, 1950–December 29, 1950), ABC (January 1, 1951–September 26, 1952), NBC (summer reruns July 1951–September 1951), and after the sponsor, Kellogg's, canceled the series, the Dumont network picked it up (August 29, 1953–May 22, 1954). The show's final season was sponsored by Kraft and appeared on NBC (December 11, 1954– January 25, 1955).

The regular cast included Frankie Thomas Jr. as Tom Corbett in both the radio and television versions. On television, this program was the first to utilize a number of special video effects and create a unique video switcher dubbed *the Gizmo.* Some of these included traveling mattes. The television program also generated ancillary publications, including 14 comics published by Dell and Prize (1952–55), eight books, and both daily and Sunday comic strips, as well as 100 licensed products.

### Space Patrol

Set on the man-made planet Terra, where the Space Patrol was headquartered, the show was created for children but also attracted a large number of adult viewers. It was created by Mike Moser, a World War II navy pilot, and starred Edward Kemmer as Buzz Corry, a former air-force fighter pilot and prisoner of war. The show began broadcasting March 9, 1950, on the West Coast as a 15-minute daily program (five days a week) on KECA-TV (channel 7) with Dr. Ross Dog Food as one of the local sponsors, while national sponsors included Ralston-Purina and Nestle Chocolate. Interestingly, when Edward Kemmer first started acting on the program, he earned eight dollars per show. Its popularity growing, *Space Patrol* became a Saturday-morning ABC network program on December 30, 1950. The same cast was featured in all of the *Space Patrol* versions, which included 210 half-hour segments, 200 radio shows, and 900 15-minute programs. The last broadcast of the series was on February 26, 1955; however, the program continued in syndication from 1957 until 1959 and was distributed by Comet Productions.

### Rod Brown of the Rocket Rangers

This show began with a stirring introduction written to provide an exciting prelude for children anticipating the start of the program. It began:

CBS Television presents—Rod Brown of the Rocket Rangers! Surging with the power of the atom, gleaming like great silver bullets, the mighty Rocket Rangers space ships stand by for blast off. Up, up, rockets blazing with hot fury, the man-made meteors ride through the atmosphere, breaking the gravity barrier pushing up and out, faster and faster then . . . outer space and high adventure for the Rocket Rangers.

Set in the year 2153 on Omega base, these cadets used the spaceship Beta to patrol the solar system and keep the peace. Starring Cliff Robertson, who later became a famous Hollywood actor, *Rod Brown of the Rocket Rangers* was modeled after *Tom Corbett, Space Cadet,* and indeed, the similarities were so evident that Rockhill Productions, which owned *Tom Corbett,* sued CBS for copyright infringement. That's probably the reason for the program's short-lived broadcast history (April 18, 1953–May 29, 1954) and the lack of archival material such as old kinescopes. For almost its entire run the program appeared opposite *Space Cadet* and *Secret Files of Captain Video.*

### Rocky Jones, Space Ranger

For this venture into space, the heroes used the XV-2 Orbit Jet and the XV-3 Silver Moon. Set in the year 2054, *Rocky Jones,* with the title character portrayed by Richard Crane, was a syndicated program with somewhat inconsistent distribution. A Roland Reed production, there were about 39 episodes that were broadcast, and production values were above average. During the run of the show (January 1954–December 1955), there were a large number of programs that had multiple story lines. Any premiums from the show were associated with Silvercup Bread.

### Atom Squad

Broadcast Monday through Friday on NBC as a 15-minute program (5:00–5:15) originating from WPTZ in Philadelphia, *Atom Squad* featured Robert Cortleigh and Bob Hastings as scientists Steve Elliott and David Fielding. They worked in an ultrasecret U.S. government agency in a New York lab, averting cold-war threats from nuclear weapons and radiation. They successfully overcame communist spies, saboteurs, and even an occasional alien. The program began with an eerie opening segment of an actor in a radiation suit moving slowly toward the camera. Some of the cast were television veterans, having been recruited from the *Captain Video* series. The actors had a rigorous schedule, usually rehearsing from noon until the beginning of the live broadcast at 5:00 P.M. The series ran from July 6, 1953, to January 22, 1954.

### Commando Cody: Sky Marshal of the Universe

As serials were a popular form of theatrical entertainment in the 1940s and into the 1950s, it's not surprising that some Hollywood studios used them to launch television series. Two of these were *King of the Rocket Men* (Republic, 1949) and *Commando Cody: Sky Marshal of the Universe* (1952), which was an offshoot from the Republic Pictures serial *Radar Men from the Moon*. The press release for *Commando Cody* reads:

> The Ruler, a diabolical scientist who wants to enslave the solar system, learns of *Commando Cody's* design for a rocket ship that can go anywhere in outer space. He is determined to sabotage Cody's work.[1]

As a top-secret scientist wearing a mask to conceal his identity, Cody is made a sky marshal of the universe to combat the Ruler. To that end he develops an ingenious "cosmic dust blanket," which destroys enemy aircraft on their descent to Earth. The 12-episode theatrical series, starring Judd Holdren, was distributed to NBC by Republic's television subsidiary Hollywood Television Service and broadcast from July 16, 1955, to October 8, 1955. Hoping to generate a theatrical audience from the television series, Republic unsuccessfully rereleased *Radar Men from the Moon* to theaters.

### Captain Z–Ro

The universe was a fantasy playground for early television programming when *Captain Z-Ro* started as a local 15-minute daily program broadcast live from KRON-TV in San Francisco. Like so many of the early science-fiction broadcasts, it began with a dramatic introduction intoning the heavenly virtues of the character.

*Captain Z-Ro!* Research explorer in time and space. Somewhere in a remote uncharted region of a planet called Earth stands the laboratory of Captain Z-Ro. In this secret location, known only to a few in the outside world, *Captain Z-Ro* and his associates experiment in time and space to learn from the past—to plan for the future. Contact has been established. We now transmit you direct to the laboratory of *Captain Z-Ro*. Please stand by.

Although the special effects were crude, and the set could only accommodate three actors at a time, this program had a loyal local audience following. It ran locally from 1952 to 1955 and then was filmed in 30-minute episodes and syndicated nationally. Its creator, writer, and star was Roy Steffens, and his young sidekick was played alternatively by Bobby Trumbull and Bruce Haynes. Along with chasing intergalactic villains, the program offered didactic lessons on history.

### Johnny Jupiter

When it was broadcast on the Dumont television network (March 21, 1953–June 13, 1953), *Johnny Jupiter* was a cleverly written satirical program featuring puppets commenting on modern American society. It featured the character Ernest P. Duckweather, a janitor at a television station who fiddles with the levers and controls in the studio and contacts Johnny on the planet Jupiter. Along with his buddies B-12 and robots Major Domo and Reject, Johnny comments on the foibles and inconsistencies of humans. For example, he notes that on Jupiter, television is used as a punishment for children who spend too much time reading and playing with their slide rules (a tool used for higher-level mathematical computations before the age of personal computers).

The puppets were brought to life by Carl Harms. Ernest P. Duckweather was alternatively played by Vaughn Taylor and Wright King, and Jerome Coopersmith was the writer. Much of the edgy humor was lost when the program moved to ABC (September 5, 1953–May 29, 1954).

### Operation Neptune

With a clever title, this NBC summer replacement series (June 28, 1953–September 21, 1953) starred Tod Griffith as Bill Hollister (alias Captain Neptune), who, with his colleague Dink Saunders, played by Richard Holland, worked for the navy warding off undersea enemies.

### Out There and Science Fiction Theatre

Two science-fiction anthology programs that were popular in the 1950s, *Out There* (CBS, October 28, 1951–January 13, 1952) and *Science Fiction*

*Theatre* (April 19, 1955–April 1957), were precursors of hit television shows like *The Twilight Zone* and *The Outer Limits*. Both dealt with themes that were uniquely strange and bizarre. Distributed by Ziv Television, *Science Fiction Theatre* was hosted by Truman Bradley and created an archive of 78 episodes, with later programs appearing in color. On CBS, *Out There* was short-lived, with only 12 episodes, with the introductory tagline of "zooming viewers to adventures in space."

### Space Barton on Mars and Beyond

This NBC series (September 18, 1950–March 23, 1951), while not an animated program, was part of the daily 4:00–4:15 Telecomics series. There were 135 episodes, and each featured comic art that appeared as a comic-book page that turned. There were several short programs under the series title, including *Danny March* and *Kid Champion,* with *Space Barton* broadcast between the two. Characters on *Space Barton* included Commander Varrick, Jackie Barton, and Princess Thursta. Writers were always creative with the names of space vehicles, and Jackie Barton's was called *Vulcan.*

### Men into Space

In today's universe, the mere title of this program expresses a gender bias, especially with the number of women involved in the space program. It was syndicated by Ziv Television with an alternate title, *Space Challenge,* and appeared on CBS, which broadcast 30 episodes (September 1959–September 1960). The series starred William Lundigan as Colonel Edward McCauley, head of America's space program, and the challenges he encountered battling saboteurs, budget cuts, and defective equipment. The only two sustaining characters were McCauley and his wife, Mary, played by Joyce Taylor. In the pilot episode, however, actress Angie Dickinson, who later became a movie star, portrayed Mary.

This was television's first serious attempt to treat America's pursuit of conquering space with a realistic format. Noted rocket scientist and space expert Wernher von Braun was a consultant to the producers, and they also had the cooperation of the Defense Department and the air force.

Although somewhat dull and pedantic at times, *Men into Space* demonstrated television's ability to enlighten its audience and enrich their ability to understand the dynamics and obstacles of space exploration. And with its special effects it helped to nurture the dream of space travel among Americans, along with the excitement, risks, and rewards such an endeavor entailed.

## ENDURING TELEVISION COMIC CHARACTERS

### Blondie

There were other comic-book characters that jumped from their ink-rendered images to the phosphorescent flickers of the small television screen. One of the most beloved was *Blondie,* which was created in 1930 by Chic Young. When Dagwood Bumstead, the heir to the Bumstead Locomotive Works, went on a 28-day hunger strike to protest his parents' refusal of permission to marry Blondie, he was disinherited but won the hearts and minds of readers around the country. Over the years the adventures of the Bumstead family have been syndicated in 2,000 newspapers, 55 countries, and 35 languages, and reached 250 million readers.

In 1957 *Blondie* moved to television on NBC Friday evenings at 7:00 P.M. It had been a success on radio and in a series of motion pictures starring Arthur Lake and Pamela Britton. However, this attempt ran for 26 episodes (January 4, 1957–July 5, 1957). An effort to revitalize the concept was made in 1968 when *Blondie* returned to television on CBS. This version, starring Will Hutchins and Patricia Harty, was also short-lived.

### Dennis the Menace

There's a certain comfort we derive from familiar characters in settings that are well known. In the vast library of comic art, one of the most beloved characters is Dennis the Menace. Created by Hank Ketcham in 1950, the strip struck a responsive chord in readers and became one of the most successful comic characters. His antics and adventures, along with the relationship with Mr. Wilson, increased its circulation to 1,000 newspapers in 48 countries, appearing in 19 languages. In October 1959, *Dennis the Menace* moved to prime-time television on the CBS network and ran until 1963. The cast featured Jay North as the irrepressible Dennis; Herbert Anderson as his father, Henry Mitchell; Gloria Henry as his mother, Alice; Joseph Kearns as Mr. Wilson (in the last season after Kearns's death, Gale Gordon appeared as his brother); and Sylvia Field as Mrs. Wilson. Two animated versions followed the live-action sitcom, one on CBS in 1988 and *The New Dennis the Menace* on CBS from 1993 to 1994. There was also a *Dennis the Menace* feature film released in 1993, written by John Hughes, starring Mason Gamble as Dennis and two notable character actors in the roles of Mr. and Mrs. Wilson, Walter Matthau and Joan Plowright.

### Hazel

This loveable maid created by Ted Key first appeared in the *Saturday Evening Post* in 1943. After the magazine ceased publication, the comic strip was picked up for syndication by King Features and eventually attracted 29 million readers. Adapted for television in 1951 on NBC, the series starred veteran stage actress Shirley Booth. Her portrayal of the meddling but loveable maid Hazel, who held the Baxter family together and was part of the family dynamic, helped to set the tone for other sitcoms featuring a similar character. Her costars included Don DeFore and Whitney Blake. The program ran on NBC from 1961 to 1964 and then moved to CBS during its last season, 1965–1966. In all, 154 episodes were produced, making *Hazel* one of the most successful live-action television series adapted from a comic strip.

Children and adults have a unique relationship with comic-book characters and their adaptation to television. Interestingly, before television, they provided children with a rich tradition of fantasy and delight. As television searched for content, the comic heroes provided a well-defined preestablished identity for audiences. Having followed their stories in the comics, television audiences were delighted to see their favorite characters leap onto the television screen. Some, of course, were live action, and others appeared in an animated format. These characters have cultivated an intimate association with their audience and nurtured close relationships with the characters. Some, like Batman and Superman, have been spun off innumerable times with various incarnations. The most recent Superman program is the enchanting *Smallville,* a prequel to the saga.

## NOTE

1. www.tvtome.com/tvtome/servlet/EpisodeGuideSummary/Showid-9784/ Commando_Cody/.

# 8

---

# TELEVISION DRAMA: FROM THE GOLDEN AGE TO THE SOAP FACTORY

Television's ability to adapt legitimate drama and conceptualize it as literary form was demonstrated by a number of ambitious television series. It was 1956, and America was enjoying a vibrant economic expansion while facing the paranoia of the cold war. However, that year was a threshold in the development and production of teleplays of substance and daring that clearly articulated that television drama could rise beyond the formulaic and create a compelling narrative form comparable to Broadway.

An essential component for the nurturing and growth of this genre was the high caliber of talent, both in front of the camera and behind it. Many featured live dramas as well as filmed, and the artists associated with their development read like a who's who in Hollywood: Rod Serling, Paddy Chayefsky, Reginald Rose, Martin Manulis, John Frankenheimer, Paul Monash, Jerome Coopersmith, Arthur Hailey, Dorothy and Howard Baker, Red Skelton, Jack Palance, Charlton Heston, Boris Karloff, Felicia Farr, Imogene Coca, and many others. It was indeed a treasure of riches and included *Playhouse 90* (CBS), *Armstrong Circle Theatre* (NBC), *Actors Studio, Studio One* (CBS), *The U.S. Steel Hour, Alcoa Hour* (NBC), *Kaiser Aluminum Hour* (NBC), *Robert Montgomery Presents, Kraft Television Theatre* (NBC), *Lux Video Theatre* (NBC), and *G.E. Theater.*

With literate adaptations and original scripts, television in the mid-1950s created a new proscenium for challenging drama featuring the best talent that the visual arts had to offer. *Actors Studio* from 1948 to 1950 featured actors like Jessica Tandy, Martin Balsam, and Marlon Brando in a groundbreaking television anthology series. *Studio One*, which ran under various titles from 1948 to 1958, was a vehicle for high drama that included such notable efforts as "12 Angry Men," written by Reginald Rose. Broadcast live on CBS on September 30, 1954, and directed by Franklin Schaffner, the play presents a timeless portrait of 12 men on a jury struggling with the reasonable doubt of a single juror about the guilt of a young Latino accused of stabbing his father to death. The television drama, of which only half survives, featured actors Franchot Tone, Edward Arnold, and Robert Cummings. At the Emmy Awards in 1955, both the actor Robert Cummings and director Franklin Schaffner won awards for their work on the program.

Several adaptations of this drama throughout the years speak to its resilience and relevance. In 1957 Henry Fonda starred in a theatrical feature-film version of the play, with Sidney Lumet making his directorial debut. In 1997 there was another adaptation, with the play once again returning to its television roots, this time on the Showtime pay cable network. This two-hour version, directed by Academy Award winner William Friedkin, featured an illustrious cast, including Jack Lemmon, George C. Scott, Ossie Davis, Dorian Harewood, James Gandolfini, Edward James Olmos, Tony Danza, and Hume Cronyn. As a testament to the versatility and timeliness of "12 Angry Men," the Roundabout Theatre Company presented its Broadway premiere in the fall of 2004.

Two individuals who were responsible for introducing the live 90-minute dramatic format to television were Worthington C. Miner and Hubbell Robinson, who at the time were both employed by CBS. They had a vision of television as an inclusive medium, embracing writers, artists, and performers and offering them an opportunity to create narrative fiction and nonfiction that tested the limits of the technology. In their vision, Robinson and Miner wanted to create high-quality programming, "mass with class." One of the first of the series on CBS was Miner's *Studio One*. It ran for 10 years and in 1958 moved from New York to Hollywood, when the name was changed to *Studio One in Hollywood*. It went off the air toward the end of 1958.

Indicative of the programs was one about Sister Mary Aquinas, a Franciscan nun who ran a unique after-school workshop and was also the first nun to earn a pilot's license. It starred actress Margaret Sullivan and featured an appearance by Sister Mary Aquinas at the end of the program.

The other anthology series that helped define dramatic television was CBS's *Playhouse 90,* created by Hubbell Robinson, which ran from 1956 to 1961. On its stage such memorable productions as "Requiem for a Heavyweight," "The Miracle Worker," and "Judgement at Nuremberg" were created. When *Playhouse 90* premiered in October 1956, it was viewed as a welcoming departure from traditional television fare.

From the standpoint of introducing a daring programming concept (particularly in a season characterized by a return to orthodox programming fare) CBS-TV rates kudos. Add to this the calculated risk of slotting it back-to-back with the full-hour "Climax" show for 150 minutes of dramatic presentation (tantamount to an evening in the theatre), then the emergence of "Playhouse 90" in the Thursday night 9:30–11 slot practically becomes revolutionary in the scheme of TV network schedules.[1]

The second week into its season, *Playhouse 90* broadcast Rod Serling's "Requiem for a Heavyweight," one of its most notable productions. A compassionate drama about a washed-up fighter, Serling's original teleplay presented a poignant yet abrasive drama about the unseemly world of prizefighting. The program featured a stellar cast, including Jack Palance, father-son actors Ed and Keenan Wynn, Kim Hinter, and director Ralph Nelson. In his portrayal of the once proud and vulnerable Mountain McClintock, Jack Palance gave one of his finest performances.

Palance did the finest acting job he's yet turned in in any medium socking across the genuine bewilderment, inferiority's [*sic*], but straight forward [*sic*] decency and pride of a boxer who's learned he's washed up but doesn't know anything else than the ring. Call it the grunt 'n' groan school of acting, but Palance's stuttering and stumbling characterization is easily the best of the new season and one of the alltime [*sic*] television greats.[2]

At this time in television's history, many advertisers were named in the title of the programs they sponsored. Whether it was *The United States Steel Hour, Alcoa Presents,* or *Kaiser Aluminum Hour,* their repertoire of drama was often superlative. For example, on CBS's *United States Steel Hour,* veteran actor Ed Begley teamed with a young William Shatner (who would later portray Captain James T. Kirk in *Star Trek*), featured in the original 1958 drama "Walk with a Stranger." It was compelling drama, with a theme of absolution for a young man embittered by his physical challenge.

Interestingly, *The U.S. Steel Hour* made its debut on ABC in November 1953 with the impressive drama "P.O.W.," an original teleplay by David Davidson about a group of American Korean War veterans repatriated to a hospital in the United States. Featuring the collective talent of actors including Brian Keith, Phyllis Kirk, Gary Merrill, and Richard Kiley, the story presented a compelling look at the problems confronting these veterans. After making its debut on ABC, the sponsor switched to CBS in 1955 because of the former network's inability to control affiliates who bumped the show to a different time slot.[3]

On NBC, *Armstrong Circle Theatre* in 1953 presented an original drama about a wife's infidelity entitled "Judgement." When a husband left his family on a business trip, his son learned that his mother was having an affair. The theme of marital infidelity was certainly one that was a challenge to the sedate mores of that time. And Armstrong, to its credit, stood by the program.

While the writers, actors, and directors were a transcendental force in the evolution of live television drama, it was the producers in many cases who were the visionaries. In particular, Fred Coe, a producer for *The Philco Television Playhouse* and later *Playhouse 90,* was a major influence on the dramatic television genre.

The characteristics of a producer are varied and include a keen eye for recognizing the creative work of artists, including writers, actors, directors, and technicians. Attracting talent was one of Coe's greatest assets, along with his determination and discipline. In the 1940s he ran a successful theater company in Columbia, South Carolina, and the Nashville Community Playhouse, where he met and worked with the directors Arthur Penn and Delbert Mann. He moved to NBC Television New York in 1945, where Penn and Mann later joined him as directors on *Philco-Goodyear Television Playhouse* (formerly *The Philco Television Playhouse*) and later on CBS's *Playhouse 90*.

There was always a sense of urgency about Coe, which probably emanated from working in live television. Producing live drama required the patience of a saint, the logistics of a general, the fortitude of an athlete, and the eye of an artist. He chose scripts, commissioned writers, battled with sponsors over using blacklisted actors, and scouted for new talent.

Working in the high-pressure environment of live television, Coe had to juggle actors in tiny studios with multiple sets while breaking away huge, bulky cameras with thick, snaking camera cables to cover their action. Everyone baked under the intense heat of the bright television lights, with temperatures reaching 100 degrees. There was no second chance, and actors had to know their lines and always be on their mark for their shots.

In today's global media marketplace, content has become king, transcending the vehicle that is the medium that delivers the message. As an artist, Coe knew how important good writers were for television, and he nurtured the talents of individuals like Paddy Chayefsky, Horton Foote, Tad Mosel, Bo Goldman, and Rod Serling. His instinct as a television producer for recognizing talent was uncanny. He cast Grace Kelly in her first television dramatic lead two years before her starring role in the movie *High Noon*. After James Dean's tragic death, Coe used a relatively unknown Paul Newman in his place for a television drama based upon a Hemingway story.

In addition to finding new talent, Coe was able to attract established stage actors to television. He brought Humphrey Bogart, Lauren Bacall, and Henry Fonda together for a *Producer's Showcase* adaptation of *The Petrified Forest*. For a staging of *Our Town*, Frank Sinatra had a leading role. And in 1955 Coe earned the highest rating for any television program up until then with his classic production of *Peter Pan* starring Mary Martin.

For NBC, *Peter Pan*'s adaptation to television was a stroke of genius by producer Fred Coe and director Jerome Robbins. It was broadcast on March 5, 1955, as part of the *Producer's Showcase* series. It fulfilled several needs for the network described by Sylvester "Pat" Weaver, who was a vice president and head of programming. He was the architect of the "spectacular," which is how *Peter Pan* was defined. It brought a certain cachet to the network, providing publicity while somewhat diluting the influence of individual sponsors, who couldn't afford to undertake such an expensive programming endeavor. It also provided a singular opportunity for the network and RCA, NBC's parent company, to promote color television. At that time it was one of the biggest hits on television, prompting *New York Times* television critic Jack Gould to write that *Peter Pan* was "perhaps television's happiest hour."

In the mid-1960s network television once again attempted to provide a stage for the adaptation of serious drama. Legendary producer and sometime talk-show host David Susskind worked with notable playwrights Tennessee Williams and Arthur Miller on adapting their plays *The Glass Menagerie, Death of a Salesman,* and *The Crucible* for television. The 1966 CBS broadcast of Arthur Miller's *Death of a Salesman* was compelling television, with Lee J. Cobb and Mildred Dunnock reprising their Broadway roles. It was a unique experience for legitimate drama adapted to television, and the audience was appreciative. However, the Western *Bonanza*, broadcast at the same time on NBC, earned a higher rating.

Nevertheless, legitimate theater continued on television, with Katharine Hepburn making her dramatic television debut on December 16, 1973, in ABC's *The Glass Menagerie*. Many more dramas were broadcast, and they included some of the finest actors of the time. There was Walter Matthau in Clifford Odets's *Awake and Sing,* Ingrid Bergman in Jean Cocteau's *Human Voice,* Dustin Hoffman in Ronald Ribman's *Journey of the Fifth Horse,* and Estelle Parsons and Susan Sarandon in Ring Lardner's *June Moon.* Although commercial television has abandoned its role as a purveyor of the arts, public television has broadcast and intends to offer more of these classic dramas. For example, on January 5, 2002, WNET, public television's channel 13 in New York, broadcast Eugene O'Neill's *Moon for the Misbegotten.* This 1975 classic was directed by Jose Quintero and starred Jason Robards and Colleen Dewhurst.

The opportunity to revisit these classic television dramas on television is the result of a company called Broadway Theater Archive, which has restored, remastered, and digitized these classic productions for distribution on videocassette and DVD. In addition, a company called Kultur, well known in the field of performing-arts programming, is distributing a number of these titles to retail stores.

Hollywood's interest in television drama led to several successful film adaptations, including *Marty* (Oscar for best picture, 1955), *Requiem for a Heavyweight, Bachelor Party, The Catered Affair, The Rainmaker,* and others. Recently, television programs have once again provided material for theatrical feature films. These retreads have included *Mission Impossible, The Fugitive, The Brady Bunch, My Favorite Martian, Dennis the Menace,* and others.

The television traditions championed by Coe and asserted by the writers of that era have contributed to the structure of the dramatic form on television. Indeed, television has created its unique form of narrative as part of the episodic-series format. It developed story arcs with broadened exposition, which in some instances is provided to the viewer at the beginning of the program by edited scenes from previous episodes. Presented as "Previously on . . . ," this technique provides members of the audience who have missed a program with unresolved plot entanglements from the past an opportunity to get caught up. It was introduced, albeit in a different format, on ABC's hit television series *The Fugitive*.

A program that helped to refine the narrative story arc was Steven Bochco's *Hill Street Blues*. It had a number of intricate plots and subplots involving its ensemble cast, and the audience had to remain current with all of the developments. Episodic television drama also became more relevant, reflecting issues and themes prevalent in American society. They became relationship-oriented, exploring the dynamics of family and friends.

Programs like *Once and Again* demonstrate the tone of television relationship drama. Created by Edward Zwick and Marshall Herskovitz, who were also the producers of *thirtysomething*, the series is a parable of extended family relationships created by divorce. It evolves around the characters of Lilly Manning (Sela Ward) and Rick Sammler (Billy Campbell) and is an intimate portrayal of family dynamics. When it premiered on September 21, 1999, it was hailed as one of the new season's most polished, accomplished series. Not every critic was so laudatory, as some found the program to be too immersed in the psychology of need, or more like "a sensitivity training session in drama drag."

Commenting about the theme of the program, Winnie Holzman, one of the writers, talked about *Once and Again* and compared it to other popular television shows. She addressed the notion of ordinary people and their routines.

I watch a lot of T.V. and I love "The Sopranos," "West Wing," "Sex [and] the City." But I guess we all feel there isn't a show doing exactly what we're doing. It isn't about huge, earthshaking events. It's about smaller people and the smaller moments of their lives. In the end, it's about how people's minds work.[4]

But smaller moments are not always as compelling as larger ones, especially those taken from the news headlines. Perhaps that's why *The West Wing*, a drama about politics and the president, is so popular. As President Josiah Bartlet, actor Martin Sheen provides an intimate portrayal of the personal and professional challenges of the office. He is investigated by a special prosecutor for concealing his illness, multiple sclerosis, and in another episode consults a psychiatrist about a sleep disorder. Dramatic news events are woven into the plot, such as the dilemma of telling the public about an instance of mad cow disease, a missing American submarine in the hostile waters off North Korea, and the U.S. practice bombing runs off the island of Vieques in Puerto Rico.

There is also a certain irony in the series as a result of the September 11 attacks. Americans looked toward President George W. Bush as the embodiment of leadership, courage, and fortitude. As fans of *The West Wing*, the television audience saw these traits in their fictional president Josiah Bartlet. Interestingly, the qualities merged into a character profile that accommodated reality and fiction. Produced by Warner Brothers television and distributed on the NBC television network, *The West Wing* has won numerous Emmy Awards for its writers and actors. It was created by Aaron Sorkin, an executive producer, with John Wells (*E.R.*) and Thomas Schlamme (*Sports Night*) as co-executive producers.

Cable television has also demonstrated its creative tendencies toward drama with pay networks HBO and Showtime delivering gripping programs with appealing characters. HBO's series about mobsters, *The Sopranos*, created a resounding proscenium for examining both the family dynamics and hierarchy of an underworld family steeped in the routines of family life while engaging in the regimen of the family business. For the most part Anthony "Tony" Soprano (James Gandolfini) seemed like a regular guy, outwardly dealing with his family's needs while inwardly conflicted about his professional role as a "boss."

The thematic similarities to Shakespearean drama are vivid, with a conniving mother, Livia (the late Nancy Marchand), who influences her brother-in-law Corrado "Junior" Soprano (Dominic Chianese) to assassinate her son. The plot fails, and Junior winds up under house arrest because of a RICO federal indictment.

The writers attempt to humanize Tony, portraying him as a devoted father and a caring husband. He is a man, however, with many chinks in his armor, fraught with insecurity, landing him in therapy with psychiatrist Dr. Jennifer Melfi (Lorraine Bracco). His infidelities and "business" dealings at times are a contradiction to his personality. On a trip with his daughter, Meadow (Jamie-Lynn Sigler), to visit out-of-town colleges, Tony recognizes a squealer who had been placed in the witness-protection program and murders him. He burns down the restaurant of Artie Bucco (John Ventimiglia), his boyhood friend, and to satisfy the gambling debt of a neighbor's son, who is also Meadow's high-school friend, Tony bankrupts his business.

Critically acclaimed as an outstanding dramatic series, *The Sopranos* hit a responsive chord with the television audience. Although it touched upon the familiar theme of dysfunctional family life, it did so within the context of a narrative structure that embodied elements of values morphed into the hierarchy of crime. It became must-see television, with restaurants and clubs emptying on the evening of the season finale. There was a sense of heroism in Tony, who labored under the shadow of his father and was reminded about his father's leadership by Hesh (Jerry Adler), a Jewish friend and confidant of his late father. As the feds started closing in on him, wiring an old lamp in his basement conference room, the audience was relieved when Meadow unknowingly moved it to her Columbia dorm, compromising the surveillance. Rather than root for the idealistic virtues of law and order, *Sopranos* fans respect the role of Tony's criminally rebellious behavior. He is the outlaw pursued by the gunslingers of justice and by a ruthless underworld of savage mobsters. He responds to all of this with a fierce individualism that is a characteristic of American literary tradition.

Another HBO series focusing on a dysfunctional family involved in an unusual family business is the comedy-drama *Six Feet Under*. The series focuses on the Fisher family, which runs an independent mortuary in Los Angeles. The characters must struggle with their own weaknesses as well as the stress of operating a business that addresses the needs and sorrow of the bereaved.

Historically, television has not been particularly enamored with addressing the business of death in its purest form. Of course, television drama has incorporated scenes of eulogies, funeral processions, and interment, but has never pursued the mortuary business as a thematic construct for storytelling. There is a precedent for humor, comedy, and drama associated with death, as seen on HBO's *Tales from the Crypt* and the stand-up routines by various comedians. There's also the Sci Fi Channel's *Crossing Over with John Edwards,* featuring a medium who communicates with the dearly departed. However, *Six Feet Under* is distinctive for television because it examines the rituals of death within the context of a family whose angst is more with the living than the dead. It presents us with the concept of dying within the routinized world of work. In effect, one family's loss is another's gain.

The Fisher family has the requisite dysfunctionality, with two sons, one a closeted homosexual, the other with an insatiable sexual appetite and a girlfriend who coaxes him to have sex in all the wrong places, not unlike the Woody Allen film *Everything You Always Wanted to Know about Sex but Were Afraid to Ask* (1972). Mother Ruth disdains offensive speech, loses money at the races, and loves to have sex anywhere with almost anyone. Her daughter, Claire, compensates for her relatively homely appearance by being creative and bright while accommodating her boyfriend's needs by doing things like sucking on his big toe.

The program was created by Alan Ball, who won a 1999 Oscar for his original screenplay *American Beauty*. It presents viewers with a not-so-subtle irony about life and death, placing it in a shrouded portrait of guilt, resentment, and fear. As a pay-cable offering, language and situations can be especially vivid, and the humor can be somewhat scatological. Critics and audiences embraced *Six Feet Under* as innovative and daring. Some, however, were not as enthusiastic, calling it sleazy and mendacious, describing the cast as "cardboard props" and their characters as "cartoons." Indeed, one reviewer appeared outraged by the arrogance of the concept and ineptness of the actors. "It is a sensibility of overriding smugness, a self-congratulatory disdain for both characters and audience that precludes any possibility of real understanding, substituting preposterousness for imagination."[5]

As both cable and broadcast television attempt to explore thresholds of dysfunctional relationships, they do so within the constructs of defining the limits of sexual dynamics. Two programs on cable, *Queer as Folk* on Showtime and *Sex and the City* on HBO, present their audience with an intimate, vibrant look at sexuality among homosexual men and heterosexual women.

In dealing with issues of sexuality, broadcast television was extremely cautious in approaching serious themes of both homosexuality and heterosexuality. One of the first network television dramas to deal with the issue of AIDS and its effect on a gay man, his family, and his coworkers was the 1985 telefilm *An Early Frost*. Rather than present a clinical study of the disease, this movie showed the human side of the story, focusing on Michael Pierson (Aidan Quinn) as he and his family, coworkers, and friends struggled with the tragic consequences of AIDS. The talented cast included Ben Gazzara as the bitter father and Gena Rowlands portraying a mother having to face the inevitability of losing a child. The writers, Ron Cowen and Daniel Lipman, created an intimate portrait of a family in crisis attempting to deal with a lethal disease and a behavioral dynamic that was not a traditional construct of their lifestyle.

In a departure from the high drama of *An Early Frost*, Cowen and Lipman returned to the theme of gay men in the Showtime cable series *Queer as Folk*. Adapted from the British series with the same title, it provides a portrait of five young gay men living in Pittsburgh who are sexually active and suffer some discrimination because of their lifestyle. The 22-hour series premiered on December 3, 2000, in New York and was cosponsored by Showtime and the Gay Men's Health Crisis.

Cable television is no stranger to the depiction of sex or the use of profanity. The series *Dream On* on HBO; the stand-up comedy routines of Richard Pryor, George Carlin, Eddie Murphy, and Chris Rock; and the program *Oz*, which depicts life in a maximum-security prison, have demonstrated cable's initiative in allowing a freedom of expression to explore adult themes. Also, HBO's *Sex and the City* shows how urban women can be just as demonstrative about sex and its pleasures as their male counterparts. However, as one critic noted, *Sex and the City* has more talk than sex, while *Queer as Folk* has more sex than talk.

As such, the producers of *Queer as Folk* have embraced their material with a resonance of realism, depicting a reservoir of sexual behavior among men that includes rape and fondling along with anal and oral sex. Unlike NBC's *Will and Grace*, where asexuality is de rigueur, *Queer as Folk* is an unsanitized amalgam of gay behavior without any pretense and a confirmation of their way of living.

Being gay, writer-creator Ron Cowen is an advocate for portraying gay men in a realistic way and not as cartoon characters or stereotyped as tortured teens and victims of AIDS. As a writer, he feels an obligation to reveal how gays are discriminated against and treated as second-class citizens. However, some critics find that the tone of the series is "preachy" and judgmental and that it delineates a behavioral context that punishes the gay men when they exit their world and become victims on the outside.

While *Sex and the City* focuses on four women—Carrie, Miranda, Charlotte, and Samantha—and their perpetual longing for meaningful heterosexual relationships, it has also explored gay sexuality. As the series has matured, so have the plots, which included Carrie dating a bisexual and Charlotte getting involved with a group of power lesbians. The exploration of lesbian love occurred in an episode when Samantha had an intimate relationship with Sonia Braga.

There's also a reoccurring gay character, Stanford Blatch (Willie Garson), who is Carrie's friend. Although he's effeminate and might be viewed as a gay stereotype, his character has been integrated into the heterosexual thematic context of the story. Instead of the contemptuous relationship between gays and straights in *Queer as Folk,* there is an inclusive quality toward Stanford's relationship with heterosexuals.

One of the most ambitious and vividly defiant dramatic series on television is *Oz.* It premiered on HBO in 1996 (with a finale in 2003), and its gritty portrayal of life inside a maximum-security prison has made it a critical success. The men of Oz, which is short for Oswald Maximum-Security Prison, live in an experimental block called Emerald City. There, they face the rituals of prison life and the violence perpetuated by incarceration.

An ensemble cast of characters yields compelling narratives nuanced by the racial and socioeconomic dynamics of the prison population. Here, manhood is tested daily within the rigors of sexuality and the dynamics of ethnic and religious conflicts. There is a brutal and unforgiving dimension to the sometimes lurid behavior, which includes murder, rape, bondage, and predatory and violent same-sex relationships that include biting off the tip of a man's penis when an inmate is forced to perform oral sex.

The series, created by Tom Fontana, presents an array of issues associated with the sociological dimensions of the criminal justice system within the context of a political, moral, and legal milieu. There's an unsettling tone fueled by hostility, corruption, and the mesmerizing fear that consumes the inmates and guards. It's compelling drama that raises the threshold of realism to an unrestrained dynamic and a relentless pursuit of authenticity.[6]

## SOAP OPERAS

Drama has always been a genre offering artists an opportunity for growth and development. It nurtures emotions that are both serious and voyeuristic. A format that provided audiences with an opportunity to become involved with the day-to-day problems of fictional characters is the daytime serial drama, euphemistically known as the *soap opera*. With a mass audience appeal and a commercial imperative, soap operas gave radio and television an alternative to legitimate drama. They also provided a fertile field for nurturing writers and actors, featuring plots that evolved around lost love, infidelity, illness, and greed.

The daytime serial drama was a staple of radio programming that started in 1935 and reached its peak in 1940. By then the four radio networks had a combined total of 75 weekly hours dedicated to this programming genre. Indeed, 9 of every 10 sponsored daytime hours were associated with this programming. Programs like *The Romance of Helen Trent,* which started in 1933 and ran for 27 years; *Ma Perkins* (1933); *Back Stage Wife; Our Gal Sunday,* which began in 1937 and ran for 22 years; and *Guiding Light* offered listeners an escape from the drudgery of their daily routines. Their story lines, which evolved very slowly, included situations that were compelling to the audience, many of whom were lonely housewives. The 15-minute segments, which were broadcast at the same time every day, had taglines like "What it means to be the wife of a famous Broadway star" and "Can this girl from a mining town in the West find happiness as the wife of a wealthy and titled Englishman?"

Perhaps one of the most banal of these voice-over introductions was the one that was read at the beginning of every episode of the radio soap opera *The Romance of Helen Trent.* It offered a compassionate and compelling, albeit cliché-ridden, reason for a divorced woman of 35 to be optimistic about finding romance.

And now "The Romance of Helen Trent," the real-life drama of Helen Trent, who, when life mocks her, breaks her hopes, dashes her against the rocks of despair, fights back bravely, successfully, to prove what so many women long to prove—that because a woman is thirty-five or more, romance in life need not be over, that romance can begin at thirty-five.

The longevity of some of the actors and actresses who played featured roles on the soap operas was long-standing and sometimes lasted for decades. Their format was simple in design and usually began with the somber tone of organ music accompanied by a narrator's voice-over providing a recap of previous episodes. Then there would be a commercial break between the action and the reprise of the narrator, who wrapped things up.

The soap opera owes its creation to several producers, including Frank Hummert, an advertising executive with the Chicago agency of Lord and Thomas. His success as a copywriter was legendary, and by the time he was 41 years old, he had accumulated a great deal of wealth and retired. Eventually, he became bored and returned to the world of advertising, taking a position with another agency, Blackett and Sample. He married his longtime assistant, Anne Ashenhurst, and as a team they created some of the most popular soap operas.

There was a certain creative genius about Hummert and the way he conceived the genre. He thought that radio could duplicate the success of continuing dramas that had been a part of the kinetoscope's success. The kinetoscope was a personal viewing machine where for five cents one could see a one-minute film. Later this concept was adapted for movie-screen serials like *The Perils of Pauline*. Hummert and Anne Ashenhurst used this concept to develop radio's first soap opera, about an ordinary Midwest barber, *Just Plain Bill*. (*Betty and Bob,* starring Don Ameche, on the NBC Blue radio network, was another early entry.)

Shortly after the success of *Just Plain Bill,* Anne and Frank created *The Romance of Helen Trent*. This radio series was a novel departure, because its theme was related to a woman's failed marriage and her quest for romance after the age of 35. At a time when so many women married in their early 20s and had families, the idea of an older woman looking for love was an attractive story line for many housewives and proved its popularity by running for 27 years.

After establishing themselves as the premier producers of radio "soapers," the Hummerts moved to New York and created a separate production company. Although they started out developing and writing most of the material, because of the enormous amount of work they soon had to hire dialogue writers to assist them. They received $25 a script or $125 a week for a five-script series. Other writers who contributed to radio soapers were Elaine Carrington and Irna Phillips.

With the development of the soap opera, women had a unique opportunity to become empowered in an industry controlled by men. As a young schoolteacher in Dayton, Ohio, Irna Phillips thought about writing and producing programs for radio. She traveled to Chicago and convinced station WGN to give her 15 minutes a day for her serialized saga *Painted Dreams.*

Phillips, along with her protégé, Agnes Nixon, produced some of the longest-running soap operas in radio and television, including *Guiding Light, The Road of Life,* and *Woman in White*. In 1956 Irna Phillips, in a dramatic departure from tradition, created the first half-hour soaper (the usual format was 15 minutes), *As the World Turns,* which was later joined by another original Phillips production, *The Edge of Night*.

Like Phillips, Nixon was not bound to the customs of the genre and also believed in departing from the usual story lines. The turbulent times of the 1960s, with its civil unrest, sexual revolution, and drug culture, provided the substance for the development of soap operas that would have more relevance to a new and younger audience. The two daytime serial dramas, *One Life to Live* and *All My Children,* hit a vibrant cord, addressing substantive issues of the day, including abortion, drugs, and the Vietnam War.

Another influential writer-producer of soap operas was Roy Windsor. His instincts as to what the 1950s American housewife wanted to see on her television screen proved to be prophetic. The daytime serials he created, *Search for Tomorrow* (1951–86) and *Love of Life* (1951–80), proved to be some of the longest-running daytime dramas in television's history. Their focus included themes evolving around marriage, romance, and family. One can only appreciate the magnitude of his achievement when reviewing the cast lists, scripts, and writers that spanned three decades and more for the series, which aired daily.

As a creator-producer, Windsor had impressive credentials. In addition to his long-running network soaps, he also created *Hotel Cosmopolitan* (1957); *Ben Jerrod,* a prime-time network series; and *Another Life* (1981). He was also an executive producer for *The Secret Storm.*

Another husband-and-wife team, William and Lee Phillip Bell, created the long-running *Young and the Restless,* which is still appearing daily on the CBS network. The series, which is owned by the advertising agency Young and Rubicam, celebrated the taping of its 7,000th episode on September 28, 2000. It has been a consistent number-one in the daytime ratings.

In radio (and later television), the advertising agencies, representing their clients, were prominent in creating programming and supplying it to the networks. In the 1940s soap operas cost the sponsor about $18,000 a week, with $3,000 paid to talent (writers, actors, and directors). The balance, less the 15 percent agency commission and payments to affiliated stations carrying the programs, went to the network. These programs became cash cows for CBS and NBC, netting about $10,000 per program.

The radio soap operas proved to be tremendously popular, attracting half the women at home as listeners. Many in the audience developed a close personal bond with the characters, sending gifts and cards marking fictional birthdays, anniversaries, and other scripted events. To a large number of the audience, there was a special affinity between them and the featured players that superseded the boundaries between fiction and reality. They tuned in to nurture their own egos, for companionship, and to escape from their boredom. Many of the women sought guidance, refuge, and moral support from the characters that they identified with.

The identification an audience has with a character in a continuing television series is a staple of television programming. Ratings for daytime and prime-time dramas usually spike when a main character consummates a relationship, gets married, gives birth, dies, or comes out of the closet. It's a reflection of the intimacy that is sustained between characters in long-running series and their fans.[7]

The soaps moved to television and captured an equally devoted audience. Perhaps the earliest daytime serial drama to be telecast was *Last Year's Nest,* which aired on a local Philadelphia station (channel 3) in 1942. By 1950, CBS began *First Hundred Years.* Soon, these were followed by the successful, long-running CBS series, including *Guiding Light,* which started on radio and is still televised daily at 10 A.M.; *Love of Life; Search for Tomorrow;* and *As the World Turns.* The first daytime serial television drama to go from 15 minutes to half an hour was *As the World Turns,* which has been on the CBS schedule since 1951.

As a legendary programmer, Fred Silverman, at ABC, didn't always like the status quo. In 1977 he expanded *All My Children* to an hour, and soon after, he moved *One Life to Live* and *General Hospital* from 30 minutes to 45 minutes with the intent of also making them an hour. He brought in Jackie Smith to coordinate production of the soaps and supervise their new long form. She, in turn, hired Gloria Monty, a talented writer, to produce *General Hospital,* and A. J. Russell, a writer from television's golden age, who wrote the "bible" for the new *General Hospital.*

As an executive producer, Jackie Smith possessed the multiplicity of talents necessary to run a soap opera "factory" with each series producing five shows a week. She dealt with monumental egos, maintained oversight of the writing, and managed the promotion for ABC's daytime dramas. Her most successful promotional effort was the theme "Love in the Afternoon," which became the catch phrase that helped catapult ABC's daytime serial dramas into a ratings leader for network television.

*General Hospital* proved to be such a popular daytime drama that many established celebrities asked to be written into the show. This led Smith on another unique promotional endeavor called "Prime-Time Stars for Daytime." No matter what caliber of star power the actor was, they all received the same honorarium, $1,000 for each appearance. When celebrity icon Elizabeth Taylor expressed an interest in appearing as a guest on *General Hospital* for a weeklong stint, Smith was elated. The network didn't have the kind of money to pay Taylor for an appearance, and now they would get her for scale, and all of the free publicity her name would buy.

But in most businesses there's no free lunch, and Smith quickly learned that. Most stars travel with an entourage, and Taylor had 25 in her party, including a hair dresser, footman, doorman, press agent, and marine specialist to set up her aquarium. In addition, she insisted that each of them appear as an extra, which slowed down production because they kept missing their lines. With the lavender roses and special food she required, and everything billed to ABC, it cost the network $100,000 for the five days—still quite a bargain.

Every successful television executive has a programming instinct that involves a sense of risk and challenge. This was true for Leonard Goldenson, the CEO of ABC. He had a screening room in his Mamaroneck, New York, home where each week he would watch several films with friends. After viewing Lana Turner's *Imitation of Life,* which he thought was a theatrical soap opera, he felt that such a genre also had a place in prime time. So he told several of his executives to find a soap-opera property that would be suitable for an evening schedule.

But serendipity interceded. Occasionally, Goldenson carpooled to Manhattan with his neighbor Spyros Skouras, the head of Fox. One morning on their ride into town, Goldenson asked Skouras if he had something that would make a "deluxe soap opera" for prime time. After a few seconds of thought, Skouras mentioned a property Fox owned called *Peyton Place.* His instinct at the ready, Goldenson jumped at the opportunity and quickly acquired the title.

The premiere of *Peyton Place* on September 15, 1964, had a phenomenal effect on the success of ABC. The half-hour show was broadcast on Tuesday and Thursday evenings at 9:30. There was some concern because the series was based upon a sexually explicit novel of the same name. Several strategic scheduling factors added to the success of the series, and they included a lead seasonal premiere week (ahead of CBS and NBC) and the debut of *Bewitched,* a hit program that preceded *Peyton Place* on the schedule.

Those three weeks gave ABC number-one ranking for the first time in its history. Of course, casting also helped, with Dorothy Malone, a veteran actress, in the lead, and Ryan O'Neal, Barbara Parkins, and Mia Farrow as the young stars in *Peyton Place,* and Elizabeth Montgomery as the star of *Bewitched.* Both programs were blockbusters, and ABC added a third night of *Peyton Place* to its schedule.

The reviews were also enthusiastic about the prime-time soap. Using adjectives like *blockbuster, superior,* and *sharp,* the program seemed to please most of the critics.

Its cup runs over with the commercial ingredients of the lovelorn columns and the stuff that packs 'em in at the drive-in-movies—the ripening sex urge in teenage kids, wretched marriages, illegitimate offspring, adultery and assorted other concupiscent adventures. Also, it is favored with a good looking cast, skilled to a man in the art of the deep sigh and with highly favorable slotting in ABC's two strongest nights of the week. . . . The show is a slick job all around, with good soaper performances and knowledgeable direction. And lest it be thought strictly a woman's dish, who's to deny that men dig sex?

. . . "Peyton Place" is gossip raised to its highest video level. It's easy to deprecate this night time sudser, but in fairness it is a good example of a tear-and-trauma drama. The acting is good, production values are superior for this type of show. The scripting is sharp and the editing is astute.[8]

Although *Peyton Place* was an example of the successful transplanting of the daytime soap format to prime time, the other networks were less sanguine about the genre's relevancy to their evening schedules. However, the same characteristics that were incorporated into the soap-opera genre became integrated into prime-time programs that were deemed to have family values. One of the first of these was *The Waltons.* As is so often the case, the creative forces involved with the program, writer Earl Hamner Jr. and Lee Rich, hadn't anticipated making it into a series. The idea evolved from a made-for-television movie, *The Homecoming,* written by Earl Hamner Jr., about a close-knit family enduring the Depression in the mountains of Appalachia.

The chairman of CBS, William Paley, saw the movie and felt that it would be a terrific series. He made a comment to producer Lee Rich, saying, "I want that one on the air. We've taken out of the barrel for too long; it's time we put something in."[9]

Once again, Paley's instinctive acumen was on target, as *The Waltons*, after making its debut in 1972, became a ratings success and a very popular television program. Its characteristics were very similar to soap-opera themes. There was no overt or gratuitous violence. Instead, there was a dialogue between generations: grandparents, parents, and children.

As a programmer, Paley had great success in both television and radio. When he was asked about his ability to recognize successful concepts and superior talent, he offered a measured response. "I believe the most important and virtually unfailing indication of a good program—over and above basic good writing, direction, casting, costumes, and sets—is likeable, intriguing characters who capture the imagination, interest, or concern of the audience."[10]

The Paley instinct for programming struck gold (black gold) for CBS in 1978 with the premiere of *Dallas* (1978–91). In his portrayal of the villainous oil baron J. R. Ewing, actor Larry Hagman personified the evils of wealth, power, and greed. The series was a tribute to prime-time soap-opera themes, with infidelity, love triangles, and illegitimacy hovering in the shadows of family dynamics.

In 1980 *Dallas* created one of the most anticipated cliff-hangers in the history of television, evocative of the speeding-train moment in the short features of *The Perils of Pauline*. At the end of the 1980 season, J. R. Ewing was shot by an unidentified assailant. When the program resolving the mystery aired on November 21, 1980, 350 million fans in 57 countries tuned in.

Actor Larry Hagman was an experienced television actor who had appeared with Barbara Eden in *I Dream of Jeannie*, another hit television series that ran for five years. He also starred for two years in the daytime soap opera *The Edge of Night*. His feature film credits include *Fail-Safe* (1964) and *Primary Colors* (1998).

The best accolade of success is imitation, and *Dallas* spawned several copycat versions, including *Falcon Crest* (CBS, 1981–90), *Dynasty* (ABC, 1981–89), and *The Colbys* (a *Dynasty* spin-off; ABC, 1985–87). Oil was a common theme for *Dynasty* and *The Colbys*, while wine and the lush setting of California's Tuscany Valley were the setting for *Falcon Crest*. The success of these programs proved to be an attraction to movie stars like Charlton Heston and Barbara Stanwyck, stars of *The Colbys*, and Oscar winner Jane Wyman, who was the lead in *Falcon Crest*.

A telling example for the audience attraction to prime-time soap operas was the success of three imported British television series, *The First Churchills*, *The Forsyte Saga*, and *Upstairs Downstairs*. For American network television, the revelation was that these imported programs, which featured soap-opera themes, could be so successful in prime time. Indeed, the premiere of *The Forsyte Saga*, based upon the Victorian-Edwardian novels of John Galsworthy, was an immediate hit with American audiences and helped increase donations for public television. Eventually, *Mobil's Masterpiece Theatre* (1971) became an umbrella title for popular British imports, including *Upstairs Downstairs,* which was a phenomenal success in America. The program, which had a soap orientation, documented the lives and events surrounding an aristocratic family living in a London town house circa 1900. It contrasted the servants (downstairs) with those of the family that employed them (upstairs), showing a vivid portrayal of the distinctions and similarities in their lives.

## MINISERIES

*Masterpiece Theatre,* which premiered in 1971 with a season that included *The First Churchills, The Six Wives of Henry VIII,* and *The Last of the Mohicans,* has been a fixture on public television for three decades.

The ABC television network was one of the first to try the miniseries format in prime time, although they called the programs *novels for television.* They started with *QBVII,* based upon Leon Uris's bestselling novel, and followed with *Rich Man, Poor Man.*

The decade of the 1980s was ushered in by an ambitious miniseries event that set the tone for the popularity of this genre for the remainder of the decade. The NBC television network broadcast the 12-part miniseries *Shogun,* based upon James Clavell's novel and filmed entirely on location in Japan. It starred Richard Chamberlain, who had played Dr. Kildare on television and had become a popular leading actor in miniseries events. In an unusual casting occurrence, Toshiro Mifune, a well-known Japanese actor (not popular in the United States), and Yoko Shimada, a relatively unknown Japanese actress, had costarring roles. In addition to the leads, 28 principal roles were cast with Japanese actors.

*Shogun* served as the benchmark for network miniseries production on an ambitious and grand scale. It was followed by *Massada* (1981), *The Winds of War* (1983), and *The Thornbirds* (1986, starring Richard Chamberlain). As miniseries costs mounted, the networks were concerned about the production costs relative to the ratings that these programs achieved.

The development of a miniseries is an arduous and challenging experience. Several examples, including *Roots, The Winds of War,* and *War and Remembrance,* are indicative of the obstacles that must be surmounted.

When ABC became interested in adapting Alex Haley's *Roots* to the television screen, they didn't realize that he hadn't started writing the book yet. The network wanted the project, and the screenwriters worked on the script while Haley wrote the novel. The only thing they were concerned about was not getting ahead of Haley's work. As the program was being shot, ABC executives Fred Silverman and Fred Pierce found the material so rich and compelling that they agreed to extend the miniseries to 12 hours. There was also the concern of a television event with a mostly black cast. At that time, no program like that had been successful on television. All of these concerns were mitigated by the overwhelming response of the audience, which tuned into the program's January 1977 premiere in record numbers, making it the highest-rated miniseries in broadcast history.

When ABC and Paramount decided to adapt Herman Wouk's bestselling novel *The Winds of War* for television, they faced a number of obstacles that proved to be quite daunting. The author wanted a faithful screen interpretation of his work and didn't want interruptions by commercials for deodorants, toilet-bowl cleaners, and feminine-hygiene products. Within the dynamics of the Hollywood community, it was unheard of to give an author control of the marketing characteristics of the event. The compromise agreement with Wouk, a first in the industry, limited the kind of participating sponsors, the number and length of commercials, the level of network promotion, and the show's format, and guaranteed that specific scenes from his novel would be included. In addition, Herman Wouk received a generous fee for the network serialization of his novel.

It took two years to write the *Winds of War* script, and casting was also a lengthy process. Five years would pass before *The Winds of War* made its television debut, in February 1983. One of the most expensive miniseries produced for television was based on another of Herman Wouk's novels, *War and Remembrance*. Everything about *War and Remembrance* was on a monumental scale. The script consisted of 1,492 pages, and there were 757 sets, 2,070 scenes, two years of preproduction, 21 months on location, one year of postproduction, 358 speaking parts, 30,310 extras, and 2 million feet of film.

The final installments for *War and Remembrance* were broadcast on ABC in May of 1989. The ratings fell below advertiser guarantees, thus prompting the network to raise the loss projection of the miniseries to between $30 and 40 million. After the disappointing ratings performance of *War and Remembrance*, the miniseries genre was reevaluated by network television. They were expensive to produce and earned lower ratings during network reruns. The consensus was that audiences preferred shorter miniseries.

During the late 1980s the broadcast television networks experienced a steep decline in their average audience share. However, the CBS miniseries *Lonesome Dove*, based upon Larry McMurtry's popular novel, helped CBS, then the number-three network, out of its rating slump. The series was broadcast during the February 1989 sweeps period and earned respectable ratings and shares for the network.

As broadcast-network television moved away from the miniseries format, cable television, especially HBO, adopted it. After almost four years of planning and two years of production, *Band of Brothers,* the 10-part HBO miniseries, made its debut on September 9, 2001. Based upon Stephen E. Ambrose's bestseller about Easy Company, a World War II parachute division, jumping into Normandy on D-day, the $120 million series had the cachet of having as executive producers Steven Spielberg and actor-director Tom

Hanks, who had teamed up for the World War II theatrical feature *Saving Private Ryan*.

The most expensive miniseries ever produced for television, *Band of Brothers* was the most ambitious undertaking in the history of HBO, a division of AOL/Time Warner. It was treated as "event" television, with an unprecedented promotional campaign and a substantial $15 million advertising budget. Part of that effort was transporting 47 of the 51 surviving members of Easy Company, who were flown to Normandy for a special screening in conjunction with the 57th anniversary of D-day. They also held a premiere at the Hollywood Bowl, the largest in the history of HBO.

As a part of AOL/Time Warner, HBO benefited from the ability to cross-promote the miniseries on its different platforms. Subscribers to AOL saw a *Band of Brothers* logo when they logged on to the "welcome" screen. In addition, there was a state-of-the-art interactive Web site that provided details about the series. Cable television was another platform effectively utilized as a promotional tool. The Turner Classic Movies channel scheduled an 11-week, 36-hour extravaganza of war movies every Monday night leading up to the miniseries premiere.

Schools were another target for the HBO publicity machine. Tapping the resources of Time Inc.'s School Publishing unit, 3 million 10th and 11th graders were targeted and received student magazines, posters, and study guides. In addition, cable operators cooperating with HBO sent a mailing themed to *Band of Brothers* to 51 million subscribers that were not affiliated with HBO, offering incentives to sign up for the service. Indeed, HBO executives had scheduled the series premiere for June but delayed it for strategic reasons pertaining to summer viewing patterns, the start of the new season, and the beginning of the school year. They also arranged for some of the Easy Company veterans to visit schools and make presentations at various community centers.

A major advertising print campaign was also part of the overall strategy. For this event the cable network purchased more newspaper and magazine ads for a single event than at any other time in its history. One of the most unique promotional aspects for the series was a partnership between the Chrysler Group division of DaimlerChrysler and its Jeep brand. The intent was to celebrate the 60th anniversary of the military jeep, which was manufactured by Willys-Overland for the Allies during World War II. In the 10-hour miniseries, these vintage vehicles are seen at least 1,000 times. Six Jeep commercials were created for network broadcast, each prominently mentioning the HBO miniseries. Indeed, the first was shot on Utah Beach in Normandy.

It was a shrewd coordinated effort, because the traditional broadcast networks have been reluctant to sell advertising spots to HBO promoting their original programming. However, the networks could not decline to run the

Jeep advertisements, as DaimlerChrysler is a major advertiser on network television.[11]

## DOCUDRAMA

While some miniseries addressed realistic themes integrated with fictional characters, the docudrama format attempted to reconcile reality with the dramatic needs of television. These programs created some controversy concerning the accuracy of the events they portrayed, their chronology, and the characters involved. Nevertheless, the genre became popular on American television, addressing many stories from newspaper headlines.

One story that appeared to grip the country was the relationship between Amy Fisher and Joey Buttafuoco. The two had an affair, and Amy shot Mrs. Buttafuoco in the head, severely injuring her. Newspapers and television stations fell over themselves reporting the bizarre circumstances of the relationship. Eventually, CBS, ABC, and NBC each broadcast a docudrama television movie about the event.

Perhaps one of the most interesting examples of how television can be politicized and become a pawn in international politics was the case of the docudrama *Death of a Princess*. In 1977, PBS (Public Broadcasting Service) acquired the license to broadcast this British-produced docudrama about a Saudi Arabian princess who, along with her lover, was executed for committing adultery. After its broadcast in Great Britain, the Saudis recalled their ambassador as a sign of protest. They argued that the program was an unfair depiction of Saudi culture and that the actual events were distorted by compromising the facts with fictional narrative. After learning that PBS had acquired the American rights, the Saudis threatened a similar response if the program was broadcast in the United States.

As a major underwriter of public television in the United States, and with extensive oil interests in the Middle East, the Mobil Oil company initiated a public-relations effort to persuade PBS against distributing the program. In addition to Mobil's advertising campaign, the Saudis hired an influential law firm in an effort to obtain a restraining order prohibiting broadcast of the program. The docudrama was broadcast; however, several PBS-affiliated stations declined to carry it, resulting in a number of community lawsuits against those stations.

Television drama is an essential part of the fabric of television. Whether prime-time or daytime soap operas, miniseries, regularly scheduled dramatic series, or special events, these narratives offer television audiences relevant entertainment based upon compelling themes. It's difficult to assess the components of successful television drama. One of the longest-running series (14 seasons, 1979–93) was *Knots Landing,* a spin-off of *Dallas*. Although it was a prime-time soap opera, it had all of the ingredients to make it a success: love triangles, addictions, swindles, and sex. While it certainly had limited literary value, it provided audiences with the type of fiction that fulfilled a need for escapist entertainment.

The longest-running prime-time drama on television was *Gunsmoke* (CBS, 1955–75). Although not a contemporary program, *Gunsmoke* addressed the universal theme of good versus evil within the context of the frontier. Its characters were imbued with the strengths and weaknesses that are common to everyone. In addition, the lead, Marshal Matt Dillon, portrayed by James Arness, was a strong yet compassionate individual, very independent but also reliant upon the close friendships he had with the other ensemble cast members: Doc Adams (Milburn Stone), Kitty Russell (Amanda Blake), and Chester Goode (Dennis Weaver, 1955–64). Their qualities of loyalty, love, and professionalism were attributes that could be respected by the audience and associated with the dynamics of their own relationships. Indeed, *Gunsmoke* served as a template for modern serial television police dramas that adapted the same themes of justice and retribution.

The second-longest-running prime-time television program is *Law and Order* on NBC (October 30, 1990, and renewed to May 2005). Many of the story lines for the series are taken from the news headlines and adapted to the format of the program. This series is an excellent example of the program as a starring vehicle, as cast members have been changed without weakening the quality of the program. It has many similarities to *Gunsmoke,* with a close-knit group of dedicated detectives and prosecutors who are sometimes victims of their own overzealousness. As with *Gunsmoke,* the characters in *Law and Order* have the same allegiance to each other and strive to uphold their values and the citizens they protect as part of the dynamics of the series. Although one program takes place in the frontier town of Dodge City, Kansas, in the 1890s and the other in present-day New York City, the principal workplace characters are clearly defined and nuanced by their own foibles that measure the essence of their being.

## NOTES

1. *Variety,* 10 October 1956.

2. *Variety,* 17 October 1956.

3. Leonard H. Goldenson and Marvin J. Wolf, *Beating the Odds* (New York: Charles Scribner's Sons, 1991), p. 167.

4. Samuel G. Freedman, "The Subtle Drama Found in Silence and Rue," *New York Times,* 22 October 2000, p. AR27.

5. Wendy Lesser, "Here Lies Hollywood: Falling for 'Six Feet Under,'" *New York Times,* 22 July 2001, p. 28.

6. Julie Salamon, "A Chance to See 'Salesman' as if for the First Time," *New York Times,* 5 August 2001, p. AR25; Alan James Frutkin, "The Return of the Show that Gets Gay Life Right," *New York Times,* 6 January 2002, p. AR33; Bernard Weinraub, "Cable TV Shatters Another Taboo," *New York Times,* 20 November 2000, p. E1; Lauren David Peden, "The Inmates of 'Oz' Move into a New Emerald City," *New*

*York Times,* 15 July 2001, p. AR24; Caryn James, "High Tech Prison and the Face of Horror," *New York Times,* 12 July 1992, sec. 1, p. 11; Bill Carter, "Sex and the Serious," *New York Times,* 13 August 2001; Peter Nichols, "50's TV Dramas in Stores Soon," *New York Times,* 18 January 2001; Susan King, "Video Log," *Los Angeles Times,* 15 November 2001.

7. Christopher H. Sterling and John M. Kittross, *Stay Tuned: A Concise History of American Broadcasting* (Belmont, Calif.: Wadsworth Publishing Company, 1978), pp. 165–66, 224; Robert Metz, *CBS: Reflections in a Bloodshot Eye* (Chicago: Playboy Press, 1975), pp. 75–82.

8. *Variety,* 23 September 1964.

9. Robert Metz, "The Hear and Now," in *Reflections in a Bloodshot Eye* (Chicago: Playboy Press, 1975), p. 403.

10. William S. Paley, "Entertaining You," p. 269.

11. Sally Beatty, "HBO Marches into Battle," *New York Times,* 18 July 2001, p. B1; Bill Carter, "HBO Bets Pentagon-Style Budget on a World War II Saga," *New York Times,* 3 September 2001, p. C1; Stuart Elliott, "Jeep's Manufacturer Seeks to Capitalize on the Vehicle's Featured Role in 'Band of Brothers,'" *New York Times,* 10 September 2001, sec. C, p. 8.

# 9

## REALITY TV: SURVIVING THE TREND

Perhaps the cultural imperative of reality television evolved from true events that were nurtured by the media to create a frenzy of attention, celebrating the mission of audience pleasure. They can be manufactured by the media, creating total audience immersion by continuous coverage with a high rate of redundancy. Since the Lindbergh kidnapping trial of 1935, and with the arrival of television and the Internet, the media have created a new genre of sensation buttressed by role models who, if not already celebrities, achieve that status as a result of the coverage.

The realistic drama of Monica Lewinsky created a compelling electronic canvas that enthralled a global audience, which breathlessly waited for any new morsel of salacious information. A 22-year-old woman thrust into the gaze of a culture consumed with a voyeuristic need, she was ill prepared to deal with it and the misconceptions and define herself. The media made assumptions about her that were not true. Her father was not a Beverly Hills doctor, but had a practice in the Valley; she was raised in Beverly Hills, but hadn't lived there for 10 years; and her family was comfortable, but not wealthy. As the media circus pervaded her life, she became adept at adopting their tools to her own needs.

Training for fame since he was a kid, O. J. Simpson was no stranger to the bright lights and attention of the media. From football star to fleeing murder suspect, Simpson's journey through the media's gaze seemed bizarre and rehearsed. It was a story made for American tabloid journalism steeped in the culture of newspapers like the *National Enquirer*. Indeed, it spoke to the character of the reality programs, with the game being played out in a courtroom and the lawyers, Simpson, and Judge Ito as the principal contestants.

In the culture of entertainment, reality has taken on new dimensions, and truth has been massaged and compromised for entertainment value. In an effort to be competitive with the reality market, Fox created the short-lived *Who Wants to Marry a Multimillionaire*. As the winner and television bride-to-be, Darva Conger met a new reality posed by the media's scrutiny and pervasiveness. She faced off with the insatiable appetite of the media, with their constant harangue for more. Along with her pseudomillionaire, Rick Rockwell, they became the global couple lavished with attention and victims of incessant curiosity.

They were captured in a bubble of grotesque imagery and pursued by a warped culture that values the lurid, taking pleasure in the pain of its victims. As part of the dynamic, there was also a deceit, which revealed that Rick Rockwell wasn't the person he claimed to be. The marriage was never consummated and eventually annulled. For Darva Conger it wasn't a lesson of love, but exposure to the base instinct of the media and its demand for full disclosure.[1]

But the deception that Rick Rockwell perpetrated planted a seed for one of the biggest reality hits of the 2002–2003 season. Plundering the realm of tasteless fiction, *Joe Millionaire* (Fox) challenged women to vie for the affections of a young man who they were told inherited $50 million. His name was Evan Marriott, a construction worker who didn't mind perpetuating a myth that he was wealthy while wooing a bevy of unsuspecting, vulnerable women lusting for his "wealth." This show, along with other reality-based programming, gave Fox its first sweeps rating win in its 16-year network history, with the finale of *Joe Millionaire* attracting 40 million viewers. There was even a sequel to the show, *Joe Millionaire: The Aftermath,* where the couple, Evan and Zora, provides a revealing glimpse of the true nature of their relationship—a reality toast to the essence of tabloid TV.

## THE ROOTS OF REALITY

There has always been reality television. Over the years it has come to television viewers in many guises and formats: sometimes as entertainment, when Steve Allen originated the man-on-the-street interview; as news documentary, under the watchful eye of Edward R. Murrow; or as a carnie sideshow, with teary-eyed contestants telling the audience about their terrible troubles. This last was a show called *Queen for a Day,* and its purpose was to showcase the unfortunate plight of women in a time of dire need.

Its popularity can be measured by its longevity, starting in 1945 on radio and moving to television in 1955. The program was so successful that NBC lengthened the format from 30 to 45 minutes, increasing its inventory of commercial spots, which were selling for $4,000 per minute.

The program's format was simple and direct: 20 women were chosen from the studio audience, and after each had been interviewed, 5 finalists were selected. The criteria for winning was solely based upon the saddest and most compelling story of woe that the contestant could conjure. Judgment was made by the studio audience via an "applause meter." Prizes like refrigerators, bedroom sets, bicycles, and washing machines were provided by the manufacturers in exchange for product announcements.

Some critics described the program as being self-indulgent and exploitative, which it was. Its host, Jack Bailey, a former carnival barker, was well suited for his role posing as the compassionate host. Indeed, the characteristics of this program are vividly evident in most of the reality programs on television today.

One entertainment reality-based program that was a precursor to shows like *America's Funniest Home Videos* (ABC, 1990) and *Totally Hidden Video* (Fox, 1989) was *Candid Camera*, created by Allen Funt. It started on ABC radio as *Candid Microphone* (1948) and made its television debut on NBC in 1949 as *Candid Camera*. It was quite an achievement to capture unsuspecting people in somewhat awkward situations, especially in early television, with cumbersome equipment, prominent lighting, and hidden microphones. But the concept clicked with the audience, and *Candid Camera* became one of the most popular programs on television and one of the first to succeed as reality-based. When CBS provided the program with a permanent time slot in 1960, it was able to build a weekly audience, and for the next seven years consistently rated as one of the top 10 shows.

In addition to creating a unique and funny reality-based program niche, Funt also pioneered in the use of guest cohosts. He was often joined by popular celebrities of the era, including Durward Kirby, Bess Meyerson, and Arthur Godfrey. The program entered syndication from 1974 to 1978 with old and new material, and theme segments such as *Candid Camera Goes to the Doctor* were produced and distributed on CBS until 1990. That year a new syndicated version of the program was distributed by King Productions and hosted by Dom DeLuise. But the ratings never materialized, and the program was not renewed.

Interestingly, one of the first experiments with the current genre of reality television appeared on public television in March 1973 and was an expression of the 1960s cinema verité movement, focusing on unscripted action and portable equipment. For months a camera crew documented the lives of the Santa Barbara, California, Loud family: Bill, Pat, and their five children. *An American Family,* a 12-hour cinema verité series produced by Alan and Susan Raymond, was a revealing portrait of a family in crisis and a disintegrating marriage. It was compelling television, exposing a family dynamic to the scrutiny of an audience 10 million strong.

The Public Broadcasting Service (PBS) had approached the Raymonds to produce a 10-year anniversary program on the Louds in 1983; however, after budget cuts, the project was canceled but revived by HBO. In 1990, PBS distributed *An American Family* as an encore presentation in two six-hour blocks, and in January 2003 the Raymonds produced *Lance Loud! A Death in an American Family*.

In 1999, public television revisited the concept of profiling a family with the 10-hour *American Love Story*. Produced and directed by award-winning filmmaker Jennifer Fox, the Sims family from Queens, New York, was the subject of the documentary. Fox lived with the family, an interracial couple with two daughters, for two years, and interviewed them, along with three generations from either side of the family, over a period of five years. In addition to portraying the dynamic of this family, the race issue and how it's viewed within the context of the family as well as in American society was paramount to the project.

It was *An American Family* that served as a model for a new generation of reality television. This series was a precursor to the updated reality genre and an antecedent to MTV's *The Real World*. Placing reality within the context of entertainment was the theme for the MTV series *The Real World*. Catering to its audience and capitalizing on the network's strength reaching a young demographic, this series, which started in 1991, was one of the first American attempts to adapt the genre to a wider commercial audience with a more compelling demographic.

The team responsible for creating and producing *The Real World* is Jonathan Murray, a former news producer, and Mary-Ellis Bunim, who was the executive producer of network-television soap operas like *Search for Tomorrow, As the World Turns,* and *Santa Barbara*. The experience each of them had in their respective genres was a catalyst in combining the dynamics of soap opera with nonfiction narrative. The three-act dramatic structure for each of the 24–26 half-hour episodes is a substantive tool that evolves along the themes presented by the participants and choreographed by the producers.

Each year the series takes seven young people who are strangers and moves them to a spectacular residence in an unfamiliar city while watching the drama unfold in their interpersonal relationships. Those chosen suit a preconceived notion about character so that the theatrical environment can accommodate the various soap-opera themes of the program. There is usually a smart guy, an attractive girl, a gay person, a shy small-town girl, and a young man with a roving eye. Selecting the seven-member "family" from approximately 35,000 applicants each season is a monumental task. However, the producers utilize a disciplined set of criteria, including diversity, appearance, and emotional accessibility, as tools for selection.

These distinctions add drama and pathos, albeit in a contrived and manipulated setting. The series has addressed many of society's problems and ills through the eyes of these youths, including AIDS, alcoholism, unwanted pregnancy, and sexual promiscuity.

No doubt one of the reasons for the enduring success of this series is the close attention to selecting the "family" members and the painstaking care of production values. A total environment of camera presence is achieved both in the residence and on location. The thousands of hours recorded on video are sorted by a team of experienced editors who understand the nuances of dramatic interaction and have a good sense of narrative structure. Scenes are not reshot; thus, staging events are avoided. With an audience estimated at 3.1 million, small by broadcast standards but impressive for basic cable, a modest cost of $300,000 per episode, and a core audience of ages 18–25, *The Real World* makes economic sense for MTV.

Although there is a certain familiarity with the interpersonal dynamics of the series, the players are always different, and the distinctions of their background and personalities create a compelling narrative. The producers developed *Road Rules* for MTV in 1995, which has six youthful participants who travel together in a recreational vehicle and are given a set of missions to accomplish. *The Real World* created a template for other iterations of the formula, although its followers have prioritized it with commercial imperatives. For the seven strangers coming together in *The Real World,* there is no ultimate prize for their efforts. They are given a sumptuous place to live (a glorious brownstone in New York's Greenwich Village for 2001) and food, but no winnings. Indeed, they are sometimes faced with the hardships associated with "family" life, having to come to terms with each other on various emotional levels. So often, their youthful illusions are shattered by the harsh reality of daily life. Unlike its followers, *The Real World* does not appear contrived within the context of its structure. Other reality programs have incorporated the style but not the substance, and instead pander to the base instincts of jealousy and greed.

## COLOR COMMENTARY

It is indeed ironic that the current trend of reality programs was started by CBS, once considered the Tiffany of network television. With its demographics skewed toward an audience equipped with "dentures and Depends," CBS took a giant step in the summer of 2000 with *Survivor.* The theme is simple: place a group of strangers in a potentially hostile environment, create a sense of competition, force them to fend for themselves, allow them to rid themselves of excess baggage, and reward the lone "survivor" with a check for $1 million. The formula clicked with the young-adult audience CBS wanted desperately to attract, generating ratings second only to the Super Bowl, the highest-rated program on television.

The dramatic structure of this reality series is similar to soap opera, which preys upon the interpersonal dynamics of the fictional characters. However, *Survivor* tests the fortitude of the contestants within the context of their community—always with the caveat that they could be voted out of the competition by their peers, realizing the pain of rejection.

Within the realm of reality television, *Survivor* is a success because it panders to an audience steeped in the tradition of escapist and sometimes exploitive movies. The essence of this drama is that it takes ordinary people and places them in extraordinary situations. Like a sporting event, the audience members become fans of particular individuals, rooting for them as players in a game of survival. The same lust for victory in the sporting arena applies to this one; however, the sense of drama is heightened because the participants are not professionals.

## KEEPING IT REAL

Interestingly, the "reality" in *Survivor II: The Australian Outback* was questioned when it was learned that some material was reenacted. The executive producer of the series, Mark Burnett, admitted that some scenes were reenacted by stand-ins but that it never affected the results of the contest or the show itself. He dismissed the concerns, saying, "I absolutely couldn't care less—I'm making great television."

Reenactments should be of concern in the news and documentary genre. However, *Survivor* is more fiction than fact, and essentially, like most mass entertainment, contrived. Like the old television show *Truth or Consequences,* these real people are part of a fictional narrative. But where is the truth in *Survivor?* It's created and carefully massaged by the show's producers, who understand the weaknesses and strengths of their characters and how to use them for the ultimate in entertainment value.

As for Burnett's remark about making "great television," it must be measured within the context of the marketplace of entertainment today. If the yardstick Burnett used to measure his success includes programs like MTV's *Jackass,* featuring gross-out antics and dangerous stunts, then perhaps there is cause to elevate the status of what he does. However, some critics would like to think that television has much more to offer, and based upon historical precedent, there is reason to believe it does.

Interestingly, there have been concerns about the potential manipulation of reality-program polling results and the exploitation of responses by contestants. On programs like *American Idol,* which require the analysis of telephone votes, Fox hired iTouch U.K. to monitor the results and determine if any abuses occur. This includes determining the origin (area code) and location of calls to discover group calling, and surveying Internet chat rooms to uncover any rumors or attempts to manipulate the results. It broadcasts the show twice on consecutive days, with a three-hour delay to the West Coast allowing voters from California and Hawaii to respond, and announces the winner on the second night. The totals for telephone calls to the program are very revealing, with 110 million calls in its first season and 15.5 million for the finale. For ABC's *Are You Hot?* all audience votes must be placed on the Internet, and results are announced the next week.

On European television, some studio audiences have openly articulated their displeasure with the selection of a winner. On the *Superstar* program in Germany, the studio audience loudly hissed and booed the winning contestant. Responding to the hostile crowd, Michelle Hunzicker, the sexy co-moderator, stared into the camera with an unflinching gaze and announced, "I'm not doing this anymore."

An interesting case occurred on the British version of *Who Wants to Be a Millionaire* when Major Charles Ingram was accused of cheating to win the $1.6 million jackpot on a segment recorded in September 2001. He is alleged to have a friend in the studio who is a college lecturer using coughing signals to alert him to the right answer. The show was never broadcast, and the producers stopped payment on the check pending an investigation and trial. The defendants were ultimately convicted of fraud and sentenced by a British court.

Since the debut of *Survivor*, the inventory of reality television programs has increased exponentially. As a study in exploitation, some offer sexual tension, some are based upon a subtext of fear, and others are mindless attempts to manipulate and entertain. But they are an alluring aphrodisiac for the American television audience, with a 13 percent inventory of reality programs on prime-time television in February 2003, an increase of 5 percent over February 2002, with an average of 25 prime-time weekly hours dedicated to that genre.

One of the reasons for the increase in hours devoted to reality is the redundancy of successful formulas. The most reverential form of validating success in television is copying what is perceived to be a winning programming format. For example, ABC's *I'm a Celebrity—Get Me Out of Here!* was an unbridled rip-off of *Survivor* with a setting in the Australian outback. The concept was imported from England, where they had the sense to cast it with individuals who had little or no public sympathy for their past indulgences. The American version clearly redefined the term *celebrity* by including Alana Stewart (Rod's ex-wife), veteran of *Lifestyles of the Rich and Famous* Robin Leach, and the well-coiffed George Hamilton. Indeed, after Mr. Leach was voted off the campsite by viewers, he wrote an indignant e-mail to his friends pillorying his teammates.

Repositioning a reality concept by populating it with "celebrities" is part of the network programming dynamic. The precedent, of course, is using celebrities in game shows such as *Hollywood Squares* and *Who Wants to Be a Millionaire*. And so it was to be expected that ABC would revisit *The Mole*, calling it *Celebrity Mole Hawaii*. The original concept consisted of 14 contestants who would face physical, intellectual, and emotional challenges. One of them was the "mole" planted by the producers to undermine the rest of the group. When *The Mole 2* was produced, most of it was filmed in Italy. In this iteration, seven celebrities—Stephen Baldwin, Corbin Bernsen, Kathy Griffin, Kim Coles, Michael Boatman, Erik Van Detten, and the model

Frederique—made up the team, with the show hosted by Ahmad Rashad. Fortunately, it had a six-episode limited run and was more taxing on the audience to watch than on the celebrities to participate.

As a venue, Hawaii is a great place for reality television because of the temperate climate, romantic atmosphere, and opportunities for capturing unscripted risqué video—a "compelling" unscripted paradise. As such, the WB network used the locale to host *High School Reunion,* transporting 17 high-school graduates from the Oak Park/River Forest, Illinois, class of 1992 to Maui for two weeks for a reunion. Of course, the cast of characters included a retinue of the usual suspects, like "the popular girl," "the nerd," "the shy one," "the flirt," "the clown," and others, including a former *Playboy* centerfold. The concept is hardly original and is a hybrid of *Temptation Island* and *The Real World.*

## ROMANCE À LA CARTE

Programs whose themes evolve around the relationships between men and women within the context of game theory include *Temptation Island, Chains of Love,* and *Sex Wars.* None of these themes are new to television. Their predecessors include the now innocent-looking *The Dating Game* and a not-so-innocent older HBO program, *Anything Goes,* a televised version of strip poker.

Fox's *Temptation Island,* from the network that gave television *Who Wants to Marry a Multimillionaire,* created a palette of tawdry exploitation by tempting so-called committed couples into infidelity. Although the theme of infidelity has been explored in many dramatic forms, *Temptation Island* is so contrived and heavy-handed that it is an insult to its participants and audience. It's a sexist, hedonistic romp with an appeal to prurient interests compromising any virtues associated with romance.

If *Temptation Island* speaks to reality associated with tasteless situations, then *Chains of Love,* on UPN, offers even more of a base orientation toward the dynamics of heterosexual relationships. In this iteration of reality, a single man or woman is chained to four members of the opposite sex for a week, eliminating each as a prospective partner until one is left. It's an exploitive environment for emotional and physical interaction. The former president of the UPN Network, Dean Valentine, described *Chains of Love* as "mainly very, very funny in a physical comedy sense," adding that "there's something very powerful about being chained up to somebody else."[2] There's also something very Freudian about it having to do with bondage.

Another reality program that would have explored the sexual dynamics and prurient interest of men and women placed in a controlled situation is Fox's *Love Cruise,* produced by Mary-Ellis Bunim and Jonathan Murray of *The Real World.* Based upon the popular television series *Love Boat,* the show was placed on hiatus after Fox's debacle with *Who Wants to Marry a Multimillionaire* and the criticism it received for *Temptation Island*.

For reality television, the pursuit of a mate (husband or wife) has defined a dynamic that defies the Judeo-Christian virtues of morality. Instead, it is being deconstructed as a tabloid for virtual behavior defined by a culture of cruelty and fear. The program *Married by America*, on Fox, integrates several classic reality formats—*I've Got a Secret*, *The Bachelor*, and *The Dating Game*—to match 3 single people with 15 possible mates. Family and friends of each of the singles are invited to quiz the prospective suitors, and the audience makes the final match. In a conspicuous attempt at creating some tension, each of the "postulants" must reveal a secret, like the young woman who admitted she posed nude for *Playboy*. She was quickly voted into the semifinals.

The bread-and-circuses mentality of television's sense of romance is one that is fraught with voyeuristic tendencies and showbiz priorities. This equation of indulgent, suggestive programming articulates a trend that clearly is evocative of a theme associated with the base values of sexual exploitation. This was evident in the March 2002 premiere of Warner Brothers Television's *The Bachelor* on the ABC television network. Interestingly, this program was produced by the same people who did the ill-fated *Multimillionaire*, which featured Rick Rockwell and Darva Conger having their 15 minutes of fame. And, of course, it wasn't long before Trista Rehn told Ryan Sutter how much she loved him on *The Bachelorette*, providing equal gender television time. After all, T-and-A programming swings both ways.

With a devastating 2001–2002 television ratings season, ABC hit a peak of 9.8 million viewers with the premiere episode of *The Bachelor* in March 2002. In this formulaic attempt at matchmaking, Alex, the stud bachelor and Harvard grad, gets to pick from a bevy of beauties that included "the butcher, the baker, and the candlestick maker." His guide and confidant throughout the six-week "ordeal" was program host Chris Harrison. Yes, Alex did find his "true love," and they lived happily ever after on the talk-show circuit, pledging their fidelity and wondering what they'll do when the camera is turned off.

The CBS program *Big Brother* smacks of an Orwellian theme with sexual innuendo, yet the interpersonal dynamics of the program couldn't be less compelling. Of all the reality programs, this iteration is almost a carbon copy of *The Real World*. On July 5, 2000, 10 individuals embarked on an 88-day self-imposed seclusion in a specially built house on a CBS soundstage in California. Cameras and microphones were present throughout to record every nuance of interaction between the participants.

The winner was decided by viewers, who voted various participants out of the house, somewhat akin to the applause meter on *Queen for a Day*. The last person remaining would win the $500,000 prize. The formula was a hit in other countries, and CBS hoped it would be successful in the United States.

Unfortunately, most of the time there wasn't much going on, and the interactive dynamics were very boring. Indeed, at one point CBS desperately offered one of the six remaining contestants $10,000 to leave the program so that they could introduce a pretty 22-year-old Florida blond into the mix. However, none of them accepted the bribe.

Although the critics ravaged the series, it was a modest success for CBS. During its run it averaged 9.1 million viewers and attracted a young demographic, one that is coveted by advertisers. Since *Big Brother* had better ratings than other summer programming, CBS reprised the series in July 2001 as *Big Brother 2*. Changes in the protocol included increasing the household pool to 12, enlarging the residence from 1,800 to 2,400 square feet, changing to contestant voting for elimination, and broadcasting the show three nights a week instead of six. The only compelling and disturbing moment came when a male contestant made a threat against a woman participant and it was revealed that he had a prior arrest (charges dismissed). It was relevant because his background was checked but failed to reveal his record.

Perhaps the WB should have pursued celebrities with more accomplished biographies for their reality smorgasbord *The Surreal Life* (January 2003). The tagline for the show is "When the stars fall from sight . . . this is where they crash." None of the "celebrities" were shooting stars even in their prime. The list read like a who's who of television-land and included once rapper MC Hammer; Emmanuel Lewis of *Webster;* Brande Roderick, former Playmate of the Year (2001) and *Baywatch* star; Corey Feldman of *Bad News Bears, Stand by Me,* and *The Lost Boys;* Gabrielle Carteris of *Beverly Hills 90210;* Vince Neil from the band Motley Crue; and Jerri Manthey, former *Playboy* bunny and contestant on *Survivor II*. The seven were placed in a home for 10 days and nights with no cell phones or personal assistants. Perhaps it's a fitting testimony to reality television that Jerri Manthey, former teammate on *Survivor,* is now validated as a celebrity because of her status as a reality show veteran. Also, even more fitting is that the home these "stars" were sequestered in was the old Glen Campbell estate on Mullholland Drive in the San Fernando Valley, a reminder of another faded career.

Combining the tawdry concept of *Big Brother* with the interrelationships of *An American Family* and *The Osbournes* produced ABC's *The Family,* hosted by George Hamilton. Invoking the theme of *The Prince and the Pauper,* a middle-class family from Manalapan, New Jersey, is relocated to a Palm Beach mansion. Their behavior and interrelationships are not being judged by the producers or viewers, but rather by the staff of servants. The family member voted to have the best relationship wins a million bucks! It's kind of like the *Upstairs Downstairs* of reality TV.

Tempting reality with a mix of romance are low-budget shows modeled after traditional game-show programs like *The Dating Game* and *The Newlywed Game*. However, the new generation of this genre is free from the rigors of being bound to conventional morality and instead pursues a promiscuity encouraged by a perception of youth and their view toward sex. The programs *Sex Wars, Blind Date, Change of Heart,* and *Strip Poker* are all part of a dynamic that is both voyeuristic and titillating. Their titles are indeed suggestive and pander to the basest instincts of their audience. They are indeed indicative of the lush film and television environment that presents an endless array of mindless content driven by sexual innuendo.

Although it is a competition in the nontraditional sense, MTV's *Undressed* is a program that follows young men and women (actors) through various casual sexual liaisons. Each episode focuses upon a different age group: high school, college, and postcollege. There's a lot of suggestive sex and language that is titillating and spicy. In one show, a high-school couple is contemplating attending a school dance. "We've got a week before the dance to brush up on our sexual smarts. . . . Tomorrow night we'll shelve the science project and get to work on the sex project."

## SEX, LIES, AND VIDEOTAPE

Perhaps it's a human frailty or need to search for the best. In sports, teams play against each other to determine championships. In the arts, awards are bestowed recognizing outstanding performers, movies, plays, music, etc. For reality television, excellence has become a commodity merchandised to the masses as a vehicle to satisfy the lowest common denominator of programming. It's a raw form of television that panders to an audience's alter ego of defiant and cruel behavior that is normally suppressed.

For *Are You Hot? The Search for America's Sexiest People* (ABC), the measure of excellence is clearly articulated by the comments of host Lorenzo Lamas to a contestant: "What's your breast size? Because it's hard to see your breasts in that dress."

Or the comment that Mike Fleiss, creator and executive producer, made while watching prospective contestants from the television monitors in the control room: "There's too many good-looking people in a row. When do we get some clunkers?"

And then, of course, there are the intuitive critical assessments of the "judges," Randolph Duke and Rachel Hunter, who, along with Mr. Lamas, excel at their benign assessments of fat knees and buckteeth. One wonders how they would view the human form as perceived by great masters like Salvador Dalí and Pablo Picasso. It is indeed comforting that they are not influential art critics, nor are they equipped to measure anything more than buns, boobs, and brawn.

On *Are You Hot?* the singular criterion for excellence is anatomical perfection, whereas, at the very least, *American Idol: The Search for a Superstar* (Fox) makes an attempt to quantify talent while conforming to the rigors of reality television by invoking the venomous cruelty of its host Simon Cowell.

Television has a long, distinguished history of talent shows, beginning with *Major Bowes Amateur Hour* on radio, which later became *The Original Amateur Hour* (also known as *Ted Mack's Original Amateur Hour*) on television. The concept was inexpensive to produce and attracted people from around the country for auditions in New York City. The audience determined the winners by either writing or telephoning in their preferences. It proved to be a very successful television format, starting on the Dumont television network in 1948 and running for over 20 years, finding a berth on each of the major television networks. Although most of the winning contestants never achieved stardom, some did, including pop singers Teresa Brewer, Gladys Knight, and Pat Boone.

Unfortunately, *American Idol* has debased the essence of the good-natured amateur talent competition and transformed it instead into a gladiator contest, with the up or down thumb signal from the judges, accompanied by a verbal lashing, condemning the contestant's lack of talent. It dehumanizes them, manipulating their emotions by perpetuating their fantasy and then crashing it by propelling them into a morass of failure, condemning them for their weight ("You don't look like an American idol"—did he forget Cass Elliot from the Mamas and the Papas?) or telling a contestant not to bother with voice lessons because she's beyond help. Of course, the contentious environment these hostile remarks create between the other judges, Paula Abdul and Randy Jackson, along with the contestant provide the requisite anxiety that creates the tension for the show. The audience revels in the in-your-face judgments, especially when delivered by an aspirant: "Kiss my natural-born black ass." Yes, we've come a long way from Ted Mack with his corny jokes and gushing platitudes.

## DOYEN OF DETRITUS

In television, leadership is quantifiable by success, and there have been many individuals that have popularized certain genres, like Goodson and Toddson (game shows), Aaron Spelling (prime-time soaps), Steven Bochco (police and lawyers), Dick Wolf (lawyers and police), Roone Arledge (sports), and Edward R. Murrow (news), and added to this distinguished list is Mike Fleiss, peddler of pulchritude and reality-show producer. He began his career as a newspaper sports reporter, and then, inspired by the Howard Stern show, he was led to Hollywood and became an executive producer on *Who Wants to Marry a Multimillionaire* and hasn't looked back, creating hits like *The Bachelor, The Bachelorette,* and *Are You Hot? The Search for America's Sexiest People*. While admitting that his shows have little thought-provoking substance, Fleiss does argue that he is providing an alternative to the predictable, formula-driven sitcom and dramas on television today. He feels that he's doing television that is somewhat sensational but more relevant than the usual formats. Invoking the credo of providing distraction for television viewers returning from a difficult day at work, Fleiss rationalizes reality TV as the pacifier for weary audiences.

Producers working with Mr. Fleiss ascribe him with a creative karma and an instinctive sense of what the television audience wants. For example, he created the concept for *High School Reunion* while his wife was planning hers, and developed *The Will*, a program about heirs battling for their share of an inheritance, after he had a similar experience with his own family.

At the moment, Mike Fleiss is the emperor of reality television, ritualizing the genre and positioning it within the context of being unique and compelling. However, the history of television programming is distinguished by cycles that merit attention and then disappear from the programming landscape. This was the case for variety programs, quiz shows, and Westerns at a time when there were only three major television networks. Now, with many more networks on broadcast, cable, and satellite, the opportunity for oversaturation has increased exponentially, and the threshold of tolerance faces accelerated diminishing returns. Indeed, Mr. Fleiss may take heed from the title of one of his shows, and instead of *Are You Hot?* change it to *When You're Hot.*[3]

## FRONTIERS OF FEAR, CHALLENGE, AND INTIMIDATION

As the reality television genre has evolved, the trends in programming have taken on a more defiant and abrasive point of view. Even the game show, whose characteristics have long been personified with charming hosts, has entered the realm of offensive annoyance. There is little charm and lots of hostility in the manner of Anne Robinson, the host of NBC's *The Weakest Link*. Although it's contrived, like her severe hairstyle, clipped speech, and minimalist behavior, she nevertheless has the ability to offend her contestants and the audience.

Offensive behavior is not a new tactic for television. It has been a staple for some daytime talk programs for years, where trash talk and rudeness have a prominent spot in their staging. Even some of the courtroom shows, like *Judge Judy,* rely upon a sense of arrogance as justice is dispensed. So in addition to the sexuality promoted by many of these programs, there is also a bias toward creating an unsettling, harsh environment to titillate the viewers.

In describing the NBC program *Fear Factor,* the term *harsh* is rather mild. Reviewers have been highly critical, calling it "televised degradation," and Ted Koppel, host of *Nightline,* devoted an entire evening asking if the program will "move us any closer to the end of civilization." What could possibly have motivated such an outpouring of disgust and revulsion? Perhaps one could call it high-concept junk with a measure of bad taste included. Contestants compete for a $50,000 prize by allowing themselves to be placed in grotesque situations. The premiere episode, on Monday, June 11, 2001, featured a contestant who shared a pit with 400 rats. In another episode, the eye on the prize was taken quite literally when contestants were asked to consume sheep eyeballs.

*Fear Factor* represents a move toward "extreme reality" personified by programs like ABC's *The Chair* and Fox's *The Chamber.* Hosted by former tennis pro John McEnroe, *The Chair* literally parlayed trial by fire into a game show. After contestants are strapped into a chair and wired to a heart monitor, they must answer trivia questions while sustaining a steady heartbeat as flames intermittently shoot up around them. If the heart rate is increased, they lose their winnings.

Fox took the concept to another level, raising the intensity of discomfort, in *The Chamber,* its short-lived theater of "torture." In this incarnation, contestants were strapped to a chair and placed in a chamber where they had to endure extreme temperatures while answering inane questions. Although *The Chamber* was canceled, the competition for ratings caused a litigious confrontation between ABC and Fox, each claiming the other stole their idea.[4]

The frantic competition to be first with a reality ratings blockbuster once again created a confrontation between ABC and Fox for the 2004–2005 television season. The ABC television network thought it had an exclusive with *Wife Swap,* planned for the fall 2004 season. The concept is somewhat akin to the "Prince and the Pauper," in which a wife from an affluent home is supplanted in a middle-class environment and vice versa. The Fox version of the same show is *Trading Spouses: Meet Your New Mommy,* which trumped ABC by premiering it during the summer of 2004 while earning strong ratings. Responding to Fox's "theft," Stephen McPherson, president of ABC entertainment, expressed his dissatisfaction. "It's pretty sad that unethical behavior can deny people their intellectual property."[5]

Indeed, Fox has been very shrewd in playing reality "poker," bluffing its way to success. Literally an hour after ABC closed a deal with a British company for a reality series entitled *Super Nanny,* Fox negotiated its own deal with another British producer securing rights to another nanny-oriented reality series. Fox's approach of "copy and conquer" was again articulated when Fox appropriated NBC's format for *The Contender* with their reality boxing series, *The Next Great Champ,* which beat NBC to the punch with an earlier premiere.

Television has always been susceptible to programming trends, indulging in the greatest form of flattery, copying a format and perpetuating it. Industry executives provide rationales for these programs, defining their popularity according to their needs and those of the audience. Instant access to real-life situations like O. J. Simpson and Monica Lewinsky played out on television are seen by some as the reasons that the 18–34 age group is attracted to reality television.

There are always generational shifts that cause television programming to change. Entertainment programming has long been subject to the vagaries of the market place, changing its focus from Western, variety, medical, detective, and legal programs to ones that are perceived to be more relevant to current audiences. The success of programs like *Friends* and *Sex and the City* reflects how more youthful audiences, who are coveted by advertisers, are empowered to change the programming landscape.

Attracting a younger audience as being critical to their survival has been the mantra of television executives trying to increase profits in a very competitive entertainment marketplace. More youthful audiences have often been a priority for network television. In some instances, programs that were still highly rated—like *Gunsmoke; Lawrence Welk;* and *Murder, She Wrote*—were canceled because audiences grew old with the programs. In the 1970s the traditional stand-up comedy of Bob Hope and Jack Benny led to the more irreverent style of *Saturday Night Live* and the cutting-edge humor of Eddie Murphy, catering to a more hip, youthful audience.

In addition to accommodating the needs of their audience, the issue of controlling costs and increasing profits provides another rationale for pursuing the basest elements of programming. Prior to September 11, the television broadcast networks were already experiencing a $3 billion decline in advertising revenue. With the licensing costs of programs like *Friends,* which for NBC is $5.3 million, as opposed to the $400,000 per-episode cost of *Spy TV,* the financial justification for the network is compelling. But what about artistic merits and serving the public interest?

Although networks aren't licensed by the Federal Communications Commission, the affiliates they serve and the stations they own are. Nevertheless, their commitment is defined by serving the needs of their shareholders and advertisers. *Fear Factor* may have little redeeming social value; however, it attracts teenage viewers, is inexpensive, and provides cheap thrills for its audience. Indeed, the argument for servicing the bottom line and rationalizing the value of such programming is a compelling one. As a connoisseur of fine taste, William Paley, the founder and chairman of CBS, was a diligent sponsor of the arts. So when critics and some of his highbrow friends attacked the wildly popular *Beverly Hillbillies* as cheap programming for mass audiences, Paley responded indignantly. He said that he personally liked the program because that kind of slapstick comedy amused him, that it was well done, and that a vast number of television viewers enjoyed it.[6]

Creating a challenge that is attractive to reality audiences is a priority for producers of the genre. In Fox's *Boot Camp,* a show that takes contestants and treats them as recruits in a mock Marine-type setting with real drill instructors, the objective is to survive the rigors of training and win a $500,000 prize. Physical challenge involving real people, like in *Survivor,* appears to be attractive to audiences. In its debut episode on Fox, *Boot Camp* had 19 percent of 18–49-year-olds in its audience, the kind of demographics that advertisers clearly desire.

Although physical challenge is a theme for some of these reality programs, Fox's debut of a show called *Celebrity Boxing,* which featured Tonya Harding "battling" Paula Jones (who was a last-minute replacement for Amy Fisher), was another tawdry display of tabloid titillation. Dredging up the graveyard of principals involved in scandal is a debasing, lurid attempt at catering to the prurient interests of an audience smothered in the gossip of their lost virtue.[7]

Television was never totally devoid of reality-type programs, with shows like *Real People, That's Incredible!,* and *Candid Camera* in the 1960s and 1970s. Indeed, there are many examples, like *Spy TV,* that are clearly derivatives of these earlier programs. Indeed, NBC's *Spy TV* is an edgier version of *Candid Camera.* Where *Candid Camera* dealt with silly stunts, *Spy TV* takes a harsher, more confrontational tone. In one segment, which was canceled in the wake of the September 11 terrorist attack, a car taking an off-road route lands in a mine field with simulated bombs going off.

Creating stunts that will either attract or intrigue a youthful audience is a formidable task for producers. The MTV show *Jackass* combines the genre of reality with gross-out antics that in some instances have generated harsh criticism. Some of the stunts are benign and disgusting, like the man who stuffed a live earthworm up his nose and spit it out of his mouth along with vomit. Others, however, can have more dangerous implications. On one *Jackass* episode, Johnny Knoxville, the "star," set himself on fire after the cameras showed that he was wearing heavy protective gear. That, however, did not stop a Connecticut boy from imitating the stunt without the needed protective garb. The program does, however, issue textual screen warnings about the dangers of imitating the stunts at home; but, of course, there are always the naive and curious.

Television programming trends are always interesting to examine within the context of cultural determinism. There is, of course, an agenda that the television networks have in pursuing a particular genre over another. During the 1950s it appeared that a postwar audience at the height of a resurgence in consumerism was attracted to quiz programs with ordinary people vying for blockbuster monetary prizes. So the networks responded, as they are now with reality television and a remarkable degree of redundant programming. Many of the characteristics of today's reality genre share the same rhythm with the 1950s game shows. There is, of course, the nature of the competition: soundproof booths in the 1950s, remote islands in the new millennium; questions that required broad knowledge in the 1950s, skills for survival in the current marketplace; revelations that answers were given to contestants in the 1950s, disclosure that some scenes in *Survivor* were re-created. The television audience and the Justice Department were shocked by the quiz scandals, and for a while quiz programs disappeared from the screen, but they eventually returned, albeit under closer scrutiny. But the audiences of today don't seem to care about manipulation: they just want to see a good game, with attractive contestants and tense competition.

Television is also a means to providing the status of celebrity to game and reality program participants. Contestants, whether they win or lose, become

part of the media hierarchy that bestows recognition and rewards achievement. It's a curious mix of fiction and reality measured by a contrived agenda
of manipulation. In the 1950s Charles Van Doren and Herbert Stempel received recognition for their knowledge of facts and trivia and then, of course,
became infamous figures in the quiz-show scandals. It was a time defined by
the culture of celebrity, with Charles Van Doren, the handsome English professor challenger from Columbia University, and Herbert Stempel, the reign-
ing 29-year-old working-class student champion from City College of New
York. The producers, Daniel Barry and Jack Enright, decided that the quiz
show *Twenty-One* needed a new star. Both men had their responses scripted,
were given answers to the questions, and were told when to make a wrong
answer. Annoyed at being forced to relinquish his crown, Stempel went public
with the fix, which prompted a congressional investigation. Many years later,
of course, Darva Conger suffered her indignation from the false declarations
of her millionaire husband-to-be on *Who Wants to Marry a Multimillionaire*.
And Sarah Kozer, who was bumped after Evan Marriott chose Zora on *Joe
Millionaire*, was featured in *Playboy* ("Sarah Nude: What Joe Millionaire
Missed," June 2003) and appeared on the cover. Celebrity does have its "virtues."

The broadcast networks state that young audiences appear to crave programs that are unscripted because they provide more excitement and intimacy. They're also looking for the biggest bang for their buck. They also
admit that the spiraling costs of production prevent them from scheduling
shows like *The West Wing* five nights a week. Nevertheless, those same executives who praise the qualities of the reality genre must also beware of
dumbing down television content. Television audiences are notoriously fickle
when it comes to superficial, one-dimensional programming. The start of the
2001 season appeared to confirm that factor.

One of the most anticipated "alternative" programs for the new season was
ABC's *The Runner*, produced by actors Ben Affleck and Matt Damon. The
concept involved an individual who would go cross-country fulfilling a set of
assignments without being identified. Any viewer could be a potential prize-
winner if they were able to capture and identify "the Runner." There were a
number of reasons for the cancellation. One was the tragedy of September
11 and the sense that, as the country remained on alert for anticipated terrorist actions, there would be little interest in tracking the contrived exploits
of a reality contestant.

In addition, by the start of the 2001 season there had been considerable
audience erosion in the ratings for programs like *Survivor, Who Wants to Be
a Millionaire,* and *The Missing Link*. Also, ABC canceled *The Mole,* a hit
during the 2001 season, in the midst of its run, because of low ratings. The
program, which was also on British television, consisted of 10 contestants
having to perform different challenges with the knowledge that there is a

saboteur among them. Other reality-based programs such as *The Amazing Race* (CBS) and *Love Cruise* (ABC) also suffered low ratings.

The most startling success of the reality genre for the 2001–2002 television season didn't appear on network television but was a program on the MTV cable network entitled *The Osbournes*. The show featured a real family—including perennial heavy-metal rocker and former Black Sabbath band member Ozzy (née John Michael); his wife, Sharon; and their teenage children, daughter Kelly and son Jack—in an updated, unbridled, sometimes obnoxious cinema verité sitcom labeled as *"The Cosby Show* in Hell." For six months a television crew filmed the family and their day-to-day routines at their home in southern California. Although this genre of reality television appeared in the 1970s on public television with the documentary television series *An American Family,* which profiled the Louds of Santa Barbara, the substance, of course, is distinctly different. The theme of *An American Family* was a serious exploration of the dynamics of family life placed within the context of the values and traditions of American mores and culture. It was a serious attempt to document and archive the components and hierarchal structure of family living. With *The Osbournes,* the singular purpose was to provide a proscenium for the theatrics of the Osbournes, mixing the thematic sense of sitcom parody with the antics of *The Rocky Horror Show.*[8]

Television can take celebrities and reconstitute them into the reality context, redefining their attributes and characteristics within the milieu of a mass audience. *The Apprentice,* featuring Donald Trump playing "the Donald," was a breakout hit during the spring 2004 television season. It was a ruthless portrayal of contestants literally clawing their way up the ladder of success, with the emperor Donald Trump relishing his role as arbitrator, benefactor, guru, and kingmaker. In an era of corporate malfeasance and excess, *The Apprentice* was a testament to the myths and reality associated with the greed and wanderlust associated with Wall Street. In a *Wall Street Journal* editorial, Professor Jeffrey Sonnenfeld expressed his disdain for the way the program defined the sensibilities of success in corporate America.

So why are 18 million Americans glued to the puffery, pushiness and deception of "The Apprentice"?

The selection process resembles a game of musical chairs at a Hooters restaurant where sexual baiting and pleading is confused with effective salesmanship.[9]

Indeed, Trump could be categorized as the comeback kid teetering on the brink of bankruptcy and reinventing his corporate empire. And for the winner, Bill Rancic, he becomes part of the Trump family working on the new 90-story Trump Tower on the banks of the Chicago River. As of this writing, the *Chicago Sun-Times* building occupies the site and investors have not confirmed their support. Like so many of Trump's pronouncements, this one can be measured by hyperbole and hot air.

Donald Trump, featured as "The Donald" in *The Apprentice,* with contestants poised "to claw their way up the ladder of success." (Photofest)

## THE MOST DANGEROUS GAME

The ultimate reality program for the spring 2003 television season was the embedded reporting and vivid video portraiture of America's war with Iraq, which had its own series title, *Operation Iraqi Freedom,* and included the stark real-time reality imagery of the bombing of Baghdad; the rapid deployment of troops; and bloodied enemy, civilian, and coalition corpses lying still on the field of battle. It incorporated every component of reality television with the ultimate challenge of life and death, a compelling game of conflict, and the decisive prize of conquest. The program dynamics also included colorful characters like Saddam Hussein, thumbing his nose at the coalition threat; the curt, measured remarks of Defense Secretary Donald Rumsfeld; the unbridled confidence of General Tommy Franks; and the daily theatrical multimedia briefings by an unflappable, articulate General Vincent Brooks from CENTCOM in Qatar. Indeed, the central command had anticipated the need for a high-end television set, and they got one, replete with large flat-panel screens emblazoned with a clawing American eagle and a walnut lectern for General Brooks to brief the press corps.

It was compelling drama with winners and losers, heroes and villains. In many ways it echoed the narrative of the television Western with long wagon trains in hostile Indian territory. The tragic circumstances of a supply convoy making a wrong turn and the dramatic rescue of PFC Jessica Lynch by Special Forces were seen via recorded point-of-view video around the world. Other images included more rescues, defiant young soldiers recovering from their wounds, emotional homecomings, photographs of the casualties, joyous crowds, the toppling of a statue, and angry anti-American mass demonstrations. All of these images combined to create a stirring dynamic of America at war but with the added dimension of providing the most intimate portrait of battle and its aftermath.

Indeed, the Pentagon had the best teachers providing lessons in reality television. They learned about the need to capture the dynamics of the moment, create a narrative structure, and have reoccurring characters, each with strengths and weaknesses, while manipulating the tension of the interactions. They understood the nature of drama, with its story arcs and three-act structure. In the end they orchestrated a symphony of visual melodies that embodied their values and demonstrated their deeds. And they did it with the unwitting support and demonstrated bias of the embedded journalists, who became prominent characters in the narrative of war.

After this most visual affectation of war as a game of reality television, it is interesting to assess what its effect will be on the reality-television genre. Clearly, the expectations of audiences may rise and become more demanding in the pursuit of even greater intimacy and challenge. Or audiences may recognize the tawdry and voyeuristic enterprise of most reality television and, after being witnesses to unbounded realism, may become bored with the ordinary contrived and weary settings of reality television. As for the merits of this genre, network programming executives are expressing less enthusiasm for devoting even more of their schedules to reality television.

## NOTES

1. Frank Rich, "The Age of the Mediathon, The Real Reality TV," *New York Times Magazine,* 29 October 2000, sec. 6, p. 58.

2. Caryn James, "Nervous Hunger for Torture Games and Gross-Out Stunts," *New York Times,* 4 February 2002, p. E1.

3. Alessandra Stanley, "Blurring Reality with Soap Suds," *New York Times,* 22 February 2003, p. B9; Craig Tomashoff, "A Barnum of Reality Chases the Relatable Concept," *New York Times,* 23 February 2003, p. AR43; Alessandra Stanley, "Reality-Show Inbreeding: Some Mutations Have Survival Value," *New York Times,* 3 March 2003, p. E1; Bill Carter, "Reality Shows Alter Way TV Does Business," *New York Times,* 25 January 2003, p. A1; Emily Smith, "Reality Bites TV Comedy," *Wall Street Journal,* 24 February 2003, p. B1; Charles Goldsmith, Emily Nelson, and Matthew Karnitschnig, "Reality TV: It's No Mean Feat Keeping It Real," *Wall Street Journal,* 7 March 2003, p. B1.

4. James, "Nervous Hunger for Torture Games and Gross-Out Stunts," p. E1.

5. Bill Carter, "In Reality TV, Is It Thievery or Flattery?" *New York Times,* 2 August 2004, p. C1.

6. William S. Paley, *As It Happened: A Memoir* (Garden City, N.Y.: Doubleday, 1979), p. 256.

7. Caryn James, "And Now the 16th Minute of Fame," *New York Times,* 13 March 2002, p. E1.

8. Seth Schiesel, "Down to Raucous Wire, Osbournes in MTV Deal," *New York Times,* 30 May 2002, p. C1.

9. Jeffrey Sonnenfeld, "Does This TV Program Paint a 'Real' Picture?" *Wall Street Journal* online, www.careerjournalasia.com/columnists/managersjournal/20040302-managersjournal.html.

# 10

# TALK TV: RUNNING AT THE MOUTH

Banter, substantive discussion, humor, and confrontation are all characteristics of the all-inclusive genre of talk television. Both radio and television have countless day- and nighttime hours devoted to this programming. The genre has taken on various guises over the years, becoming a hybrid of news, entertainment, and tawdry kitsch. It is indeed part of the cultural fabric of America, offering a modicum of empowerment to listeners who can call a radio or television station and vent an opinion or ask a question. Every day, talk television and radio consume part of the viewing and listening schedule, and they have become a pervasive presence on the media landscape.

## RADIO'S RHETORIC: THE BEGINNING OF TALK

The early 1930s marked the beginning of talk radio, and there were three developments that helped to shape its style and substance. The first was an invitation by John J. Anthony, a disc jockey at a local station, for his listeners to call him up with any comments and questions. He repeated what was said into the open microphone for the audience. Although it was a clumsy attempt, Anthony's innovative approach was probably the first call-in program on radio.

Another aspect of talk was the discussion or panel format. *The University of Chicago Roundtable* started as a local radio program in 1931 and in 1933 was picked up by the NBC Red network, while on the NBC Blue network, *America's Town Meeting of the Air* started in 1935. These programs proved to be popular with listeners, as *America's Town Meeting* took questions from the studio audience, and *University of Chicago* had a network run of 25 years.

As a radio personality, Steve Allen, the veteran entertainer and late-night talk-show host, also contributed to the genre while at KNX radio in Los Angeles. Starting as a disc jockey in 1948, Allen was able to attract local celebrities who, although unscheduled, stopped in for live chats. The live interviews with these surprise guests became a popular part of the program and were also adapted to Allen's later work in television.

A New York City disc jockey, Barry Gray at WMCA radio, had also decided to interview guests after he became bored with playing records. He started in radio at station WOR as a $59-a-week announcer for name bands, introducing them on the quarter hour and half hour from 6:00 in the evening until 2:00 in the morning. One evening in 1945, while doing his radio show, the legendary bandleader Woody Herman called up, and Gray decided to talk with him instead of playing records. His new format was tremendously successful, and Gray played less music while filling more time interviewing studio guests and taking listeners' calls. His innovative approach distinguished Barry Gray as "the father of talk radio."

The talk show became a hybrid genre of information and debate. The first radio personality to combine controversy with commentary was Joe Pine at KABC in Los Angeles. He created a forum for listeners to air their concerns and hostilities in a barrier-free environment. As a host, Pine was tolerant, to a point, quickly establishing a niche for the rebukes toward listeners that are a standard of the "insult" genre today.

Another host whose style was deliberately provocative and bombastic was Alan Burke, host of the syndicated *Alan Burke Show* (1966–69) on WNEW, New York, then a Metromedia station. Instead of celebrity guests, Burke invited unique characters on his show and then insulted them. As a provocateur, Burke instigated hostile encounters, like the takeover of his show by hippies in a mock guerilla-warfare event. His confrontational style became the hallmark of the short-lived *Morton Downey Jr. Show* on WWOR-TV, New York. Both programs were created by Larry Fraiberg.

One of Pine's best students was Bob Grant, who has been a radio talk broadcaster for over 50 years. After graduating from the University of Illinois, Grant held a number of positions on Chicago radio stations as a newsman and actor before moving to Los Angeles. At KNX he was a radio personality and television talk-show host and then moved to KABC as sports director. On several occasions he was asked to fill in for Joe Pine, and in 1964 he took over Pine's program.

Controversy has been a hallmark of Grant's career. At WABC radio he distinguished himself as an ultra-right-wing conservative with a penchant for denigrating African Americans, homosexuals, lesbians, and other minorities. His radio constituency, however, was politically attractive to Republicans seeking public office, who regularly appeared on his program. There were, however, limits to the language of hostility that the network would bear, and WABC dropped him from its lineup. It didn't take long for Grant to find another berth, at WOR radio in New York, where he is still broadcasting from.

The tradition of conservative politics in broadcasting was a benchmark for William F. Buckley Jr. As the host of *Firing Line* on PBS for 34 years, Buckley was a monument to the politics of the right. His eloquent rhetoric, laced with a pompous, mercurial manner, provided a staunch defense for conservative traditions that he espoused. From 1966 to the final segment, taped at the University of Mississippi on December 3, 1999, Buckley's acerbic wit and defiant posture set a new threshold for the tone and substance of television debate.

As one of the most recognized program hosts in the world, Larry King has become an international icon of talk, reaching a potential global audience of 150 million people in over 200 countries. Born in Brooklyn, New York, King (née Larry Zeiger) moved to Miami, Florida, in 1957 and worked in radio, as well as becoming a newspaper columnist and color commentator for the Miami Dolphins' broadcasts. On January 30, 1978, his radio program *The Larry King Show* made its debut on the Mutual Broadcasting Network and was distributed to stations in 28 cities, running from midnight to 5:30 A.M. In a move that would confirm King as a compelling presence in pop journalism and bestow him with an endowed global pulpit, *Larry King Live* premiered on CNN in 1985. In February 1983 his radio program was moved to afternoon drive time, and in 1994 Westwood One began simulcasting his CNN show on radio, and King ended his syndicated radio program.

On CNN, King's television program is much like it would look like on radio. He sits at a desk with a large microphone (which may be a prop) and his guest sits opposite. However, other guests who appear live are remotely delivered on-screen, akin to Edward R. Murrow's *Person to Person*. Callers have an opportunity to question the guests, and King paces the program with an accomplished rhythm. He subscribes to a philosophy of "talk-show democracy," with a humanistic approach to his questioning. His preparation is a measured balance of knowledge and intuition. He is one of the most practiced and skilled interviewers on television, combining knowledge, wit, discipline, and style.

## TALK COMES TO TELEVISION

The talk show was a perfect match for television, and the technology expanded the genre in substance and style: late-night talk, with a mix of comedy and entertainment, and morning and afternoon talk, with their combination of interviews, political panels, and confrontational histrionics. One contributor who helped shape the content of television talk was Sylvester "Pat" Weaver, who created the signature NBC programs *The Today Show* and *The Tonight Show,* bookending them at the beginning and end of the day. His first attempt was *Broadway Open House,* which was a late-night offering on NBC from May 1950 to August 1951. It featured two veteran stand-up comedians, Jerry Lester and Morey Amsterdam, as hosts. The show had a variety orientation with singing, dancing, and humor as its format.

As the father of late-night and daytime talk, Weaver tried different approaches, attempting to find an appropriate balance between talk and entertainment. He eventually abandoned the slapstick routine for a more relaxed conversational style. In 1950 CBS invited Steve Allen, who was then a disc jockey and radio talk-show host at KNX, a CBS affiliate in Los Angeles, to New York, where he was the host of the half-hour *Steve Allen Show*. He moved to WNBT in 1953, which was then the local outlet for NBC. After 15 months his show, which was the predecessor of Johnny Carson's *Tonight Show*, moved to the NBC network late-night lineup.

Allen created a format that included many of the stylistic components that still endure as late-night talk fundamentals today. His announcer was Gene Rayburn, and Skitch Henderson was the bandleader. He had a regular group of celebrities, including the comedians Don Knotts, Bill Dana, Pat Harrington, and Louis Nye. There was also a prominent group of singers that often appeared, including Steve Lawrence, Eydie Gorme, and Andy Williams.

On the program Allen was a genius at conceiving funny situations that involved guests and the studio audience. These stunts included having his hair cut, selling hot dogs, and using weight-training equipment. Often he would stroll into the studio audience with an open microphone, urging their participation, and would take the camera outside for his man-on-the-street interview.

His genius for ad-libbed comedy and impromptu sketches was legendary. Allen was a natural for television, using the intimacy of the screen as a measure for the type of performing he felt was apropos for the smaller screen. His antics were legendary and set the standard for television humor and variety. He found humor in the simple acts of everyday life, like reading the newspaper. Allen would read the letters to the editor of the *New York Daily News* on *The Tonight Show*, noting the content and how they were signed, for example, "Disgusted, from the Bronx." Possessed of an unrelenting cache of creative energy, Allen was the author of 52 books; thousands of songs, including "This Could Be the Start of Something Big" and the theme song for the movie *Picnic*; and the film *On the Beach*.

In 1956 Allen curtailed his *Tonight Show* appearances to star in *The Steve Allen Show*, NBC's Sunday prime-time offering competing against *The Ed Sullivan Show* on CBS and the hit Western *Maverick* on ABC. By January 1957 Allen decided not to return to late-night television. He had three other regularly scheduled programs on network television, *The Steve Allen Comedy Hour* on CBS during the summer of 1967 and a similar variety program on NBC in 1980 and 1981. He was also the moderator of *Meeting of the Minds*, a 1970s show that offered imagined conversations with famous people from the past. Steve Allen, a youthful 78, was active until his death on October 21, 2000.

After Steve Allen departed from *The Tonight Show,* NBC attempted a number of different stylistic changes in the content and format. From January 1957 to July of that year, most of the changes that were implemented were unsuccessful. The title was changed to *Tonight: America after Dark,* and the show featured reports from correspondents in different cities covering celebrity parties, film premieres, and nightclub acts. While Jack Lescoulie was the designated host, his role was more of a moderator, providing a transition from one report to another.

The changes were greeted with audience defections, resulting in low ratings, and the network quickly moved to plug the loss. The original band, the Lou Stern Trio, was replaced by the Mort Lindsey Quartet, and then they were axed in favor of the Johnny Guarnieri Quartet. The host of the revised program was Al "Jazzbeaux" Collins, an inventive jazz disc jockey with a flair for imagination. On the overnight shift at WNEW radio in New York, he invented the Purple Grotto, an imaginary subterranean studio replete with characters like Harrison, a Tasmanian owl. His tenure as a *Tonight Show* host was short-lived, and soon NBC was once again searching for a replacement.

That person turned out to be Jack Paar, a man with intelligence, wit, and a knack for conversation. Having worked in radio, Paar entertained troops in the South Pacific during World War II, pleasing the enlisted men with his imitations of officers. After leaving the service, he returned to radio as an occasional host for Don MacNeil on the popular program *The Breakfast Club,* turned up as a panelist on *The $64,000 Question,* and in 1947 was Jack Benny's summer replacement.

His film career started at Paramount, where he made his debut in the 1950 film *Walk Softly, Stranger,* with veteran actor Joseph Cotten. The following year he was at Twentieth Century Fox, appearing in *Love Nest* opposite a young starlet named Marilyn Monroe. In television, Paar started as a host of game shows, including *Up to Paar* (1952) and *Bank of Stars* (1953). In 1953 he was the host of a CBS daytime variety series, and his cast of regulars included Edie Adams, Jack Haskell, and pianist Jose Melis.

His most visible venture in television, which gave him the most prominence prior to *The Tonight Show,* was when he replaced Walter Cronkite on CBS's *The Morning Show* in 1954, which was a competitor to NBC's popular *Today Show* with Dave Garroway. It was during this time that Paar honed his skills as a raconteur and worked on the relaxed style and format of the talk show. Once again CBS called upon Paar to host an afternoon program, this time a variety format. During this time Paar also appeared as a guest on *The Tonight Show,* and NBC took notice of these well-received appearances. On July 29, 1957, Paar became the new host of *The Tonight Show.*

The network's mandate was for Paar to restore the late-night franchise to the prominence it held when Steve Allen reigned as host. He immediately

assembled a staff, including writers Jack Douglas and Paul Keyes, who established the opening monologue as a key extemporaneous component of the
show's format. There was also a pool of talented regular performers that
included Cliff Arquette (*Charlie Weaver*), Oscar Levant, Hans Conreid, Bea
Lillie, Peter Ustinov, Hermione Gingold, and Elsa Maxwell. Also, Paar had
an instinct for talented young comedians, helping to nurture the careers of
the Smothers Brothers, Bob Newhart, Dick Gregory, Godfrey Cambridge,
Woody Allen, and Bill Cosby.

*The Tonight Show* with Jack Paar proved enormously successful. It started
with 46 NBC network-affiliated stations, but the number soon increased to
170. This prompted Paar and the network to rename the show *The Jack Paar
Tonight Show.* As part of the program's format, Paar sometimes engaged in
the controversy of realpolitik. He supported Fidel Castro and was questioned
for his stand by the U.S. House of Representatives. Never one to shun controversy, Paar was the first entertainer to originate a program from the Berlin
Wall. This event appeared to be the catalyst for his departure from late-night
television, as there were U.S. troops filmed in the background as Paar spoke
from the Brandenburg Gate. The world press viewed the event as having
militaristic overtones, and it resulted in a Defense Department inquiry and
the censure of the U.S. Commander in West Berlin.

Paar's television audience relished the ongoing feuds that Paar, as an enfant
terrible, carried on with other celebrities, like Steve Allen, Walter Winchell,
and Ed Sullivan. The audience waited with anticipation for the sparks to fly.
And so they did in 1960, when NBC censors edited a joke Paar made about
a water closet, which is a British word for bathroom. By then he was taping
the show early in the evening and broadcasting four nights a week, with
Friday reserved for reruns, *The Best of Paar.*

Upset over the edit and not being informed, the next evening Paar walked
out and, in an emotional address, announced that he was leaving the show.
A shocked Hugh Downs, his announcer, was left to finish the show. Paar
captivated the news media for five weeks as they speculated on his where-
abouts and whether or not he'd return to the program. He returned from
Hong Kong and stayed with the show until March 29, 1962, when he retired
from late-night television after logging more than 2,000 hours.

After Jack Paar left *The Tonight Show,* NBC once again faced a transitional
period until a new permanent host was available. During this 26-week period,
a number of guest hosts filled in, including Soupy Sales, Art Linkletter, Groucho Marx, Merv Griffin, and Jerry Lewis. And during this time the late-night
talk show showcased its first female host, Arlene Francis.

At the start of *The Tonight Show Starring Johnny Carson,* on October 1,
1962, a new genre of late-night programming was created. As an entertainer,
Carson placed his imprimatur on the format, manipulating its essence to suit
his personality and the culture of the time. He distinguished the program
with his superb timing as an accomplished interviewer, monologuist, and

comedian. For 30 years Johnny Carson held reign on America's psyche, commenting with humor and pathos on some of the most turbulent times in American history. He became a cultural icon, instilling the virtues of comedy and challenging the boundaries of humor within the context of changing times.

Born in Iowa and growing up in Nebraska, Carson listened to his favorite radio comedians, Jack Benny and Fred Allen, emulating their style. He also performed card tricks for family and friends.

After serving in the navy in the Pacific during World War II, Carson earned extra cash writing radio comedy while still a student at the University of Nebraska. In Los Angeles Carson became an accomplished announcer and soon had his own television programs, including *Carson's Cellar* (1953), *Earn Your Vacation* (1954), and *The Morning Show* (1954). These programs were short-lived, but nevertheless *Carson's Cellar* attracted the attention of comedian Red Skelton, who hired him as a writer for his television show. In a classic Hollywood tale of serendipitous circumstance, Carson substituted for an ailing Red Skelton one evening and made an impressive, memorable television debut. Soon ABC came calling, making him host of a game show called *Who Do You Trust?*

There had been a tradition created by Groucho Marx that established the television game-show format as a forum for comedy. As host of *You Bet Your Life* (NBC, 1950–61), Groucho integrated humor and the art of banter into the program, combining it with the comedy of one-liners. The program rarely gave away a lot of money, but that's not why viewers tuned in. They watched to see Groucho leering at the pretty female guests and making wry comments about almost anything. There was also the secret word ("Say the secret word and win a hundred dollars"), which was revealed by lowering a toy duck at the beginning of each show. Groucho's irreverence and charm made this a popular evening program.

The success of *You Bet Your Life* wasn't lost on Carson or ABC when they created *Who Do You Trust?* (1956–63). Although broadcast on the East Coast at 3:30 in the afternoon, the show became ABC's most popular daytime program. Carson, like Marx, humorously bantered with his guests, testing the limits of television censorship.

After initially declining to become host of *The Tonight Show* (he had made a guest appearance in 1958), succeeding Jack Paar, Carson accepted and made television history with his former game-show announcer, Ed McMahon. For 30 years, 10 in New York City and 20 in Burbank, California, Carson provided a unique perspective on American culture while becoming a profit center for NBC. By 1979 *The Tonight Show Starring Johnny Carson* attracted a nightly audience in excess of 17 million people and represented 17 percent of NBC's profit. That same year Carson threatened to quit, and a settlement was reached affording a more generous salary and additional vacation time and shortening the program from 90 to 60 minutes.

The list of casualties of those who attempted to compete with Johnny is substantial and includes *The Les Crane Show* (ABC, 1964); *Joey Bishop* (1967–69), which included sidekick Regis Philbin; *Dick Cavett* (1969–74); *Merv Griffin* (CBS, 1969–72); and *Pat Sajak* (CBS, 1989). While these programs attempted to imitate the *Tonight Show* format, they were unable to capture the spontaneity and personal dynamics that Johnny Carson brought to late-night television.

As the consummate icon of nighttime programming, Carson earned numerous awards, including Emmys, the Kennedy Center Honors Lifetime Achievement Award, and the Presidential Medal of Freedom. After taping 5,000 shows and interviewing 23,000 guests, Carson faced a new competitive television landscape in the 1990s. There were more networks and therefore greater competition. He and Ed McMahon were in their 60s; their producer, Freddie DeCordova, was older; and the face of late-night television had changed with the political and satirical irreverence of *Saturday Night Live*. Always conscious of his entries and exits, Carson didn't want to be perceived as Jack Benny or Bob Hope, gasping for a last laugh and sympathetic applause, so on May 22, 1992, he taped his last *Tonight Show*.

Show business is fraught with duplicity, manipulation, and intrigue. During the year's time from Carson's retirement announcement to his final program, there was a great deal of speculation about who would succeed him. At one time Joan Rivers was Johnny's permanent guest host, and she was succeeded by Jay Leno. As for David Letterman, he was already hosting his own late-night program, *Late Night with David Letterman* (1982), on NBC, immediately following *The Tonight Show*. Both Letterman and Leno anticipated taking over Carson's role as late-night owl. However, anticipating Carson's imminent retirement, NBC had already prepared for the transition by offering Leno a contract. Wanting to be on top of the perch, Letterman accepted an offer from CBS, and *The Late Show with David Letterman* debuted August 30, 1993.

As a successful late-night talk-show host, David Letterman had a good sense of how to serve his audience. He had Paul Shaffer, his bandleader from *Late Night,* and incorporated a number of successful features, including his famous Top Ten list. Upon its premiere on CBS, *The Late Show* was a ratings success, and for the first time in NBC's illustrious history the network no longer had a monopoly in the landscape of late-night talk television.

The 1990s also saw other entries into the nighttime talk-show circuit, including Arsenio Hall and Dennis Miller (who had more success after moving his show to HBO in 1994) and *Bill Maher's Politically Incorrect* in 1993. Others who attempted to create a run in the curtain of late-night talk and weren't successful included Bob Costas, Greg Kinnear, Tom Snyder, Craig Kilborn, and Keenen Ivory Wayans.

Even at a time with increased competition from cable and satellite, Letterman and Leno still dominate late-night talk television. The competition be-

Host David Letterman with guest and politician Al Gore on *The Late Show with David Letterman.* "The Letterman epic was steeped in the psychology of greed, impudence, and lies." (Photofest.)

tween the two is intense, as there is a great deal of money and prestige at stake. When CBS and Letterman wanted to celebrate his 15th anniversary as a late-night host and include clips from his NBC show *Late Night,* NBC refused, offering no reason for the declination.

In March 2002 CBS faced its greatest crises with David Letterman, as his contract was near its end and the network failed to come to terms with the star during an exclusive negotiating period. It was during this time that the tension of network-television dynamics reached a peak in a revealing and sordid pas de deux of obfuscation, pandering, and mendacious manipulation. The ABC television network could nearly taste the winning elixir of profitability from a late-night talk show. Suffering from a decline in its bottom line from network ad revenue and declining theme park attendance, Disney, the parent company of ABC, embarked on an adventure, attempting to seize the opportunity and catch a big fish, chatting him up with boastful guarantees.

And Letterman was posturing, nibbling at the bait. He was not enamored with Leslie Moonves, then president of CBS Entertainment (as of June 2004, copresident and co–chief operating officer)—indeed, the two men were like fire and ice. Also, the talented comedian suffered ratings losses against Leno because NBC had a stronger lead-in prime-time schedule than CBS. And so Bob Iger, the president and chief operating officer of the Walt Disney Company, alumnus of Ithaca College and heir apparent to Michael Eisner, the CEO of Disney, was dispatched to woo the recalcitrant and insecure entertainer. And so, on a cold February day in 2002, Iger and Lloyd Braun, chairman of ABC Entertainment, acting like stage-door johnnies, were freezing their tushies off waiting, without an appointment, outside the Ed Sullivan Theater in New York, hoping to talk with Mr. Letterman. After killing time in a nearby coffee shop and doing some impulse shopping, they had a cordial one-hour meeting with the late-night television star.

All successful dramas with compelling characters have a backstory, and the Letterman epic was steeped in the psychology of greed, impudence, and lies. It was the dance of the seven veils, and as each one fell, the temptation for ABC reached a climactic height of enduring passion with a careless abandon for those whose talent and loyalty were a testament to ABC's late-night schedule.

Political turmoil knows no time, and as the essence of such drama unfolds, there are those who are enabled to observe and report on the events at hand. For Roone Arledge, then ABC president of news and sports, and Ted Koppel, the event was the capture of Americans in Iran, an enduring saga that served as the catalyst for the production of ABC's *America Held Hostage* (1979), which in 1980 morphed into *Nightline*. The program filled a compelling need at a time when Americans faced anonymous adversaries in a part of the world they knew little about.

The ABC television network had been experimenting with an occasional 11:30 news half hour addressing breaking national and world events, but when Americans were taken hostage in Iran, the program *The Iran Crisis: America Held Hostage* became a regularly scheduled late-evening program hosted by the distinguished ABC correspondent and anchor Frank Reynolds. Sadly, Reynolds was suffering from lung cancer, and Ted Koppel, who was hosting a Saturday-morning news program for ABC, was chosen for the 11:30 time slot. In 1980 *Nightline* went to four nights a week, and in 1981 it added a fifth evening.

A regularly scheduled time slot on network television is a coveted piece of real estate—so much so that when Letterman began negotiations with CBS, his representatives, as part of the negotiating process, asked that his company, Worldwide Pants, be given control over the 11:30 time slot even after he retired. In television, the bricks and mortar is programming content, the foundation of any network. CBS declined the request and also mistakenly thought that it had the right to match any other offers. Representatives of Letterman found the CBS position wanting, and after the exclusive CBS negotiating term expired, the mating dance began.

There were compelling reasons for ABC to pursue Letterman, and all of them had to do with money. As a disappointed Bob Iger said later: "But I don't have any second thoughts or misgivings. This was David Letterman, for goodness sakes, and the economic issues were extremely compelling. I think we would have deserved criticism if we hadn't tried to get him."[1]

In categorizing Mr. Letterman as a major talent who is deserving of pursuit, Iger is probably right. After the tragedy of September 11, Letterman distinguished himself from others of the same ilk by making a sincere, heartfelt statement articulating his personal grief. It was a message that demonstrated Letterman's appeal not only as a clown but as a compassionate human being. And so Mickey came calling with money (never an issue with either party), a new high-tech theater, and (more importantly) an aggressive promotional blitz on Disney's ESPN targeting a younger audience with greater appeal toward advertisers. The Letterman camp had often complained to CBS, which is owned by Viacom, that its promotional efforts toward the younger demographic on MTV and VH1 were inadequate.

However, Letterman had an additional concern that was uncharacteristic for a celebrity of his stature and therefore remained incalculable as a potential sticking point for ABC. He wanted assurances from the network that was wooing him that it had a firm decision to move *Nightline* out of its time period, whether it was for him or someone else. Also, as someone who respects the traditions of broadcast journalism, he didn't want to be viewed as the catalyst for the cancellation of the long-running program.

While David Letterman was being forthright in his concerns for Koppel's program, the management of Disney and ABC, including Bob Iger, Lloyd Braun, and CEO Michael Eisner, engaged in duplicitous deceit by not informing David Westin, the president of ABC News, or Ted Koppel of its intentions. The executive suites of corporate America have a long tradition of deliberate mendacity and obfuscation within their own ranks. Sometimes the most loyal individuals are the last to know about changes directly impacting them. This, of course, was true for Ted Koppel.

As a seasoned veteran of ABC News with his own reliable network of sources, Koppel soon learned about the threat to his position. An experienced professional, he chose not to use his chosen instrument of television for his response, but instead turned to the op-ed page of the *New York Times*. Under the heading "Network News Is Still Serious Business," Koppel provided some personal history and documented how *Nightline* has consistently earned second place in its broadcast time period. In addition, he noted that in times of crisis the ratings peak to some of the highest in late-night broadcast programming. He also wrote about the unique public-service dimension of the program and how profitable it has been for its parent company. Offering no illusions, Koppel articulated his understanding of Disney's pursuit of Letterman and the company's need to be concerned about the bottom line. However, he took particular umbrage at a comment made by a company executive that *Nightline* had lost its relevance. Responding, Koppel made it abundantly clear that the global political dynamic today offers the most compelling argument for *Nightline* to continue.

I would argue that in these times, when homeland security is an ongoing concern, when another terrorist attack may, at any time, shatter our sense of normalcy, when American troops are engaged in Afghanistan, the Philippines, Yemen, and Georgia, when the likelihood of military action against Iraq is growing—it is, at best, inappropriate and, at worst, malicious to describe what my colleagues and I are doing as lacking relevance.[2]

The drama ended with Letterman deciding to stay at CBS and ABC having to engage in damage control. There were conciliatory telephone calls to Koppel by Iger and Eisner. But the battle of entertainment versus news so boldly articulated by Edward R. Murrow, an icon of broadcast news, in his 1952 speech "Wires and Lights in a Box," will certainly endure.

Part of drama is a denouement that provides reconciliation for the characters and an opportunity to mend their differences. For Disney and ABC, the need was compelling, as they had no replacement for *Nightline* if Koppel jumped ship to either CNN or PBS, which expressed an interest in the program. Rather than interrupt a revenue stream of $13.1 million, which is what the program earned in 2001, an accommodation was reached with Koppel and his production team. Although the terms were confidential, sources revealed that he was guaranteed the 11:35 P.M. time slot for two years. All the parties were satisfied that a settlement had been reached. In a statement, Robert Iger, the president of Disney, voiced his pleasure with Koppel's decision to stay at ABC. "We want to renew and reaffirm our support for *Nightline*. We look forward to working with ABC News to make a strong program even stronger in the coming years."[3]

Although Koppel felt betrayed by Disney in its failed attempt to sign David Letterman, he nevertheless articulated his confidence in the network's commitment to the program.

For our part, my colleagues and I renew our commitment to making *Nightline* the best news program it can possibly be. It is especially gratifying for me and everyone at *Nightline* to have questions about the future of the broadcast so warmly and enthusiastically resolved at the highest levels of the corporation.[4]

And so the troops demonstrated their commitment to each other, expressing their allegiance to the corporate mantra of unity, knowing well how tenuous their relationship really is.

## DAYTIME TALK

Historically, daytime talk shows evolved from radio, and as television became more popular, the format was adapted to it. One show that set the tone for daytime talk within the context of news was the NBC program *Meet the*

*Press.* Created by Lawrence Spivak and Martha Rountree, the show was first broadcast on radio on October 5, 1945; moved to the NBC television network on November 6, 1947; and began broadcasts on the NBC radio network on May 4, 1952. Starting at a half hour, the program was expanded to 60 minutes on September 20, 1992. It is the longest-running (over fifty years) regularly scheduled panel-discussion show on network television.

Before entering radio and then television, Spivak was the editor of *American Mercury* magazine. He was associated with the program as creator-moderator until he retired in 1975. As cocreator and moderator, Martha Rountree was an experienced public-affairs producer for radio and television. She produced *Leave It to the Girls,* which began as a radio program in 1945, was a local program in New York City in 1947, and moved to NBC in 1949, where it ran until 1954. Each week the women panelists, which included Ann Rutherford and Harriet Van Horne, would bash men and ask the male guest to defend himself. She also produced *Keep It Posted* (also known as *The Big Issue*) from 1951 to 1954; *Washington Exclusive* (1953), which featured six senators discussing current events and military affairs; and *Press Conference* (1956–57). She was the only female moderator on *Meet the Press,* serving from 1947 to 1953. There have been a number of moderators over the years, including Ned Brooks; Bill Monroe; Marvin Kalb; Roger Mudd; Chris Wallace; Garrick Utley; and Tim Russert, the current host.

## THE CHICAGO SCHOOL OF TELEVISION

Defining the dynamic of daytime television in the 1950s became a pioneering effort by a number of talented and creative individuals. One of the most notable achievements in innovative television was at the NBC-owned Chicago station WNBQ, which later changed call letters to WMAQ-TV. Under the ever-inquisitive and sharp-eyed Jules Herbuveaux, who was the station's first general manager, a number of programs and their artists distinguished themselves as unique and entertaining. There was the sophisticated and literate humor created by the genius of Burr Tillstrom on *Kukla, Fran, and Ollie,* where puppets interacted with Fran Allison. For the preschoolers, there was the delightful *Ding Dong School,* with Miss Frances (Dr. Frances Horwich) and famed naturalist and animal expert Marlin Perkins profiling exhibits from Chicago's Lincoln Park Zoo.

Although all of the programs from WNBQ were trendsetters in their form, style, and function, there was one, *Garroway at Large,* that was apart from all the rest. It was a Sunday-evening talk-variety program that found humor in life's smaller moments. Hosted by Dave Garroway, whose relaxed demeanor was in opposition to the more strident tone of television comedy, it was original, perceptive, and daring. Deliberately excluding a studio audience, *Garroway at Large* featured an ensemble of players who ad-libbed in a semi-scripted format and who genuinely enjoyed each other's company. The show lasted for one season, ending its run in June 1951.

In television-land, innate talent doesn't go unnoticed, and Garroway's timing was perfect. With the genius of Sylvester "Pat" Weaver, who was NBC's vice president of television and who created the concept of bookending the morning *Today Show* and evening *Tonight Show,* there was a spot for Garroway, who seemed perfectly matched as the first host of the network morning show. It was serendipity that brought them together. As a Chicago resident, Garroway lived in the Ambassador East, a residential hotel, and wandered into its restaurant to have breakfast, something he rarely did. While there, he found a discarded copy of the show-business broadsheet *Daily Variety,* which announced NBC's upcoming morning show. His show, *Garroway at Large,* had been canceled because Procter and Gamble, the most powerful advertiser in television, wanted the prime-time spot for its own use. A Chicago meeting was set with Mort Werner, a *Today Show* producer, so that Garroway could make a pitch for hosting the show. According to *Daily Variety,* several notable comedians were being considered, including Fred Allen, Bob Hope, and Milton Berle. The meeting went well, and Garroway flew to New York for a test and two days later was notified that he got the job.

At NBC, Weaver was an innovator who encouraged his staff to think out of the box. His success included Sid Caesar's *Your Show of Shows,* and his vision for a morning program, tentatively called *Rise and Shine,* was radio with pictures. He felt that morning television should not be defined as all-consuming but instead must serve as a mild distraction from the routine of the day.

We cannot and should not try to build a show that will make people sit down in front of their sets and divert their attention to the screen. We want America to shave, to eat, to dress, to get to work on time. But we also want America to be well informed, amused, to be lightened in spirit and in heart and to be reinforced in inner resolution through knowledge.[5]

*The Today Show* premiered at 7:00 A.M. on Monday, January 14, 1952, to less-than-enthusiastic reviews. One television critic, Jack Gould, writing in the *New York Times,* found the show to be pretentious but admitted that it had some merit. He also said that the show lacked creativity and was a slave rather than a master to its inventiveness and ingenuity.

The ratings were low, the advertisers were not interested, and the program was in the red. At *The Today Show* the mood was less than sanguine, until one serendipitous day when two former NBC pages, Carmine "Buddy" Menella and Roy Waldron, showed up with a "friend" at the NBC casting office. Their "friend" was a baby chimpanzee named J. Fred Muggs, and it was decided to put the adorable chimp on the show. Although some critics expressed their dismay about mixing news with the funny, frantic antics of our hereditary predecessors, the audience and the advertisers loved it, and so J. Fred Muggs was on his way to stardom. If adults didn't watch *The Today Show,* their children did, reveling in the unscripted adventures of Muggs, and soon they got hooked on the information and entertainment value of the show.

With its newfound talent and attractive advertising rates, the sponsors started lining up. One of the first was Dow Chemical, hawking a product called Saran Wrap. On the show, Dave Garroway demonstrated how clear the product was by wrapping it over the television camera lens. What better venue was there for advertising a material for wrapping leftovers than on a morning show with housewives in the audience? Soon, *The Today Show* was recognized as a formidable tool to create an awareness for national branding. It did that for Saran Wrap, Smuckers, and a host of other products that were little known before venturing to the sandlot of morning television.

*The Today Show* set became a frolicking playpen for Muggs, who, during his four-year run, shrewdly learned the ins and outs of the television business. He was dressed in costumes, written into skits, and eventually became a commanding presence on the program. His salary was in excess of $500 a week— not bad for the budding chimp thespian and his owners, who paid $600 for him. Although *The Today Show* was seen in the United States, the madcap antics of Muggs had repercussions around the world. Suddenly, the TV chimp became a worldwide celebrity, and the royal family was part of the drama.

It was during the 1953 coronation of Queen Elizabeth, and in those days, before satellite broadcasting, *The Today Show* covered the event with live audio and recent still photographs. There were some cutaways of Muggs and his playful antics, and during one critical moment, as the Queen was crowned, there was a shot of Muggs climbing over a chair with his butt in full view. In a moment of aplomb, Garroway said to his cohost, "Ah, don't you wish that you too could be a king in a far-off land where you originated?" It created an international incident, with the matter being addressed in the House of Commons. Indeed, the British outrage was so pronounced that when Muggs was scheduled for a world tour, the British made it known that his presence was not welcome in the land of pomp and pompousness.

In 1961, after nine consecutive years of hosting *The Today Show,* Dave Garroway left the program. His wife had committed suicide, and his grief and depression had taken its toll. The network decided to place John Chancellor, a seasoned news veteran, as host of the program. However, Chancellor's inexperience as an entertainer was clearly a detriment, and so in 1962 Hugh Downs replaced Chancellor, and Joe Garagiola, the quick-witted former St. Louis Cardinals catcher, was added as an on-air talent.

The 1960s were also a time for women to become more prominent in the dynamic of morning television. Interestingly, in the 1940s and 1950s the daytime face of television was mostly female. In the late 1940s there were several programs hosted by and themed to women. They included *The Mary Margaret McBride Show* (NBC, 1948); *Pauline Frederick's Guest Book* (ABC, 1948); *Maggi's Private Wire* (NBC, 1949); *Leave It to the Girls* (NBC, 1949);

*The Kathi Norris Show* (NBC, 1950); *All Around the Town,* with Mike Wallace and his first wife, Buff Cobb (CBS, 1951); and *The Lilli Palmer Show* (CBS, 1951). Some of these programs had limited runs of 13 weeks and targeted women as their prime audience. One of the first First Ladies to become involved with television was Eleanor Roosevelt, with her 1950 program *Mrs. Roosevelt Meets the Public* on NBC.

*The Today Show* with Dave Garroway had a number of women dubbed *Today Girls* associated with the program. The first of these was Estelle Parsons (1953–54), who later became a Hollywood actress. Others associated with Dave Garroway's *Today Show* included Helen O'Connell (1956–58); Betsy Palmer (1958–59); Florence Henderson (1959–60); and Barbara Walters, who was hired as a writer but became an on-camera reporter covering the 1963 Kennedy assassination. She was a host of the program from 1963 to 1976.

While *The Today Show* set the standard for morning and daytime television talk, there were other programs, many of them syndicated, that helped to set the tone of this genre. In the 1960s there were several syndicated programs that were hosted by women whose content was oriented to that target audience. One of the most popular was *Girl Talk* (1963–70), with Virginia Graham as the original host and Betsy Palmer assuming that role in 1969. Most of these programs focused on celebrity interviews, and the well-known hosts included Pamela Mason (wife of actor James Mason), Gypsy Rose Lee, and Lee's sister, June Havoc. The first 1960s talk program to seriously address women's issues was *Outrageous Opinions,* hosted by noted feminist Helen Gurley Brown.

Nationally syndicated daytime talk shows have historically been an important part of the television landscape. Two entertainers, Merv Griffin and Mike Douglas, successfully parlayed their talent into successful programs. As a fledgling entertainer, Griffin performed for talent shows and sang on KFRC radio in San Francisco. In 1950 he recorded "I've Got a Lovely Bunch of Coconuts," which became a hit, selling 3 million copies. His first regularly scheduled television program, in 1958, was *Play Your Hunch,* which was followed by another quiz program in 1963 entitled *Word for Word.* As a talk-show host, Griffin's career received an energy boost in 1962 when he was named as a substitute host for Jack Paar on *The Tonight Show.* As a result of his success, NBC gave him his own hour-long *Merv Griffin* talk show that year. Also, his fascination with the television game program format led to a bonanza of wealth with his creation of *Jeopardy* and *Wheel of Fortune.*

Another performer who became a successful daytime talk-show host was Mike Douglas. He started in 1961 with a 90-minute local program out of Cleveland, Ohio, and the show was nationally syndicated in 1963 and ran until 1982. In 1965 the program moved to Philadelphia and changed its format, including a weekly celebrity cohost, and in 1967 it was the first nationally syndicated daytime talk show to win an Emmy. In the 1970s Douglas moved to Los Angeles, where his access to celebrities became more available.

The most successful syndicated daytime talk program in the history of television is *The Oprah Winfrey Show.* Distributed nationwide on more than 120 channels, with an audience in excess of 10 million viewers, Winfrey has turned her show into a cottage industry with a steady stream of revenue. The show, which started in 1986, grossed more than $125 million after its first year, earning Winfrey $30 million. As the principal of Harpo Productions, Ms. Winfrey arranged to acquire ownership of her program, and in 1988 purchased the rights and assets from Capital Cities ABC. As a result, she became the first woman to own and produce her own television talk show.

In the process of creating a unique niche on television, Oprah Winfrey has diversified into film and television production and publishing. Her company, Harpo Productions, produced the award-winning 1989 miniseries *The Women of Brewster Place* along with other projects. In the publishing arena, there is *Oprah's Book Club* and *O: The Oprah Magazine.*

Beginning her broadcasting career in radio at Nashville station WVOL, Winfrey moved quickly to television as a reporter-anchor at WTVF-TV in the same city. In 1976 she became coanchor at WJZ-TV news in Baltimore and demonstrated a flair for being the talk-show host of *People Are Talking.* Recognized as a rising talent in the daytime talk genre, she was invited to Chicago in 1984, a major broadcasting market, to host the troubled *A.M. Chicago.* Hosting a talk show in a competitive market was a formidable task, especially going against rival host Phil Donohue. In less than a year Winfrey surpassed Donohue's viewing audience by 100,000, and her show became first in the ratings. The program was expanded to an hour and in 1985 was renamed *The Oprah Winfrey Show.* (Phil Donahue returned to prime-time television in 2002 on MSNBC, but his effort was short-lived).

As some daytime talk shows embraced the exploitative trend of trash talk, Winfrey refused to succumb to it. Her perseverance and determination are notable assets. When she was sued by a group of Texas cattlemen for defaming beef on her talk show (Oprah is a vegetarian), she moved the show's production to Amarillo, Texas, for the duration of the trial and was vindicated. As an advocate for children's rights, Winfrey was instrumental in the passage of the Oprah Bill, aimed at protecting children against child abuse.

## THE EASE OF SLEAZE: MAURY POVICH, JENNY JONES, AND JERRY SPRINGER

The trash-talk trend on daytime talk shows has had a number of orientations, mostly to do with exploiting the voyeuristic need of the viewing audience. Programs feature guests desperately seeking attention who reveal intimate details of their lives with lurid, sexually explicit enhancements. Infidelity is one of the most popular of the themes, fitting perfectly into the carnie atmosphere of these programs. As a tool in the hands of talk-show producers, the lie detector was an instant hit. The tension and drama unfolding as the guest contestant was asked questions with responses that were measured for validity by the detector entertained audiences who assessed the guest's guilt or innocence in their own mind.

Driven by the challenge for more compelling personal drama, talk producers pushed the limits of good taste by using their stage to determine issues of paternity. Creating a game-show-like atmosphere that could be called *Name That Sperm,* the talk shows have embraced DNA testing as a means for identifying a father. Genetic science has entered the realm of the big top, with a nod toward the cultural implications of mass disclosure. The confirmation, or lack of it, bestowed on the father while providing a legitimate means to pursue parenting issues does not and cannot address relationship issues of the couple.

But in a culture of instant gratification where technology provides the ability for everyone to experience their 15 minutes of fame, these themes reflect the public's fascination with the lifestyles of the not-so-rich-and-famous. One talk-show producer noted that using television as a confessional has become routine and no longer has any stigma associated with it. For Maury Povich, host of the third-highest-rated talk show, the DNA birthright programs have all the dimensions of classical drama. "These are classic themes of betrayal, revenge, truth and the search for resolution."[6]

However, the more substantive issues associated with this trend are the implications involved in the personal dynamics of the people involved. Unfortunately, these programs are not noted for their ability to provide exhaustive background checks on the couples relating to spousal or child abuse. Although they claim to have postprogram counseling, their level of effort is minimal.

Some social workers feel that the short-term gratification associated with the buzz and glamour of being on syndicated television, along with the modest cash rewards, suspends the reality of the situation. Most agree that the parties involved cannot address the myriad of issues associated with their predicament in a half-hour television show.

Perhaps the most notorious event associated with the tawdry midway antics of daytime talk was on the 1995 *Jenny Jones Secret Crush* program. The unsuspecting Jonathan Schmitz was surprised to learn that his secret admirer was another man, Scott Amedure. Three days after the taping, Schmitz killed Amedure and implicated Jenny Jones when he admitted to a 911 operator that Amedure had humiliated him on national television. Although the program was never broadcast, Jones was called to testify at Schmitz's murder trial and appeared somewhat aloof with her responses pertaining to her involvement with her own television program. Observing her courtroom demeanor, a California columnist wrote, "In a performance brimming with evil, Jones swore under oath that she has little influence on the show."[7]

In retrospect Jones feels that it was a mistake for her not to be more aggressive in defending herself immediately after the incident occurred. On her
program she articulated her regrets and remarked that the tragedy was about
the actions of one individual. Since then she embarked on what has been
dubbed as her "rehabilitation tour," with guest appearances on radio and
television talk shows around the country, defending herself against any im-
plication in the sordid affair and contradicting claims that Mr. Schmitz was
ambushed. She reiterates this defense in her book, *Jenny Jones: My Story*, and
asserts her belief that Schmitz's troubled history of alcoholism, depression,
and attempted suicide could have led him to kill Amedure even if they had
not appeared together on her show.

Although Schmitz was convicted of second-degree murder, the legal action
persists, with the family of Mr. Amedure pursuing a civil action, suing the
*Jenny Jones* program for $50 million in damages. The suit alleges that Ms.
Jones manipulated Mr. Schmitz, luring him on the show by implying that his
secret admirer was a woman. In 2002 the damage award was dismissed.

Another sleazy proponent of the gutter instincts of talk TV is a former aid
to Robert Kennedy, a lawyer, and the former mayor of Cincinnati, Jerry
Springer. After serving as mayor, Springer distinguished himself as the leading
news anchor in Cincinnati. Then, in 1991, he became host of *The Jerry
Springer Show*, one of the most debased and contrived talk shows on television. Utilizing every trick to titillate the audience with trash talk, provocative
posing, lurid tales, and nudity, Springer revels in the gluttonous pornography
of pulchritude. Indeed, his program was accused of provoking this behavior
by coaching contestants to get into fights and admit to actions that they never
engaged in—in other words, creating a fiction of voyeurism to provoke a
nihilistic level of crudity that presumed to be factual.

The premise of many of these daytime talk programs is to create confrontational situations manipulating the personal dynamics of the parties involved.
These shows are driven by priorities other than the needs of the contestants.
They have an agenda that articulates the ideals of television entertainment,
which focus on ratings and competition. These are the singular ideals that
drive programs like *Jenny Jones* and *Jerry Springer*, littering the television
landscape with monuments to crass, indulgent, lowest-common-
denominator programming.

## NOTES

1. Bill Carter, "How ABC's Full-Court Press Almost Landed Letterman," *New York
Times*, 18 March 2002, p. C1.

2. Ted Koppel, "Network News Is Still Serious Business," *New York Times*, 5 March
2002, p. A23.

3. Joe Flint, "ABC Is Said to Have Pact on 'Nightline,' " *New York Times*, 9 April
2002, p. C1

4. Alessandra Stanley, "The Yin and Yang of Late-Night TV," *New York Times,* 10 March 2002, p. WK6.

5. Sylvester Weaver, *The Best Seat in the House: The Golden Years in Radio and Television* (New York: Knopf, 1994), p. 21.

6. Universal, www.uni.television.com/maury

7. Dan Trigoboff, "Jenny Talks Back; Host Campaigns to Distance Herself and Show from 1995 Shooting," *Broadcasting and Cable,* 12 January 1998.

# 11

## KIDS, CARTOONS, PUPPETS, AND MUPPETS

The evolution of children's television programming in the United States has a rich history and tradition associated with creativity, enrichment, entertainment, and education. Some of the earliest of these programs were retreads of old studio Westerns that featured stars like William Boyd as Hopalong Cassidy. One of the most popular of the Western television stars was Roy Rogers, who—with his wife, Dale Evans, and horse, Trigger—led many children down the happy trails of their youth. There were also theatrical cartoons that were reedited for television. However, soon original children's programming appeared, and some were based upon popular radio characters such as Captain Midnight.

### PUPPETS

One of the most endearing children's television formats features puppets. Indeed, the art of puppetry dates back to ancient India, China, and Turkey. Children are fascinated with the fantasy world that puppets create, and adults are also enamored with them. Perhaps one of the greatest testimonies to their allure was the Edgar Bergen and Charlie McCarthy show on radio, which was also known as *The Chase and Sanborn Hour.* The irony of the success of this show on radio was the enduring illusion that ventriloquist Edgar Bergen created without being seen by his listening audience. Although the audience knew that Charlie was a puppet, they suspended their sense of reality and accepted him as a character on the show. The audience that was present in the studio had the same reaction and would urge Charlie to move his mouth closer to the microphone so that they could hear him better!

Although Edgar Bergen and Charlie McCarthy never became popular on television, the idea of creating a show around a ventriloquist and his dummy was revisited with *The Paul Winchell–Jerry Mahoney Show*. The style was very similar to Edgar Bergen and Charlie McCarthy, with Paul Winchell playing straight man to his dummy, Jerry Mahoney. With the success of the show, Winchell commented that his puppet, Jerry Mahoney, was getting more fan mail than him.

The duo first started on NBC's *The Bigelow Show* in 1948. In 1949 the program moved to CBS and was canceled after a year, but in 1950 they appeared on NBC's *The Speidel Show* on Tuesday evenings in a variety format oriented toward children and adults, and the show was eventually renamed *The Paul Winchell–Jerry Mahoney Show*. In a move to consolidate children's programs on Saturday morning, it was renamed *Winchell and Mahoney*, with an audience of children and a set that included a clubhouse. The program ran until 1956 and was one of the first dedicated children's television programs. They appeared as a team on various other variety-oriented television programs and did television commercials through the 1960s. With an ability to create distinctive voices for animated characters, Paul Winchell's work could be heard on many Saturday-morning cartoons, and he was the voice of Tigger in Disney's *Pooh* series.

## Howdy Doody

Television culture embodies virtues associated with pro-social behavior that is a valuable construct in children's television programs. Children's television programming can address issues of play integrated with lessons about responsibility, honesty, and friendship. One program that created a benchmark in the genre and served as a model for children's programming was *The Howdy Doody Show* (1947–60). It was a fun-filled environment that consisted of a group of children on the set (the peanut gallery); some silly characters (Clarabelle the Clown, Mayor Bluster, Flub-a-Dub); sing-along segments; and the stars, Howdy Doody and Buffalo Bob Smith.

The character of Howdy Doody first appeared in the guise of Elmer, a radio voice on Buffalo Bob's *The Triple B Ranch Show*. In 1947 NBC introduced Howdy Doody on a show called *The Puppet Playhouse*. The name was officially changed to *The Howdy Doody Show* in 1949, and the show was sponsored by a gaggle of advertisers, including Poll-Parrot Shoes, Ovaltine, Colgate, Wonder Bread, Welch's Grape Juice, Kellogg's cereal, Blue Bonnet Margarine, Nabisco, Royal Pudding, and Ideal Toys.

As an early contender in the children's television marketplace, *The Howdy Doody Show* set a number of precedents on the video landscape, including the first network children's series to run five days a week and the first program of the day preceded in the beginning only by the test pattern. It was also the first program to broadcast over 1,000 continuous episodes and the first to be broadcast in color (130 episodes from 1955–1960).

### The Kuklapolitan

Interestingly, two puppet-oriented children's television programs that were conceived at about the same time couldn't be more different in character. While *The Howdy Doody Show* typified a somewhat carefree, frantic, playful environment, the puppets on *Kukla, Fran, and Ollie* were less frenetic and more idiosyncratic. Their characters had all the human frailties and strengths of people, and the sophisticated language they used was at times more appropriate for adults than children. That's why it was difficult to categorize this show as either adult or children, but it was probably targeted to both.

The creative genius behind *Kukla, Fran, and Ollie* was Burr Tillstrom, who started building his own marionettes when he was 14. After working in theaters, carnivals, fairs, and nightclubs, Tillstrom went to Chicago in 1941 and performed with his puppets on station WBKB. Working the puppets required someone else to interact with them, and he chose Fran Allison, a former schoolteacher from Iowa who was playing Aunt Fanny on *Don McNeil's Breakfast Club*. Soon the program moved to WNBQ, the NBC Chicago affiliate, and RCA, the original sponsor, was joined by such national brands as Sealtest and Ford. It was broadcast on NBC Monday through Friday from 6:00 to 6:30, Chicago time, and was canceled at the end of the 1953–54 season.

At times the essence of the humor in the show was quite literary, as when they did their version of *The Mikado* and Ollie made a dramatic entrance as Lieutenant Pinkerton, thinking that they were doing the opera *Madame Butterfly*. Ollie was the single-toothed Mr. Oliver J. Dragon, whose long puppet body looked like leopard skin, and Kukla had a boyish appearance, with a bright-red doorknob-shaped nose. And Fran Allison provided a counterpoint, interacting with the puppets on a human level. *Kukla, Fran, and Ollie* won 16 awards in 1949, which articulated its distinction as a show that entertained and enriched its audience.

### The Muppets

Being a visionary in the entertainment industry has its rewards and penalties, but for Jim Henson it realized a destiny of virtue that created a lingering love for the enduring characters that were his creation. At an early age he exhibited an artistic talent that was nurtured by his grandmother, who was a painter and seamstress. She introduced Henson to needlework and soft-sculpture technique.

In high school Henson was an outstanding art student who pursued his interest in theatrical puppetry's interface with television. He was interested in using the television camera to crop puppeteers from audience view, thus freeing them from the confines of box-type stages. As a senior at Northwestern University, he debuted his Muppets (marionette and puppet hybrids) on a Saturday-morning children's show from Washington. Later, at television station WRCTV, an NBC affiliate, Henson created *Sam and Friends*, a 5-minute, twice-a-day filler program following the two daily newscasts. On that show he introduced the audience to an early version of Kermit the Frog. During this time, Henson and his Muppet characters made guest appearances on some of the most popular early television programs, including *The Steve Allen Show* and *The Jack Paar Show*, along with programs hosted by celebrities Milton Berle, Red Skelton, and Ed Sullivan.

His appearances on these shows helped to popularize his endearing characters, and soon considerable demands were made upon him for Muppet appearances on variety programs and commercials. In 1961 he created Muppets Inc. and enlisted Don Sahlin and Frank Oznowicz (Frank Oz) to help him and his wife, Jane Anne Nebel, meet the demands. By 1963 Henson and his family settled in New York, and his Muppets were a weekly feature on *The Today Show* and *The Jimmy Dean Show*. Indeed, it was on the latter program that Henson introduced his first nationally recognized character, Rowlf, the famous floppy-eared, piano-playing pooch.

Generating income from television and advertising, Henson utilized those assets to create Muppet designs and produce several short features, including *The Cube, Youth 68*, and *Timepiece*. In an auspicious collaboration, Henson and his Creature Shop joined with Children's Television Workshop (CTW) to create both human and animal Muppet characters for *Sesame Street*, an innovative preschool program on public television. His creations, which included Bert and Ernie, Grover, Cookie Monster, Oscar the Grouch, and Big Bird, became universal icons of children and adult entertainment, creating an industry of licensed merchandise, videos, recordings, television shows, and feature-length films.

In 1976 Henson and his associates realized their goal of creating an original television series, *The Muppet Show*, featuring Muppet characters Kermit, Miss Piggy, Fozzie Bear, Gonzo the Great, and pseudoband Dr. Teeth and the Electric Mayhem. The series was seen in 100 countries and ended original production in 1981. Returning to the needs of young audiences, Henson created the HBO series *Fraggle Rock* and the animated television program *Muppet Babies*. As the Muppet characters became a global phenomenon, their popularity provided a rationale for the production of several theatrical features, including *The Muppet Movie, The Great Muppet Caper*, and *The Muppets Take Manhattan*.

The influence that Jim Henson had on the development of family television entertainment was profound. He was responsible for taking the art of puppetry and integrating it with television, creating a seamless transition to enriching fantasy. His creatures have become international symbols of goodwill,

"In an auspicious collaboration, Henson and his Creature Shop joined with Children's Television Workshop (CTW) to create both human and animal Muppet characters for *Sesame Street*, an innovative preschool program on public television." (Photofest.)

nurturing children around the world and demonstrating that family-value-oriented entertainment can be stimulating, compelling, and profitable.

## Puppets: Pushing the Envelope

Humor has limitless boundaries. In Shakespeare's work, both high- and lowbrow humor was used to entertain the audience. Fun was made of bodily parts and functions, and no character, regardless of class or stature, was immune. Today, American society has evolved into a culture of permissiveness, where some critics decry the tasteless direction that comedy has taken. However, our culture has become more accommodating toward language and situations that previous generations found lewd and contemptible. We are far removed from the time when Johnny Carson's utterances of God and Hell were bleeped from the screen.

In the spring of 2002, *Crank Yankers* premiered on the Comedy Central cable television network. Creating an interesting dynamic between puppets and reality, the format was used to re-create the crank telephone calls made by comedians, with real characters re-created by the puppets. It's an interesting concept, and one that helps to ameliorate some of the situations and language used on the show. There's a psychological determinant that may allow us to be more accepting of embarrassing humor if it's placed in the realm of fantasy. Transferring identities was certainly not unfamiliar to Shakespeare.

## CARTOONS

The funny pages, or comics, in the newspapers were always a major attraction for children and adults. Indeed, Hearst and Pulitzer, major newspaper publishers at the turn of the century, fought over the exclusive rights to a comic strip called *The Katzenjammer Kids*. Comic strip characters have become entrenched within the fabric of American culture, integrating into the industry of entertainment. With the art of animation and the era of sound recording, these characters and others leaped from the printed page to the silver screen, radio, and then television, bursting through the boundaries of art and creating global icons of humor, mirth, and adventure.

### Hollywood and Movie Cartoons

As a pioneer in the art of animation, the Fleischer Studio, headed by Max Fleischer, was responsible for inventing the rotoscope and the first to use sound in an animated film. The rotoscope, which Fleischer developed in 1917 and patented, was a device that projected live-action footage onto the animator's drawing board, allowing the artist to trace the projected image and produce lifelike drawings. He created cartoon versions of Popeye, Superman, and Betty Boop. Experimenting with hybrid animation, Fleischer's animated series *Out of the Inkwell* was a unique concept that allowed Koko the Clown to escape from the drawing, interacting with Fleischer on the screen.

One of the most enduring of Fleischer's cartoon characters was Betty Boop. She first appeared as a club singer in the 1930 film *Dizzy Dishes* and was modeled after Helen Kane, a singer under contract to Paramount known as "the Boop Oop a Doop Girl." She was a sexy little character that ran afoul of the Motion Picture Production Code, which required that her skirt be lowered and garter belt removed.

The artistic and technological advances in animation and the appearance of cartoons on television can be attributed to the efforts of Walt Disney. With the shrewd business acumen of his brother, Roy Disney, Walt created the rudiments of an entertainment giant that nurtured iconic animated characters, reflecting his values and what he perceived to be the tastes of the American public. The Disney studio was started in 1923 with a hybrid animation series entitled *Alice's Wonderland*. He moved quickly toward technical innovation and was the first to add music and sound effects to a cartoon. As part of his early experience, Disney learned that protecting his intellectual property was crucial, because one of his first cartoon characters, Oswald the Rabbit, was stolen from him.

Although it's assumed that Disney either created or adapted his popular cartoon characters from fairy tales, there were artists working for Disney who originated characters. As an animator who worked for Disney from 1935 to 1942, Carl Barks first introduced his Donald Duck character in a short entitled *The Wise Little Hen,* where he was a loud, agitated comic extra. During his time at Disney, Barks worked on 35 projects, all centering around the Donald Duck character and his extended family, which included his nephews, Huey, Dewey, and Louie, and his miserly uncle, Scrooge McDuck. At Disney, Barks was promoted to the story department, where he met Jack Hanna, who later became a principal in Hanna-Barbera, an animation studio specializing in cartoons for television.

The decade of the 1930s proved to be a defining moment for Walt Disney, as he incorporated the Technicolor process into his productions and bet the studio (so to speak) on his first animated feature, *Snow White and the Seven Dwarfs*. The movie was a resounding financial and critical success, and he followed it with *Pinocchio* and *Fantasia,* two movies that defined Disney's sense of artistic animation.

Owning a successful Hollywood studio, Walt Disney pursued his passion to build Disneyland, a theme park in California. However, as his company's stock was selling for seven dollars a share, he had difficulty raising the investment money. He approached Leonard Goldenson, the president of AB-PT (now ABC, owned by Disney), and as part of a financing package Disney agreed to a $40 million television-program deal. It was for seven years at $5 million a year and resulted in the hit *Disneyland* television program, which made its debut on October 27, 1954. This was followed with the even more successful *Mickey Mouse Club* in 1955. The two, however, parted company after seven years when RCA/NBC spirited Disney away for a color production of *Walt Disney's Wonderful World of Color,* which would prove to be a boon for the sale of color television sets with color patents owned by RCA.

The Disney studio was an incubator for a number of talented animators, including Hugh Harmon and Rudolph Ising, who had worked there in the early 1920s and departed along with a number of other artists in 1929. They entered a partnership with Leon Schlesinger and produced an eight-minute musical cartoon entitled *Sinkin' in the Bathtub,* distributed by Warner Brothers Pictures, featuring new characters Bosko; his girlfriend, Honey; and later a dog named Bruno.

In their efforts to create a new cartoon studio, they produced a pilot film called *Bosko the Talk-Ink Kid,* which pioneered the technology of synchronized speech. Warner Brothers liked what it saw and decided to distribute a series of cartoons featuring Bosko and his friends. The new series was named *Looney Tunes,* which was a direct reference to Disney's *Silly Symphonies,* as Bosko, Honey, and Bruno were referenced to Disney's Mickey, Minnie, and Pluto. After a year of success with *Looney Tunes,* a second series of cartoons entitled *Merrie Melodies* was created.

Warner Brothers' *Looney Tunes* has appeared on American television for over four decades, helping to define America's culture of entertainment. Its stable of cartoon characters, featuring Bugs Bunny, Road Runner, Tweety, and Daffy Duck, has had an enduring presence, entertaining generations with humor and their wild antics.

## Cartoons Come to TV

Cartoons were a natural fit for television, and the first to appear were silent theatrical animated shorts. One of the first was the series *Farmer Al Falfa and His Terrytoon Pals,* by Paul Terry. In 1953 CBS broadcast these cartoons on *Barker Bill's Cartoon Show* with new titles and sound effects, renaming the show *Farmer Gray.* His sidekicks included Ignatz Mouse and Kiko the Kangaroo. This package of cartoons went into syndication in 1956.

While Disney became an early presence on television, the rudiments of regularly scheduled animated programs and the development of original animated television characters were pioneered by William Hanna and Joseph Barbera, who created the successful Hanna-Barbera studio. Their stable of cartoon celebrities included some of the most enduring cartoon personalities ever created: Tom and Jerry, the Flintstones, Yogi Bear, and Scooby Doo.

Although trained as an architect and an engineer, with some experience in journalism, Hanna moved into animation during the Great Depression, when he utilized his previous training to become a letterer with the Pacific Art and Title Company, headed by Leon Schlesinger. He was spirited away by Rudolph Ising, who was a principal in the HarmonIsing studios, which produced *Looney Tunes* and *Merrie Melodies.* There, Hanna became a writer, editor, and lyricist. He left with Ising in 1937 to join Metro-Goldwyn-Mayer's animation department, where he met his longtime collaborator, the artist Joseph Barbera. Their first teamed effort was an MGM short film entitled *Puss Gets the Boot,* which introduced the Tom and Jerry characters. With that success, the studio gave them the freedom to work exclusively for the next 17 years on *Tom and Jerry* features.

After working at MGM for 20 years, the studio closed its animation division, which was a devastating blow to Hanna and the other animators. How-

Fred and Barney take their wives, Wilma and Betty, for a ride on the Flintmobile in Hanna-Barbera's prehistoric series *The Flintstones*. (Photofest.)

ever, that event turned into an enterprising opportunity when Hanna joined with Barbera to form the Hanna-Barbera Studio and create cartoons for television, the technology that prompted the closing of the MGM animation division. There were, however, a number of compelling challenges that the new team had to face, particularly trimming animation production costs for a weekly half-hour television series. They achieved this by pioneering a limited-cell animation technique with Hanna, reconfiguring the cartoon narrative from action to plot-centered dialogue.

Their first television cartoon series, *The Huckleberry Hound Show,* which was the first completely animated series on television, debuted in 1958 and was the first cartoon ever to win television's prestigious Emmy Award. The studio became a prominent producer of animated films, with an inventory of 150 television programs and 3,000 half-hour programs.

In addition to the proverbial Huckleberry Hound, other legendary characters in their animation stable included the Flintstones (1960–66, syndicated over 30 years), which was modeled after Jackie Gleason's successful series *The Honeymooners,* and Yogi Bear, also a takeoff on actor Phil Silvers and his *Sergeant Bilko* show. Other landmark comic adventures included *Space Ghost, The Jetsons,* and *Scooby Doo,* which was released as a live-action film in the summer of 2002.

The creative dynamic at Hanna-Barbera sustained generations of children growing up with television, nurturing them on the funny antics of frantic characters caught in the fantasy of time and space while enduring a legacy of wit and charm.

## Winky Dink and Interactive Television

As technology has become a potent force of empowerment in the entertainment industry and has created a palate of interactive programming on television and the Internet, its precedent can be traced to early broadcasting. In a pioneering effort, the CBS television network introduced a cartoon character named Winky Dink in a Saturday-morning program in the fall of 1953 called *Winky Dink and You*. The unique aspect of this was that children viewing at home could purchase Official Winky Dink Kits for 50 cents that included a thin sheet of acetate to be placed on the television screen and held up by static electricity, magic crayons, and a cloth for cleanup. This pixielike character would have adventures and get into tense situations and a child could use his or her imagination to draw a means of escape (bridge, rope) on the acetate. Hosted by Jack Barry, the program became a phenomenon, with 1955 sales of kits reaching 2 million.

There were also Winky's cartoon pals, which included Mysto the Magician; Dusty Dan; Mike McBean; and, of course, his dog, Woofer. The program also included live-action skits featuring Jack Barry and his awkward sidekick, Mr. Bungle. Although many children owned the kits, there were quite a number that drew directly on the television screen, to the consternation of their parents. The program was canceled by CBS in 1957. The series was resurrected in 1969 for syndication with 64 new segments and accompanied by a new Winky Dink drawing kit.

Another children's program that used art and drawing as a theme was *Ding Dong School*, featuring Dr. Frances Horwich. Known as Miss Frances to her "children," the program originated locally in Chicago and was added to the NBC weekday schedule in 1952. Children participated by sending in their artwork, and Miss Frances would display and discuss it on the air.

## Adult Cartoons

While children's cartoons have been a staple for decades of television programming, edgy adult cartoons have also captured the imagination of viewers. A pioneer in animation featuring adult themes was Ralph Bakshi, who produced *Fritz the Cat* (1972), the first adult-themed animated feature. He learned his craft as an 18-year-old paint opaquer at Terrytoons and became a director of the television cartoons *Deputy Dawg* and *The Mighty Heroes*. He followed *Fritz the Cat* with *Heavy Traffic* (1973) and *Coonskin* (1975), which was an offensive satire of Disney's *Song of the South*. The film was removed from distribution by Paramount after virulent protests. In 1992 he produced *Cool World*, which combined live action with animation and featured Kim

Basinger as the sultry comic-strip vamp who attempts to seduce her cartoonist to move from the "cool world" to the real world.

It is indeed fitting that Bakshi's talented protégé John Kricfalusi was a pioneer in producing one of the first adult-themed cartoons for television with *The Ren and Stimpy Show,* featuring the mutant Chihuahua and the foul feline, a demented duo that captured the imaginations of the valued 18–49 audience. Seeing an opportunity to serve a niche audience, in 1992 Viacom (corporate parent of CBS) acquired *Ren and Stimpy* along with *Rugrats* and *Doug,* two other animated series with a flair for the bizarre, at a cost of $40 million for their Nickelodeon cable network.

Of course, there was *Looney Tunes,* but *looney* is not an adjective that best describes the antics of Beavis and Butthead, perhaps the strangest and longest-running duo of neurotic teens on the planet. These two hyperventilating heroes of the counterculture expressed a defiance toward everything normal and struck a resounding chord with young and older audiences. The mutant embryos were created by Mike Judge, premiered on MTV's *Liquid Television,* and eventually became the highest-rated featured program on the network, running from 1991 to 1998.

Perhaps one of the most dysfunctional families to be featured on television was Matt Groening's Simpsons. Starting with the comic strip *Life Is Hell,* Groening moved on to his offbeat family of the plodding dad, Homer; his strident wife, Marge; their delinquent son, Bart; and Maggie, the family's toddler. Their animated exploits started as a short on Fox's *Tracey Ullman Show,* which was followed by a 1989 Christmas special, and in 1990 it became a regularly scheduled weekly prime-time series on Fox.

## NURTURING HOSTS

### Captain Kangaroo

Television has created celebrities who were icons for the first generation of kids growing up with the tube. They included the zany, kinetic antics of Pinky Lee and Soupy Sales and the more reserved, low-key, warm-and-fuzzy approach of Bob Keeshan (Captain Kangaroo) and Mister Rogers. Indeed, Keeshan's television career started at NBC, where he was a receptionist and was given bit parts to play on a program called *The Triple B Ranch Show,* hosted by Bob Smith, who later became Buffalo Bob and host of the program *The Howdy Doody Show.* Eventually Keeshan assumed the role of Clarabelle, a mute clown who communicated by honking a horn. In 1952 he left *The Howdy Doody Show,* moved to WABC-TV in New York, and hosted the afternoon cartoon show *TV's Time for Fun.* His work on the early-morning program *Tinker's Workshop* became the genesis for *Captain Kangaroo.*

In 1955 CBS approved the concept for *Captain Kangaroo,* and the program ran until 1985, distinguishing it as the longest-running children's series

"[*The Simpsons'*] animated exploits started as a short on
Fox's *Tracey Ullman Show,* which was followed by a 1989
Christmas special, and in 1990 it became a regularly scheduled weekly prime-time series on Fox." Featured here (from
left to right): Santa's Little Helper, Marge, Homer, Bart,
Lisa, Maggie, and Snowball II. (Photofest.) © Fox Broadcasting Co.

on commercial network broadcast television. As the host of the program,
Keeshan embodied all the virtues of a warm, compassionate figure reassuring
to children and their parents while leading them through the nonintimidating
activities of the Treasure House.

In 1981 CBS trimmed a half hour off the program to provide a berth for
*CBS Morning News.* The show was renamed *Wake Up with the Captain* and
first moved to 7:00 A.M. and then to 6:30 A.M. By 1982 the Captain was
relegated to an hour on weekends, and after being canceled, Keeshan moved
the program to the Public Broadcasting Service (PBS), where it ran for two
years. A children's advocate, Bob Keeshan also provided oversight of the products advertised on the program, choosing those that he felt had potential for
creative play. His contribution to children's programming embodied a spirit
of inquiry and a commitment to the values of education and enrichment.

## A Special Neighbor

Over 30 years ago Fred Rogers and his neighborhood changed the landscape of children's television, creating rituals that personified the trust and caring that an adult can convey to children. The show started in 1954 as *The Children's Corner* on WQED, the Pittsburgh educational television station (a PBS affiliate). By 1963 Rogers had developed the format for *Mister Rogers' Neighborhood* and produced a 15-minute version for Canadian television. He returned to Pittsburgh's WQED with the concept, and in 1969 *Mister Rogers' Neighborhood* was distributed nationally by PBS. It has since become the longest-running program on PBS.

An ordained minister, Fred Rogers was the ultimate nonintimidating, loving father figure who embraced children with an honest, warm approach. His sincere rendition of the welcoming theme song was an invitation that evoked a sense of belonging and feeling of security: "Would you be mine, could be mine, won't you be my neighbor?" His philosophy was based upon the ideals and value of family and community. "The whole idea is to look at the television camera and present as much love as you possibly could to a person who might feel that he or she needs it."[1]

Children take comfort in repetition, which ritualizes the ordinary and mundane, providing them with comfort and reassurance. Fred Rogers was a master at this, changing from his loafers into canvas boat shoes, which provided a transition from his living room to the neighborhood of make-believe. His warm, fuzzy cardigan sweaters were symbolic of his friendship and love.

In his pursuit of communicating confidence, he addressed issues of substance that could upset and confuse a child. When a pet goldfish died, Rogers used the event to discuss loss and sadness. He tried to allay the fears of children that can be so damaging if they are not addressed by an adult. His nurturing provided children with an approach to fantasy and reality that exuded trust, loyalty, and caring.

In 1971 Fred Rogers created Family Communications Inc., which produced his program and served as a conduit for commercial ventures and child advocacy. He retired in 2001 and died two years later, but his program, with 33 years of inventory, continues to air and is a testament to him and the essence of the family values he stressed.

Pro-social values are inherent in the dynamic of many children's television programs, and two that have had a prominent impact upon the genre are *Barney and Friends* and *Teletubbies,* both distributed on PBS. Barney is, of course, the purple dinosaur that has generated a treasure trove of licensed product merchandising for its creators. He and his friends—Baby Bop and her big brother, BJ—offer enrichment and instruction on health and safety habits, manners, and self-esteem. Indeed, the vastness of the *Barney* revenue machine and its $2 million funding by the Corporation for Public Broadcasting (CPB) to the Lyons Group, the program's creators, became a cause of controversy in the mid-1990s. Former senator Bob Dole called *Barney* a cash cow with only a fraction of the licensing revenue returning to the coffers of the CPB. Indeed, in 1993 *Barney* merchandise generated a gross revenue of $500 million, netting the Lyons Group about $20 million. However, the CPB renegotiated its contract with the production company in the mid-1990s, which allowed public television to recoup the costs for the program's new season within four years.

A British Broadcasting Corporation production, *Teletubbies,* and its retinue of characters, including Tinky Winky, Dipsy, Laa-Laa, and Po, were an instant hit when the show was distributed by PBS in the United States starting in 1997. These cuddly characters became endearing creatures to preschoolers (infants and toddlers) and also created a bonanza in licensed product merchandising. In 1999 a family-values issue associated with Tinky Winky was raised by Reverend Jerry Falwell, who alleged that the character was secretly gay. Once again, like in the case of *Murphy Brown,* the crusaders of the airwaves were policing the ether and branding the fictional characters with real-life virtues. Fortunately, no one seemed to care whether or not Tinky Winky was gay.

Perhaps the most significant development in children's television programming is the elimination of some of the abusive practices that were inherent in the programs: the advertising associated with them and the number of commercials inserted. Today, there are limits as to the number of commercials allowed and the type of products advertised. For example, children's vitamins are not allowable, and hosts of programs cannot endorse products. In addition, there are stipulations concerning programs that are based upon popular toys, which can be construed as program-length commercials. Also, legislators have voiced their concerns about the need for family values and the integration of pro-social material in children's television programming.

Television is a window on the culture and values of our society. It provides a consuming experience for children that envelops them in glowing images that feed their psyches, nurturing their will. Young children learn from television, and those rudiments serve as an important foundation for learning in their later years. Unfortunately, television has been used by parents as an electronic babysitter, paying little heed to the nature and content of programs that children are viewing. Although federal regulation has attempted some oversight, the parent must serve as the child's mediator of selection. As with the Internet, children's access to television content should be monitored, and parents should watch television with their children.

The television viewing experience, especially for young children, should be pleasant, nonintimidating, and nurturing. A parent can help to ameliorate confusion and fear that a child may have as a result of seeing something disturbing. Indeed, in today's television landscape, with its myriad of channel offerings via broadcast, satellite, and cable, there is a more compelling need to be more proactive about parental supervision.

## NOTE

1. Interview with Don Swaim, June 1, 1987, http://wiredforbooks.org/fredrogers.

.

# 12

## TELEVISION'S TELLTALE TUBE: FANTASY, SCIENCE FICTION, AND THE OCCULT

Throughout literature, the expressive nature of the bizarre and occult has been part of the fabric of drama. The work of Edgar Allan Poe demonstrated the popularity of narrative themes that wove an intricate web of mystery, murder, and a taste for the strange and extraordinary. Creating a sense of dread and doom can be a compelling and captivating experience for an audience. Indeed, filmmakers have embraced the genre, producing a visual array of substance and kitsch but always hearkening back to the classical elements of this genre.

As radio evolved, it adapted the dramatic form to suit its format as a mass medium. One of the most innovative talents to produce drama for radio was Orson Welles. Along with John Houseman, he established *The Mercury Theatre on the Air* in 1937. As an actor, Welles had already taken advantage of radio's opportunity, appearing quite regularly on *The March of Time* and as the lead character in the popular radio series *The Shadow*. In the summer of 1938 he was given a nine-week berth on network radio to produce drama for *The Mercury Theatre on the Air*. Notably, the first adaptation was of Bram Stoker's classic gothic horror tale of the living dead, *Dracula*.

The radio series attracted talented performers like Katharine Hepburn, Helen Hayes, Laurence Olivier, and Lionel Barrymore, and writers like Lucille Fletcher, whose *The Hitchhiker* and *Sorry, Wrong Number* created compelling stories with themes that were supernatural and mysterious. One dramatic program on *The Mercury Theatre on the Air* became a defining moment of the series. It was an adaptation of H. G. Wells's *The War of the Worlds*, broadcast on Halloween eve 1938, which created a panic in some cities by listeners who thought that the country was under a gas attack from Mars.

While Orson Welles directed the live broadcast from a CBS studio in New York and played a role in the drama, the story was adapted to radio by Howard Koch and John Houseman. The broadcast received so much attention that the Campbell Soup Company became the sole sponsor, renaming the series *The Campbell Playhouse* and scheduling it for 9:00 P.M. Fridays.

In the 1950s television embraced the dramatic form with challenging and evocative dramas. Young writers created drama original to television, capitalizing on the small screen's intimacy. One of them was Rod Serling, who, as a young playwright, helped to define the medium of television with provocative teleplays, including "Requiem for a Heavyweight" (*Playhouse 90*, 1956) and "Patterns" (*Kraft Television Theatre*, 1955). As a dramatist, Serling challenged convention and moved toward narrative fiction that shattered barriers of tradition, moving toward themes that stretched the realm of imagination. His anthology series *The Twilight Zone* (CBS, 1959–65; 134 half hours) was indicative of this, with its manipulation of time and space and somewhat didactic endings. It created a unique dynamic within the genre, establishing a foundation for the synergy between the known and unknown.

While *The Twilight Zone* addressed themes of science fiction, Serling's subsequent series *Night Gallery* (NBC, 1969–72) dealt with horror and the macabre. Each program opened with Serling standing before several portraits, each suggesting the mayhem that was about to occur. He introduced each with these ominous words:

"As a dramatist, Serling [the creator of *The Twilight Zone*] challenged convention and moved toward narrative fiction that shattered barriers of tradition, moving towards themes that stretched the realm of imagination." (Photofest.)

Good evening, and welcome to a private showing of three paintings displayed here for the first time. Each is a collector's item in its own way—not because of any artistic quality, but because each captures on a canvas, suspends in time and space, a frozen moment of a nightmare.

Each two-hour program featured segments of different lengths. In the pilot program, Steven Spielberg made his directorial debut in "Eyes," featuring Hollywood legend Joan Crawford. During the first season, *Night Gallery* was included as a segment in NBC's experimental programming cycle *Four in One*. The following year, after winning an Emmy nomination for "They're Tearing Down Tim Riley's Bar," which was written by Serling, the program was given its own dedicated time period. In the third season NBC cut the series from an hour to a half hour and asked for a "refocus" of the dramatic content. However, Serling was nominated for another Emmy for the teleplay "The Messiah on Mott Street." The program was canceled in 1973 after 15 shows.

With his characteristic deadpan humor and sardonic smile, Alfred Hitchcock became a television celebrity with a series that exploited his talent for the macabre and his pursuit of the extraordinary. While his feature-film career brought him notoriety and fame, television brought him recognition, making his name a household word. He embraced television, using it as a tool to experiment with different styles and themes. Indeed, his cinematic masterpiece, *Psycho,* was highly influenced by his work in television and its need for economies of scale.

The program *Alfred Hitchcock Presents* was broadcast on CBS and then on NBC from October 2, 1955, to June 1962. A total of 268 episodes were aired during this time. As the host of the program, Hitchcock would introduce each teleplay with a humorous reference and reappear at the end with a clever witticism. Often evil would triumph over good, which was in defiance of the television code of ethics. Sponsors were concerned about the material, and in one case Revlon, an alternating sponsor, blocked the telecast of a program that featured a deranged magician's assistant who tries to saw a woman in half.

In 1962 the series was expanded to an hour and renamed *The Alfred Hitchcock Hour;* it ran from September 1962 to May 10, 1965, with 93 filmed episodes. Interestingly, five years after Alfred Hitchcock's death, NBC broadcast an original series entitled *Alfred Hitchcock Presents* from September 1985 to July 1986, creating original scripts and new versions based upon stories from the series. After concluding its run on NBC, additional episodes were produced and broadcast on the USA network during the 1987–88 season. Using digital techniques and colorized enhancement of his original introductions, Hitchcock introduced each of the episodes. It had a bizarre effect, but it was certainly apropos for the master of the macabre to return from the grave and host a new television series based upon his original inspiration.

In a time of racial unrest, war, and political turbulence, *The Outer Limits* provided television viewers with compelling science-fiction dramas that addressed issues of substance. In the early 1960s, when America faced some of its most daunting challenges, this program provided thought-provoking themes that challenged the boundaries of tradition.

The inspiration for the ABC series came from Leslie Stevens and Joseph Stefano. As a boy of 15, Stevens got a job as a gofer with Orson Welles's *Mercury Theatre on the Air*. Eventually he made it to New York City and became a songwriter and a playwright. By 1963 Stevens had created the Western *Stoney Burke* for ABC and proposed the concept for his science-fiction series, known as *Please Stand By*, to the network. Busy with other creative commitments, Stevens turned to his friend Joseph Stefano, the Academy Award–winning screenwriter of Alfred Hitchcock's *Psycho*, to take over the day-to-day running of the production. He had a clear vision and set his agenda for the themes he wanted to address, which included discrimination, censorship, capital punishment, and man's inaccessibility to man.

The beginning of each program set the tone of the series, when a disembodied control voice uttered these menacing words:

There is nothing wrong with your television set. Do not attempt to adjust the picture. We are controlling transmission. If we wish to make it louder, we will bring up the volume. If we wish to make it softer, we will tune it to a whisper. We will control the horizontal. We will control the vertical. We can roll the image, make it flutter. We can change the focus to a soft blur or sharpen it to crystal clarity. For the next hour, sit quietly and we will control all that you see and hear. We repeat: There is nothing wrong with your television set. You are about to participate in a great adventure. You are about to experience the awe and mystery which reaches from the inner mind to . . . *The Outer Limits.*

The pilot episode, "The Galaxy Being," written and directed by Stevens, showcased the style and narrative structure of the series and set the dramatic tone. It was broadcast on the ABC television network from September 1963 to January 1965. Each episode had a budget of approximately $150,000 with $40,000 dedicated to makeup, and mechanics for creating special effects. In its first season, *The Outer Limits* was scheduled for Monday evenings at 7:30, opposite two quiz programs, *To Tell the Truth* (CBS) and *I've Got a Secret* (CBS), and a movie on NBC. Midway into the first season, ABC renewed the series but repositioned it against the formidable *Jackie Gleason Show* on Saturday evenings. That move was disastrous, and in the middle of the second season, *The Outer Limits* was canceled. The original series has been a syndication favorite for the last 30 years, and a new version is being produced by MGM Television and is syndicated and also distributed by the Sci Fi Network.[1]

Although most of the programs with a theme oriented toward the bizarre or occult were broadcast in prime time, there was one series, *Dark Shadows,* on ABC, that was a daytime serial. It was conceived by Dan Curtis and was very much in the style of the gothic thriller *Jane Eyre*. Indeed the plot was almost a carbon copy except for the presence of the wildly popular character Barnabas Collins, the 175-year-old resident vampire. Set in a small fishing village in Collinsport, Maine, the youthful Vicki Winters has taken the job of governess to 10-year-old David Collins, heir to a family fortune, and also acts as companion to Elizabeth Collins Stoddard, the mistress of Collinwood. The series made its debut on ABC on June 27, 1966, broadcast 1,225 episodes, and ran until April 2, 1971. It was one of the most successful soap operas on television and one of the first to feature a famous Hollywood celebrity, Joan Bennett. In 1973 Dan Curtis produced a *Dracula* feature film for television starring veteran actor Jack Palance.

Taking advantage of its success, *Dark Shadows* was made into a theatrical feature film in 1970. In 1975 the program went into syndication until 1990, when the Sci Fi Channel purchased the exclusive rights to broadcast the show. An NBC attempt to reinvent the series failed and only lasted from January 13 to March 22, 1991.

For the 1995 television season, CBS tried its hand at gothic drama with *American Gothic,* featuring the town of Trinity, South Carolina, and its murderous sheriff, Lucas Buck, portrayed by actor Gary Cole. Ten-year-old Caleb Temple's sister Marlyn returns as a ghost to protect her younger brother from the sheriff's evil. It lasted only one season and was canceled in 1996.

With the uncertainty of the 1970s, which was immersed in the intrigue of Watergate and the cold war, the success of the short-lived *Kolchak: The Night Stalker* reflected the insecure sensibilities of the American public. Produced in 1972 as a television film for ABC and shot in 12 days on a budget of $450,000, *Kolchak: The Night Stalker* was one of the most successful movies ever produced for television. It featured Darren McGavin as a Las Vegas reporter covering a serial killing who discovers that the suspect is a vampire. In 1973 a sequel, *The Night Strangler,* was produced. After the success of the features, the television series *Kolchak: The Night Stalker* was produced and included 20 episodes broadcast from September 13, 1974, to August 30, 1975.

In the series McGavin reprises his role as a Chicago reporter on the trail of unearthly beings responsible for heinous crimes. Interestingly, David Chase, creator of *The Sopranos,* was the story editor of the series, and Robert Zemeckis, of *Forrest Gump* and *Back to the Future* fame, was a writer. The movies and the series have been acknowledged as an inspiration for *The X Files* by its creator, Chris Carter.

Another series that could have been a precursor to *The X Files* was the short-lived *Eerie, Indiana.* Created by Karl Schaefer and Jose Rivera, with several episodes directed by Joe Dante (*Gremlins*), the program was offbeat, funny, and bizarre. It's about a 13-year-old boy, Marshall Teller (Omri Katz), who moved with his family from a New York suburb to the town of Eerie, Indiana, where he witnesses strange events and bizarre goings-on. There's Elvis in a bathrobe getting his morning newspaper, and the Foreverware Twins, who have stayed 1960s teenagers by sleeping in airtight plastic containers aptly called *Foreverware*. The show had a funny, surrealistic tone to it and was on NBC from September 15, 1991, to April 1992. It was resurrected for a single episode on NBC in December 1993, then was on Disney in 1994 and on Fox Kids in 1997.

There was a singular television event in 1990 that captured the imagination and interest of the American viewing public and created a buzz of watercooler conversation. Scheduled as a limited-run miniseries midseason replacement on ABC, *Twin Peaks,* written by David Lynch and Mark Frost and directed by David Lynch, was heralded as a significant departure from traditional narrative, exploring the shadows of the dark and sinister. In his cinematic body of work, David Lynch is known as a master of the unconventional, creating a vivid visual style and language that compels the audience to watch, listen, and think. Nothing is what it appears to be, and the nuances of the narrative unfold in a cadence of suspicion with a threatening sense of awe.

Prior to its premiere, the critics were touting the series as a unique and distinctive television event. As an auteur, Lynch had a significant body of work, including the cult classic *Eraserhead* (1978), *The Elephant Man* (1980), *Dune* (1984), *Blue Velvet, Wild at Heart,* and *Lost Highway.* He and Frost were well suited to uncover the bizarre turn of events in the murder investigation of high-school prom queen Laura Palmer, found trussed in a plastic bag floating in a lake in the town of Twin Peaks. Although the series was canceled after the second season, it served as an inspiration for other programs, especially *The X Files,* which featured David Duchovny.

In *The X Files,* creator-producer Chris Carter evolved the narrative genre of film noir to an entertaining mix of plots and characters within a dynamic of psychoses dealing with threats from without and within while acknowledging the validity of the paranormal. FBI special agents Fox Mulder (David Duchovny) and Dana Scully (Gillian Anderson) entered an uncharted dimension where their partnership and training were tested by the strain of unexplainable events. For Agent Mulder there was little doubt that within the confines of reality there were nuances of doubt that offered ripples of opportunity with doors that opened into portals of time and space. However, Agent Scully, with her medical degree, was more skeptical and demanding in her search for cause and effect.

The series was broadcast on Fox from 1993 to 2002 (Duchovny left in 2001) and became a hit as well as a cult classic. It successfully integrated the genres of drama, mystery, science fiction, and horror. The series had a welcome edge that looked, sounded, and felt ominous while desperately seeking the glitter of light as it moved toward the edge of darkness. There was humor, pathos, dread, and fear associated with some very inventive plots. Technically, each program had a compelling visual dynamic, with great care placed upon cinematography and lighting, using these elements as components of story-telling. Although *The X Files* completed its network run in 2002, it is presently syndicated on television stations around the country.

Another television series that blends humor with horror and the occult is *Buffy the Vampire Slayer*. The television series evolved from a 1992 feature film with the same title that received tepid reviews and was less than a modest success. However, screenwriter Joss Whedon adapted the format to a successful television series that premiered on the WB network in 1997 and has been a favorite with critics and audiences alike. Indeed, in 2002, when speculation surfaced that the series and its star, Sarah Michelle Gellar, would be

The cast of *Buffy the Vampire Slayer* (left to right): David Boreanaz (as Angel), Sarah Michelle Gellar (as Buffy Summers), Alyson Hannigan (as Willow Rosenburg), Anthony Stewart Head (as Rupert Giles), Charisma Carpenter (as Cordelia Chase), and Nicholas Brendon (front, as Xander Harris). (Photofest.)

moving to the United Paramount Network (UPN), it created a stir in the media. From 2001–2003, *Buffy the Vampire Slayer* appeared on UPN and is currently syndicated on FX.

The premise is based upon a myth that in every generation a vampire slayer is born, and Buffy Summers, who moved with her mother to Sunnydale, California, is the young woman chosen to slay the demons with the aid of her compatriots, Willow, Giles, Xander, Anya, Tara, Spike, and Dawn. The program is a lively mix of horror and humor that has a special appeal to younger viewers. Another program with a similar audience demographic is *Sabrina the Teenage Witch,* which in 1971 was an animated television series. It featured Melissa Joan Hart as Sabrina Spellman, who lives with her aunts, Hilda and Zelda, in Massachusetts, and the mishaps she endures as a young witch. In a clever plot development, Barbara Eden, who wasn't a witch but a genie in *I Dream of Jeannie,* the classic television sitcom, appeared in a guest role as Sabrina's great-aunt, Irma. The program also ran on UPN.

Cable television has been a repository for several horror-fantasy series. Another of these, produced by Trilogy Television and created by Richard Lewis, is *Poltergeist: The Legacy,* which ran from 1996 to 1999. It was about a secret society called the Legacy that fought evil forces threatening all of humanity. The series featured some veteran television performers, including Daniel J. Travanti (*Hill Street Blues*) and Helen Shaver (*The Education of Max Bickford*). Another science-fiction cable-television series was *Swamp Thing,* based upon the comic book with the same title. It was originally broadcast on the USA network from 1990 to 1993. The main character is Dr. Alec Holland, who was badly burned, disfigured, and sprayed with toxic chemicals in a lab accident instigated by his nemesis, Dr. Anton Arcane. As a result, Holland has adopted a plantlike appearance and has mysterious powers over the vegetation.

There's a rich literary and cinematic tradition associated with stories of the macabre and tales of doom and horror. From *Nosferatu* to *Friday the 13th* and its many sequels, audiences have relished the sinking quagmire and anticipation of murder and mayhem. Television has accommodated this lust for blood by satisfying the thirst with such innovative and sinister programs as *The Hitchhiker* (HBO, 1984–94) and *Tales from the Crypt* (HBO, 1989–96), based upon the 1950s EC comics *Tales from the Crypt* and *The Vault of Horror.* There is a psychological manifestation associated with recreational terror that creates the tension and satisfies a need for fear and absolution. It appeals to every emotion and sensibility associated with death and the spiritual reckoning that is part of that dynamic. Movies like *The Exorcist, Poltergeist,* and *The Sixth Sense* evoked a fascination and fear of the paranormal, manufacturing a compelling sense of awe that has sustained itself on television. Whether it's ghosts, aliens, vampires, or mutants, there is a compelling audience interest based upon a tradition of horror that transcends the arc of drama and sinks its audience into a shivering abyss of darkness. Television is equal to the task and can create the numbing sensation of overwhelming fear and the pleasure that is derived from it.

## NOTE

1. John J. Flynn, "From the Inner Mind to the Outer Limits," http://www.towson.edu/~flynn/tol.html.

# 13

## SETTING THE AGENDA: TELEVISION NEWS STYLE AND SUBSTANCE

The news marketplace has been a battleground of competition driven by technology and creative entrepreneurship. With a faster printing press, the enterprising businessman and journalist Benjamin Day had his newspaper, the *New York Sun,* hit the streets for a penny apiece (known as *the penny press*), hawked by newsboys and undercutting the competition by five cents. As the *New York Sun*'s volume grew, its readership increased, attracting advertisers that subsidized production and distribution.

In moving the newspaper toward mass distribution, the area of content had to be addressed. The era of the news-gathering journalist was initiated by James Gordon Bennett, who started the *New York Herald* in 1835. He instituted beat reporting by sending staff to police stations to report on crime, to city hall to cover politics, and to sporting events.

By the late 1880s the power and riches of the press were embraced by men of vision and determination who built empires and earned the distinction of "press baron." Individuals like Joseph Pulitzer, who purchased the *New York World* in 1883 with a modest circulation of 20,000, in less than a decade made it into a powerhouse reaching 374,000 readers. He was challenged in the New York market by William Randolph Hearst, who assumed control of the *New York Journal* in 1895 and used screaming headlines to sell newspapers. His instinct concerning popular taste was in tune with the times, as he articulated his philosophy to the readers. "It is the *Journal*'s policy to engage brains as well as to get the news, for the public is even more fond of entertainment than it is of information."[1]

An interesting comment, made before the onslaught of the mass media and the recontextualization of television news within the imperatives of entertainment. There were several personalities and a number of events that helped to define the role of the mass media—first radio, later television—as tools of the news trade. The news defined these moments of historical significance that were shaped by the essence of radio and television.

It was the summer of 1925 in the sleepy town of Dayton, Tennessee, when two of America's foremost legal scholars descended on a courthouse to take up the case of a 24-year-old high-school biology teacher, John Scopes, and whether or not he violated state law by teaching Charles Darwin's theory of evolution. The defense was represented by Clarence Darrow, with William Jennings Bryan serving the prosecution. There was so much interest in the case, known as "the Monkey Trial," that WGN, a local Chicago radio station owned by the *Chicago Tribune,* leased a telephone line for $1,000 a day to provide live commentary from the scene. It was the first time radio was used to provide coverage of a courtroom proceeding.

As television evolved and technology has become more sophisticated, Marshall McLuhan's axiom about a "global village" has become even more profound. With live satellite transmission, events around the world can be seen transmitted live. The dissemination of news is instantaneous, with reporters in the field using compact, mobile satellite video cameras for live video feeds.

One of the first live events that radio news covered was the tragic explosion of the German airship *Hindenburg* as it was ending its maiden voyage and docking in Lakehurst, New Jersey. On May 6, 1937, Herb Morrison of Chicago station WLS was present to record the event on a disc for the station's archives. He witnessed the hydrogen-filled dirigible explode, with passengers on fire jumping to their deaths. In New York, radio station WHN carried the news first, and then the story was picked up by CBS and NBC. The recording was expedited back to Chicago and broadcast on WLS the next morning. It clearly demonstrated the power of radio to provide on-the-spot coverage of news.

That power of immediacy and urgency that radio could provide was viewed suspiciously by the newspaper industry. In the 1930s radio received most of its news feeds from the wire services: Associated Press (AP), United Press (UP), and International News Service (INS). These were controlled by the newspapers, and because of radio's threat, the service to radio was eliminated. In response to the aggressive posture of the newspaper industry, the radio networks began their own news-gathering operations, sometimes nothing more than using the newspapers as a source for stories. In an attempt to reign in the ambitions of radio, newspapers decided to stop publishing free listings of radio programs, classifying them as advertising and demanding payment.

As tensions between radio and newspapers increased, a secret agreement was reached in 1933 at New York City's Biltmore Hotel, subsequently known as the Biltmore Agreement. The terms included restricting radio stations to two five-minute newscasts a day, at 9:30 A.M. and 9:00 P.M., providing a buffer of protection for the morning and evening newspaper editions. Also, only interpretation and commentary could be broadcast, no hard news, and only stories provided by the newly created Press-Radio Bureau, which received news copy from the wire services. In addition, radio had to cease its own news-gathering operations and could not broadcast sponsored news.

Interestingly, only the radio networks signed off on the Biltmore Agreement, leaving independent stations and some affiliates to create their own news-gathering service. Soon Transradio Press Service became one of the largest bureaus providing news to radio. Also, the wire services—INS, UP, and AP—reevaluated their position and started providing news to radio stations and networks. Almost a year later the Biltmore Agreement was effectively dead.

The development of a culture of news at the radio networks was a function of competition. As CBS took on its formidable rival, NBC, it had greater amounts of unsold time, which it used for news programming. Coordinated by Paul White, CBS soon had one of the most formidable stables of news commentators on radio, including H. V. Kaltenborn, Edward R. Murrow, Eric Sevareid, William L. Shirer, and Elmer Davis. In 1938 the network introduced *The CBS World News Roundup,* with shortwave connections from around the world. In 1936 CBS broadcast the abdication of Great Britain's King Edward VIII and the coronation of King George VI. The coronation was one of the first radio broadcasts to be heard around the world.

One of the most dramatic news stories of the 1930s was the kidnapping of pioneer aviator Charles Lindbergh's baby and the subsequent apprehension and trial of the perpetrator. The 19-month-old child was kidnapped in 1932, but it wasn't until 1935 that a trial for the suspect, Bruno Richard Hauptmann, was convened. It was a massive media event, with photographers, reporters, and radio broadcasters vying for the best location. Indeed, Gabriel Heatter, a reporter for the Mutual Radio Network, was given a first-row seat because the judge's wife was a special fan of his. All sense of decorum was lost in the circuslike frenzy of pandemonium that followed the trial and ensuing guilty verdict. In a move to prevent further encroachments by the media into courtroom proceedings, the American Bar Association adopted Canon 35—later Canon 3A(7)—as a rule of judicial procedure, placing restrictions upon reporters and photographers and also limiting radio coverage. As of 1952 the rule included television.

The beginning of World War II created a need for the dissemination of breaking stories about the war prior to America's entry and, afterward, about the Allies' progress. The CBS war-correspondent news team was lead by Edward R. Murrow, who had become a familiar voice on CBS, reporting from London about the drama of the British resistance against the Germans. He began each broadcast with his signature phrase, "This . . . is London." A talented reporter who used radio and then television to provide a more intimate portrait of the news for his listeners, he flew on a B-29 during an air raid over Berlin (against the orders of his superiors) and later broadcast a vivid description of the experience. His commentary was articulate, descriptive, and poignant, as was demonstrated by his April 15, 1945, report from Buchenwald, the liberated concentration camp.

Permit me to tell you what you would have seen, and heard had you been with me on Thursday. It will not be pleasant listening. If you are at lunch, or if you have no appetite to hear what Germans have done, now is a good time to switch off the radio, for I propose to tell you of Buchenwald.

. . . Murder had been done at Buchenwald. God alone knows how many men and boys have died there during the last twelve years. Thursday I was told that there were more than 20,000 in the camp. There had been as many as 60,000. Where are they now?

The CBS radio network had an ambitious agenda, with journalists covering the major fronts of battle including Eric Sevareid on the fall of France, Howard K. Smith from Europe, Charles Collingwood reporting from North Africa, William L. Shirer from Europe, and Webley Edwards in the Pacific theater. Other reporters remained based in New York as anchors, and they included Lowell Thomas, John Daly, and Robert Trout.

Perhaps one of the most important radio broadcasts during the war was the coverage of D-day and the Allied invasion of France on June 6, 1944. For CBS, reporter George Hicks recorded amphibious troops landing from a naval ship with the natural sound of battle in the background. That recording was transmitted via shortwave back to the United States for broadcast.

Radio reported President Franklin Roosevelt's death on April 12, 1945, the first radio report on the passing of a sitting president, and then covered the momentous events of the end of the war in Europe and the celebrations that followed, the atomic bomb dropped on Hiroshima and Nagasaki, and the subsequent surrender of the Japanese on the battleship *Missouri* in Tokyo Harbor.

With the rise of television, the networks created their own niche for news with daily 15-minute broadcasts. At NBC, John Cameron Swayze anchored *The Camel News Caravan*, while CBS hosted *Douglas Edwards with the News*. Each of them narrated newsreel footage. Indeed, the theatrical newsreels served as a foundation for creating documentary news programs on network television.

One of the first documentary news programs was *The March of Time*, which made its radio debut on March 6, 1931. It finessed the news by using actors to re-create events and evolved into a theatrically distributed newsreel with film footage covering two to four stories in 22 minutes. The format serves as a model for the popular magazine-style news programs like *60 Minutes*.

A documentary-style radio program, *Hear It Now*, hosted by Edward R. Murrow and produced by Fred W. Friendly, moved to television as *See It Now* in 1951 as a weekly half-hour program. It was television's first regularly scheduled public-affairs program, with Murrow and Friendly using it to address some of the more compelling issues of their day. The program had a definite point of view and developed a style of advocacy journalism. It championed unpopular causes and personal injustices. One of the most compelling was a program on Senator Joseph McCarthy, the junior senator from Wisconsin, who had been using the issue of communist infiltration into American society as a bully pulpit.

Documentary television became a regular component of network programming with the creation of *CBS Reports, NBC White Paper,* and *ABC Close-Up.* These programs distinguished themselves by addressing critical issues of the day and presenting them within the context of serious discussion and debate. At CBS, network president Frank Stanton created *CBS Reports,* and its first program was "Biography of a Missile." Sustaining the journalistic mission of Edward R. Murrow, *CBS Reports* examined the plight of migrant workers in "Harvest of Shame," and the public-relations effort of the Pentagon and the military-industrial complex in the program "The Selling of the Pentagon."

At NBC, network president Robert Kintner created *NBC White Paper* to compete with *CBS Reports.* It was not a regularly scheduled series and was programmed several times a year, with its debut on November 29, 1960. It had a team of top-notch producers and journalists, which included producers Irv Gitlin and Al Wasserman and correspondents Chet Huntley, Fred Freed, Edwin Newman, Frank McGee, and Robert Northshield. It addressed national and international issues that had serious implications for American values and culture. In "The U-2 Affair," the program examined the deception of President Eisenhower's administration in its attempt to cover up America's use of spy planes after the Soviets shot one down and pilot Francis Gary Powers survived. Clearly, *NBC White Paper* had a focused approach to setting an agenda to provide analysis and in-depth reporting.

At ABC, John Secondari developed the theme of the *Close-Up* series by applying Aristotle's classic definition of drama, "men in action." His mission was to focus on the dramatic structure of people, places, and events. It also used the technique of cinema verité to provide an intimate portrait of the subjects chosen. For example, in "Walk in My Shoes," the program explored the anger and frustration of black Americans. Another program, "Meet Comrade Student," explored the strengths and weaknesses of Russian education. After a number of years the *Close-Up* series was relegated to occasional status, until it disappeared from the schedule entirely.

A new dynamic within network news programming occurred on September 24, 1968, with the premiere of *60 Minutes* on the CBS television network. By that time the three major television networks had grown disenchanted with long-form television documentary and were looking for an alternative vehicle to present longer stories in a more entertaining format. With *60 Minutes,* executive producer Don Hewitt created a new genre (pioneered by theatrical newsreels) known as the *newsmagazine* program, which included three 15-minute in-depth stories for every program segment.

As a veteran news producer who worked as a director for Edward R. Murrow's *See It Now* and also directed the first televised Kennedy-Nixon debate, hosted by correspondent Howard K. Smith, Hewitt felt that long-form documentary television was no longer a viable programming format. "There is no story you can do in an hour documentary that we couldn't do in a *60 Minutes* segment. And nobody looks at [documentaries] when they're on the air."[2]

The *60 Minutes* formula has been a huge success, making it the longest-running newsmagazine program on television and one of the most profitable, earning the network approximately $70 million a year. It has established a reputation for providing coverage of timely events and personalities without trivializing the facts. At a time when celebrity confessionals have been an integral part of television, *60 Minutes* has prevailed as a serious arbitrator of news and pubic affairs.

Indeed, even prior to the events of September 11, *60 Minutes* correspondents did stories on bioterrorism and the Al Jazeera satellite channel and provided in-depth coverage of the Middle East. With seasoned correspondent Mike Wallace at its helm, the program boasts some of the most talented newspeople in the business, including Ed Bradley, Steve Kroft, Andy Rooney, Morley Safer, Lesley Stahl, Bob Simon, and Christiane Amanpour, who is an occasional contributor. Of course, success creates imitation, with ABC's *20/20*, NBC's *Dateline,* and *60 Minutes II.*

For NBC, the quest to develop a successful newsmagazine program proved to be somewhat elusive, frustrating, and challenging. In 1969, shortly after the debut of *60 Minutes,* NBC introduced *First Tuesday,* but that program ran for only a couple of seasons and was later resurrected as *Special Edition.* The network continued to search for a viable newsmagazine format with programs like *Weekend, NBC Magazine, Prime Time Sunday,* and *Real Life with Jane Pauley,* until finally coming up with *Dateline* in 1993, hosted by Jane Pauley and Stone Phillips.

At ABC, the premiere of *20/20* was marked by the disastrous pairing of two male anchors, one an Australian whose speech was unintelligible. They were literally yanked from the show and replaced the following week by the indomitable Hugh Downs, who was eventually joined by Barbara Walters. This news franchise has proven very successful for ABC, with anchor Barbara Walters joined by John Miller, and another iteration of the program called *20/20 Downtown,* with anchors Elizabeth Vargas, John Quinones, and Cynthia McFadden. In September 2004, Elizabeth Vargas joined John Stossel as co-anchor on *20/20,* replacing Barbara Walters.

When Diane Sawyer was wooed away from CBS in 1989, Roone Arledge, then president of news and sports at ABC, needed to create a one-hour regularly scheduled prime-time newsmagazine program for her, which became *Prime Time Live.* Originally teamed with veteran newsman Sam Donaldson, the program was resplendent with a glitz that included a $400,000 video wall. Originally taped before a live audience, the format and teaming of the two anchors once again proved to be less than auspicious. Of her relationship with Donaldson, Sawyer described it as "fire and ice" and embellished it further by adding that it was "a date between Emily Dickinson and the Terminator." Uncomfortable with the live format, Sawyer appeared a bit awkward in the face-to-face confrontation with the audience. Eventually the live concept was jettisoned, and Donaldson was moved to Washington while Sawyer remained in New York.

Attractive, intelligent, and articulate, Diane Sawyer has created her own brand of journalism, easily moving between the genres of serious news and tabloid television. After graduating from Wellesley College, Sawyer returned to her home state of Kentucky and began her television career as a weather reporter on a Louisville station. In 1970 she moved to the Nixon White House and joined the staff of press secretary Ron Ziegler. She remained there until 1974 and then worked with the former president on his memoirs. In 1978 she became a CBS news correspondent in the Washington bureau and was the first woman correspondent on CBS's *60 Minutes,* where she distinguished herself as a serious journalist. At ABC, the network has recognized her worth as a commanding news presence and asked that she return to morning television to prop up the ratings of *Good Morning America* with her cohost, Charles Gibson.

As the networks have pursued the newsmagazine programming genre, there has been no commitment to long-form documentary on broadcast television. However, both public television and cable have provided a comfortable berth for the long-form genre.

## PBS: BILL MOYERS AND KEN BURNS

There is a rich tradition of documentary television that has an enduring heritage hearkening back to the days of Edward R. Murrow. Indeed, the virtues of this genre, while neglected by the commercial broadcast television networks, have been embraced by public television. Perhaps one of the most articulate and dedicated of this breed of journalists is Bill Moyers. His voice has addressed some of the most challenging issues in America and across the globe, providing in-depth analysis and commentary. As a journalist, Moyers has a narrative style that is both questioning and deliberate, offering thought-provoking observations. His probing style is moderated by a sense of compassion, which is probably a reflection of being an ordained Baptist minister.

There are few journalists that have the practical experience of working in the White House with a sitting president. In the Johnson administration, Moyers served as special assistant to the president and later as press secretary. Prior to moving into television, he was the publisher of *Newsday* and then produced *Bill Moyers' Journal* for PBS. He was equally comfortable working in the worlds of commercial television and public broadcasting and was able to accommodate their different dynamics and needs. At CBS he was the chief correspondent for *CBS Reports* and was a senior network news analyst.

Since 1986, when he established his production company, Public Affairs Television, Moyers and his team have produced more than 240 programming hours of literate television for PBS. The topics chosen are part of eclectic themes that range from the sublime (such as *Joseph Campbell and the Power of Myth*), reverential (*God and Politics*), and philosophical (*The Power of the Word*) to American culture (*Sports for Sale*). From the environment to the Constitution, Bill Moyers has sustained and cultivated the essence of serious broadcast journalism, refining it to a conscious level of discussion while re-defining the art of serious conversation. In 2002 he returned to weekly tele-vision on the PBS network with *Bill Moyers Now.*

## Ken Burns

One filmmaker who has reconceptualized the cultural and educational dy-namic of long-form documentary is Ken Burns. His body of work is repre-sented by exhaustive research and concern for detail. The subjects he has chosen are marked by history, culture, and tradition. In his 1990 work *The Civil War,* Burns presented a compassionate and knowledgeable documen-tary that illustrated the hardships of war and the challenges for the men who fought. With a keen sense of timing, his epic documentary *Baseball* was shown in 1994, the year that major-league baseball players went out on strike. Not one to pander to popular culture, Burns explored the history and industry of our first mass medium in *Empire of the Air: The Men Who Made Radio* (1992). His other films have included *Jazz* (2001), a definitive television portrait of Mark Twain (2002), and *Horatio's Drive: America's First Road Trip* (2003), about the historic journey of motorist Horatio Nelson Jackson, and most recently, *Unforgivable Blackness: The Rise and Fall of Jack Johnson* (2004).

In many ways Ken Burns has become a cinematic television auteur, delving at length into personalities, events, and icons past and present. His work is indicative of legitimate scholarship presented in familiar terms. It resonates with interesting and compelling information that is both enriching and en-tertaining. He has pursued his subjects with the vigor of a scholar and the discipline of a writer, compelled to share his quest for information and knowl-edge with a wider audience. His body of work is a legacy to both the cultural and historical roots of America, painting a portrait to help define the rituals, personalities, and traditions that are part of this country's fabric.

## PBS Public Affairs Programming

PBS, along with the Corporation for Public Broadcasting, has a long tra-dition of producing exemplary public-affairs and news programming. At times some of the themes they've addressed have been controversial, but they

are always on the cusp of relevance and ethical reporting. Series like *POV,*
*Frontline, Nova, American Masters,* and *The American Experience* have provided insightful and challenging programming. With a distinctive style and a
unique voice, public television has created a niche for relevance in news and
public-affairs programming.

Pursuing themes and subjects that may have been lost in the archive of
time is part of their programming dynamic. A program like *The Orphan*
*Train,* which provided viewers with a narrative about the relocation of
100,000 urban children to rural America for work on farms from 1854 to
1929, was indeed a compelling saga. Also, tracing the historical roots of
American events in films like *Gold Rush* and *The Oregon Trail* helped to
illustrate the drama and challenge of the experience.

Addressing issues of substance is a recurring theme on PBS. For example,
the concerns of global overpopulation were discussed in *Paul Ehrlich and the*
*Population Bomb.* Understanding the diabolical mind of a mass murderer in
*The Trial of Adolf Eichmann* offered a disturbing yet enlightening profile of
a deranged man. On *Nova,* "Fire Wars" explored the dangerous yet necessary
work of the men and women who fight wildfires, and on *Frontline,* the world
of pornography and its cultural and legal implications were explored. The
pursuit of art is also a priority of the network, with the *American Masters*
series and its entertaining and informative profiles on artists and entertainers
like Quincy Jones.

Clearly, public television has become an important place for the production
and distribution of documentaries. It has assumed a responsibility for nurturing this genre in the face of commercial broadcast television's neglect.

## CABLE TELEVISION AND THE DOCUMENTARY FORMAT

One of the most distinctive features of cable is the niche television networks
that are themed to a particular programming format. There are several of
these networks in the area of public affairs and documentary.

### A&E Networks

One of the most visible, productive, and successful cable networks operates
under the single entity of A&E Networks, which is owned by Hearst (37.5%),
ABC (37.5%), and NBC (25%). There are three discrete network platforms,
which include A&E (Arts and Entertainment), the History Channel, and
Biography. Each of these networks attracts between 60 and 80 million viewers
and has received a number of Emmy Awards. Some of the outstanding programs include *Investigative Reports,* hosted by Bill Kurtis, which devotes a
weekly two-hour segment to a single contemporary issue, each themed to an
hour program. Subjects have included the war against terrorism ("Two
Young Americans: The Patriot and the Taliban"), law enforcement ("Inside

SWAT"), and contemporary issues facing American workers ("Wage Slaves: Nickel and Dimed in America").

The History Channel serves as a canvas for portraits of the past that are related to the evolution of culture and civilization. It provides a distinctive voice with compelling narratives that make history speak to the present. Another popular network is Biography, which offers profiles of personalities, creating intimate biographies of people from various professions and disciplines.

### Court TV

Covering legal proceedings in a court of law by television and radio has been the subject of some controversy and debate since radio's coverage of the Lindbergh kidnapping trial. Since 1991 Court TV has televised more than 700 trials and also has provided viewers with feature news and public-affairs presentations, including its weeknight one-hour documentary series, *The System*. Other regularly scheduled documentary programs on the cable network include *The Elite*, which focuses on highly trained law-enforcement officers like those who work in prisons, as profiled in the segment "Prison Squad." The program *Forensic Files* gives the audience an intimate look at how investigators use their scientific tools of investigation to solve crimes.

The network, which is owned by Time Warner Entertainment and Liberty Media Corporation, has been proactive in gaining access to closed courtrooms by filing suits such as the one brought against the state of New York in September 2001 challenging the prohibition of cameras in the courtroom.

### Cable News Network

As a 24-hour news and public-affairs network, CNN has come a long way since Ted Turner's launch of the service in 1980, when it was ridiculed as the "Chicken Noodle Network." Since then it has grown into a global news presence, with bureaus around the world. The network distinguished itself during America's first Gulf War, when CNN's Peter Arnett remained in Iraq as the only Western journalist during its bombardment. He also had an exclusive interview with Iraq's leader, Saddam Hussein, which was seen and heard in 105 countries. During the 2003 invasion and subsequent occupation of Iraq, CNN once again played a prominent role with its embedded journalists and comprehensive coverage of the theater of war and its aftermath.

Evolving as a prominent source of international news, CNN has developed into several discrete networks and program services, including CNN International, CNN Headline News, CNNfn (financial news), CNNSI (Sports Illustrated), CNN Español, CNN Airport Net, CNN Radio, and Noticas. Programs offer an eclectic approach to news, public affairs, interviews, discussion, and finance. The network also has a distinguished group of anchors and program hosts, including Judy Woodruff (*Inside Politics*), Wolf Blitzer, Lou Dobbs (*Moneyline*), Larry King, Aaron Brown, and Paula Zahn.

The compelling nature of CNN's news coverage is a function of the correspondents in the field. One of the most accomplished is Christiane Amanpour, CNN's chief international reporter. She has reported from some of the most hostile regions in the world, including Iran, Yugoslavia, Afghanistan, Bosnia-Herzegovina, Haiti, Algeria, and Rwanda. Because of her reputation, Amanpour has obtained many exclusive interviews, including Pakistan's president, General Pervez Musharraf; Senator Hillary Rodham Clinton; Jordan's president, King Abdullah; and Iranian president Mohammed Khatami. Her work on the 1985 four-week documentary series *Iran: In the Name of God* was instrumental in earning CNN its first Alfred I. duPont–Columbia University journalism award.

A former senior White House correspondent for CNN from 1992 to 1999, Wolf Blitzer is the anchor for *Wolf Blitzer Reports* and also the Sunday-morning *Late Edition,* which is seen in more than 200 countries and territories. He received an Emmy Award for his coverage of the Oklahoma City bombing and in 1991 was one of the first journalists on the scene in Moscow after a failed coup. Prior to CNN, Blitzer worked for Reuters and was the Washington correspondent for the *Jerusalem Post.*

## SATELLITE NEWS: AL JAZEERA

The terrorist attacks of September 11 created a compelling marketplace for news and information by an anxious and frightened American public. In the United States, audiences were tuning into broadcast-network coverage of the events along with cable outlets, including CNN. In the aftermath of the attacks, the global audience became aware of Al Jazeera, an Arab-language network founded in 1996 that became a conduit for the dissemination of videos by Osama bin Laden. Also, the network provided a valuable link to the Arab world and a tool for educating the American public about the fervor of Islam and its emotional and political ties.

Founded in 1996 and operating from the Gulf emirate of Qatar while broadcasting in Arabic, Al Jazeera has had a profound influence in shaping public opinion in the Arab world and among the Arabic community in the United States. As the Gulf War catapulted CNN into news prominence, the tragedy of September 11 created both popularity and legitimacy for the Arab-language network. Owned by the Al Jazeera Satellite Channel, it professes an editorial policy based upon neutral, unbiased reporting, sometimes angering Arab states and the United States.

Among its broadcast, cable, and print competitors in America, there has been some skepticism about the neutrality of Al Jazeera, with the *New York Times* claiming that it has an anti-Israel and anti-American bias. In Great Britain, the *Daily Telegraph* referred to the station as "Bin Laden TV"; Dan

Rather, of CBS, speculated that bin Laden might have helped finance the network; while National Public Radio (NPR) sarcastically noted that Al Jazeera's coverage should "come with a health warning."

Although some have expressed doubts about Al Jazeera's claim to impartiality, the network nevertheless provides a serious forum for the presentation and discussion of issues pertaining to terrorism, Islamic fundamentalism, and the political dynamics of the Arab world. In addition to the satellite feed, which is, of course, available to subscribers in the United States, anyone with a computer can access its Web site (http://www.aljazeera.net), which is managed by Afkar Information Technology. The Web site provides a full script from the main programs of Al Jazeera's satellite channel, along with audio, 24–36 hours after broadcast.

The Web site employs a staff of 60, with 36 described as researchers and journalists. After the September 11 terrorist attacks, visits to the site went from 700,000 page views a day to 1.2 million. Visits also increased significantly after the American invasion of Afghanistan and the coalition war on Iraq, and there is also an English-language version of the Web site, english .aljazeera.net/Homepage.

In February 2004 an American-sponsored satellite-television station broadcasting in Arabic and known as Al Hurra ("the Free One") began service. Based in Virginia, its budget for the first year of operation is $62 million. The mission of the station is to repudiate and challenge attacks on the United States by Al Jazeera and other Arab-based media. It's based upon a legacy of other American-sponsored propagandistic media like Radio Free Europe and the anti-Castro broadcasts of TV Marti.[3]

## RELICS AND DINOSAURS

In the era of the Internet and the age of technology, there is much more empowerment for gaining access to news and information. At one time, news was the exclusive domain of newspapers, until radio came along, then television, cable, satellite, and the Internet. There is an aging stable of broadcast-network news anchors: Dan Rather in his 70s, and Peter Jennings and Tom Brokaw each in their 60s. For the television audience there's no compelling need to watch any of them, and their combined audience fell from a 1981 high of 84 percent to a current figure of 43 percent. And the audience that does tune in is made up of aging baby boomers, who are eschewed by advertisers hoping to reach the 18–24 demographic. They are also white, male, and perceived by many as artifacts from another era.

Indeed, that time was in the 1940s and 1950s, when CBS and NBC began regularly scheduled evening newscasts with Douglas Edwards's *CBS World News Roundup* on radio and *Douglas Edwards with the News* on television and John Cameron Swayze and his *Camel News Caravan* on NBC. Each of them was a pioneer broadcaster, creating a new genre of television that became the foundation for televised news.

At CBS Douglas Edwards began reporting a 15-minute five-night-a-week television news program in 1948. He was a reporter in Atlanta and Detroit before joining the legendary Edward R. Murrow in Europe to cover the end of the war. After returning to the United States, Edwards became the anchor for the *CBS World News Roundup* network radio broadcast. When his nightly newscast began, it was broadcast in only five East Coast cities. Eventually, however, it generated an audience of 34 million viewers. Upon his death in 1990, he was heralded as a distinguished broadcast journalist and a trailblazer.

Although John Cameron Swayze started out in print journalism in 1930 at the *Kansas City Journal-Post*, he got his start in radio at that newspaper. Radio station KMBC had a live microphone in the newsroom for late-breaking bulletins, and Swayze provided the narration. In 1933 he was involved in experimental television broadcasts at the Kansas City Power and Light Building. Then, in 1940, he moved to radio at KMBC for a weekly salary of $30. Hoping to break into network radio news, Swayze went to Hollywood and got a desk job with NBC's Western News Division. He was transferred to New York to another desk job and proposed a quiz program called *Who Said That Quote,* which the network liked and landed him back on the air. During the 1948 Republican and Democratic conventions, Swayze reported on television for NBC and eventually became the anchor for *The Camel News Caravan*. His signature closing line, "Glad we could get together," moved into the lexicon of American culture. Audiences became familiar with his style and appearance, making him "the nightly monarch of the air." He ended his anchor career in 1956 and was replaced by the team of Chet Huntley and David Brinkley; however, his career on television resumed as a game-show host and pitchman for Timex watches. Another of his phrases that became a popular reference that was product-related to Timex watches was "It takes a licking and keeps on ticking."

When men like Douglas Edwards and John Cameron Swayze began their careers as television newsmen, they were known as *news readers*. Indeed, the word *anchor* wasn't a part of popular usage until 1952, with a number of executives claiming its coinage. At the time there wasn't a clear definition of what an anchor would be or the influence he could have over an audience or as the executive editor of a newscast.

In 1956 the landscape of television news resounded with a distinctive change by the teaming of Chet Huntley and David Brinkley in the *Huntley-Brinkley Report*. The two men had first been teamed to anchor the Republican and Democratic national conventions in 1956. Their coverage for NBC generated the largest television audience share for the conventions at the time. This led to a regularly scheduled 15-minute weekly news program (increased to 30 minutes in 1963) with Huntley in New York and Brinkley in Washington, D.C., a first for television.

A Montana native, Chet Huntley started working in radio while attending the University of Washington and working at Seattle station KPCB, where he was an announcer and writer. Eventually he moved to Los Angeles station KFI and then made the network rounds: first CBS News West, where he worked for 12 years; then to ABC in 1951; and finally to NBC New York. At times he was criticized for using his position to editorialize, such as his endorsements for the beef industry. However, he was an outspoken critic of Senator Joseph McCarthy's demagoguery and false allegations. He also made headlines when he crossed the picket line of the American Federation of Television and Radio Artists, stating that news anchors didn't belong in the same union as actors, singers, and dancers. At the conclusion of the broadcast, each anchor would end with the salutations "Good night, David" and "Good night, Chet," which became a pop-culture American idiom. His last broadcast was on August 1, 1970, and he died in 1974.

At NBC it was news producer Reuven Frank who recognized the synergy between Chet Huntley and David Brinkley, creating the most memorable anchoring team in the history of network television. In 1943 David Brinkley joined NBC radio and eventually became the Washington reporter for John Cameron Swayze's *Camel News Caravan*. As an anchor, Brinkley had a lean writing style and focused delivery. His use of prominent declarative sentences was a characteristic of his formidable style. He was also aware of how important the pictures were in television news and that the reporter had to use them to tell the story. As Reuven Frank said about Brinkley's ability, "Brinkley writes silence better than anyone else I know."

With a career distinguished by literate reporting, David Brinkley was one of the most respected broadcast journalists in the history of television. He was associated with some of the most compelling news and public-affairs programming, including *David Brinkley's Journal* (1961–63), *NBC Nightly News* (commentator 1971–76, coanchor 1976–79), *NBC Magazine with David Brinkley* (1980–81), *This Week with David Brinkley* (1981–98), and *ABC's World News Tonight* (commentator 1981–98).

Defining the characteristics of a television news anchor can be a daunting experience. There are many variables that come into play, including camera presence, trust, and professionalism. A national news anchor that epitomized these traits and set a standard for anchoring was Walter Cronkite. He was responsible for creating a new dynamic that provided a unique kind of intimacy for television. Although he started in radio, Walter Cronkite joined the UP wire service in 1939 as a reporter covering World War II. He was in the thick of battle, landing with the troops on D-day, parachuting with the 101st Airborne, and flying bombing missions, and was the chief correspondent covering the Nuremberg trials. It was Cronkite who assumed Douglas Edwards's anchor position at *The CBS Evening News* in April 1962, and shortly thereafter the program was expanded to 30 minutes, the first network news program to achieve that status. On the first broadcast of the newly formatted program, he had an exclusive interview with President Kennedy, and only two months later reported his assassination.

At CBS Walter Cronkite helped to define the character of the anchor as a role model for the television generation. A news producer, Don Hewitt, created a set that reflected the empowerment of the position, with the anchor sitting behind a horseshoe desk with a staff of writers toiling away near its edge. He was also the first anchor to become a managing editor of a network news broadcast.

During his tenure at CBS, Walter Cronkite became a vaunted father figure, earning the trust and reverence of a television nation. He became a source of comfort in the difficult time during the Kennedy assassination; was an advocate for NASA's space program; and, most notably, changed his point of view on America's war in Vietnam, indirectly impacting on the country's foreign policy.

As a broadcast journalist, Walter Cronkite was a model of ethics, rarely imposing his opinion in the CBS News broadcasts. However, there was an instance in the 1960s, during the Vietnam War, when Cronkite, feeling betrayed by the Johnson administration's foreign policy, spoke strongly for U.S. withdrawal. It was February 1968, and the Vietcong and North Vietnam regular troops violated a truce for the Tet Lunar New Year, unleashing a savage attack across South Vietnam, ravaging 35 cities, towns, and provincial capitals. Reporting from the battle zone, Cronkite articulated his position in a dramatic manner, invoking phrases like "darkest clouds" and "bloody experience." In the end he uttered a phrase that would echo in the chamber of President Johnson's oval office, influencing his foreign policy. "It is increasingly clear to this reporter that the only rational way out then will be to negotiate, not as victors, but as an honorable people who lived up to their pledge to defend democracy, and did the best they could."

For President Lyndon Johnson, Walter Cronkite's frustration with America's involvement in Vietnam was a reality check with public opinion. With the family interests of his wife, Lady Bird Johnson, including ownership of a CBS affiliate in Texas, he understood the power and influence television had. For example, he once observed that after he made a speech, one sentence of coverage by then CBS Washington News correspondent Dan Rather would reach a wider audience than all of the newspaper columns addressing his speech the next day. Indeed, he felt that Walter Cronkite was watched and listened to by the "good folks" of America. According to White House insiders, Johnson was "stunned" by Cronkite's commentary and felt that the newscaster's popularity and prestige with the American public caused him to lose credibility. Indeed, a poll had revealed that 70 percent of Americans trusted Walter Cronkite more than any other public figure. A little more than a month later, Johnson announced that he ordered all air and naval bombardment of North Vietnam to cease, and at the end of his speech expressed

"As a journalist, Walter Cronkite was a model of ethics, rarely imposing his opinion in the CBS News broadcasts." (Photofest.)

his resolve not to seek or accept the Democratic Party's nomination for another term as president.

At CBS, Cronkite's position was unchallenged except in 1964 when, under pressure from the competition of Huntley-Brinkley, the network replaced him with the team of Robert Trout and Roger Mudd for coverage of the presidential nominating conventions. Although in public he appeared undaunted by the change, privately he expressed his dismay. At one point he contemplated leaving CBS; however, after learning that the network had received 11,000 letters critical of the change, he decided to stay on. And stay he did, becoming "Uncle Walter," a father figure for millions of Americans and a trusted mediator of the news.

### Anchors Away

The French have a saying: "The more things change, the more they stay the same." That can be attributed to the broadcast-network news anchors on CBS, NBC, and ABC. Each of them lays claim to a regal dynasty of decades anchoring the news and posturing on behalf of their network. Perhaps, however, they're relics of another time and place. In the heyday of the evening network news in the early 1980s, NBC's *Nightly News*, CBS's *Evening News*, and ABC's *World News Tonight* collectively attracted 84 percent of the audience. In today's news marketplace, their combined audience has dropped to 43 percent of share. As aging diplomats in a world consumed by youth, they're derisively referred to as members of the Viagra and Depends set.

Three aging white men experienced with covering every nuance of every story, battle-worn and sometimes scarred, they epitomize the essence of what was the jewel in the crown of network news. In today's fragmented television environment, where mass audiences have become more of a niche, with 24-hour news and anchors that have cultivated the entertainment side of the business, it seems that they may be part of a dying breed.

They are indeed the holy trinity of network news, steadfastly manning their desks, editing their copy, and reading the news. They're relics of another age, a time when women were relegated to the more mundane job of housewife and men were empowered with a voice of reason and confidence. Although women have become important to the fabric of broadcast news, the three old-guard networks have stubbornly clung to their anchoring values, faithfully staying with the suits and avoiding the skirts. The network legacy, however, has recently ended for Tom Brokaw, who has been replaced by Brian Williams, and Dan Rather, with speculation as this book goes to press that his replacement will be either John Roberts, chief White House correspondent, or Scott Pelley, a *60 Minutes Wednesday* reporter.

## The First Princess of Network News

Celebrity has always been an important feature of the network evening news. At the ABC television network, John Daly was the resident anchor, and he was succeeded by Ron Cochran. When Elmer Lower, formerly of NBC, became the head of ABC news in the early 1960s, ABC's news budget was a trifling $4 million, a fifth of CBS's and NBC's news budgets. By 1967 Lower managed to increase ABC's news and public-affairs commitment to $35 million. In 1970 Elmer Lower teamed veteran journalists Harry Reasoner and Howard K. Smith, creating one of the most successful news-anchor teams on television, making ABC competitive with CBS's Walter Cronkite and NBC's John Chancellor. After Lower moved up in ABC's corporate hierarchy, William Sheehan replaced him as head of news.

Hoping to generate even higher ratings for the ABC evening news, Sheehan decided to make Reasoner the sole evening news anchor. Ratings dipped initially and then stayed static, prompting another change in 1976. For the first time in the history of network television news, a woman was made co-anchor of a nightly network newscast.

Early television was ripe for talent and opportunity, and Barbara Walters possessed the tenacity and fortitude to succeed. She became one of the youngest producers in television and was also booking guests for CBS's *Morning Show.* Soon she became a writer for the successful *Today Show,* eventually moving into a spot as a "Today Girl," and in 1974 was made the first female cohost. Hoping to give Reasoner a rating boost, Sheehan teamed him with Walters. Although there was an initial increase in ratings, the resentment harbored by Reasoner, a veteran journalist, against Walters, who was perceived as a novice with little or no hard news experience, created visible tension on the set. The team lasted for two years, after which Reasoner returned to CBS and *60 Minutes* while Walters continued as a news and public-affairs personality at ABC. In September 2004, after 25 years as a cohost of ABC's *20/20,* Walters stepped down from that position. However, she continued her affiliation with ABC, doing six interview specials a year and remaining as executive producer and cohost of the daytime talk show *The View.*

## The Second Coming

Experienced in the rigors of politics and a veteran broadcast journalist, Connie Chung was the first Asian American woman to reach prominence as a network-television journalist. After graduating with a journalism degree from the University of Maryland, she began her journalism career in 1969 as a copy person at WTTG-TV in Washington, D.C. At that station she eventually became an on-air reporter. Her first network assignment, in 1971, was with CBS news as a Washington correspondent. In 1976 she moved to Los Angeles, working on local and network broadcasts at the CBS-owned station KNXT (KCBS-TV). From 1983 to 1989 Chung was an NBC news correspondent and anchor. In 1989 she returned to CBS, anchoring *Face to Face with Connie Chung* and *Saturday Night with Connie Chung.* Then, in 1993, Ms. Chung was given one of the greatest opportunities of her career, when she assumed the coanchor position on *The CBS Evening News with Dan Rather.*

When she was named as coanchor, Rather's network newscast was third in the ratings; however, Chung's popularity was confirmed by her Q ratings. This is a measurement made by a company known as Marketing Evaluations, which computes a rating based upon the popularity of the person. At the time Chung was made coanchor, she had the highest Q rating of any female journalist on network television. She also became the second woman in the history of evening broadcast-network television news to be named as an anchor.

The rationale for CBS to move Chung in with Rather was to help with the program's flagging ratings. However, she faced a great deal of hostility from Rather, who viewed her as an interloper interested more in entertainment than in hard news. Her magazine-style programs were viewed as infotainment, and she was also criticized for her tabloid approach to broadcast news. This criticism was reinforced by a prime-time interview with Kathleen Gingrich, mother of then House Speaker Newt Gingrich. During the interview, Kathleen revealed that her son once made a disparaging remark about then First Lady Hillary Clinton. Using a manipulative interviewing technique, she set Kathleen Gingrich up by asking her to whisper the pejorative remark to her, saying that it would be "just between us." The whisper that was heard round the world was the word "bitch," and soon after, Chung left the network. Several years later she became a featured correspondent on CNN, anchoring her own program. Since assuming her role at CNN, Chung has been criticized for the tabloid orientation of her program, which included frequent interviews with Rabbi Shmuley Boteach, Michael Jackson's former spiritual adviser, and contestants from *American Idol*. One of her harshest critics is Ted Turner, the founder of CNN, who has described her show as "just awful." In 2003, during the Iraq war, Chung's program was removed from the CNN schedule, and she resigned from the network.[4]

## The It Girl

There's a special attraction toward women television-news correspondents that help an audience define who they are. A new generation of viewers has a different sensibility of how televised news is covered that is shaped by the mediation of technology and content. Indeed, as the events of September 11 have demonstrated, television reporters become characters in the breaking news they cover, acting in the story as it unfolds. At times the distinction between an event and the reporter covering it blends together in an amalgam of time, space, and drama. We have a different visual culture from what was predominant 25 years ago that is not particularly attuned to "grave old white men with weird hair."

These changed sensibilities are reflected in the personae of younger television personalities, who help to define the news in their own image—specifically, Ashleigh Banfield, formerly of MSNBC. Criticized for her lack of substance and commitment to style, Banfield has become the doyen of a new breed of hip journalists who provide a connection to a younger audience longing for someone who communicates in their lingua franca.

She changes her hair color, dresses fashionably, and suddenly appears with titanium-framed eyeglasses. But she can also be a tireless reporter, sometimes yielding to hyperbole. Many news personalities have a moment that served as a catalyst in their career. For Ashleigh Banfield there were three: leaving Fox for MSNBC, reporting on the most controversial presidential election in modern times, and covering the collapse of the World Trade Center.

Like so many other reporters, she was stunned by the event, racing from her New York City West Side apartment downtown to get the story. It was a test of her mettle and her ability to synthesize a voluminous amount of confusing information into a cohesive narrative. She was in danger, as reporters often are. After all, their calling is similar to that of the firefighter: "We run in when others run out." She protected a mother and child as the second tower collapsed and was a bundle of conflicted emotions as she reported the horror and tragedy that she witnessed firsthand. Human emotions were a part of what she experienced, and she wasn't ashamed to share them with her audience. In news, objectivity is a prized commodity, but there are times when the audience expects more . . . and wants to know that the person they're watching feels like they do. Working 20-hour days, as so many reporters did, Banfield was a continuous on-scene presence, guiding the audience through the pace of a tragedy and its aftermath.

Being a war correspondent is like a badge of courage among journalists, who take a pen or camera to battle instead of a gun. It may involve flying bombing missions (as Edward R. Murrow did) or parachuting behind enemy lines (like Walter Cronkite), or it may mean sleeping on a cold concrete floor, subsisting on very little food, and not bathing for days. Reporting from Afghanistan, Banfield endured these discomforts but, more importantly, was reporting from an unstable hostile region, anchoring and directing an hourlong live prime-time show four nights a week.

She's unapologetic for the way she perceives and reports the news. Her sense is that if some of the audience finds her entertaining, then she's accommodated a void and a need. She wants to be informative and doesn't offer any excuses for her style. Indeed, she considers herself a news veteran with 15 years of experience. She may be somewhat self-indulgent, but Banfield has earned the coveted stripes of a journalist muddied by her critics yet resolute in her purpose: to tell the story . . . in her own words. Ms. Banfield's role at MSNBC was diminished because of slipping ratings. In addition, she raised the ire of her superiors after delivering an articulate, thoughtful, and provocative speech at Kansas State University in Manhattan, Kansas, on April 24, 2003, criticizing television's coverage of the Iraq war and the tenor of broadcast journalism.

Women television correspondents are more vulnerable than men to criticism associated with their appearance and poise. An editorial published in the *Wall Street Journal* by Tunku Varadarajan was especially harsh on Christiane Amanpour. By labeling her the "diva of parachute journalism," Varadarajan berated her appearance as a "fearless she-man" outfitted in a flak jacket and accessorized by other "tough girl raiment." In an acutely microscopic examination of Ms. Amanpour's looks and voice, Varadarajan noted that her "alluring dark looks are thought to convey an anti-Barbie seriousness of mind." However, the author's most vacuous and condemning statement was that Ms. Amanpour's British accent could be construed as erudition by Americans.

Interestingly, the author of the editorial found Ashleigh Banfield to be the "anti-Amanpour," describing her as a "fine-boned lady" and praising her ability to report on the events with "genuine rather than feigned" enlightenment. Also cited was her abandonment of the flak jacket as *couture de guerre* for simple cotton shirts. Ms. Banfield's change of hair color from blond to brown for her move as a war correspondent raised the ire of one South Asian Web forum participant, who declared that it was ludicrous for a white woman to think that she could blend in by dying her hair.

However, Varadarajan did find one woman correspondent who appeared to measure up to the "high standards" of fashion, skin tone, hair color, intonation, and erudition espoused in the editorial. Declaring that Lyse Doucet of the BBC had neither Ms. Banfield's insecurity nor Ms. Amanpour's "gaudy egotism," he elevated her to the Mount Olympus of broadcast journalism.

As for her foreign reporting credentials, Ms. Doucet's experience includes service in many Muslim countries. After graduating from college in 1982, her assignment was in the Ivory Coast of West Africa, her first experience in a Muslim country. She spent 1983–88 at the BBC's newly inaugurated West Africa bureau, covering countries like Senegal, Mali, and Burkina Faso. In 1989 she spent a year reporting from Kabul, covering the Soviet troop withdrawal from Afghanistan. After completing her assignment there, she moved to Tehran, covering Iran after the death of the Ayatollah Khomeini. Then, from 1990 to 1993, she was the BBC's Pakistan correspondent.

As one of the most experienced journalists with credentials reporting from Muslim countries, Lyse Doucet has the political acumen and cultural familiarity with the region that enables her to provide insight and provocative thought. Immersed in the dynamic of Islamic fundamentalism, with firsthand experience associated with its leadership, she is an articulate spokesperson offering balanced coverage and insightful commentary.[5]

## Reporter's Boot Camp

Concerned about providing greater access for reporters to cover the war with Iraq (2003), the Defense Department created a five-day defense-combat training program for journalists at Camp Barrett, a Marine base in Quantico, Virginia. During that time they had to endure overnight hikes and ambushes and were schooled in nuclear, chemical, and biological weapons; embarking and disembarking from a helicopter; and reacting under fire. During this time the journalists were embedded with the troops, sleeping, eating, and interacting with them. After training, each journalist received their "graduation" attire: flak jackets, Kevlar vests, helmets, and camping gear.

Another option for journalists is to take a five-day, $2,300 course with Centurion Risk, a company founded by several former British Royal Marines, located at the Massanatten Military Academy in Virginia. Since 1995 the company has trained 10,000 reporters in the art of surviving battle coverage.

So much has changed in the coverage and dissemination of news. It has become an instantaneous commodity with a shelf life of seconds. News can be accessed from a multitude of different platforms—television, radio, the Internet, PDAs, satellite, newspapers, and mobile phones—so that on any day, at any instant, anyone can get an update. The interface of these technologies has redefined the characteristics and dynamics of news. There no longer is a need to wait for your newspaper to be delivered or reach the newsstand to get your news, as you can read that same newspaper on the

Internet, and no need to wait for a scheduled television or radio newscast, because of 24-hour news on cable. In essence we have all become mediators of the news, defining its access by our own terms and determining our needs.

Indeed, more than ever, each of us has become a gatekeeper of the news, setting our own agenda, determining our order of access, and assimilating what we want when we want it. There's no longer the act of grasping at a partially missed headline or the confusion of a garbled reference. We can gain access to any news niche, past or present, and archive or discard it at our whim.

There's a reconstitution in the global dynamic of news with almost no boundaries and unlimited access to foreign sources. We can now see and hear many messengers while determining the worth of their information within the context and hierarchy of news. It's an invigorating process of empowerment that places a greater burden on the consumer to determine truth, relevance, and bias.

## NOTES

1. Lewis H. Lapham, "The Consolations of Vanity—William Randolph Hearst and Ted Turner," *Harper's,* December 1997, p. 1.

2. Burton Benjamin, "The Documentary: An Endangered Species," occasional paper, no. 6, Gannett Center for Media Studies, October 1987.

3. Neil MacFarquhar, "Washington's Arabic TV Effort Gets Mixed Reviews," *New York Times,* 20 February 2004, p. A3.

4. Jim Rutenberg, "Inside CNN, a Struggle to Be Less 'Tabloid,'" *New York Times,* 24 February 2003, p. C1.

5. Tunku Varadarajan, "Windswept, Inept, Ashleigh Banfield Hits the Road," *Wall Street Journal,* 22 August 2002; Tunku Varadarajan, "Parachute Journalism Redux," *Wall Street Journal,* 12 November 2001.

# 14

## MINISERIES/DOCUDRAMA: A DELICATE BALANCE

### THE BRITISH INVASION

One of the most formidable programming genres created for television was the miniseries. It's interesting, however, that the idea for a more short-form, limited-run series was not conceptualized by Americans but was the brainchild of British producer Donald Wilson. In 1955 he developed the idea of adapting John Galsworthy's novels about an aristocratic British family to television. The books were published in three volumes from 1906 to 1920 and became popular reading on American college campuses during the Roaring Twenties. Indeed, Galsworthy won the Nobel Prize for Literature in 1932.

The BBC (British Broadcasting Corporation) had to obtain the rights to the novels that were held by MGM (Metro-Goldwyn-Mayer). At the studio, Galsworthy's novels were the substance of one film, *That Forsyte Woman* (1949), starring MGM's stable of stars, and the cast included Errol Flynn, Greer Garson, Walter Pidgeon, Robert Young, and Janet Leigh.

The BBC had reservations about attempting such an ambitious project, and executives wondered if the miniskirted 1960s generation and Vietnam-era audience would be interested in the trials of a wealthy Victorian family. However, the BBC was about to introduce a new channel, BBC 2, and wanted a programming event to inaugurate the service. They gave the go-ahead, and production began.

*The Forsyte Saga* introduced the genre of prime-time soap opera, in a limited run, to television. Its 26 installments ran from January through July in 1967 on BBC 2 and were filmed in black and white, costing $728,000. It was the most expensive series the BBC had ever produced and was the last drama in black and white. The miniseries was also the first BBC serial to be sold to the Soviet Union. On BBC 2, the miniseries attracted an audience of 6 million viewers, and when it was reprised on BBC 1, it was seen by an audience of 18 million.

In the United States the series was brought to public television with the assistance of the Ford Foundation, which paid National Educational Television (NET) to distribute it. The program became an audience phenomenon with Americans, who found the drama and ethos of the characters to be very compelling. They tuned in every week, creating the cultural concept of "appointment television." Critics also praised the series, with author James A. Michener saying that *The Forsyte Saga* was "one of the significant cultural events of this century." On October 6, 2002, a new adaptation of Galsworthy's work, coproduced by Boston's public television station WGBH and Britain's Granada TV, made its debut on American television. Based upon two of the novels, *The Man of Property* and *In Chancery*, and distributed by PBS, this $10 million, eight-hour adaptation is a stunning tribute to the legacy of the original series.

The original *Forsyte Saga* had a profound influence on American television. Stanford Calderwood, then president of public station WGBH in Boston, was so pleased with the success of *The Forsyte Saga* that he created Mobil's (now Exxon Mobil's) *Masterpiece Theatre* as a showcase for British drama. In 1971 it premiered with a 12-part miniseries, *The First Churchills*, written and produced by Donald Wilson. *Masterpiece Theatre* has provided a window for American audiences to experience dramatic television from England and the United States. It has also provided a foundation for the development of original drama conceptualized for television.

One of the most successful *Masterpiece Theatre* productions was *Upstairs Downstairs*. It was produced in England by Sagitta Productions for London Weekend Television (LWT), was not an adaptation of a literary work, and was created specifically for television. It was about the Bellamys, an upperclass British family, and their servants, who lived with them in a five-story London town house. There was an interesting dynamic between those who were born to privilege and those who faced the daily drudgery of dealing with their needs. The stories were historically driven, and meticulous attention was paid to period detail as the 55 episodes moved from 1903 Edwardian England to World War II, ending shortly after the stock-market crash in the summer of 1930. This series was the highest-rated program on public television as American audiences enthusiastically followed the exploits of the characters. Cycles of 13 episodes were shown on *Masterpiece Theatre* in 1974, 1975, and 1976, and in 1977 a final cycle of 16 segments were seen. As the series has been syndicated around the world, it's estimated that 1 billion people in more than 40 countries have seen *Upstairs Downstairs*.

Another British export to *Masterpiece Theatre* was the 13-part historical miniseries *I, Claudius*, coproduced by the BBC and London Film Productions. As a fictionalized account of the Roman Emperor Claudius, the program as shown in the United States was a critical success and popular with American audiences. The production, which was based upon two novels by poet and essayist Robert Graves, presented a sympathetic portrait of Claudius, who succeeded the notorious Caligula as emperor of Rome and reigned for 13 years. The character of Claudius, played deftly by actor Derek Jacobi, was based upon a factual portrait of the character, who was born with a physical deformity and spoke with a stammer.

The miniseries was seen in the United States in 1977 and 1978, and there was some concern about the vivid imagery of how some of the decadence was portrayed. The Boston public-television station WGBH, without consulting with Mobil Corporation, decided that some selective editing was needed to moderate scenes of nudity, gruesome violence, and aggressive sexuality. The station defended its decision based upon the rationale that some viewers in selected parts of the country might find the material offensive.

For more than three decades, *Masterpiece Theatre* provided Mobil (now Exxon Mobil) with an excellent vehicle to cultivate and nurture its corporate image. The program's success helped to personify the company as a citizen of the arts and a patron of quality television. There are, however, critics who portrayed the corporation as an arrogant proponent of its own agenda that defined art as preproduced foreign historical dramas that offered a safety net without the potential risk of funding a work in progress.

Responding to the criticism pertaining to the emphasis that *Masterpiece Theatre* placed upon British drama, a new series of programs entitled *Exxon Mobil Masterpiece Theatre's American Collection* premiered in October 2000. Focusing on the literary and dramatic works of American authors and artists, the series received a $15 million grant from the Corporation for Public Broadcasting (the largest single grant to PBS) along with generous support from Exxon Mobil. A commitment to produce nine films over three years has resulted in works by Langston Hughes (*Cora Unashamed*), Henry James (*The American*), Willa Cather (*Song of the Lark*), and Eudora Welty (*The Ponder Heart*). In the spring of 2004, Exxon Mobil ended its funding of *Masterpiece Theatre*. This is an annual loss of approximately $9 million. Over the past three years PBS has lost 32 percent of its corporate underwriting.

## AMERICAN NOVELS FOR TELEVISION

With the success of limited-run series like *The Forsyte Saga*, the three major broadcast networks of that era took particular note of the genre. The ABC television network was the first to implement the concept for American audiences. It commissioned the adaptation of a Leon Uris novel, *QBVII*, about a concentration-camp survivor, played by actor Anthony Hopkins, who distinguished himself as a physician only to be accused at the height of his career of castrating a concentration-camp inmate. It was six hours long and broadcast in 1974. It was a success with television audiences and was soon followed by an adaptation of Irwin Shaw's novel *Rich Man, Poor Man*. Although no longer associated with ABC, Barry Diller, a former programming executive at the network, had commissioned the adaptation of the novel, and the miniseries was produced by Universal Pictures. At the end of the football season, ABC had a nagging gap in its prime-time Monday schedule and moved the 12-part, six-night, two-hour-per-segment series into it. It was broadcast during a seven-week span from February 1 to March 15, 1976, and was an immediate hit. As with the novel, the miniseries profiled the fictional Jordache family and the adversarial relationship between brothers Rudy (played by Peter Strauss) and Tom (played by Nick Nolte). Like *The Forsyte Saga*, the plot integrated various historical events during the 1945–65 time span of the story.

## MINISERIES REDUX

It was 1977, and Jimmy Carter made *Time* magazine's cover as Man of the Year, and in July there was a blackout in New York. On the ABC television network from January 23–30, the miniseries *Roots* was broadcast on eight consecutive nights, instead of weekly installments, creating a new scheduling pattern for the genre. Prior to *Roots*, the miniseries was scheduled as a weekly event. The program was adapted from Alex Haley's "symbolic" novel of the same name and became a viewing phenomenon with American television audiences. At the time, it generated the highest rating of any prime-time network television program, earning an average 44.9 rating and a 66 share, with 85 percent of all television homes having watched all or part of the series.

Bringing *Roots* to television was the result of a confluence of forces that involved personalities, industry dynamics, and economic realities. Knowledge about Haley's historical novel tracing his African ancestors became apparent to David Wolper, a documentary producer known for his ability to combine fact with fiction, in 1972. At that time he expressed an interest in buying the rights to the novel, but Columbia Pictures had an option on the property. After the option expired, Wolper purchased the rights from Haley for $50,000.

Although executives at ABC had concerns about the viability for success of a miniseries featuring blacks in leading roles and about the audience reaction to the brutality of white slave-owners toward their chattel, they decided to produce the program. In an effort to mediate the harshness of the white characters, scriptwriters created the role of a ship's captain plagued by his conscience about transporting his first "cargo" of slaves. This character and some others did not appear in the novel.

Although executives at ABC were enthusiastic about the series, they nevertheless were concerned about its impact. To this end, *Roots* was scheduled on consecutive nights in an effort to conclude the series before the ratings sweep month of February. Also, the network heavily discounted advertising rates, anticipating that the ratings would be weak.

No one at the network or in the entertainment business could have predicted the enormous success that *Roots* became. It was "appointment" viewing for the majority of American audiences, who happened to be white. During the eight-night run, business at bars, restaurants, and movie theaters suffered as people stayed home to watch the show.

Perhaps more than anything else, *Roots* defined a new protocol for the television miniseries. It created a unique dynamic by integrating historical relevance within a cultural context. In a society where racial stereotyping and issues of integration had a relevancy toward the shaping of values and attitudes, *Roots* was an important barometer, measuring the tolerance that American television audiences had toward this genre and the material it addressed. Network fears of defiance by white audiences toward the portrayal of slaveowners never materialized. Instead, the miniseries became a valued tool for discussion and dialogue. Although its narrative style incorporated some of the well-worn tools of soap opera, the dramatic context of *Roots* had a compelling theme that helped audiences understand the black diaspora and its relation to the American experience.

Creating an understanding about the rich diversity of other cultures was also part of the substantive content of the 1980 miniseries *Shogun*. Based upon James Clavell's bestselling novel, this 12-hour epic, presented in five consecutive parts on NBC, gave viewers a unique insight into seventeenth-century feudal Japan. The $20 million miniseries featured prominent Japanese actors, many of whom were unknown to American audiences. Indeed, Japanese actors were cast in 28 principal roles, with two leads played by Toshiro Mifune and Yoko Shimada. Richard Chamberlain played the principal American lead, John Blackthorne, who was marooned with his shipmates.

The 1980s realized an ambitious schedule of miniseries on network television. They addressed a variety of themes, including biblical events (*Massada*, 1981) and adaptations of bestselling novels (*The Winds of War*, 1983, and *The Thornbirds*, 1986). Indeed, it was another adaptation of a Herman Wouk novel (he had written *The Winds of War*) that became one of the most expensive television programs in history and soured television's taste for epic miniseries. It was the 30-hour, $100 million miniseries *War and Remembrance*. The monumental scale of the production was daunting, with a 1,492-page script, 2,070 scenes, 757 sets, two years of preproduction, 21 months on location, one year of postproduction, 358 speaking parts, 30,310 extras, and 2 million feet of film. In May of 1989 the ABC television network broadcast the final installments of *War and Remembrance*. The audience response was rather tepid, as reflected in the low ratings, which fell below the advertiser guarantee pledged by the network. This led the network to announce that the loss projected from the miniseries would reach between $30 and 40 million.

Although the three major broadcast networks were disappointed with the performance of miniseries, the genre was somewhat revitalized by the program *Lonesome Dove*. The manner in which this story was adapted for television provides insight into what is, at times, the serendipitous process of program development. In 1972 writer Larry McMurtry and film director Peter Bogdanovich wrote a screenplay, *The Streets of Loredo*, which was conceived as a vehicle starring veteran Western actors John Wayne, Henry Fonda, and James Stewart. The project never materialized, and McMurtry went on to expand it into an 843-page Pulitzer Prize–winning novel. Prior to its publication, McMurtry had a chance meeting with Motown Films president Suzanne de Passe, who purchased the film rights to the unpublished novel. It was broadcast on CBS in February 1989 and featured actors Robert Duvall, Tommy Lee Jones, Anjelica Huston, Diane Lane, Robert Urich, and Danny Glover.

In the 1990s the miniseries genre embraced a myriad of thematic elements, including Greek mythology, classic literature, popular fiction, headline stories, celebrity families, and a British female cop who became an American icon. Betrayal is a familiar theme of the spy genre and also a compelling subject for miniseries and serial television. A landmark miniseries produced by the BBC and distributed in the United States by PBS in 1979 was *Tinker Tailor Soldier Spy*, based upon the John Le Carré novel. It was one of the first of this genre to be adapted to the short serial format. The 1990 four-hour miniseries *Family of Spies*, about Chief Warrant Officer John Walker, starring Powers Boothe, was a chilling portrayal of a navy veteran implicating his family and friends in spying for the Russians. On a similar theme, in November 2002 CBS broadcast its two-part, four-hour miniseries *Master Spy*, based upon FBI agent and spy Robert Hanssen, also known as "the undertaker." It was developed and written by Norman Mailer and Lawrence Schiller, who collaborated on other television projects, including *The Executioner's Song* and *American Tragedy*. Also in 1990, on NBC, was the four-hour miniseries *Phantom of the Opera*, produced by Image Entertainment and directed by Academy Award winner Tony Richardson. Profiling one of the most famous American families can be a daunting task; however, the 278-minute, three-part series *The Kennedys of Massachusetts* chronicled 55 years in the life of the family. It was based upon Doris Kearns Goodwin's book *The Fitzgeralds and the Kennedys*, with a teleplay written by William Hanley.

On public television's *Masterpiece Theatre*, actress Helen Mirren played DCI (Detective Chief Inspector) Jane Tennison, who, after the death of a well-respected male DCI, must assume responsibility for a murder investigation. She faces the brutality of a serial murderer and endures the hostility of a male-dominated police force that jealously guards the integrity of their deceased predecessor while protecting their turf. The compelling narrative structure and the realistic character portrayals made the series popular with American television audiences. There were five additional *Prime Suspect* series, ending with *Prime Suspect Six: The Last Witness,* all of them capturing the pathos and emotional conflicts that Tennison must face in her personal and professional life.

Surely network television in the 1990s viewed the miniseries as a viable product, but one that needed to be shorter while embracing more fiscal restraint. Indeed, many of the miniseries were in two or three parts, which could have designated them as television movies years ago. One producer who has been especially bullish on the genre is Robert Halmi Sr., who helped produce *Gulliver's Travels,* starring Ted Danson, in 1996, and *Merlin,* a four-hour, $30 million project starring Sam Neill, both on NBC. For ABC, Halmi produced *Cleopatra,* a $28 million, four-hour miniseries that was broadcast in 1999, and *Moby Dick,* starring Patrick Stewart as Captain Ahab, which cost approximately $20 million and premiered on the USA cable network in 1998. During the 1990s Halmi was the most prolific television miniseries producer, adapting works of literature as well as classics to the screen. In 1997 NBC broadcast the $40 million, six-hour miniseries *The Odyssey,* a coproduction of Halmi's Hallmark Entertainment and Francis Ford Coppola's American Zoetrope, starring Armande Assante, Isabella Rossellini, Vanessa Williams, and Geraldine Chaplin. That epic was followed by *Noah,* a four-hour Hallmark Entertainment event broadcast on NBC in May 1999.

The end of the 1990s, especially 1997, proved to be a benchmark for the distribution of miniseries on American broadcast and cable television networks. That year ABC ran a six-hour, $23 million adaptation of Stephen King's *The Shining,* and CBS broadcast a six-hour miniseries based upon the Mario Puzo (author of *The Godfather*) novel *The Last Don,* starring Danny Aiello. Biological hazards and deadly viruses, with their devastating impact upon the world population, have been a recurring theme in miniseries development and production. In 1997 NBC broadcast the miniseries *Robin Cook's Invasion,* starring Luke Perry, about a deadly escaped virus that needs human life-forms to replicate. There was precedent for this theme in the 1995 miniseries *Virus,* by the same author, and in the 1994 miniseries *Stephen King's The Stand,* about a virus that destroys 99 percent of the earth's population, which also addressed the theme of tribal division between good and evil.

Themes of impending Armageddon surrounding natural disasters have been a popular plot device in feature television miniseries events. In 1999 CBS broadcast *Aftershock: Earthquake in New York,* a two-part miniseries starring Cicely Tyson, Charles Dutton, and Tom Skerritt, with all the requisite special effects featuring falling rubble and buildings collapsing. Legendary heroes like Joan of Arc provide ample historical context for a miniseries, and one about her exploits was broadcast on CBS in May 1999. Also on CBS in 1999 was the four-hour *Shake, Rattle, and Roll: An American Love Story,* about the roots of rock 'n' roll.

The start of the new millennium brought the CBS miniseries *Jackie Bouvier Kennedy Onassis: A Life,* shown in two parts on CBS. It was also a technical benchmark that was postproduced on a 1080/24p High Definition television platform. The Kennedy women, specifically the sisters-in-law, were profiled in the 2001 NBC miniseries *Jackie, Ethel, Joan: Women of Camelot*.

A more notorious subject for a miniseries, which was also broadcast on CBS in 2000, was *An American Tragedy,* profiling the "dream-team" defense lawyers of the O. J. Simpson case. It was based upon the bestselling book by Lawrence Schiller and starred Ron Silver, Christopher Plummer, and Ving Rhames. Also on CBS in 2000 was *Haven,* a two-part miniseries based upon the exploits of Dr. Ruth Guber, who in 1944 escorted 982 Holocaust refugees to a community established for them in Oswego, New York. Biblical themes have an enduring sensibility in television miniseries, and that was the intent for *Jesus* on CBS, starring Jeremy Sisto in the title role, with Gary Oldman and Jacqueline Bisset. In development for five years, the project was originally intended for Turner Network Television (TNT); however, director Lorenzo Minoli moved it to CBS after confronting "artistic differences" with TNT. Another miniseries with a religious tone, focusing on Bible stories from Creation to the Ten Commandments, was *In the Beginning,* broadcast on NBC in 2000. Produced in association with Hallmark Entertainment, the four-hour series featured an all-star cast including Martin Landau, Diana Rigg, Jacqueline Bisset (who starred in *Jesus*), and David Warner.

Blockbuster bestsellers have provided television with ample material for miniseries development. Indeed, adapting popular novels to the television miniseries provides the program with a target audience familiar with the author's work and eager to commit the time and effort to tune into the event. Authors like Stephen King and Dean Koontz have a "presold" audience that can be perceived as potential television viewers, especially if the author's name appears in the title of the miniseries. This was the case in the 2000 Fox broadcast of *Dean Koontz's Sole Survivor,* based upon the novel, which explores the tragedy of a plane crash, a family that perished, and a husband's quest for answers. It was also true of the Sci Fi cable channel's successful three-part 2000 miniseries based upon Frank Herbert's *Dune*.

For bestselling author Stephen King, the television miniseries offers a latitude of expression that the constraining time limits of feature films do not. He's been associated with seven miniseries produced for the ABC television network, which include adaptations of his novels and original scripts for television. The first of his adaptations was of *It*, King's 1,138-page novel, which was broadcast in 1990, and his first original miniseries for television was the 1999 three-part *Storm of the Century.* The author's second original miniseries was the six-hour *Rose Red,* the ultimate haunted-house story, which was broadcast on ABC in January 2002.

Not to be outdone by the macabre work of Stephen King, CBS created its own 2002 miniseries broadcast with an occult theme, *Living with the Dead*. It starred Ted Danson as a psychic loner asked to assist the police in a murder case.

With the advent of the Internet and the success of video games, it's not surprising that a television miniseries would be modeled after a game. *Myst* was produced by Mandalay Pictures, Columbia TriStar Domestic Television, and Cyan, the studio that created the game. In addition to games, miniseries based upon historical epics were part of the television landscape, with the USA cable network and its production *Helen of Troy* in 2003.

The advantage of the miniseries is that it creates a branding for the television viewer that offers an affiliation to the event, dedicating the viewing effort to a particular station, day, and time. It does not require a long-term commitment, as does the traditional television serial, which has a longer continuous life span. Also, a miniseries can attract celebrity talent that could or would not make a commitment to a continuing television series. Associated with the content is the ability to provide excellent promotional opportunities, especially during sweeps ratings cycles. Indeed, hyping the event can result in "appointment" viewing, with audiences changing their routines in order to watch the program. There are also, of course, risks, which include competitive programming, accelerated viewer falloff if the initial segment is wanting, and high cost. Indeed, reruns of miniseries do not fare well, and that limits the network's ability to recoup its investment.

However, as a genre, the miniseries has provided television with outstanding and compelling drama on cable and broadcast, addressing themes of substance and relevance. With a competitive marketplace and greater fragmentation of the audience, the miniseries may offer an opportunity for a network to distinguish itself amid the clutter of entertainment choices. Indeed, Hallmark Entertainment is clearly an advocate for the television miniseries, as it produces about 40 projects a year.

# 15

## SPORTS AND TELEVISION: THE TORTOISE MEETS THE HARE

One of the greatest influences on the economics of sports is television. No other medium has provided the access, intimacy, and drama that have helped to portray athletes and their game as icons of American culture. Television attracts huge audiences to these contests, supplementing live attendance in the arena. Indeed, the excitement created by television serves as a catalyst for increasing the volume of ticket sales and thus the revenue at the gate. As a mass medium, television has the unique ability to coalesce the emotions of its audience into a convergence of emotional fervor and feelings of national pride that are expressive of its character.

Perhaps the harbinger for the role that the mass media was to have in sports came first in 1936 and then in 1938, with two boxing matches featuring the same fighters. It was the famous Joe Louis versus Max Schmeling bout in 1936, which was one of the greatest upsets in the history of the sport, with the champion Joe Louis losing his crown to the German. For the rematch, on June 22, 1938, when Louis avenged his loss and regained his championship, the radio audience was the largest ever assembled. It was a defining moment for radio and one that clearly demonstrated the role that radio and television would have on sports culture.

There are few who doubt the influence that television has had on the way sports are perceived and games are played. From *Monday Night Football* to World Series and Olympic coverage, television has served its own agenda, manipulating sports to suit its own needs. It has taken marginal sports like golf, tennis, and wrestling and popularized them (although it wasn't able to do so with soccer). Television's fiduciary relationship with professional sports has made ordinary people with athletic promise and ability into symbols of a consuming culture, providing them with wealth and power that is far beyond their expectations.

One of the most unique incarnations between television and sports has been in the realm of wrestling. Wrestlers have become cultural icons, performing to frenzied fans in the stands and on television. Indeed, two of their biggest stars, the Rock (Dwayne Johnson) and Mankind (Mick Foley), became bestselling authors, with their autobiographies listed as numbers one and three on the *New York Times* bestseller list. Can these blundering figures of brazen brutality reinvent themselves as literati and cast personae of themselves as the new heroes of the information age?

They brought show business to wrestling with brawling matches, sexy women in scant costumes, outrageous story lines, and cartoon characters. This is the stuff that has lubricated the well-oiled $1 billion machine of Vince McMahon's World Wrestling Federation (WWF) and driven its juggernaut to set records for live attendance and ratings for cable and pay-per-view television. It's gross, profane, and staged, yet its allure has captivated a loyal fan base and made it a force to be reckoned with in the competition for the sports and entertainment audience.

In the spandex wrestling universe, the powers of good and evil are played

*Monday Night Football* sportscasters Howard Cosell, Don Meredith, and Frank Gifford, during the NFL Hall of Fame Game, 1972. (Photofest.)

out inside and outside the arena. Indeed, the wrestling canvas is only a prop and is the proscenium in a staged theatrical spectacle of entertainment. There are few rules of sport that govern these events, as simulated combat spills outside the ropes and "unscheduled" fights propel the action. Wrestlers wear bizarre costumes, step to unique dances like Scotty Too Hotty's "the worm," and use parts of their anatomies as shameless tools of sport. The fans revel in this show world of obscenity, relishing the "spontaneous" choreography of mayhem pursued by hard-bodied and overweight Goliaths matched with bosom babes bursting with bravado through the seams of their costumes.

This mindless transmutation of sport gushes millions of dollars into the coffers of the WWF and into the pockets of its principals and entertainers. Its weekly televised *Raw Is War* event is the highest-rated show on cable television, with an audience of 5 million households, while *Smackdown,* another weekly cable program, is the highest-rated show on the UPN cable network, attracting the same number of viewers. There are also the pay-per-view events, which cost the fans $30 for each show. In addition to the revenue streams of television and live attendance, there is also the licensed product merchandising of the WWF (now known as the WWE): action figures (which outsell Pokemon's) and home videos, which usually are the leaders in sports. No slouch in the area of new media, the WWF was one of the first to offer World Wide Web surfers streaming video on its Web site as a profitable enterprise. All this yields several hundred millions of dollars in revenue and a street value for the company in excess of $1 billion.

Television has also contributed to the tawdry spectacle of debasing the essence of sports culture, demonizing its values and making a mockery of its competition. In the spring of 2002 the Fox network introduced a special called *Celebrity Boxing.* Although it hit a ratings bonanza of 15.5 million viewers and was watched by more viewers than any other Fox show, it was the bread and circuses of carnie television. Quoting Andy Warhol, "Everyone gets their 15 minutes of fame." That was certainly the case for the celebrity boxing matches, which included the once famous Tonya Harding versus Paula Jones and Vanilla Ice versus Todd Bridges. Even the still famous ring announcer Michael Buffer got into the act, intoning his trademark phrase, "Let's get ready to rumble."

Boxing is a sport requiring skill, discipline, experience, and knowledge. With this incarnation, one is reminded of the traveling carnival, with its resident pugilist offering ordinary people the opportunity to step in the ring and do battle with the best. That was a form of mass entertainment invoking a fantasy at a mythical chance of toppling a champion. However, for these participants their only achievement was to mock themselves and remind the audience of their ill-gained fame and transgressions. They sullied their reputations even further by losing their self-esteem. This is another example of the dumbing down of television toward the basest level of voyeurism.

Women in the boxing ring is not a new phenomenon, and in a sport that measures muscle and brawn as the tools of a champion, competitive bouts between equally matched women opponents can be interesting. There are, of course, legendary boxing bouts that have been relegated to the archives of history, and the three matches (including "The Thrilla in Manila") between Muhammad Ali and Joe Frazier have the distinction of offering some of the most compelling drama in boxing. And so, with Frazier and Ali in retirement, with only the echoes of cheering crowds sustaining their memories, their daughters, Laila Ali and Jacqui Frazier-Lyde, laced up their gloves.

Of course, it was a promoter's dream to cast the daughters of one of boxing's greatest rivalries in the role of opponents meeting in the ring to avenge a lingering score. Both women had professional bouts prior to their match. A practicing criminal attorney in Philadelphia and mother of three children, Frazier-Lyde had an unbeaten record, with three knockouts, and was 39 years old when she fought Laila Ali. A more experienced and younger boxer, 23-year-old Ali was unbeaten after eight fights, with seven knockouts.

The event was held at Turning Stone Casino in Verona, New York, and attracted a crowd of 8,000 in a tent set up in the parking lot outside the casino. With almost every seat filled, each of the women was guaranteed a six-figure purse. The fight was scheduled as an eight-round match, and it turned out to be quite a slugfest, with Ali taking the decision.

While women boxing women can have a certain allure, a woman boxing a man can be somewhat disorienting. Some critics found the boxing match between Margaret MacGregor and Loi Chow, which was sanctioned by the state of Washington, an aberration. Although MacGregor was victorious, and each fighter was awarded an equal purse of $1,500, some critics called it a sideshow and feared that it would diminish the sport of women boxing.

## MISSIONARY OF MAYHEM

Perhaps one of the shrewdest entrepreneurs in sports marketing, Vince McMahon managed to circumvent an onerous tax that the state athletic commissions impose on pay-per-view broadcasts. The McMahons redefined their product as *sports entertainment* and convinced the commissioners that the matches are scripted and the results fixed. Indeed, the writing resembles the raunchiest of soap operas, and includes the McMahon clan—Vince; his wife, Linda; and their children, Stephanie and Shane—as principal protagonists.

A part of American culture is the allure of the bizarre and the offbeat. This is what attracts the public to a carnival, its midways, and boardwalks. Here, the audience can get close to some of the weirdest anomalies, real or imagined, to walk the earth. Two-headed people and the bearded and fat ladies are fixtures in a culture that has a voyeuristic fascination with the strange and the abnormal. The wrestlers of the WWF are a breed of men and women who provide their audience with the titillation, sexuality, and entertainment that is the basis for its success. They perform in the arena of cultural kitsch, showboating their behavioral excess to enthusiastic fans who revel in the gluttony of bad taste and vile language.

## PIGSKIN AUTEUR

The irony of wrestling's success is that network television has become interested in attracting the same audience. To that end, NBC and Vince McMahon announced the formation of a new football league, the XFL. NBC's partnership with World Wrestling Federation Entertainment Inc. created the eight-team league with different regulations of play and more intimacy through the placement of cameras and microphones.

As a partner in the XFL, NBC brought $30 million to the table and the cachet of broadcast-network legitimacy. There is a history between Vince McMahon and Dick Ebersol, the chairman of NBC Sports. In the 1980s the two men worked together, producing a wrestling show for NBC, and made millions for their efforts. They've embarked on an ambitious project, one that has not met with much success in the past. Indeed, in 1998 NBC and Turner Sports attempted to create a summer league of 12 teams, but abandoned the idea in 1999.

Indeed, there have been a number of attempts to create additional football leagues; all have failed. These included the World Football League; the United States Football League (USFL); and the World League of American Football (later NFL Europe), which was an NFL product. Chet Simmons, who was a commissioner for the USFL, which lasted for three seasons and disbanded in 1985, noted how the fans were disappointed with the level of play and the precipitous decline in ratings.

Promoting the new league as smashmouth, in-your-face football, McMahon, the tireless promoter, encouraged the kind of play that the NFL discourages. This includes harder hitting, end-zone celebrations, and sexy cheerleaders in skimpy attire. To assist in the creation of the mise-en-scène, XFL officials, coaches, and players were wired for sound. Also, camera people wore helmets and pads.

Some of the technical improvisations, while well intended, suffered from poor execution. The 30 microphones fielded by the league were subject to extraneous noise and interference, and an innovative attempt of stringing a television camera on a wire above the field provided an awkward perspective on game play.

With NBC reserving Saturday nights from 8:00 to 11:00 prime time for the XFL, with TNN and UPN airing the games on Sundays at 4:00 and 7:00 eastern time, respectively, Ebersol and McMahon exuded a high level of confidence. That was reflected in the 10.0 Nielsen rating guarantee for the combined three-network telecast.

Another issue, raised by psychologists and psychiatrists, is the level of violence that teenage fans of the WWF are exposed to. Their concerns relate to the ambient violence level and the values associated with the way the XFL was played, based upon their experience with the WWF. Indeed, McMahon proudly cites the prime-time audience demographics for the WWF as 15 percent 12 and under and 15 percent 12 to 18.[1]

Following the military's style of not abandoning a position, Dick Ebersol, the chairman of NBC Sports, and Jeff Zucker, the president of NBC entertainment and group president for entertainment, news, and cable, uttered the usual platitudes of endorsement for the XFL. Perhaps it was the elixir that Vince McMahon used to sell them the sizzle on what was a tawdry display of hedonistic, lurid amateur sport. McMahon is the consummate pitchman, conjuring up his perception of entertainment and pushing the envelope of crudity and vulgarity.

American audiences understand the dynamics of televised wrestling. They understand that what they're watching is not legitimate competition. Televised wrestling has a history in American culture that defines it as an entertainment commodity and not as professional sport. Unfortunately, some salesmen start to believe their own hype, which manifests itself in a dynamic that pursues all forms of wanderlust. McMahon and his partners at NBC thought that they could shed the discipline of football, never realizing that it's the pretentiousness, the rules, and the hallowed ground of professional sports that they attacked.

For NBC, the struggle to sustain the credibility of the XFL amid a critical storm of protest managed to slam the network to the mat. The ultimate embarrassment occurred at the beginning of the season, on the second Saturday-night prime-time broadcast. A power interruption caused a 90-second delay, and NBC was dark for the first minute and a half. Father Time's mantle of disruption was even more evident when the game ran 45 minutes over and into the coveted time period of *Saturday Night Live,* which was featuring actress Jennifer Lopez as the guest host. Because of her popularity, the network was expecting to spike the ratings of the show, but instead the XFL game was a washout for the network. It enraged Lorne Michaels, executive producer of the show, who went to videotape instead of the live broadcast. This instance clearly created a crisis of confidence at NBC over the fate of the XFL. The next day NBC entertainment president Jeff Zucker reiterated how important it was to the network that *Saturday Night Live* start on time and stated that it was a priority.

Clearly the XFL was not the rating juggernaut that NBC had hoped it would be. While Dick Ebersol, the chairman of NBC sports, indicated that it's a work in progress and that it would be a challenge to start a new league, declining ratings alarmed NBC affiliates. The president of Belo Broadcasting and head of the NBC affiliate board of governors, Jack Sander, expressed his dismay over the continued ratings freefall and was concerned about his West Coast stations preempting their local newscasts to carry the program live.

Amid all the doom and gloom surrounding the XFL, two networks, UPN and TNN, were mostly pleased with their results. At UPN the games boosted Sunday-night ratings, increased revenue, and appeared a good fit with the UPN audience demographics. A UPN affiliate, WUPV in the Richmond-Petersburg, Virginia, market was earning record revenue from the games, turning away advertisers, and was sold out for the third quarter. At TNN the key demographic audience, 18–49-year-old adults, tripled.

But not all advertisers were happy with the XFL. The Japanese automobile manufacturer Honda made a hasty exit in February, giving both content and ratings reasons for leaving. According to a company spokesperson, after seeing what the first game was like, they felt that the venue wasn't appropriate for a conservative company. What could Honda possibly have objected to? Cheerleaders in revealing costumes sought out by the cleavage cam? Or filling a hot tub with bikini-clad babes posturing suggestively to the audience watching a game between the Los Angeles Extreme and Chicago Enforcers?

As part of the hype-driven atmosphere of the XFL, Vince McMahon used his WWF scribe skills to publicly harass and criticize the NFL. He referred to certain NFL rules as "pantywaist," implying that the league was sissified. At an XFL game in Los Angeles (the NFL had left the city six years before), the Rock, a WWF star, harangued the NFL with off-color trash talk. His broadcast remarks said that the NFL executives who left Los Angeles six years ago should use the suitcases that they left with, "turn them sideways and stick them straight up your candy ass."[2]

The hostility expressed toward the NFL caused concern for the Anheuser-Busch Company, one of the biggest sports advertisers on television. It disapproved of the denigrating tactics and strongly urged that they be stopped.

There also appeared to be some ill feeling between some UPN affiliates toward NBC stations for cutting their rates and offering the games for a third less than UPN stations.

At the start of the XFL season, McMahon was brazen about the new league and its ability to invigorate what he perceived to be the leaden, overregulated NFL. "The timing is right for a game that middle-class America can relate to and afford to come to. They enjoy the XFL and football, and a little sexuality going along with the aggressive nature of football. That works."[3] Maintaining that the NFL is a tame alternative to the XFL is a gross misstatement of reality. Players in the NFL face a punishing career replete with concussions, broken bones, and postcareer disabilities. As some critics have pointed out, the XFL is not sport, and it's not entertainment. In its attempt to bring bread and circuses to the arena, it has debased the essence and spirit of the game while mocking its traditions. How can one explain the tawdry attempt at a pregame interview with a female television reporter sitting in the lap of a Hitmen player? Instead of a Peabody, it should earn a gross-body award.

When asked about his audience, a television network executive once remarked that they are the people he flies over when he goes from the East

Coast to the West. Perhaps Vince McMahon and NBC had similar thoughts when they tried to foist a bunch of has-beens and wannabes on the American sporting public. The ratings were an indication that the XFL should gather for its last huddle and hike the ball into oblivion. A game between Birmingham and Las Vegas on a Saturday night in March earned a 2.1 rating and a 4 share, which was down 25 percent from the previous week. Perhaps the only distinction earned by the XFL was that it achieved the lowest rating of any sports-related prime-time program in television history. The previous record was held by game three of the 2000 Stanley Cup finals on ABC, with a 2.3 national rating and a 5 share.

For NBC, the XFL was a bad dream and was canceled. As is often the case, there are some positive elements to every debacle. The army, which had severe recruiting problems, had an overwhelming response to its XFL advertising, signing record numbers of recruits at stadiums and generating enormous traffic at its Web site. Attendance at XFL games was high, averaging 23,000 a game in the eight XFL cities. And miking players in their line of scrimmage so that the gritty sound of play could be heard on the air proved to be a crowd-pleasing innovation.

Perhaps the biggest problem for the XFL was not the flesh-baring cheerleaders, the ignorance of the commentators, or the leveraged rules of play; no, the biggest problem was Vince McMahon. He certainly didn't display any elegance, nor was he eloquent in his interview with Bob Costas (*On the Record with Bob Costas,* HBO). Hostile and belligerent, McMahon verbally wrestled with Costas, and when he couldn't parry with an articulate response, he was abusive, telling Costas to shut up. Without a script and cues, McMahon appears to be a target for his own hype. That, however, hasn't stopped him from becoming the missionary of mayhem with the XFL, the WWF, and most recently AOL/Time Warner's Championship Wrestling. He may be down, but he's not out.[4]

As the XFL season was winding down with a lingering thud, the Arena Football League (AFL) season was just getting started. The league has 19 teams, and after 15 seasons has been under the watchful eye of the NFL. Indeed, some AFL teams are owned by NFL franchises, including those of William Clay Ford Jr. (Detroit) and Jerry Jones (Dallas). In addition, there's also crossover ownership from other sporting venues like Jerry Colangelo (Phoenix Suns, Arizona Diamondbacks) and Charles Wang (New York Islanders).

Unlike the XFL, arena football has been nurturing its game plan for years. It has a keen sense of who its fans are, knows how to market to them, and keeps its expenses under control with a salary cap of $1.4 million and salaries ranging from $32,000 to $170,000 a year. Not without failures (New Jersey Red Dogs, New York City Hawks), the AFL created a second league, which hopes to expand to 40 teams in the future. Although there are only modest television rights for the AFL with TNN, ESPN, and ABC, worth about $25 million, the NFL's option to purchase 49.9 percent of the league could change the television-rights issue dramatically. Also, after the XFL debacle, NBC invested $20 million in the AFL and scheduled 15 regular-season games for broadcast.

Where the XFL denigrated the NFL's rules of sport, the AFL has been more respectful of those rules, which in some cases differ. A field is 50 yards long, half the size of the NFL's, and there are 8 players, as opposed to 11 in the NFL There are also differences related to touchdowns, stopping the clock, punting, and conversions. Uniforms and the football are about the same as in the NFL. The league's goal is to reach more young fans, bringing them to affordable games in the arena.

As the XFL moves toward the oblivion of "a road poorly taken," the AFL is poised as a solid alternative to traditional football and one whose horizons appear to be set on a well-executed plan of play.[5]

In some ways television has corrupted the essence of sports with its cacophony of color commentary, its topsy-turvy scheduling needs, and its pot of gold that can provide unyielding temptation and greed. It's an electronic genie that materializes and grants its wishes, using its power of alchemy to weave athletic virtue into gold. The power it exerts over the teams, players, and owners has resulted in a dynamic of mistrust and jealously that permeates almost every venue of sports and the public it serves.

The mass media and sports have a long tradition of mutual accommodation in the production and distribution of events. Initially, however, there was suspicion on the part of some sporting venues toward radio's potential for siphoning revenue from a team's gate. In 1934 New York's three baseball teams prohibited the broadcasting of their games on radio.

For innovation to happen, there usually is a visionary who can see beyond the normal boundaries of perception and envision circumstances differently from everyone else. The general manager of the Brooklyn Dodgers, Larry McPhail, was such a person when he arrived in 1938 and sold the broadcast rights to radio for an annual amount of $70,000. With the arrival of television, baseball was redefined as a spectator sport, with a longer season and the splitting of each league into two divisions.[6]

The historical roots of broadcast sports coverage on radio dates back as early as October 1922, when AT&T and its New York station, WEAF, participated in the broadcast of a football game between Princeton and the University of Chicago. The following month a Harvard–Yale football game was broadcast over AT&T long-distance lines. Sports coverage made a substantial leap to television in May 1939 after RCA introduced the first mobile television unit. It broadcast the first baseball game between Columbia and Princeton with a single camera over NBC and followed that up with two-camera coverage of a doubleheader between the Brooklyn Dodgers and the Cincinnati Reds from Ebbets Field.[7]

Television took the ball and literally ran with it, taking sports and creating a new and visually compelling narrative with its incorporation of the classical dramatic components of rising action, conflict, and pathos. Broadcasting college and professional football games became a currency for television, with the calfskin as a symbolic metaphor for the herding and huddling of the masses before their television sets.

There is an aesthetic to the game of football that was perfect for capturing it on television. Although it involved an expansive playing field, touchdowns, and broad, animated gestures, it also provided the intimacy of the huddle, calls by referees, and close-ups of the fans and the players. The networks saw its potential as an audience-grabber and asserted themselves into the culture of the sport. In 1964 CBS paid the NFL $28 million for rights to broadcast league games for the 1964 and 1965 seasons. The cost of the licensing fee was immediately recouped by two separate $14 million sponsorship agreements from the Ford Motor Company and the American Safety Razor Company, a subsidiary of Philip Morris. Profits rolled in after additional spot announcements and station breaks were sold.

Perhaps the greatest debt of gratitude owed by television to sports coverage is to Roone Arledge of the ABC television network and his genius for turning competition into audience entertainment. As the architect of modern televised sports coverage, Arledge created intimacy by using handheld and miniature cameras, shotgun microphones, slow motion, and instant replay, using television and its unique technology to bring viewers even closer to the action. As a showman who matched William Paley's (founder and CEO of CBS) shrewd instinct for talent and extravagance, Arledge pursued sports as a programming vehicle for the masses.

His perception of sports as a means toward building a loyal audience resulted in the unique success of enduring programming franchises like *Monday Night Football* and *Wide World of Sports*. These programs presented a programming genre that offered the essence of competition within the context of a compelling saga of personal achievement. In his pursuit of drama, Arledge realized the need to provide his audience with a unique personality to provide commentary and analysis. His choices of Howard Cosell and Jim McKay, two very different personalities, proved to be one of the greatest talent coups in the history of broadcast sports. These two commentators wove the fabric of journalistic narrative into their reports, with Cosell providing the sarcasm and wit and McKay achieving legendary stature with his vivid on-scene account of the kidnapping and eventual murders of the Israeli athletes at the 1972 Munich Olympic Games.

Television and its influence on sports have created a massive merchandising venue for the commercialization of events and the compensation of its athletes. Football's Super Bowl is a good example of how network television has manipulated a competition into a showplace of entertainment, building up audience excitement into an emotional frenzy of expectation.

Football's popularity as television spectacle could not have been predicted from its rather inauspicious beginning on NBC-owned experimental station W2XBS. On October 22, 1939, announcer Allen Skip Walz and his crew of eight were at Ebbets Field to broadcast the first-ever-televised NFL game between football's Brooklyn Dodgers and Philadelphia Eagles.

Too many viewers didn't notice the broadcast, as there were only about 1,000 households that could receive the transmission. There were more people in the stands as 13,051 fans in the stadium watched the Dodgers beat the Eagles 23–14. All of the action was covered by two cameras, and at times the screen went dark when clouds blocked the sun as it moved behind the stadium.

Television has created football in its image, reflecting its value as a commercially driven enterprise that once a year lowers its hypnotic veil on a global audience in excess of 800 million viewers who watch the Super Bowl on television. From the first Super Bowl, on January 15, 1967, which matched the Green Bay Packers against the Kansas City Chiefs before a crowd of 63,035 fans at the Los Angeles Coliseum, the game has earned its cachet as a valuable tool for reaching a huge mass audience. Television networks aggressively compete for the rights to broadcast the game, and it typically rotates to a different network each year.

There are, of course, huge costs besides the license fee that are associated with covering the Super Bowl for a worldwide audience. For Super Bowl XXXIII, in 1999, the Fox television network had a 300-person production staff, 31 cameras, 25 videotape replay machines, 12 pregame announcers, and 4 game announcers for seven hours of program. The network charged advertisers $1.6 million dollars for a 30-second spot. The following year ABC charged advertisers $2 million for a 30-second spot on Super Bowl XXXIV, and for Super Bowl XXXVII, in 2003, ABC charged advertisers between $2.1 and 2.2 million for 61 30-second commercials.

The record price for a 30-second spot was $2.3 million, on CBS for Super Bowl XXXVIII, in 2004. Time Warner's America Online (AOL) subsidiary got more than it bargained for when it paid $10 million to be the exclusive sponsor of the halftime show. The show was produced by MTV (Music Television, a Viacom subsidiary) and featured Janet Jackson and Justin Timberlake in a sparring duet that ended with Justin exposing Janet's bare breast. Ironically, AOL had three advertising spots in the Super Bowl featuring its technology TopSpeed, a free service to subscribers, but it wasn't fast enough to catch and obscure Janet's flashing boob. In 2005, Super Bowl XXXIX on Fox will feature Paul McCartney—a safer bet for the halftime show—with 30-second spots between $2.4–2.5 million.

No other event in the history of American televised sports has captured the unique cultural phenomenon of the Super Bowl. It is an event made for television, mixing the drama of competition with the value of entertainment as manifested by the components of broadcast technology and the carnival midway atmosphere of the halftime show.

While the Super Bowl illustrates the spectacle of competitive sports, ABC's *Monday Night Football* is a testament to the enduring relationship among television, football, and the viewing public. In 2004, after more than 30 years of regular broadcasts, the program consistently draws a large television audience and is a top-rated show for the network, although seasonal ratings have consistently declined. It is ABC's most expensive show, costing $550 million annually. The money is reflected in the quality of the game coverage, color commentary, and the drama of the competition.[8]

The *Monday Night Football* franchise at ABC is a jewel in the crown for the network, and its legacy and tradition makes it an icon of sports television. As such, it must aspire to the very best color commentary and analysis on sports television today. Those traditions led Howard Katz, the president of ABC Sports, whose career at the network started as an assistant on the show in 1971, to push the envelope and resurrect the drama, unpredictability, and humor that Howard Cosell, Don Meredith, and Frank Gifford brought to the program in its heyday. The longtime producer and director were fired along with analyst Boomer Esiason, and veteran producer-director Don Ohlmeyer was brought in to make the fix. Somewhat of a legend in television for his creative genius, abusiveness, and extravagance, Ohlmeyer produced *Monday Night Football* from 1971 to 1977 under then executive producer and legendary showman Roone Arledge.

Declining ratings, a trend toward more bravado and intimacy in television with shows like *Big Brother* and *Survivor,* and NBC's move to invest $30 million as the first network to have equity in a football league, the new XFL, made Ohlmeyer's mission even more challenging. His assignment was to bring a sense of danger and unpredictability back to the program. He compared it to the success of NASCAR racing on network television when they changed the rules, allowing restrictor plates on air-intake valves, which adds to the drama by increasing the possibility that more cars have in winning on the last lap.

To help create that drama, Ohlmeyer hired television writer-producer David Israel to help weave a dramatic narrative associated with the players and the teams that they were matched against. He was convinced that great storytelling was a critical component of any medium.

Perhaps his most surprising hire was comedian and satirist Dennis Miller, a *Saturday Night Live* alumnus. Miller, who is an avid football fan and who, like Howard Cosell, admitted to never playing the game, was not the front-runner for the job. The controversial and confrontational talk-show host Rush Limbaugh was seriously being considered, along with Tony Kornheiser, a *Washington Post* columnist with an ESPN radio show; Billy Crystal; and Chris Rock. In the end, Ohlmeyer chose Miller because of his appeal to the younger male demographics that skew the audience of the show. While some critics were skeptical about Miller's potential as the first non-sports-announcer to be affiliated with a prominent sports telecast, he proved to be a witty and acerbic presence in the booth with Al Michaels and Dan Fouts. For the 2002–2003 television season, Al Michaels was joined by John Madden (replacing Dennis Miller), former coach of the Oakland Raiders, with Melissa Stark providing commentary from the sidelines.

Moving to bring more intimacy to *Monday Night Football,* Ohlmeyer convinced the NFL to mount tiny mini-cams on the referees' caps, providing viewers with a cinema verité look at the action, and to have more roaming reporters on the sidelines and at halftime to interview the players. No doubt the mini-cams were a hard sell, especially after the NBA coaches balked at being miked during the 1999–2000 season.[9]

The way television covered sports was changed forever on September 17, 1960, in Birmingham, Alabama, when the ABC television network broadcast its first college football game in a $6 million rights package. Roone Arledge created a unique resonance by developing a narrative punctuated by the intimacy of dramatic close-ups, natural sound, and the dynamic elements of classical drama. And, true to Arledge's credo, that day he added show business to sports.

His pursuit of a regularly scheduled football franchise for network television and ABC led Arledge into an epic struggle with the league, his bosses, and Howard Hughes. Pete Rozelle, then commissioner of football, was a dynamic force in transforming the game into a national pastime. He understood the value of television, and in 1964 sold CBS an NFL rights package for $14 million. Shortly after, NBC agreed to an $8.4 million deal to cover the new American Football League games. Prior to Rozelle becoming commissioner of the NFL in 1960, football had generated a paltry $2 million in television revenue. Football was third in popularity, behind baseball and college football. Pete Rozelle was a master at the art of negotiation and persuasion, focusing team owners on the league concept and moving them into a merger with the American Football League. His ability to envision the future allowed him to convince the Browns, Steelers, and Colts to switch into the American Football Conference (AFC). Football can thank Rozelle for the faith that television has placed in their franchises, which was expressed in 1998 when three of the networks paid $18 billion for games that at the time of the deal had not been scheduled. Once the team owners tasted television's largesse, they hankered for more, and Rozelle easily obliged. His legacy has provided each of the teams in the NFL with more than $75 million a year in network revenue, based upon the most recent football rights contract of $17.6 billion with ABC, ESPN, and Time Warner, generating substantial wealth for the owners and players.

Sunday afternoon had been the dedicated venue for football, but Tom Moore, ABC network president, wanted to try something different: offering NFL games in prime time, at night. Evenings were not a traditional forum for football, but other sports, like baseball, made the transformation. In addition, Moore had a Friday-evening void to fill with the cancellation of the

Friday-night fights sponsored by Gillette. Everything appeared to be falling into place: there was a mutually beneficial relationship between the NFL and television, and Lee Iacocca, of Ford, was ready to commit to sole sponsorship. Friday-night football looked like a done deal until a well-organized letter-writing campaign by high schools protested the telecast of the evening game for fear of diminishing attendance at the Friday-night high-school football games.

The unlikely protagonist that brought Monday Night Football to ABC was Howard Hughes. Although a recluse, Hughes had a keen eye for audience tastes and owned a company that distributed sports programming. Rozelle had a taste for the Monday-night package, and Hughes had the money, offering $9 million a year. With an offer on the table, Rozelle used it as leverage with the big three, shopping it to CBS, NBC, and ABC. With a strong Monday prime-time schedule in place, CBS wasn't interested; NBC was curious, but its late-night star, Johnny Carson, wouldn't tolerate a delay in the start of *The Tonight Show* to accommodate football; and Arledge at ABC, of course, jumped at it, and after presenting it to a reluctant management, the deal was finally approved by ABC's CEO, Leonard Goldenson, for $8.5 million a year.

Once again Arledge proved his genius, by casting the show with three distinct personalities who probably could act in any number of Shakespearean comedies: Howard Cosell, Keith Jackson, and Don Meredith. Reflecting their worth and the value of the television franchise, ABC set the advertising rate for the premiere fall 1970 season at $65,000 a minute.

The team of Cosell and Meredith—black hat and white hat, bad guy and good guy—initially didn't impress the critics or the Ford Motor Company, a majority sponsor of the series. Most of the negative reviews concerned Cosell, and when Henry Ford called Leonard Goldenson to express his displeasure and suggested that Cosell be removed, everyone listened. Changes were made, Ford was appeased, and the team persevered until the following season, when Frank Gifford replaced Keith Jackson as the play-by-play announcer. The popularity of the show continues with the team formula conjured up by Arledge 30 years ago, with the charismatic union of Al Michaels and John Madden.[10]

Lest anyone diminish the value and importance of sports and television, then one can turn to the ESPN–Major League Baseball (MLB) dispute. The problem arose when ESPN paid $600 million for the NFL rights and, to accommodate the more popular football game broadcasts, switched three Sunday-night baseball games to their lower-rated ESPN 2 network. MLB was outraged. It viewed the Sunday-night franchise as sacrosanct and were appalled at what it perceived was a violation of trust in America's national pastime. (Baseball has long been envious of football's higher ratings and rights fees.)

More significantly, the ESPN franchise is the world's most prominent and largest cable-television sports network, worth approximately $15.4 billion, with gross revenues exceeding $1 billion. Each year it disseminates 4,900 hours of live or original sports programming to 80 million households on ESPN, with 4,200 hours on ESPN 2 to more than 67 million homes. The company, owned by Disney (80%) and Hearst (20%), includes a host of subsidiary divisions, which stretch the network's reach to 150 million households in 180 countries with broadcasts in 21 languages. ESPN has aggressively pursued the baseball franchise, with a six-year, $851 million local-rights game package that runs through 2005. It includes 105 Wednesday- and Sunday-night regular-season games, including games broadcast on ESPN radio.

The matter was brought before Judge Shira A. Scheindlin, a federal judge in Manhattan. It was for her to determine the somewhat quixotic relationship between sports and television and to assess if any damages were warranted. The judge ruled that MLB, if victorious, could only receive a nominal sum. In December 1999 the parties settled, and ESPN signed a new $800 million contract which provides for 800 hours of live and studio coverage of baseball on ESPN. Reluctantly bowing to the popularity of football, the boys of summer agreed to ESPN eliminating its Sunday-night baseball package in September, with a switch of "meaningful" games to Friday nights on ESPN 1 and Sunday evenings on ESPN 2. The agreement is significant to baseball because of the network's prominent reach, with ESPN 1 seen in 80 million homes and ESPN 2 in 67 million.[11]

Another dispute involving baseball and sports rights packaging that headed for the courts was between the New York Yankees and Cablevision, the parent of the Madison Square Garden Network (MSG). After the conclusion of the 2000 baseball season and the Yankees' successful defense of the World Series against the New York Mets, its contracts with MSG and New York's local channel 5 expired. The team, once part of the now-defunct Nets-Devils ownership group, had wanted to start its own network (Yankees Entertainment and Sports Network, which would eventually carry Nets and Devils games) and signed an agreement with Trans World International, a subsidiary of the International Management Group (IMG). Interestingly, the IMG was founded by Mark H. McCormack, whose first client was golfer Arnold Palmer, a college buddy. As a result of his affiliation with IMG, Palmer's income escalated from $50,000 to $500,000 within three years and eventually to more than $10 million. The company also negotiated Tiger Woods's 2000 5-year contract with Nike for $100 million and Derek Jeter's 10-year deal with the Yankees for $189 million.

MSG had a clause in its contract that guaranteed the right to match a competing bid, and New York State Supreme Court Justice Barry Cozier ordered the Yankees to forward a fair bid and forbade them from completing the contract with TWI. The prospective deal with TWI would have brought the Yankees $898 million over the next 10 years. If, as in the past, MSG wanted to purchase exclusive rights to all of the games, then the price escalated to $1.3 billion, or, if spread over the 10-year period of the contract,

$2.4 billion with an up-front $165 million payment starting with the 2001 season and concluding with a $311 million payment in 2010. The expired deal with MSG paid the Yankees $493.5 million over 12 years, including $51 million for the 2000 season.

In November 2000, IMG made a one-year offer to carry Yankees games in 2001 for an estimated rights fee of $55 million. The team presented the bid to MSG, which had seven business days to match it. However, the significance of the bid, which is only $4 million more than MSG paid for the 2000 season, is that there is no exclusive clause allowing either entity the right to match outside bids after 2001. This is a stipulation that is especially important to MSG. Now, of course, the Yankees games are distributed by the YES network. The trend has been to create dedicated channels for various sporting venues, including the Golf Channel and the Tennis Channel.[12]

Other baseball teams have leveraged their lucrative television contracts to hire star players at budget-busting salaries. In a scenario similar to the Yankees, the Texas Rangers also threatened to create a rival network competing with Fox Sports Net. The threat paid off, and Fox Sports Net paid the Rangers and the Dallas Stars $250 million over 10 years for the local cable rights and $250 million a year over 15 years for the local broadcast rights. That deal made it possible for the Rangers to sign Alex Rodriguez to a 10-year, $252 million contract, the richest in the history of sport. His contract became even more attractive after Rodriguez moved to the New York Yankees. The Yankees will pay $112 million over seven years while the Rangers are paying $67 million of the $179 million left on his $252 million, 10-year contract and will continue payments to Rodriguez through 2025. He also received a $10 million signing bonus. In return for consideration of the $5 million devaluation in his contract, Rodriguez receives hotel suites on road trips, a buyout of his Texas home by the Rangers, along with his luxury suites at the ballpark in Arlington and American Airlines Center. All of this largesse, of course, is indirectly attributed to the lucrative television license fees with MLB.

Indeed, Fox Sports Net has been very aggressive in the pursuit of local MLB broadcasting rights. The network is the top local-rights-holder for cable, with half of the 30 MLB teams having sold broadcast and cable rights to Fox and its affiliates. Fox Sports Net has exclusive local cable rights to 26 of the league's 30 teams. Movement of local baseball games away from broadcast and to cable has been the trend. The average number of broadcast games per team fell from 52.4 in 2000 to 50.2 in 2001, which is a 4.3 percent decline. Also, the average number of baseball games per franchise on cable rose from 75 in 2000 to 80.6 in 2001, a 7.5 percent increase. Overall, in the 2001 season regional cable networks carried 2,417 games, which exceeded by 910 the 1,507 that were broadcast on television stations.

Fox Sports has also been aggressive in securing MLB's off-season baseball schedule. Fox Sports has a six-year, $2.5 billion deal for the exclusive rights to the All-Star Game, every playoff game, and the World Series until 2006.[13]

Network and cable television's pursuit of sports franchises comes at a time of increased competition and audience erosion. Televised sports are an effective tool for reaching specific demographics and serve as a foundation for promotional opportunities. Even as some events suffer declining broadcast ratings, sports programming endures as a viable distinctive venue for attracting audiences and branding the network with a sports theme.

As rights fees soar into dizzying altitudes, the persistent question is a determination of value. Assessing a dollar amount to a televised-sports package includes a number of variables, such as intrinsic value, exclusivity, distribution platforms, potential advertising revenue, merchandising, ratings, and residuals. An example of how the worth of sports programming is determined is the 1999 CBS $6 billion contract with the National Collegiate Athletic Association's (NCAA) college basketball championship tournament. At times CBS has been somewhat cavalier toward its pursuit of sports franchises.

In 1989 the network allowed its exclusive franchise with the National Basketball Association (NBA) to expire, and the same deal rejected by CBS was accepted by NBC. Once again, in 1994, CBS had an opportunity to continue its relationship with the NFL and was one of three television networks that earlier paid $1.67 billion in rights fees. The network estimated that it had lost $100 million a year on the package and allowed its expiration, ending a 40-year relationship with professional football. Of course, others were waiting for CBS to fumble the ball, and Fox quickly bought the NFC package for $1.58 billion for four years; NBC purchased the AFC package for $868 million; and TNT, along with ESPN, anted up for cable rights. It seemed as if everyone made a touchdown except for CBS, which effectively was frozen out of professional football until 1998.

In a relatively short time Fox has become a competitor in the arena of broadcast sports franchises. Guided by its CEO, Rupert Murdoch, Fox has assembled an aggressive, energetic team to pursue television sports franchises. The team of Murdoch, Chase Carey (now retired chairman and CEO of Fox Television), and David Hill (Fox Sports chairman) has been a leader in bringing athletic competition to television. Even an obscure tournament like Millennium MI Bass Fishing achieved a respectable rating. Along with the more mundane, Fox and the FX sports channel have acquired rights to football, baseball, and figure skating and acquired ownership of baseball's Los Angeles Dodgers.

One venue where Fox has a distinctive presence is the Fox Sports Net baseball franchise. It is the leading local-rights-holder for cable and is increasing its dominance in broadcast baseball coverage. It has 21 regional networks, with 10 owned and operated and 11 affiliates. Nearly half of the 30 Major

League Baseball teams have sold over-the-air and cable games to Fox. Indeed, the trend in coverage of baseball games has seen a decline in broadcasts and increase in cable. Broadcast stations are reluctant to challenge cable's lock on local coverage because of their unwillingness to preempt network programming for local baseball games. Fox has made a determined effort to make a visible presence in baseball, paying $115 million a year for the rights to postseason games and $2.5 billion to 2006. However, declining ratings have compromised Fox's mission of branding itself as a sports network. In 2002 Fox's parent company, News Corp, took a quarterly write-down of $909 million, the largest ever for a network. The sum included a loss of $387 million for the NFL, $297 million for NASCAR, and $225 million for MLB.

One of the persistent criticisms of baseball has been the length of the games. During the 2000 World Series between the Yankees and the Mets, the games became marathons of fan and audience endurance. With a running time of four hours and 51 minutes, game one of the subway series was the longest in World Series history. In 1977, when the Yankees played their last 12-inning game prior to 2000, it lasted four hours and 24 minutes, with subsequent games in that series lasting from just over two hours to two and a half hours.

## PITCH COUNTS: FAST-FORWARD ON THE BASEBALL DIAMOND

During the dog days of summer 2001, except for routine team rivalries and pennant-race logistics, baseball was pretty quiet. That is, until MLB's Sandy Alderson, executive vice president for baseball operations, sent an e-mail to umpires about the need to reduce the pitch count and enforce a rule-book definition of the strike zone. The e-mail was a substantive attempt to create a dynamic within baseball for addressing the issue of game time.

Unlike other sports, baseball does not serve Father Time. Games are scheduled for afternoon or evening time, but there is no limit of hours, minutes, or seconds that must be met within any time constraints. And so fans in the stadium and tuning in at home must patiently watch as pitchers settle themselves on the mound (the rule book says they must pitch the ball within a 20-second window, which never happens) and endure batters clicking their spiked shoes and moving in and out of the batter's box.

There were a number of issues associated with Alderson's missive. One that was most disturbing to the umpires was the maintenance of pitch-count averages as a tool to assess their individual performance. His e-mail to Jim Joyce, an experienced professional with 14 years of umpiring, questioned why there were so many pitches in a game and also why it (the game) took so long.

What was even more disturbing to Joyce was Alderson's use of language, which admonished the veteran umpire to "hunt for strikes."

The recommendation to Joyce is a result of Alderson's determination, supported by Commissioner Bud Selig's office, that there is a correlation between the misapplication of the strike zone and a high pitch count. Both Alderson and Selig endorsed a plan to enforce the strike zone as the rule book defines it, resulting in more high strikes.

Other baseball umpires were also critiqued. Alderson was critical of Angel Hernandez, an umpire with nine years' experience, observing that his most recent pitch count of 300 in Cincinnati was good but needed to be brought down. He cited that in May and June Hernandez averaged a pitch count of 310 per nine-inning game, the highest count in MLB. Another umpire, Fieldin Culbreth, was singled out because he had more than 300 pitches in a Kansas City–Detroit game and because during the months of May and June he averaged 307 pitches per nine-inning game.

Sports are a vast reservoir of statistics and minutiae that creates comparative records on almost any activity or event. A company called STATS Inc., which compiles data, including box scores, for the Associated Press, analyzed pitch counts for a number of umpires. Interestingly, John Hirschbeck, head of the umpires union, had at one point the lowest pitch-count average, with 272 pitches per nine-inning game, while umpire Scott Higgins, with 305, had the highest average. For Alderson, the ideal pitch count is 270, and after publicizing it, he initiated a public-relations dilemma. The umpires union immediately filed a grievance against MLB.

Each side used the media as its pulpit, and soon after its filing, the grievance was dropped after Commissioner Bud Selig's office decided to abandon pitch counts as a determinant of umpire performance. The umpires felt that they were being unjustly singled out using a quantitative tool that they had little control over. For them, pitch counts were the exclusive purview of the baseball pitcher.

However, this did not deter the commissioner's office from installing tracking equipment to confirm that umpires were adhering to the strict interpretation of the strike zone. The technology, designed to monitor planes and missiles, is known as the *Umpire Information System* and was developed by QuesTec and Atlantic Aerospace. A previous generation of the technology was being used on Fox Television.

The company has a five-year contract with MLB and began testing and using the system in 1991. During the 1992 season the umpires moved to end baseball's association with the company because of various fines and disciplinary actions by stock regulatory agencies against Edward Plumacher, a principal of the company. In addition, the umpires union had filed two grievances and a lawsuit pertaining to the use of the technology. Addressing issues of integrity, the union reiterated that those empowered to officially evaluate the umpire's performance must themselves have competence and integrity. In baseball, the umpires are the judges . . . baseball is a game between men, not a game of man against the machine.[14]

Although this issue may have been misinterpreted and misdirected, the matter of interminably long games is still one that requires some action. There are a number of variables that impact the length of the baseball game, including pitcher performance, batter staging, umpire strike zone, manager preference, and the designated hitter. The average baseball game lasted two hours and 55 minutes in 2001, just 3 minutes less than the previous year.

But there is something magical happening in baseball, although it's not in the majors. For the BlueClaws of Lakewood, New Jersey, a minor-league team, the game time averages two hours and 32 minutes. That's one reason their fans are so devoted and fill the seats. For the 2001 season the team had broken the all-time attendance record for the Class A South Atlantic League. Another team, the Brooklyn Cyclones, had sold out just about every seat, approximately 7,500 per game, at Keyspan Park in Coney Island.

There's a mystique for the fans as they trudge to see the minor-league teams at play. Younger players, not as professional, entertain the crowd. Their moves may not be as polished nor their performance well orchestrated, but as the song from *Damn Yankees* says, they sure have heart.

The attendance figures tell the story. Sure, on an average summer night about 500,000 people attend a major-league baseball game, but 350,000 are at the minor leagues. However, the trend in attendance favors the minors. From 1993 to 2000, per-game attendance fell 4 percent for the majors and rose 19 percent in the minors. In addition to the length of the games, another reason for the decline is the escalating cost of ticket prices. According to Team Marketing Report, a newsletter based in Chicago, since 1993 the cost of a major-league ticket, adjusted for inflation, has risen 61 percent, to $19; for the minors it's about $6, less than admission to a movie.

Some of the suggestions to speed up the game include eliminating the designated hitter, decreasing the number of commercials between innings, defining consistent strike zones, and limiting the number of times a batter can step in and out of the box. Since many games going beyond three hours are played in the evening, there is a significant loss of children at the stadium and watching at home. The loss of a youthful audience is perhaps the most critical detriment resulting from lengthy games. They are indeed the audience of tomorrow, and losing them could irreparably damage the game.[15]

One paramount reason for longer games is the need for television to recoup its investment in rights fees. Playoff and World Series games must be played in prime time because of the interest and revenue they can generate. Television audiences are forced to watch frequent commercials with endless redundancy as a means for the network (Fox) to pay MLB its generous tithe so that the teams can reward their players with budget-busting salaries and their commissioner with a $2 million annual salary. Indeed, those fans who were "fortunate" to attend one of the subway-series games between the Mets and Yankees were "treated" to $3.50 pretzels and $4 regular-size sodas.

Of course, there are different perceptions as to the worth of such sports franchises, but there is also an arrogance that manifests itself with network leadership. This was best demonstrated in the days of radio by David Sarnoff, of RCA, when young upstart William Paley was stealing the best radio talent from RCA's NBC radio network and housing them at CBS. Sarnoff built RCA and NBC, but as a nuts-and-bolts kind of guy, he didn't understand what the real attraction of radio was. His sense was that it was the technology that was most important and not the talent. Conversely, Paley loved and nurtured his talent, and knew that it was their programs that attracted radio's audience. Paley was getting NBC's best and brightest for CBS by offering the likes of Jack Benny better deals, allowing the artists to keep more of the money they earned. Sarnoff dismissed the talent defection until his lieutenants prevailed on him to offer Bob Hope, the anchor of NBC, more money not to abandon Sarnoff's network.

The irony is that, although Paley was gone from CBS, his mantra was ignored and the legacy that he established was lost on the network's leaders. Athletes are like actors, and an adoring public celebrates their efforts. There are numerous examples—Joe DiMaggio, Joe Namath, and Michael Jordan— of individuals that came to personify the very essence of celebrity. Not to have them on your air was to demonstrate an ignorance of audience taste and a conceit toward programming the network.

There were executives at CBS who understood the ramifications of these decisions and were able to make some accommodation toward rebuilding the network's presence in sports. The notion of athletes as talent and celebrities was never more apparent than at the 1994 Winter Olympic Games in Lillehammer, Norway. And it was not necessarily a high-profile event that attracted the audience. It was the rivalry and bad blood between two champion figure skaters, Nancy Kerrigan and Tonya Harding. The tension of their personal and professional competition was the highest-rated Winter Olympics event since the 1980 Games in Lake Placid.

While CBS paid dearly for the NCAA package in 1999, the deal is for 11 years, with an 8-year window allowing for renegotiation of the contract. The network was anxious to secure the NCAA rights because that same year it lost the privilege to broadcast the NASCAR races, a rising star on the televised sports front, to Fox, NBC, and TBS (who paid a combined total of $2.4 billion over six years).

The CBS arrangement with the NCAA is unique in its procurement of exclusive distribution rights on a number of platforms. Over the years, exclusivity has been a recurring theme in the network's bargaining position with the NCAA. In a seven-year, $1 billion deal with the NCAA that became effective in 1991, CBS negotiated exclusive broadcast rights, excluding any distribution on cable or independent television stations.

Its latest terms with the NCAA gives the network exclusive broadcast rights as well as cable, radio, satellite, new media, Web sites, merchandising, corporate sponsorship, e-commerce, publishing, and archiving. Broadcast networks are sensitive to the competition from other media and are aggressively pursuing exclusive agreements that allow them greater control of the various revenue streams generated by the sports franchises. These arrangements are reflected in other high-priced contracts negotiated by broadcast networks, including the NFL (CBS, Fox, ABC, and ESPN; eight years for $17.6 billion), NHL (ABC and ESPN; five years for $600 million, 176% more than the previous five-year deal), and NBA (NBC and Turner; four years for $2.64 billion, 136% more than in the previous contract).[16]

Network television faces the dilemma of paying highly inflated rights fees in an effort to secure a niche for sports-themed event television. The reality is that in some cases declining ratings have eroded the value of these packages. Ratings for network television have been in a tailspin from the competition of cable, satellite, and the Internet. However, for some leagues, like the NBA, the decline has been dramatic and indeed worrisome for NBC, the network broadcasting the games. For the 1999–2000 season, ratings for NBA basketball games on NBC were down 15 percent for afternoon games and more than 20 percent for games in prime time. When NBC signed its $1.75 billion, four-season pact with the NBA, which was more than double the previous amount, it was hoping for an embarrassment of riches. Instead, what it got was an embarrassing lesson in economics.

During the 1999–2000 season NBC averaged only about 5.9 million fans for its regular-season prime-time games, down from 7.4 million the previous season. While the NBA was in a slump, ratings for the NFL held steady, while the bizarre antics of wrestling on the UPN network is attracting 7 million viewers every Monday night. An estimated 700,000 fewer homes tuned into NBC for league basketball games during the 1999–2000 season than the year before. Indeed, when NBC broadcast a prime-time basketball game on Sunday, March 12, 2000, the network reached a historical low point in its ratings history: the lowest rating for any night in a season. Competing programs on cable television have routinely outscored the basketball games, although NBC is seen in more homes than most cable networks, including HBO.

Volume appears to be another measure for the decline in ratings. There are a large number of NBA teams, and their games are available on cable and broadcast television. The Turner cable channels sometimes distribute as many as four games a week during the regular season, while a regional network such as MSG carries the local home team's games. This abundance of NBA riches appears to be a force in eroding the television audience for the league basketball games.

Interestingly, some sports stadia have also experienced a decline in fan attendance. One of the most stunning and architecturally aesthetic of the stadia is Miami's American Airlines Arena, where the Heat plays. Like other local teams, its ratings were down 24 percent during the 1999–2000 season. However, attendance at the stadium has been somewhat sporadic, forcing management to close and block off the 3,200 balcony seats with black curtains at least seven times during the 1999–2000 season. Adding to the dilemma are the bright yellow courtside chairs that when empty are a glaring televised witness to the ambivalence of the fans. According to the Heat, however, all the courtside seats are sold.

The stadium, which opened in January 2000, holds 19,600 fans and has sold out at least a third of the time. It has a large number of luxury seats that could go a long way in increasing the team's revenue and subsidize the Heat's annual payroll of $53 million. Like baseball, basketball suffers from the perception that live attendance at a game can be a costly enterprise. At American Airlines Arena, parking can cost $25, and that, when added to the price of regular admission, which can range from $12 to $75, can be a pocketbook-busting experience suited for the most loyal of fans.

Of course, some fans have voiced their displeasure over the more arcane "weaknesses" of the stadium, including being moved backward for the $20,000-a-year seats, loud music, bright lights, rough concrete surfaces, and cooking odors from the gourmet restaurants under the stands. Amid those "hardships," there's certainly something to be said for watching the game at home or in the comfort of your favorite sports bar.

While broadcasting and league executives euphemistically refer to this phenomenon as a "transitional" period, they nevertheless attempted to provide a rationale by attributing the ratings decline to a number of circumstances. The retirement of Michael Jordan and the void left by him for a superstar of the NBA is one factor they cite. Related to the celebrity issue is the reluctance of a considerable number of young college-basketball players who have abbreviated college careers and declared their professional status. The absence of a strong collegiate presence as a venue to nurture prominent college players is another instance used to explain the declining interest in the television audience. Regular-season ratings for NCAA college basketball on the CBS television network also hit historical lows during the 1999–2000 season. In addition, the NBA lockout during the 1998–1999 season is also viewed as a factor that alienated a significant portion of the fan base.

The task of breathing life back into the NBA and creating interest in the league, the players, and the games has become a compelling mission for the principals involved. With the ushering in of the new millennium, the NBA, along with NBC, instituted a policy for miking the coaches of the teams during network broadcasts, thus providing television viewers with edited audible commentary of the behind-the-scenes action.

Taking their lead from football's NFL, where NFL Films pioneered the use of in-game wireless microphones in the 1960s, the NBA is hoping to achieve the spontaneity, irreverence, and entertainment that microphones have provided in other sporting venues.

Major-league baseball has also been wired for sound, with microphones placed around the baseball diamond, in the bases, on the foul poles, in the fences, and in the bullpen. Baseball managers are also miked, and occasionally an expletive eludes the "minders," like Yankee manager Joe Torre's curse on a Fox broadcast several years ago. But that's just the stuff that television is looking for.

Basketball, being a close-contact, rough-and-tumble sport, is not a game for wimps—either coaches or players. Why, then, did so many of the NBA coaches risk a $100,000 fine and refuse to wear the microphones? Initially, three coaches—Pat Riley of the Miami Heat, Paul Westphal of the Seattle Super-Sonics, and Butch Carter of the Toronto Raptors—forged a united front against donning the mikes. Concerned about hampering their ability to coach and the possibility of their taped coaching remarks being made available to opposing teams, the three were later joined by other coaches, including Jeff Van Gundy, formerly of the New York Knicks. After some tense days and emotional brinkmanship, the league reached a compromise with the Basketball Coaches Association. Coaches were given the option of wearing the microphone, which has an off switch, or using a boom microphone to listen into their huddles during time-outs.

In an era of the Internet, where mini–Web cameras and microphones overhearing the admonitions of basketball coaches have eroded the presumptive boundaries of privacy, it appears to be a rather benign issue. Unfortunately, sports venues have in some cases become tasteless spectacles of boorish behavior by fans, players, and some coaches. There are other, more compelling issues, such as violence and drug use, that coaches can unite against. Unfortunately, hardly a whisper is raised about them. Adding the candid audible moments to team sports provides the television viewer with a voyeuristic opportunity to be intimate with the team and feel a part of the competition. It's a realization that even some of the heretofore most private moments have succumbed to the priorities of entertainment in a culture that has a greater respect for intrusion than privacy.

In addition to the microphones, NBC juggled its prime-time schedule to include the first national broadcast of the Toronto Raptors' Vince Carter, who is heralded as being an heir apparent to Michael Jordan. Mr. Carter didn't disappoint the viewers in his debut game on national television, scoring 51 points in one of the highest-scoring games of the 1999–2000 season. Unfortunately, only 4.6 million viewers during prime time saw the game on a Sunday night. However, the need to nurture the next generation of basketball stars must be a priority for the league and television if the dynamics of professional basketball are to survive.[17]

There is a cachet of distinction associated with high-profile sporting events, and one of the most prominent is the Olympic Games. Television has created a spectacle that capitalizes on human drama, personal pathos, nationalistic zeal, and record of achievement, focusing on athletes like speed skaters Dan Jansen and Bonnie Blair going for the gold while struggling to overcome their personal tragedies, or an explosion in the Olympic staging city of Atlanta and the media and law enforcement's tyranny in wrongfully accusing Richard Jewel as the villain. This is the stuff that brings the mass audience to their sets, sits them down, and hypnotizes them for several hours each day during the event. Although ratings have declined for almost every Olympic broadcast since 1972, it remains a holy grail of television broadcasting that assumes a unique, compelling character.

There have been some missteps in the broadcasting of the games, and, unfortunately, NBC has been associated with each of them. The network suffered the largest television-ratings decline in the broadcast history of the Games in the summer of 1988 from Seoul, Korea. Perhaps it was the political unrest or the time-zone delays in televising the events in the United States. Undaunted, NBC had the resolve to bid again, winning the rights for $401 million to broadcast the 1992 Summer Games from Barcelona. But this time NBC had an ambitious plan to distribute real-time competition on cable pay-per-view.

Knowing that the media reported the results of Olympic contests prior to their free distribution on their commercial network, NBC reasoned that it could merchandise the event as a pay-per-view spectacular. The network joined with Cable Television Systems, one of the largest multiple-system operators (MSOs) with a great deal of experience in managing and distributing sports programming (owners of Madison Square Garden, the New York Knicks, and the New York Rangers). The idea was ingenious, although its implementation was flawed. They called it *Triplecast* and marketed the pay-per-view telecasts in three tiers of service. However, two of the most damaging obstacles to its success were the retail pricing and the timing of the live broadcasts to American audiences.

Cable television has enjoyed a charmed existence concerning the pricing of premium events and pay networks on its systems. There are few inhibitions to raising subscriber payment thresholds, and a cavalier attitude to what the market will bear. However, in the case of Triplecast, both NBC and Cablevision seriously underestimated the resistance of consumers to a package of $125 for 15 days or $29.95 for individual daily orders. In addition, the live Olympic events were broadcast starting at 2:00 A.M. on the East Coast and 5:00 A.M. on the West. While there are baseball fans that will camp outside Yankee Stadium for opening season, playoff, or World Series tickets, and basketball addicts that will pay several times the face value of a ticket to see their beloved New York Knicks in a championship game, the same psychology does not apply to the Olympics. Fans can see some of their favorite professional athletes go for the gold on the U.S. team, but the attraction is to the event, with little or no emotional ties to the team. Therefore, Triplecast misjudged the psyche of the fans and their attraction to the broadcasts. Expecting to have a pay-per-view audience of 2 million, they instead signed up about 250,000, and only then at heavily discounted prices. NBC and Cablevision had combined estimated losses of between $100 and 150 million, but the experience taught television an important lesson about merchandising and audience appeal.

To NBC's credit, it took the hit on the 1992 Barcelona Games but understood the inherent value of the Olympics as a foundation to its overall network programming strategy. Undaunted by its failure, the network won the rights to the 1996 Summer Games from Atlanta ($456 million) and the 2000 Summer Games from Sydney, Australia, and 2002 Winter Games (for a combined two-event total of $1.2 billion). In addition to the 2004 Games from Athens, Greece, NBC and its parent, General Electric, are paying $2.2 billion for the 2010 Winter and 2012 Summer Games. In addition, General Electric will spend $160 million to $200 million on sponsorship.

The Sydney event involved a 15-hour eastern-time-zone delay, which was accommodated by the network's expedient use of its two cable platforms, MSNBC and CNBC. The two cable networks complemented NBC's 162 half hours on prime time and weekends with total cable coverage of 172 hours. While NBC provided coverage of various events, intercutting between competitions, its cable networks stayed with an event until its end. In addition, less-popular audience-pleasers like boxing, soccer, tennis, water polo, baseball, weight lifting, and equestrian events were delegated to the cable networks.

Once again, however, NBC experienced lackluster ratings for the 2000 Olympics, and after the first week had to issue "make goods" to advertisers for ratings that fell well below the guaranteed threshold. Just the opposite occurred in 2004 during NBC Universal's coverage of the Olympic Games from Athens. The network sold over $1 billion in advertising and was able to add to its revenue with unsold commercial spots that it had set aside in case there was a repeat of the Sydney Games when the network had to provide free airtime to advertisers for failing to meet ratings guarantees. It paid $793 million for exclusive rights to broadcast the games but provided coverage 24 hours a day on any one of seven NBC Universal networks: USA, MSNBC, Bravo, CNBC, NBC, Telemundo, and HDTV. More than 1,200 hours of sports was broadcast (triple the coverage of Sydney in 2000), which totaled more than the past five summer games. According to Nielsen Media Research, the average rating for NBC Universal was 15 for NBC, an increase of 9 percent over Sydney.

The Triplecast attempt wasn't the only failure in the annals of televised sport. Indeed, some of the blame for these missteps could be attributed to the hubris and greed harbored by the promoters as well as the television networks. In 1988 CBS paid $1.06 billion for exclusive broadcast rights to league-championship playoffs, the All-Star Game, the World Series, and 12 games a season for a term of four years beginning in 1990. With a 1990 four-game World Series sweep and a 20 percent decline in advertising rates, the network suffered a loss of $500 million on its baseball contract. Sensitive to network television's reluctance to invest heavily in exclusive baseball broadcast rights, in 1993 ABC, NBC, and MLB agreed on a joint venture called the Baseball Network. For the first time, MLB produced and distributed its own games for network television. This alleviated the need for the networks to pay rights fees, and MLB sold most of the advertising time.

While the Baseball Network attempted to address a number of critical issues associated with the revenue streams of baseball, the 1994 players strike crippled the network's mission. In August 1995 both ABC and NBC terminated their relationship with the Baseball Network, effectively putting it out of business. After this collapse, negotiations returned to the traditional process of broadcast rights, and in 1995 a five-year package of national television deals was reached with Fox, NBC, ESPN, and Liberty Sports for a total $1.68 billion through 2000.

The frenzied competition for televised sports rights is not only a function of American culture but has global implications as well. In 2002 Japan and South Korea hosted soccer's premiere event, the World Cup. Said by some to be the most popular sport in the world, the rights to broadcast this event in Japan involved an interesting foreplay in the dynamics of collusive bargaining, secret agreements, obstruction, and double-dealing.

Soccer's international governing body, the FIFA, sold the worldwide licensing rights to ISL Worldwide, the mammoth global sports-marketing company. The initial cost of the global World Cup rights was $500 million, which was later reduced to $250 million. The value of the soccer television franchise escalated considerably, to more than 40 times the amount that the NHK Japan's public broadcaster paid for the 1998 World Cup, because of the increased global interest in the sport. However, Japanese broadcasters were reluctant to place competing bids and instead formed their own television consortium made up of the different networks and television stations, including the NHK. Known officially as the Japan Consortium, it consisted of the five private networks, the public television network (NHK), and 200 individual television stations. In their attempt to achieve bargaining parity, the parties agreed not to bid as individual entities, pledged to restrict broadcasting rights to members of the consortium, and jointly set acquisition fees for the games.

The document read like a manifesto, with each entity sealing its pledge with a promise to seek consortium permission to depart the membership. Accused of conspiring to manipulate Japanese World Cup rights fees, Seiji Urushido, an executive with Japan's BS Nippon television network, blamed the open competitive market in the United States and specifically NBC's bid for the Summer and Winter Olympics as the cause for increased global-rights fees.

Perhaps the most disturbing element in the Japanese television conspiracy is the role of Japan's Dentsu, the advertising agency that is considered the largest in the world. In its role as mediator, it wears two hats: one as a representative of the Japanese Consortium, the other as a 10 percent equity owner of ISL Worldwide. Indeed, Dentsu's involvement appeared to be a conflict of interest because of its control of Japan's broadcast advertising, selling one-third of all Japanese advertising and with a virtual monopoly over prime-time commercials.[18]

The implications from the Japanese World Cup soccer negotiations addresses the enthusiasm and aggressiveness of broadcasters worldwide and their quest for exclusive broadcast rights to sporting events. Although there has been a decline in America's domestic ratings for televised sporting events, there is still a compelling interest in sports by the television audience. While the economics of televised sports coverage presents substantive challenges, it nevertheless will not negate the need to satiate the audience's desire to see sports on television. There will be more shared packages, with more games on cable television and perhaps pay-per-view. Competition is the essence of sport, and it is also the singular variable that drives media entertainment in the United States. However, as inexpensive reality television has proved, television will cater to the lowest common denominator, providing the greatest thrills for the least amount of money. Unfortunately, the broadcast networks and cable have supported the teams and their gluttony for excessiveness in salaries and bonuses. Their greed, and that of the players, is symbolic of the challenges that televised sports face in this country and around the world.

Television has created an international culture of sporting significance, cultivating its own dynamics within the constructs of its substance. It has manipulated the protocols of sports to suit its own needs and has subjugated the participants to a form of voluntary indentured servitude. It has changed the way people look at sports; changed its significance; and, most of all, created its own hierarchy of judgmental behavior, acting as the gatekeeper for audience taste. It has also created a mythology for the jocks who greedily embrace the largesse of the system. However, they should realize that when you try to weave ratings into gold, there are limits to the fantasy you've created.

## NOTES

1. Richard Sandomir, "XFL, a Reality Series with Sports Thrown In," *New York Times,* 1 February 2001, p. D1.

2. Stefan Fatsis and Joe Flint, "How the XFL Became One of the Biggest Flops on TV," *Wall Street Journal,* 23 April 2001, p. A1.

3. Jere Longman, "The Finest Football February Can Offer," *New York Times,* 12 February 2001, p. D1.

4. Andrew Ross Sorkin, "Smackdown! W.W.F. to Buy Wrestling Rival," *New York Times,* 24 March 2001, p. C3; Richard Sandomir, "McMahon and Knight: Tough Interviews," *New York Times,* 20 March 2001, p. D6; Mike Freeman, "XFL May Let Teenagers Opt to Turn Pro," *New York Times,* 4 March 2001, sec. 8, p. SP1; Steve McClellan and Richard Tdesco, "Loss on the Play," *Broadcasting and Cable,* 26 March 2001, p. 5; John Leland, "Why America's Hooked on Wrestling," *Newsweek,* 7 February 2000, p. 47; "Gridiron Gladiators," Media Central, 1 April 2001, http://www.findarticles.com.

5. Richard Sandomir, "To Live Another Day in the Arena League," *New York Times,* 1 May 2001, p. D1.

6. Elliott J. Gorn and Warren Goldstein, *A Brief History of American Sports* (Urbana: University of Illinois Press, 2004).

7. Erik Barnouw, *Tube of Plenty: The Evolution of American Television,* rev. ed. (New York: Oxford University Press, 1982).

8. Richard Sandomir, "Inside 'Monday Night Football' from the Truck to the Booth, a Look at ABC's No. 2 Program," *New York Times,* 17 November 1999, p. D1.

9. Richard Sandomir, "Monday Night Shift Ends Esiason's Job," *New York Times,* 9 March 2000, p. D1; Richard Sandomir, "Esiason Fires Back after Being Dismissed," *New York Times,* 10 March 2000, p. D4; Julian Rubinstein, "Monday Night Football's Hail Mary," *New York Times Magazine,* 3 September 2000, sec. 6, p. 46; Joe Schlosser, "Miller Time on MNF," *Broadcasting and Cable,* 7 August 2000, p. 32; Richard Sandomir, "The Pressure Is on Miller, but Other Analysts Will Also Be Tested," *New York Times,* 3 September 2000, p. SP10; Bill Carter, "Making Fun of Football," *TV Guide,* 2–8 September 2000, p. 9.

10. Marc Gunther and Bill Carter, *Monday Night Mayhem: The Inside Story of ABC's Monday Night Football* (New York: William Morrow, 1988).

11. Richard Sandomir, "TV Sports," *New York Times,* 30 November 1999, p. D2; Joe Flint, "ESPN, Baseball Reach Settlement in Telecast Dispute," *Wall Street Journal,* 7 December 1999, p. B8.

12. Richard Sandomir, "Yanks' Parade of Numbers: Dollar Signs Followed by 0's," *New York Times,* 31 October 2000, p. D3; Richard Sandomir, "I.M.G. Makes Yankee TV Bid," *New York Times,* 9 November 2000, p. D11.

13. Kim McAvoy, "Baseball Gets the Bucks," *Broadcasting and Cable,* 2 April 2001, p. 26.

14. Murray Chass, "Umpires Want Ball-Strike Monitor Gone," *New York Times,* 20 September 2002, p. D3.

15. David Leonhardt, "The National Pastime Falls Behind in the Count," *New York Times,* 12 August 2001, sec. 3, p. 1; Tom Haudricourt, "Umpires Strike Back as Monitoring System Causes Controversy," *Milwaukee Journal Sentinel,* 18 June 2003, pp. 1–4; http:sportsillustrated.cnn.com, "Union Head Has Lowest Pitch Count," "End of Story, Baseball Stops Counting Pitches, Umps Drop Grievance," "Striking Back Alderson: Pitch-Count Tracking Much Ado about Little," "Crossed Signals Umps May Have Misread Pitch Count Directive."

16. Joe Flint, "CBS Signs $6 Billion Deal With NCAA," *Wall Street Journal,* 10 November 1999, p. A3.

17. Steve Popper, "Timeout Microphone: Van Gundy's Big Debut," *New York Times,* 15 March 2000, p. D1; Alan Schwarz, "NBA's Indecent Exposure," *New York Times,* 19 March 2000, p. D3; Bill Carter, "NBA Games Are a Sinker," *New York Times,* 15 March 2000, p. E10; Bill Carter, "With Jordan Gone, Basketball Ratings Hit a Slump at NBC," *New York Times,* 20 March 2000, p. A1; Harvey Araton, "Rising Star Minimized by Falling TV Ratings," *New York Times,* 13 March 2000, p. D3; Sam Walker, "Solving the Mystery of the Miami Heat and Its Empty Seats," *Wall Street Journal,* 21 April 2000, p. A1.

18. James Roman, *Love, Light, and a Dream* (Westport, Conn.: Praeger, 1998), pp. 81–82.

# 16

## TRENDS AND ISSUES

In a relatively short time, television has had a profound effect on American and world culture. It has become a behavioral model; educational tool; information provider; entertainment resource; babysitter; and source for concern, debate, and criticism. It has validated itself as an essential tool and part of the fabric of society.

Over the years many issues and concerns have been manifested about television. Before the Internet there were initiatives involving the use of television as an instructional tool to service distant school districts in rural communities. In many cases this practice evolved into the talking head, which was an ineffectual means for teaching. However, television combined with the Internet offers new opportunities for distant learning, and, of course, public television became a model for preschool and school-age children with programs like *Sesame Street* and *Electric Company.*

Television's behavioral influence on children has been concerned with modeling and imitating what they see. There have been many studies associated with the effect that violent television programming has upon children and whether or not it influences antisocial behavior. While there is no definitive correlation between television and violence, there are indications that in some cases children that may be more predisposed to violence may act out in a negative way. Also, although no direct link can be made, there were several instances where prime-time television programs were said to have motivated aggressive assaults on individuals. In one, a scene where adolescents doused a vagrant with gasoline and set him on fire was mimicked on the streets of a major urban city, and in another, a segment where a young woman was gang-raped in prison was emulated in a real prison. Both these incidents occurred shortly after the television broadcast.

Abusive behavior toward women by men was also a concern about music videos disseminated on the MTV television network. Many of them depicted women as victims of sexually explicit violence, and parents expressed their concern about the provocative nature of the music videos and their intent toward denigrating women. Indeed, parental televisual concerns also include some of the suggestive and violent lyrics associated with rap music on MTV.

As for language and situations, there has been an accelerated trend to make prime-time television programming more realistic. Indeed, television has evolved from the prudish portrayals of a husband and wife in separate beds to very vivid intimacy between couples on the commercial networks. This is a profound change from the policies of the past, which were predicated upon the oversight of content by the network standards-and-practices departments. They are responsible for assessing the propriety of language and situations on their network. Over the years there has been more flexibility in what is deemed appropriate, as defined by the changing mores in American society.

These concerns are also expressed as they relate to advertising. Networks also examine the content of commercials for their suitability and claims. Any television station has the ability to reject a commercial based upon what it perceives to be specious claims, inappropriate language, or provocative situations. For years broadcast stations and networks would not accept condom advertisements; however, now some cable and broadcast networks, along with broadcast stations, do accept paid advertising, but may limit it to a specific time of day. They may also accept nonpaid public service announcements.

There are few limitations on the frequency of commercials that are inserted into a program; however, there are regulatory policies on the number and length of commercials in children's programs. And there are prohibitions concerning commercials that advertise certain products, like vitamins.

## TECHNOLOGY

The technology of television has had a relatively short history, but in that time there have been compelling changes in both production and exhibition. The first studio television cameras were cumbersome, heavy, and for the most part immobile. Before the Zoomar lens was invented, each camera was equipped with a turret that consisted of three lenses: wide angle, medium shot, and close-up. On the command of the director, the camera person would squeeze the trigger on the turret and move the appropriate lens into position. In the early 1950s Heinz Kilfitt of Germany designed the variable focal-length lens, or Zoomar (zoom) lens, which became an industry standard for studio and home video cameras.

Television programming in the late 1940s and 1950s had no effective storage or archival capacity. Many programs were broadcast live and then lost in the ether forever. Some were recorded on 16 mm film off a television monitor (those recordings were known as *kinescopes*), and others, like *I Love Lucy*, were filmed for broadcast using three simultaneously running 16 mm film cameras. However, there was a great deal of interest in magnetic recording, which was initiated by the German development of a sound-recording device called the Magnetophon. Indeed, Bing Crosby, the famous crooner, used a prototype of this technology at ABC to record his radio program. In 1948 the Ampex Corporation introduced its first magnetic professional tape recorder model 200.

Moving from recording sound to magnetic video was the next step: in 1951 Bing Crosby Enterprises developed a crude version of a video recorder, and in 1956 Ampex introduced the first monochrome videotape recorder, the VR 1000. On November 30 of that year, *Douglas Edwards with the News* was the first program recorded on videotape, and in 1957 3M Corporation introduced commercial blank tape at $307 per reel. Consumer and industry video recorder models appeared in 1970 with the Sony U-Matic and in 1975 with the Sony Betamax, and in 1976 Panasonic and JVC developed a new standard of videotape recording called Video Home System (VHS), which eventually became the industry standard.

## Digital Television

The move toward a digital and high-definition television (HDTV) standard was initiated on November 17, 1987, when, at the request of 58 broadcasters, the Federal Communications Commission (FCC) created the Advisory Committee on Advanced Television Service (ACATS). In 1993 seven companies that designed all-digital systems formed the Grand Alliance, which included General Instrument and MIT; Zenith and AT&T; and Sarnoff, Philips, and Thomson. A number of formidable tasks faced the alliance, including the types of pixel arrays and video compression. However, in 1995 a Grand Alliance digital television system was agreed upon, and the FCC took steps for implementation. It announced an ambitious timetable for stations to begin broadcasting in the DTV format: 26 stations by late 1998, 40 stations by mid-1999, 120 stations by 2000, and every station in the country by 2006. To encourage the transition to HDTV, the FCC awarded every television licensee an additional digital frequency. The first live broadcast of HDTV occurred on October 29, 1998, with coverage of the launch of the space shuttle STS-95, which transported John Glenn back into space.

## Television Sets

The evolution of television receivers has dramatically evolved from 1908, when Campbell-Swinton and Russian-born Boris Rosing, independent of each other, suggested that a cathode-ray tube (CRT) could reproduce a television image on a phosphor-coated screen. There were several inventors who contributed to television, including Vladimir Zworykin and the Iconoscope; Philo Farnsworth and the Image Dissector; and Allen B. Dumont, an American electrical engineer who developed the CRT for use in television during the 1930s. On January 13, 1928, Ernst F. W. Alexanderson demonstrated the first home television receiver in Schenectady, New York.

After World War II, television receiver set sales blossomed, and in 1946 6,500 sets were made and sold in New York, Los Angeles, Chicago, and Philadelphia. Supply couldn't meet demand, as early picture tubes were blown and shaped by hand. In an effort to accommodate the demand and reduce prices, some of the early sets were sold as kits. The Dumont company was the first to bring mass-produced television sets to market, in May 1946, followed by RCA and Philco. Typically, the size of the receiver was from five to seven inches, with a price tag between $375 and $500. Soon, 10-inch screen sizes became standard.

## Flat-Panel Displays

Although there were earlier attempts to produce a television receiver that was flat, it wasn't until 1996 that Fujitsu produced the first plasma display panel. The inert gas is sandwiched between two glass panels, and a mild electric current stimulates an ultraviolet light image on the screen. There are also liquid crystal displays (LCD), but this technology is more suitable for smaller screens.

## DVD

Digital video disc technology was viewed as the next platform for storage capacity, replacing VHS tapes, laser discs, and CD-ROMs. In 1994 two similar yet distinctive technical systems were proposed. In May 1994 Sony/Philips announced a high-density DVD named the Multimedia CD (MMCD), with 5 to 10 times data capacity, while Toshiba and Time Warner introduced the Super Disc (SD). Each of the prototypes had distinctive features; for example, Toshiba's Super High Density Disc was double sided, thin, and could accommodate 10 gigabytes of data storage. Hoping to avoid the struggle that competing standards caused in the home video recording and playback marketplace with Beta and VHS, the companies quickly came to terms with a common standard for the super-density disc. In 1996 the first DVD players went on sale in Tokyo, and in 1997 they went on sale in seven American cities. The public's anticipation for DVD technology was very high, and in 1998 1 million DVD units were sold in the United States. In addition, computer DVD-ROM drives, which allow consumers to burn their own DVDs, have become more popular. The drives are supported by software created by companies like GEAR Software, Prassi Software, Smart Storage, and Adaptec.

## CONVERGENCE

As computer technology evolved, it prompted discussion on the convergence of platforms between the television set and the computer screen. Indeed, there has been a great deal of synergy between the two. The computer offers users the opportunity to view DVDs and streaming video and will also provide downloads of theatrical feature films. Internet-oriented services are also offered on traditional television sets, for those viewers without computers, via Web TV.

Broadcasters have also created ancillary platforms, referring viewers to their Web sites and cable channels for additional information on items they present on their broadcast networks and affiliated stations. The NBC television network was one of the first to embrace the use of alternate platforms, with cable stations (CNBC, MSNBC) and related Web sites.

There's an interesting psychological dynamic in how viewers perceive watching television and working on a computer. In most cases people watching television tend to do it from a distance, while their relationship to the computer screen is more intimate, allowing them the ease of touching the screen.

As technology becomes more portable via wireless applications with more sophisticated hardware, there's little doubt that the move toward convergence will progress. And the advent of HDTV lends even more credence to the possibility of a single screen for watching television and surfing the Web.

## REGULATION

The FCC, which Congress provides oversight for, has the responsibility of regulating the airwaves (radio and television), cable, and the Internet. There are five members on the commission, appointed by the president. The commission's regulatory oversight has consisted of a three-tiered initiative that includes the allocation of frequency space, assignment of stations, and regulation of existing stations. There are several bureaus that the FCC coordinates to accomplish its regulatory agenda. The Media Bureau makes recommendations and provides administrative oversight of licensing programs for the electronic media, which includes cable, broadcast television, and radio in the United States and its territories. It also addresses Direct Broadcast Satellite (DBS) issues. Under the guidance of the Consumer and Government Affairs

Bureau, the FCC administers a proactive posture toward providing consumers with information about wireline, wireless, television, cable, satellite, and Internet-service-provider issues. For example, the FCC provides military personnel with a "calling home" service that offers them different opportunities for reduced-cost long-distance access and provides low-income families with opportunities for telephone access via its "afford a phone" campaign. As the name implies, the Enforcement Bureau ensures that telecommunication companies provide service in a lawful and reasonable manner. It oversees various abuses, such as slamming, unsolicited faxes, obscene or indecent material, hoaxes, and contests sponsored by licensees. At the International Bureau, the issues addressed relate to foreign telecommunications markets. This division directs and articulates international telecommunication policies while protecting the interests of the American public. The purview of the Wireless Telecommunications Bureau is the enforcement of wireless telecommunications programs and policies. These regulatory issues relate to amateur, cellular, paging, broadband PCS, and public safety. Under the aegis of the Wireline Competition Bureau, its regulatory efforts are divided among four divisions: Competition and Policy, Pricing Policy, Telecommunications Access Policy, and Industry Analysis and Technology. Coordinating their efforts, these divisions help to enforce choice, opportunity, and fairness in the development of wireline telecommunications services. The bureau also encourages investment in wireline telecommunications infrastructures, fostering economic growth and widespread availability.

## CONTENT

The mass media, including the Internet, are not governed by a regulatory protocol because of First Amendment guarantees. Although there are policies associated with indecency and obscenity, radio, television, cable, and the Internet are not subject to prior restraint, which means that no entity can censor their material. All television networks and affiliated stations are governed more by self-regulatory efforts. For example, a commercial network may be sensitive about a content issue based upon the concern of its advertisers. However, the latitude of permissiveness on broadcast and cable has clearly become more explicit in both language and image. If one looks back at television from earlier decades, there's a stark distinction between the conservative pragmatism of then and the articulation of the libertarian sensibilities of now.

It's difficult to predict trends in programming genres. As this book goes to press, reality programming remains prominent on network and cable schedules. This form of television was probably reinforced by the 2003 war with Iraq, billed as *Operation Iraqi Freedom*. At least 500 journalists were embedded with the troops, and for the first time, in any battle American television audiences were witnessing the action live from their living rooms.

The dramatic scenes of bombardment and engagement created a compelling portrait of America at war and the emotions that accompany the canvas of confrontation. It was billed as the ultimate in reality television.

The interesting dynamic is that reality television is steeped in the traditions of nonfiction or documentary. Although most of the programming is a mutant of the genre, it is rooted in those foundations. Nonfiction documentary television had an auspicious beginning in the early days of television with regular network prime-time series like *CBS Reports, NBC White Paper,* and *ABC Close-Up.* Indeed, it was Edward R. Murrow who led the forefront of journalists making the transition from print to radio and then to television, with *Hear It Now* and *See It Now.* It was Murrow who helped to create a posture of advocacy journalism in the style and tone of the stories he chose to tell.

The other regularly scheduled documentary series offered provocative stories, setting the agenda for thoughtful dialogue and debate. One memorable *CBS Reports* program reported by Murrow was "Harvest of Shame," about the frustration and poverty of being a migrant worker. For the most part, these types of nonfiction programming were issue-oriented, taking a position and advocating it.

Long-form prime-time regularly scheduled documentaries were abandoned by network television because of their expense and their inability to capture large audiences. However, a new trend supplanted this genre with the creation of *60 Minutes* and other newsmagazine programs that mixed entertainment values into the journalistic narrative. The stories are shorter, with usually three being covered in a one-hour program.

Cable television, however, has become a valuable repository for documentaries. Networks like A&E and the History Channel offer viewers interesting documentaries associated with prominent figures and events. For example, A&E's *Biography* has been very successful in generating audience interest. Other cable networks, like Animal Planet, also have an ambitious schedule of themed documentary programs.

## NEWS

Daily news programs have not changed considerably over the years, and the early-evening broadcast-network programs—*World News Tonight* with Peter Jennings, *NBC Nightly News* with Tom Brokaw (succeeded by Brian Williams), and *CBS Evening News* with Dan Rather—have anchored their network nightly news programs for a total of about 60 years, each with a tenure of 20 years or more. Some critics have referred to these aging Caucasian males as "relics," the old guard of traditional evening network television news.

The style of most television newscasts, network or local, hasn't changed much over the years. On the evening news network platform with the aforementioned legendary "stars," there's a single voice providing a narrative for the news. They are the sole anchors of the newscast. In local news there's usually a team of two anchors, male and female, that read the news. Of course, the local newscast always includes additional feature items delivered by contributing reporters who do remotes from the field, sports, weather, and "style" pieces.

What has changed in news is its repositioning for a younger audience demographic. Cable networks like MTV have redefined and reshaped the news with more of an orientation toward its audience. For example, Gideon Yago, a young MTV journalist embedded with the Marines during Operation Iraqi Freedom, filed an interesting story led by a photograph of two young Marines, one's arm around the other, smiling and smoking cigars. He wrote:

I've been screening some of the photos I've taken on my laptop and there's this one snapshot I nabbed of two young Marines hanging out in the desert and smoking cigars that I really dig. They look like they could be on a hunting trip: two guys with rifles, kicking it in camo, smoking Cubans in the great outdoors. (Of course, when hunting, the game doesn't usually shoot back.) But the thing that I really love about the snapshot, and that I think is the most telling about the two guys in it, isn't their guns or their gear. It's the ring on the finger of the Marine on the left. This baby-faced PFC has a wife back home, out of contact, probably glued to a TV screen. He looks like he could be in your homeroom class, or hanging out in your student union.[1]

The piece goes on to say that in a few months America is likely to have a younger contingent of veterans from Gulf War II than from any other war. The informal style of the piece and its colloquial use of language make a connection with the intended audience.

In an age of streaming electronic information and an ever-abundant means of accessing the data, news on television is changing to accommodate the needs of the audience. Tailoring the style and substance of the news for different demographics has long been a part of newspaper publishing, offering distinctive platforms for tabloids like the *New York Post* and the more traditional *New York Times*. These changes have been reflected in television news coverage, with the Fox cable news channel offering a more strident tone to its reporting, while the other broadcast networks continue with their traditional subdued coverage.

There's a compelling need to provide audiences with television news reporting that is unbiased, fair, and comprehensive. It's also imperative to present it in a manner suitable to the target audience. Clearly, younger audiences do not identify with relics like Dan Rather, Tom Brokaw, and Peter Jennings; therefore, even more stylized versions of the news serve the needs of this demographic.

Television programming trends tend to be cyclical, with some formats being more durable than others. Prime-time quiz programs, which disappeared from the television landscape after the quiz scandals of the 1950s, returned with a vengeance with the debut of *Who Wants to Be a Millionaire*. Of course, daytime game and quiz shows continue to be a formidable part of the programming mix, either as syndicated or network-distributed material.

Another example of a genre that was once a prominent part of the programming dynamic but suffered from diminishing returns is the variety show. There were quite a few that were very popular, including *The Ed Sullivan Show, Sonny and Cher, The Smothers Brothers Comedy Hour, Lawrence Welk,* and a host of others. However, their decline could be attributed to a number of reasons, including changing audience tastes and America's loss of innocence as it pursued a more aggressive global agenda. There are conceptual remnants of the variety show in the reality formats, especially the talent-oriented programs like *American Idol.*

Quite often, programming styles and formats that fade away are resurrected in another guise. For example, the decline of Westerns and detective shows, once a staple of television, were reformulated as police and law programs. Indeed, the police programming genre is so durable that ABC and Wolf Films brought the series *Dragnet* (NBC, 1951–59, 1967–70) back to prime-time network television on ABC on February 2, 2003. Its run was short-lived and was canceled in November 2003.

Feature-length theatrical films were once part of the prime-time programming mix on network television. The NBC television network aggressively pursued theatrical feature presentations when it introduced *Saturday Night at the Movies* on September 23, 1961. The ability to popularize this format was because Hollywood studios realized television could afford them an additional revenue stream for their theatrical product, and the advent of color television made these movies more attractive for the audience to watch. The network developed a number of movie nights, including *Tuesday Night at the Movies* (1965), *Monday Night at the Movies* (1968), *The NBC Mystery Movie* (1971), and *The NBC World Premiere Movie* (1971). The *Mystery Movie* format actually consisted of three rotating programs: *McCloud, McMillan and Wife,* and *Columbo.* NBC's movie-themed nights continued with *The NBC World Premiere Movie* (1971), *Thursday Night at the Movies* (1975), *Movie of the Week* (1976), *The Big Event* (1976), and *The NBC Late Night Movie* (summer 1977).

Showing movies on television was popular because it provided the three television networks with a tested finished product. They weren't gambling on the introduction of a new program, as the theatrical feature had already had a successful run in movie theaters. It proved so successful that the combined three-network prime-time allocation to theatrical features increased to 12 weekly hours. Soon, however, it became evident that the networks were consuming theatrical film product at a voracious rate, and NBC, responding to that, created *The NBC World Premiere Movie,* featuring made-for-television movies. This was also a successful format, and by 1972 the three networks had shown almost 100 made-for-television movies.

The reasons for the decline of the movie genre were severalfold. It was a matter of economics and the changing dynamic of the entertainment marketplace. Theatrical feature films became expensive to acquire and produce, the advent of HBO and Showtime pay cable channels offered the consumer an alternative to the broadcast networks, and the introduction of low-cost and higher-definition DVD players provided another conduit for accessing recent theatrical feature films. Movies are no longer a staple of prime-time programming fare, as alternative genres have replaced them. The ABC television network relinquished its Sunday movie night in 1998. However, CBS has sporadically offered made-for-TV movie specials on Sunday evening, like *Hell on Heels: The Battle for Mary Kay,* starring Shirley MacLaine, and *Master Spy: The Robert Hanssen Story,* starring William Hurt.

Similar to movies, the miniseries, which offers a multipart story over several days or weeks, is also a genre that has declined in popularity, especially on broadcast network television. They're expensive to produce and yield low audience numbers during reruns. However, HBO and the Public Broadcasting Service (PBS) have had a very ambitious miniseries development and acquisition program. HBO's *Angels in America* and *Band of Brothers* and PBS's *Foyle's War, Prime Suspect,* and *Henry VIII* are some of the more notable miniseries events.

Television has borrowed from many artistic disciplines and has adapted those forms to its own creative needs. It has also defined new parameters of entertainment within the context of its technological virtuosity and versatility. As the landscape of television expands into the realm of high definition and becomes even more sophisticated in its distribution pattern, there'll be new, interesting, and perhaps even compelling programming formats. And content will be reflective of the ever-changing marketplace of ideas, cultural mores, and audience taste. Most certainly there will be new trends, some perhaps even more base than reality or wrestling, stretching the spandex of journalistic fiction to even more grotesque heights of voyeuristic pleasure.

## NOTE

1. www.mtv.com/news/articles/1470422/20030307/index.

# BIBLIOGRAPHY

Adelson, Andrea. "A Bilingual Way to Attract Viewers." *New York Times,* June 15, 1998, p. D8.

———. "Video Network Hopes to Copy Success of Spanish-Language Radio." *New York Times,* 26 January 1998, p. D7.

Andrews, Bart. *The I Love Lucy Book.* New York: Doubleday, 1985.

Araton, Harvey. "Rising Star Minimized by Falling TV Ratings." *New York Times,* 13 March 2000, p. D3.

Barnouw, Erik. *Tube of Plenty: The Evolution of American Television.* Rev. ed. New York: Oxford University Press, 1982.

Barron, James. "Dale Evans, No-Nonsense Queen of the West, Dies at 88," *New York Times,* 8 February 2001, p. A28.

Battaglio, Stephen. "The Big Business of Fond Farewells." *New York Times,* 29 July 2001, p. AR23.

Beatty, Sally. "HBO Marches into Battle." *New York Times,* 18 July 2001, p. B1.

Boddy, William. *Fifties Television: The Industry and Its Critics.* Chicago and Urbana: University of Illinois Press, 1990.

Bogle, Donald. *Primetime Blues: African-Americans on Network Television.* New York: Farrar, Straus & Giroux, 2001.

Bowser, Andrew. "Univision Rules with Telenovelas." *Broadcasting and Cable,* 9 November 1998, pp. 34–35.

Carter, Bill. "Another Short Second Act for a 'Seinfeld' Alum?" *New York Times,* 25 March 2002, p. C1.

———. "HBO Bets Pentagon-Style Budget on a World War II Saga." *New York Times,* 3 September 2001, p. C1.

———. "How ABC's Full-Court Press Almost Landed Letterman." *New York Times,* 18 March 2002, p. C1.

———. "Making Fun of Football." *TV Guide,* 2–8 September 2000, p. 9.

———. "NBA Games Are a Sinker." *New York Times,* 15 March 2000, p. E10.

———. "Reality Shows Alter Way TV Does Business." *New York Times*, 25 January 2003, p. A1.

———. "Sex and the Serious." *New York Times*, 13 August 2001.

———. "Shrinking Network TV Audiences Set Off Alarm and Reassessment." *New York Times*, 22 November 1998, p. 1.

———. "With Jordan Gone, Basketball Ratings Hit a Slump at NBC." *New York Times*, 20 March 2000, p. A1.

Chass, Murray. "Umpires Want Ball-Strike Monitor Gone." *New York Times*, 20 September 2002, p. D3.

Cropper, Carol Marie. "Spanish-Speaking Consumers Are the Object of a Growing Number of Marketers' Desires." *New York Times*, 10 July 1998, p. D5.

De Vries, Hilary. "In Comedies, Signs of a New Women's Movement." *New York Times*, 25 February 2001, p. AR19.

Fabrikant, Geraldine. "Diller's Latest Television." *New York Times*, 23 November 1998, p. C1.

Fatsis, Stefan, and Joe Flint. "How the XFL Became One of the Biggest Flops on TV." *Wall Street Journal*, 23 April 2001, p. A1.

Fish, Stanley. "Running Away from a Daunting Television Legacy," *New York Times*, 22 October 2000, p. 27.

Flint, Joe. "Ah, to Be Master of Late-Night TV." *Wall Street Journal*, 7 March 2002.

———. "ESPN, Baseball Reach Settlement in Telecast Dispute." *Wall Street Journal*, 7 December 1999, p. B8.

Freedman, Samuel G. "The Subtle Drama Found in Silence and Rue." *New York Times*, 22 October 2000, p. AR27.

Freeman, Mike. "XFL May Let Teenagers Opt to Turn Pro." *New York Times*, 4 March 2001, sec. 8, p. SP1.

Frutkin, Alan James. "The Faces in the Glass Are Rarely Theirs." *New York Times*, 24 December 2000.

———. "The Return of the Show That Gets Gay Life Right." *New York Times*, 6 January 2002, p. AR33.

Garcia, Guy. "Nely Galan." *New York Times Magazine*, 11 December 1994, p. 59.

Gates, Anita. "When TV Began to Be about TV." *New York Times*, 28 May 2000.

Goldenson, Leonard H., and Marvin J. Wolf. *Beating the Odds*. New York: Charles Scribner's Sons, 1991.

Goldsmith, Charles, Emily Nelson, and Matthew Karnitschnig. "Reality TV: It's No Mean Feat Keeping It Real." *Wall Street Journal*, 7 March 2003, p. B1.

Goldsmith, Olivia. "Word-Perfect Women: Out of the Mouths of Babes." *New York Times*, 7 December 1997.

Goodman, Tim. "Big Networks, Cable Ignore Latinos; Showtime's Drama 'Resurrection Blvd.' Stands Out as an Exception." *San Francisco Chronicle*, 16 September 2001.

Gorn, Elliott J., and Warren Goldstein. *A Brief History of American Sports*. Urbana: University of Illinois Press, 2004.

Greenberg, Bradley S., et al. *Mexican Americans and the Mass Media*. Norwood, N.J.: ABLEX Publishing, 1983.

Gunther, Marc, and Bill Carter. *Monday Night Mayhem: The Inside Story of ABC's Monday Night Football*. New York: William Morrow, 1988.

Hall, Carla. "For Women in Sitcoms, It's the Next Generation." *L.A. Times*, 18 May 1998, p. F1.

Harper, Phillip Brian. "Extra Special Effects, Televisual Representation and the Claims of the Black Experience." In *Living Color: Race and Television in the United States*. Ed. Sasha Torres. Durham: Duke University Press, 1998.

Hilmes, Michele. *Hollywood and Broadcasting: From Radio to Cable*. Chicago and Urbana: University of Illinois Press, 1990.

"Hispanic Trends: City Dwellers." *Hispanic Market Report*, http://209.24.148.139/trends.html.

Hogmeister, Sallie. "New Executives Tapped to Head Telemundo Network." *Los Angeles Times*, 14 August 1998, p. 3.

James, Caryn. "And Now the 16th Minute of Fame." *New York Times*, 13 March 2002, p. E1.

———. "High Tech Prison and the Face of Horror." *New York Times*, 12 July 1997, sec. 1, p. 11.

———. "Nervous Hunger for Torture Games and Gross-Out Stunts." *New York Times*, 4 February 2002, p. E1.

———. "There's a Lot of Elaine in This Star's New Sitcom." *New York Times*, 26 February 2002, p. E1.

Johnson, Allan. "Galavision Says Si to Bilingual Lineup." *Chicago Tribune*, 16 November 1997, p. 3.

Kate, Nancy Ten. "Move Over Spanish Soaps." *American Demographics*, January 1997, p. 10.

King, Susan. "Video Log." *L.A. Times*, 15 November 2001.

Koppel, Ted. "Network News Is Still Serious Business." *New York Times*, 5 March 2002, p. A23.

Lapham, Lewis H. "The Consolations of Vanity—William Randolph Hearst and Ted Turner," *Harper's*, December 1997, p. 1.

Leland, John. "Why America's Hooked on Wrestling." *Newsweek*, 7 February 2000, p. 47.

Leonhardt, David. "The National Pastime Falls Behind in the Count." *New York Times*, 12 August 2001, sec. 3, p. 1.

Lesser, Wendy. "Here Lies Hollywood: Falling for 'Six Feet Under.'" *New York Times*, 22 July 2001, p. 28.

Lidz, Frank. "The Private Eye by Twilight," *New York Times*, 7 April 2002, p. AR26.

Longman, Jere. "The Finest Football February Can Offer." *New York Times*, 12 February 2001, p. D1.

MacDonald, J. Fred. *Who Shot the Sheriff? The Rise and Fall of the Television Western*. New York: Praeger, 1987.

MacFarquhar, Neil. "Washington's Arabic TV Effort Gets Mixed Reviews," *New York Times*, 20 February 2004, p. A3.

Marin, Rick, and Veronica Chambers. "High Heels, Low Esteem." *Newsweek*, 13 October 1997, p. 71.

Marin, Rick, Veronica McAvoy, and Kim McAvoy. "Baseball Gets the Buck." *Broadcasting and Cable*, 2 April 2001.

McClellan, Steve. "Telemundo: Time for Plan B." *Broadcasting and Cable*, 9 November 1998, p. 30.

McClellan, Steve, and Richard Tdesco. "Loss on the Play." *Broadcasting and Cable*, 26 March 2001, p. 5.

"Media Usage and the Hispanic Consumer." *Hispanic Market Report*, http://209.24.148.139/trends/html.

Meisler, Andy. "A Hispanic Drama, Rejected Once, Finds a Home." *New York Times,* 16 December 2001.

Metz, Robert. *CBS: Reflections in a Bloodshot Eye.* Chicago: Playboy Press, 1975.

———. "Toplines . . . " *American Demographics,* December 1998, p. 7.

Millman, Joyce. "The Good, the Bad, the Lucy: A Legacy of Laughs." *New York Times,* 14 October, 2001, p. 30.

Moss, Robert F. "The Shrinking Life Span of the Black Sitcom." *New York Times,* 25 February 2001.

Navarro, Mireya. "Trying to Get Beyond the Role of the Maid." *New York Times,* 16 May 2002.

Nelson, Emily. "Reality Bites TV Comedy." *Wall Street Journal,* 24 February 2003.

"Networks Lose Ground on Diversifying Prime Time Picture, Study Shows." *Children Now,* 15 May 2002, in *Full Colors: Prime Time Diversity Report—2002.*

Nichols, Peter. "50's TV Dramas in Stores Soon." *New York Times,* 18 January 2001.

Oppenheimer, Jess. *Laughs, Luck . . . and Lucy,* with Gregg Oppenheimer. New York: Syracuse University Press, 1996.

Paley, William S. *As It Happened: A Memoir.* Garden City, N.Y.: Doubleday, 1979.

Peden, Lauren David. "The Inmates of 'Oz' Move into a New Emerald City," *New York Times,* 15 July 2001, p. AR24.

Pollack, Andrew. "Entering U.S. Broadcasting, Sony Buys Telemundo Stake." *New York Times,* 25 November 1997, p. D8.

———. "Univision's Success Story Attracts New Competition." *New York Times,* 19 January 1998, p. D1.

Popper, Steve. "Timeout Microphone: Van Gundy's Big Debut." *New York Times,* 15 March 2000, p. D1.

Rich, Frank. "The Age of the Mediathon: The Real Reality TV." *New York Times Magazine,* 29 October 2000, sec. 6, p. 58.

———. "The Weight of an Anchor." *New York Times,* 19 May 2002, p. 35.

Rodriguez, Clara E. *Latin Looks: Images of Latinas and Latinos in the U.S. Media.* Boulder, Colo.: West View Press, 1997.

Roman, James. *Love, Light and a Dream.* Westport, Conn.: Praeger, 1998.

Rubinstein, Julian. "Monday Night Football's Hail Mary." *New York Times Magazine,* 3 September 2000, sec. 6, p. 46.

Rutenberg, Jim. "Charlie Sheen's Redemption Helps a Studio in Its Struggle." *New York Times,* 4 February 2002, p. C1.

———. "Inside CNN, A Struggle to Be Less 'Tabloid.' " *New York Times,* 24 February 2003, p. C1.

Salamon, Julie. "A Chance to See 'Salesman' as if for the First Time." *New York Times,* 5 August 2001, p. AR25.

———. "Latino Family Values, Beyond the Tortillas." *New York Times,* 23 January 2002.

———. "A Wayans as a Father, Not a Brother." *New York Times,* 28 March 2001.

Sandomir, Richard. "Esiason Fires Back After Being Dismissed." *New York Times,* 10 March 2000, p. D4.

———. "I.M.G. Makes Yankee TV Bid." *New York Times,* 9 November 2000, p. D11.

———. "McMahon and Knight: Tough Interviews." *New York Times,* 20 March 2001, p. D6.

———. "Monday Night Shift Ends Esiason's Job." *New York Times,* 9 March 2000, p. D1.

———. "The Pressure Is on Miller, but Other Analysts Will Also Be Tested." *TV Guide,* 2–8 September 2000, p. SP 10.

———. "To Live Another Day in the Arena League." *New York Times,* 1 May 2001, p. D1.

———. "TV Sports." *New York Times,* 30 November 1999, p. D2.

———. "XFL, a Reality Series with Sports Thrown In." *New York Times,* 1 February 2001, p. D1.

———. "Yanks' Parade of Numbers: Dollar Signs Followed by 0's." *New York Times,* 31 October 2000, p. D3.

Schiesel, Seth. "Down to Raucous Wire, Osbournes in MTV Deal." *New York Times,* 30 May 2002, p. C1.

Schlosser, Joe. "Miller Time on MNF." *Broadcasting and Cable,* 7 August 2000, p. 32.

———. "What's Due for Fall?" *Broadcasting and Cable,* 7 May 2001, p. 12.

Schwarz, Alan. "NBA's Indecent Exposure." *New York Times,* 19 March 2000, p. D3.

Shales, Tom. "Connie Chung, Dishing Up the Nightly News." *Washington Post,* 26 June 2002, p. C01.

Smith, Suzanne E. *Dancing in the Street: Motown and the Cultural Politics of Detroit.* Cambridge, Mass.: Harvard University Press, 1999.

Sorkin, Andrew Ross. "Smackdown! W.W.F. to Buy Wrestling Rival." *New York Times,* 24 March 2001, p. C3.

Stanley, Alessandra. "Blurring Reality with Soap Suds." *New York Times,* 22 February 2003, p. B9.

———. "Reality-Show Inbreeding: Some Mutations Have Survival Value." *New York Times,* 3 March 2003, p. E1.

———. "The Yin and Yang of Late-Night TV." *New York Times,* 10 March 2002, p. WK6.

Sterling, Christopher H., and John M. Kittross. *Stay Tuned: A Concise History of American Broadcasting-,* 3rd ed. Mahwah, NJ: Lawrence Erlbaum, 2002.

Sterngold, James. "Strong Women in TV? They'd Sure Better Be." *New York Times,* 18 December 1997, p. AR 1.

Teachout, Terry. "If the Nightly News Goes Out, It's with a Whimper." *New York Times,* 24 March 2002, p. AR27.

Tomashoff, Craig. "A Barnum of Reality Chases the Relatable Concept." *New York Times,* 23 February 2003, p. AR43.

———. "Farewell to 'Third Rock,' Truly Out of This World." *New York Times,* 13 May 2001, p. AR21.

Trigoboff, Dan. "Jenny Talks Back; Host Campaigns to Distance Herself and Show from 1995 Shooting." *Broadcasting and Cable,* 12 January 1998, p. 21.

Varadarajan, Tunku. "Parachute Journalism Redux." *Wall Street Journal,* 12 November 2001.

———. "Windswept, Inept, Ashleigh Banfield Hits the Road." *Wall Street Journal,* 22 August 2002.

Vogue, Live Wire, July 2002.

Weinraub, Bernard. "Cable TV Shatters Another Taboo." *New York Times,* 20 November 2000, p. E1.

Weinstein, Steve. "Culture Clash's Sitcom Saga." *Los Angeles Times,* 8 January 1992, p. E9.

# INDEX

**About the Author**

JAMES ROMAN is Professor of Film and Media Studies at Hunter College, City University of New York. He is the author of *Love, Light, and a Dream* (Praeger, 1996).